JEAN-CLAUDE LEJEUNE

RETHINKING OUR CLASSROOMS, VOLUME 2

Teaching for Equity and Justice

A Rethinking Schools Publication

Rethinking Our Classrooms, Volume 2
Edited by Bill Bigelow, Brenda Harvey, Stan Karp, and Larry Miller.

Rethinking Schools, Ltd. is a nonprofit educational publisher of books, booklets, and a quarterly journal on school reform, with a focus on issues of equity and social justice. To request addtional copies of this book or a catalog of other publications, or to subscribe to the *Rethinking Schools* journal, contact:

Rethinking Schools
1001 East Keefe Avenue
Milwaukee, Wisconsin 53212 USA
800-669-4192
www.rethinkingschools.org

Rethinking Our Classrooms, Volume 2: Teaching for Equity and Justice
© 2001, Rethinking Schools, Ltd.

Cover illustration by Ann Shearer; based on an image by Skjold Photographs.

Book and cover design by C.C. Krohne.

Layout by Jeff Hansen

Project Coordinator: Leon Lynn

Editorial Assistance: Joanna Dupuis, Carol Ringo, Malaka Sanders.

Proofreaders: Elizabeth Dahlk, Joseph Hahn, Beth Murray, Danah Opland-Dobs, Kitty Ptacek, Dale Weiss.

Special thanks to the Joyce Foundation for its generous support of this project.

Special thanks to Linda Christensen, Beverly Cross, Kelley Dawson, David Levine, Robert Lowe, Barbara Miner, Bob Peterson, Kathy Swope, Rita Tenorio, Mike Trokan, and Stephanie Walters. Special thanks also to Len Mitnaul.

ISBN 978-0-942961-27-0

JEAN-CLAUDE LEJEUNE

TABLE OF CONTENTS

TABLE OF CONTENTS
CONTINUED

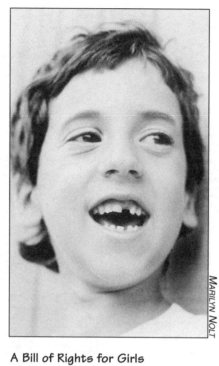

MARILYN NOLT

Introduction

Teaching for Equity and Justice

Like its predecessor, Volume 2 of *Rethinking Our Classrooms* begins from the premise that schools and classrooms should be laboratories for a more just society than the one we now live in. After more than a decade of high-profile national debate on school reform, we think this proposition is more central than ever to the success, perhaps even the survival, of public education.

Schools have crucial obligations not only to individual students and families, but to our society as a whole. Their success or failure is tied not just to personal well-being, but to the prospects of creating a multiracial democracy capable of addressing the serious social and ecological problems that cloud our future. We live in a world plagued by economic inequality, endemic violence, and racial injustice. A me-first, dollar-driven culture undermines democratic values, and seems to invent daily new forms of alienation and self-destruction. Over the long term, the production and consumption patterns of industrially overdeveloped and under-planned economies like ours threaten global ecological disaster.

Given such unpleasant but inescapable realities, education reform must be driven by a far broader vision than it has been in recent years. What happens every day in our classrooms both shapes — and is shaped by — the larger social currents that define who we are as a society and where we are headed. Accordingly, to be truly successful, school reform must be guided by democratic social goals and values that provide a deeper context for more traditional academic objectives.

Unfortunately, too many schools foster narrowly self-centered notions of success and "making it." Too

JEAN-CLAUDE LEJEUNE

many, especially in poor areas, provide a dismal experience based on tests, tracking, and a sanitized curriculum that lacks the credibility or sense of purpose needed to engage students or to connect with their communities. Too many schools fail to confront the racial, class, gender, and homophobic biases woven into our social fabric.

Years of classroom experience have convinced us that these shortcomings are intimately connected to low student achievement, including poor performance on standardized tests. The problems many schools have in teaching children to read, write, and think are, to a large extent, symptoms of the inequality that permeates our educational system. In fact, we would argue that unless our schools and classrooms are animated by broad visions of equity, democracy, and social justice, they will never be able to realize the widely proclaimed goal of raising educational achievement for all children.

Historically, efforts to expand the reach of public education or to democratize curriculum have been accompanied by extensions of the sorting and labeling mechanisms schools use to preserve pockets of privilege. (See for example the role play activity on the origins of tracking in *Rethinking Our Classrooms Volume 1*, p. 133). Today the standardization and testing movements threaten to play a similar role. They profess to raise the bar for all children, yet without dramatic increases and more equity in resources and without radical improvements in teaching and learning inside classrooms, they are more likely to create a new credentialing maze that continues to channel some students to lives of privilege and others to educational oblivion.

Teachers typically have little individual control over many of the factors that shape the conditions of schooling. But in their classrooms they often have a measure of autonomy to create a space that can profoundly affect the lives of young people. As we wrote in our earlier volume, despite many obstacles, "teachers can create classrooms that are places of hope, where students and teachers gain glimpses of the kind of society we could live in and where

students learn the academic and critical skills needed to make it a reality."

This effort to rethink our classrooms must be both visionary and practical: visionary, because we need to go far beyond the prepackaged formulas and narrow agendas now being imposed on our schools and classrooms; and practical, because the work of reshaping educational practice and countering the agendas imposed from above requires daily, school-based efforts at learning, teaching, organizing, and educational activism by those with the most at

MARILYN NOLT

stake — teachers, students, parents, and local communities.

We've drawn the articles, stories, poems, and lessons in this second volume of *Rethinking Our Classrooms* from different academic disciplines and grade levels. We hope they will offer insights and useful examples that can be adapted in classrooms of all levels and disciplines and in diverse social settings. Our goal is to provide frameworks and identify resources that can support teachers in their efforts at class-

room transformation.

A common social and pedagogical vision still unites the collection. We continue to believe, as we wrote in our first volume, that curriculum and classroom practice must be:

• **Grounded in the lives of our students.** All good teaching begins with a respect for children, their innate curiosity and their capacity to learn. Curriculum should be rooted in children's needs and experiences. Whether we're teaching science, mathematics, English, or social studies, ultimately the class has to be about our students' lives as well as about a particular subject. Students should probe the ways their lives connect to the broader society, and are often limited by that society.

• **Critical.** The curriculum should equip students to "talk back" to the world. From an early age, students must learn to pose essential critical questions: Who makes decisions and who is left out? Who benefits and who suffers? Why is a given practice fair or unfair? What are its origins? What alternatives can we imagine? What is required to create change? Through critiques of advertising, cartoons, literature, legislative decisions, foreign policy choices, job structures, newspapers, movies, consumer culture, agricultural practices, and/or school life itself, students should have opportunities to question social reality. Wherever possible student work should also move outside the classroom walls, so that academic learning is linked to real-world issues and problems.

• **Multicultural, anti-bias, pro-justice.** A social justice curriculum must strive to include the lives of everyone in our society and to examine critically their histories and inter-

connection. With some 40% of the students in public schools from communities of color, while more than 90% of the teachers are white, we need to address directly and constructively the racial, class, and gender dimensions of educational inequity and school failure. We need to move from what anti-racist educator Enid Lee calls the "soft stuff" to the "hard stuff." This means not only "celebrating our diversity," but also helping ourselves and our students understand why some differences translate into access to wealth and power, while others become a source of discrimination and injustice. Only when we face honestly the truths about our past and our present will we be able to uncover the common ground that public schools in a multiracial society need in order to thrive.

There is already a backlash against the unfinished efforts of recent years to revise traditional versions of history, literature, and other subjects, and to include the experience and voices of people of color, women, gays and lesbians, and working people. Nevertheless, we need to push this effort further and deeper. We must resist attempts by state tests and standards to push multicultural curriculum reform to the margins.

• **Participatory, experiential.** Traditional classrooms often leave little room for student involvement and initiative. They encourage a passivity that is reinforced by fragmented, test-driven curriculum, and which discourages students from taking more responsibility for their own education. In a "rethought" classroom, concepts need to be experienced first-hand, not just read about or heard about. Through projects, role plays, simulations, mock trials, or experiments, students need to be mentally, and often physically, active. They need to be involved as much as possible in explicit discussions about the purposes and processes of their own education. Our classrooms also must provoke students to develop their democratic capacities: to question, to challenge, to make real decisions, to solve problems collectively.

• **Hopeful, joyful, kind, visionary.** The ways we organize classroom life should seek to make children feel significant and cared about — by the teacher and by each other. Unless students feel emotionally and physically safe, they won't share real thoughts and feelings; discussions will be artificial and dishonest. We need to design activities that help students learn to trust and care for each other. Classroom life should, to the greatest extent possible, pre-figure the kind of democratic and just society we envision, and thus contribute to building that society.

• **Activist.** We want students to come to see themselves as truth-tellers and change-makers. If we ask children to critique the world but then fail to encourage them to act, our classrooms can degenerate into factories for cynicism. Part of a teacher's role is to suggest that ideas have real consequences and should be acted upon, and to offer students opportunities to do just that. Children can also draw inspiration from historical and contemporary efforts of people who struggled for justice. A critical curriculum should be a rainbow of resistance, reflecting the diversity of people from all cultures who acted to make a difference, many of whom did so at great sacrifice. Students should be allowed to learn about, and feel connected to, this legacy of defiance.

• **Academically rigorous.** A social justice classroom equips children not only to change the world, but also to navigate in the world that exists. Far from devaluing the vital academic skills young people need, a critical and activist curriculum speaks directly to the deeply rooted alienation that currently discourages millions of students from acquiring those skills. By addressing directly the social context and social relationships that help create school failure, critical classrooms seek to break the cycle of remedial tedium and replace it with more self-conscious, purposeful student activity.

A social justice classroom offers more *to* students than do traditional classrooms, and expects more *from* students. Critical teaching aims to inspire levels of academic performance significantly greater than those motivated or measured by grades and test scores. When children write for real audiences, read books and articles about issues that really matter, and discuss big ideas with compassion and intensity, "academics" starts to breathe. Yes, we must help students "pass the tests," even as we help them critique the harmful impact of test-driven education. But only by systematically reconstructing how and what we teach do we have any hope of cracking the cynicism that lies so close to the heart of massive school failure, and of raising academic expectations and performance for all children.

• **Culturally sensitive.** Critical teaching requires that we admit we don't know it all. Each class presents new challenges to learn from our students, and demands that we be good researchers and good listeners. These days the demographic reality of schooling makes it likely that white teachers will enter classrooms filled with children of color. As African-American educator Lisa Delpit has written: "When teachers are teaching children who are different from themselves, they must call upon parents in a collaborative fashion if they are to learn who their students really are." They must also call upon the cultural diversity of their colleagues and on community resources for insights into the communities they

> **Without social justice teaching inside classrooms, even much-needed reforms in funding equity or school governance will have limited impact.**

seek to serve. What can be said about racial and cultural differences between teachers and students also holds true for class differences.

We know from our own experience that creating successful critical classrooms is not easy. It is difficult, demanding work that requires vision, support, and resources. Finding groups and networks of support is crucial for the long haul, as is the need to build alliances for equity beyond the classroom among parents, professional associations, teachers' unions, and community groups. The success of our classroom efforts is ultimately tied to efforts at the district, state, and national levels to improve public education and to sustain the collective social obligations that a democratic system of public schooling implies.

We know too that there will be opposition from those who think critical teaching for social justice is "too political," as if traditional teaching for the status quo were not equally "political" in its authoritarian practice, its unequal outcomes, and its endorsement of the established order.

Some colleagues will resist calls to take on greater responsibility for school failure. Others will succumb to corrosive cynicism or force of habit. At times, infuriatingly wrongheaded or counterproductive mandates will be imposed upon us from above by bureaucrats or politicians. At other times the small steps we manage to take may seem painfully short of our grand visions, even isolated and utopian in the face of the broader social changes needed.

But the alternative to critical teaching for social justice is to surrender to a system that, left to its own logic, will never serve the common good. Critical classroom practice is an indispensable, and much-neglected, missing piece in the puzzle of school improvement. Without social justice teaching inside classrooms, even much-needed reforms in funding equity or school governance will have limited impact.

For all its flaws, public education exists because generations of people have fought to improve the future for themselves and their children. Whether public education continues to exist, and whether it rises to the challenges before it, remains an open question. How we as teachers respond will help determine the answer.

A classroom veteran once told younger colleagues that teachers had two choices: "We can teach for the society we live in, or we can teach for the one we want to see." *Rethinking Our Classrooms* is for those with the vision to reach for their dreams. ∎

— The Editors

CLEO

THE POWER OF WORDS

There are layers of meaning in the language we use in our classrooms. Whether it's the vernacular our students bring with them or the literary classics enshrined in the curriculum, language raises issues of culture, identity, and power that demand attention. In this section, teachers discuss ways to explore those issues and to put the power of words in our students' hands.

Where I'm From: Inviting Students' Lives Into the Classroom

By Linda Christensen

I remember holding my father's hand as he read my story hanging on the display wall outside Mrs. Martin's third-grade classroom on the night of Open House. I remember the sound of change jingling in Dad's pocket, his laughter as he called my mom over and read out loud the part where I'd named the cow "Lena" after my mother and the chicken "Walt" after my father. It was a moment of sweet joy for me when my two worlds of home and school bumped together in a harmony of reading, writing, and laughter.

In my junior year of high school, I skipped most of my classes, but each afternoon I crawled back through the courtyard window of my English class. There were no mass assignments in Ms. Carr's class: She selected novels and volumes of poetry for each student to read. Instead of responding by correcting my errors, she wrote notes in the margins of my papers asking me questions about my home, my mother, my sister who'd run away, my father who'd died three years before.

These two events from my schooling capture part of what the editors of *Rethinking Our Classrooms, Volume 1* meant when we encouraged teachers to make students feel "significant" in our classrooms:

> *The ways we organize classroom life should seek to make children feel significant and cared about — by the teacher and by each*

WHERE I'M FROM

I am from clothespins,
from Clorox and carbon-tetrachloride.
I am from the dirt under the back porch.
(Black, glistening
it tasted like beets.)
I am from the forsythia bush,
the Dutch elm
whose long gone limbs I remember
as if they were my own.

I am from fudge and eyeglasses,
from Imogene and Alafair.
I'm from the know-it-alls
and the pass-it-ons,
from perk up and pipe down.
I'm from He restoreth my soul
with a cottonball lamb
and ten verses I can say myself.

I'm from Artemus and Billie's Branch,
fried corn and strong coffee.
From the finger my grandfather lost
to the auger
the eye my father shut to keep his sight.
Under my bed was a dress box
spilling old pictures,
a sift of lost faces
to drift beneath my dreams.
I am from those moments —
snapped before I budded —
leaf-fall from the family tree.

— George Ella Lyon

other. Unless students feel emotionally and physically safe, they won't share real thoughts and feelings. Discussions will be tinny and dishonest. We need to design activities where students learn to trust and care for each other. Classroom life should, to the greatest extent possible, pre-figure the kind of democratic and just society we envision, and thus contribute to building that society. Together students and teachers can create a "community of conscience," as educators Asa Hilliard and George Pine call it.

Mrs. Martin and Ms. Carr made me feel significant and cared about because they invited my home into the classroom. When I wrote and included details about my family, they listened. They made space for me and my people in the curriculum.

In my classrooms at Jefferson High School, I've attempted to find ways to make students feel signifi-cant and cared about as well, to find space for their lives to become part of the curriculum. I do this by inviting them to write about their lives, about the worlds from which they come. Our sharing is one of the many ways we begin to build community together. It "prefigures" a world where students can hear the home language from Diovana's Pacific Islander heritage, Lurdes' Mexican family, Oretha's African-American home, and my Norwegian roots, and celebrate without mockery the similarities as well as the differences.

Sometimes grounding lessons in students' lives can take a more critical role, by asking them to examine how they have been shaped or manipulated by the media, for example. But as critical teachers, we shouldn't overlook the necessity of connecting students around moments of joy as well.

I found a poem by George Ella Lyon in *The United States of Poetry*[1] that I use to invite my students' families, homes, and neighborhoods into the classroom.

Lyon's poem follows a repeating pattern, "I am from . . . ." that recalls details, evokes memories — and can prompt some excellent poetry. Her poem allows me to teach about the use of specifics in poetry, and writing in general. But the lesson also brought the class together through the sharing of details from our lives and lots of laughter and talk about the "old ones" whose languages and traditions continue to permeate the ways we do things today.

Teaching Strategy:

1. After students read the poem out loud together, I note that Lyon begins many of her lines with the phrase, "I am from." I remind the class of William Stafford's[2] advice to find a hook to "link the poem forward" through some kind of device like a repeating line, so the poem can develop a momentum. I suggest they might want to use the line "I am from" or create another phrase that will move the poem.

2. We go line by line through the poem. I ask students to notice the details Lyon remembers about her past. After we read, I ask students to write lists that match the ones in Lyon's poem and to share them out loud. This verbal sharing sparks memories and also gives us memo-

ries to share as we make our way through the lesson:

• Items found around their home: bobby pins or stacks of newspapers, grandma's teeth, discount coupons for a Mercedes. (They don't have to tell the truth.)

• Items found in their yard: broken rakes, dog bones, hoses coiled like green snakes. (I encourage them to think of metaphors as they create their lists.)

• Items found in their neighborhood: the corner grocery, Mr. Tate's beat up Ford Fairlane, the "home base" plum tree.

• Names of relatives, especially ones that link them to the past: Uncle Einar and Aunt Eva, Claude, the Christensen branch.

• Sayings: "If I've told you once. . . ." (The students have a great time with this one. They usually have a ready supply that either brings me back to childhood or makes me want to steal their families' lines.)

• Names of foods and dishes that recall family gatherings: lutefisk, tamales, black-eyed peas.

• Names of places they keep their childhood memories: Diaries, boxes, underwear drawers, inside the family Bible.

3. We share their lists out loud as we brainstorm. I encourage them to make their piece "sound like home," using the names and language of their home, their family, their neighborhood. The students who write vague nouns like "shoes" or "magazines" get more specific when they hear their classmates shout out, "*Jet*," "*Latina*," "pink tights crusted with rosin." Out of the chaos, the sounds, smells, and languages of my students' homes emerge in poetry.

4. Once they have their lists of specific words, phrases, and names, I ask them to write. I encourage them to find some kind of link or phrase like "I am from" to weave the poem together, and to end the poem with a line or two that ties their present to their past, their family history. For example, in Lyon's poem, she ends with "Under my bed was a dress box/spilling old pictures. . . . I am from those moments . . . ."

5. After students have written a draft, we "read around." This is an opportunity for students to feel "significant and cared about," in the words of *Rethinking Our Classrooms, Volume 1*, as they share their poems.

6. Seated in our circle, students read their poems. After each student reads, classmates raise their hands to comment on what they like about the piece. The writer calls on his/her classmates and receives feedback about what is good in the poem. I do stop from time to time to point out that the use of a list is a technique they might "borrow" from their peer's poem and include in their next poem or in a revision. I might note that the use of Spanish or home language adds authenticity to a piece and ask them to see if they could add some to their poem. After a few read-around sessions I can spot writing techniques that students have "borrowed" from each other and included in their revisions or their next piece: dialogue, church sayings, lists, exaggeration.

"Where I'm From" is an opening lesson in a year of critical teaching. As we create schools and classrooms that are "laboratories for a more just society than the one we now live in," we need to remember to make our stu-

---

I Am From Soul Food and Harriet Tubman

By Lealonni Blake

I am from get-togethers
and Bar-B-Ques
K-Mart special with matching shoes.
Baseball bats and BB guns,
a violent family is where I'm from.

I am from "get it girl"
and "shake it to the ground."
From a strict dad named Lumb
sayin' "sit yo' fass self down."

I am from the smell of soul food
cooking in Lelinna's kitchen.
From my Pampa's war stories
to my granny's cotton pickin'.

I am from Kunta Kinte's strength,
Harriet Tubman's escapes.
Phyllis Wheatley's poems,
and Sojourner Truth's faith.

If you did family research,
and dug deep into my genes.
You'll find Sylvester and Ora, Geneva and Doc,
My African Kings and Queens.
That's where I'm from.

I Am From Pink Tights and Speak Your Mind

By Djamila Moore

I am from sweaty pink tights encrusted in rosin
bobby pins
Winnie-the-Pooh
and crystals.

I am from awapuhi ginger
sweet fields of sugar cane
green bananas.

I am from warm rain cascading over
taro leaf umbrellas.
Crouching beneath the shield of kalo.

I am from poke, brie cheese, mango,
and raspberries,
from Marguritte
and Aunty Nani.

I am from speak your mind
it's o.k. to cry
and would you like it if someone did that to you?

I am from swimming with
the full moon,
Saturday at the laundromat,
and Easter crepes.

I am from Moore and Cackley
from sardines and haupia.
From Mirana's lip Djavan split,
to the shrunken belly
my grandmother could not cure.

Seven diaries stashed among
Anne of Green Gables.
Dreams of promises
ending in tears.
Solidifying to salted pages.

I am from those moments of
magic
when life remains a
fairy tale.

dents feel significant and cared about. These kinds of lessons keep me going, too. When the gray days of budget cuts, standardized tests, school restructuring plans gone awry, and kid-bashing talk in the teacher room pile up one after another like layers of old newspapers on your back porch, pull out George Ella Lyon's poem and invite the stories and voices of your students into the classroom. ■

Linda Christensen is Language Arts Coordinator for the Portland, Oregon public schools and is a Rethinking Schools editor. This article is adapted from her book Reading, Writing, and Rising Up: Teaching About Social Justice and the Power of the Written Word, *available from Rethinking Schools.*

References

Bigelow, Bill, et al. *Rethinking Our Classrooms: Teaching for Equity and Justice.* Milwaukee, WI: Rethinking Schools, 1994.

Blum, Joshua, Holman, Bob, and Pellington, Mark (Eds.). *The United States of Poetry.* New York: Harry N. Adams, 1996.

Stafford, William. *Writing the Australian Crawl.* Ann Arbor, MI: University of Michigan Press, 1978.

Stafford, William. *You Must Revise Your Life.* Ann Arbor, MI: University of Michigan Press, 1986.

Notes

1. *The United States of Poetry* (see References) is a book and a video. They introduce students to political poetry as well as to some old and new poets from diverse racial and social backgrounds. The video uses a music video format and demonstrates performance poetry. I use both the book and video with my high school students. Most of the pieces are more appropriate for older students, but some pieces, like "Where I'm From," could be used with elementary students as well.

2. William Stafford, Oregon's poet laureate for many years, published many outstanding books of poetry as well a two wonderful books on writing: *Writing the Australian Crawl* and *You Must Revise Your Life.* See References.

I Am From . . .

By Oretha Storey

I am from bobby pins, doo-rags
and wide toothed combs.
I am from tall grass, basketballs and
slimy slugs in front of my home.
I am from prayer plants that lift
their stems and rejoice every night.

I am from chocolate cakes and deviled
eggs that made afternoon snacks just right.
I am from older cousins and hand me downs
to "shut ups" and "sit downs."

I am from Genesis to Exodus
Leviticus too.
Church to church, pew to pew.

I am from a huge family tree,
that begins with dust and ends with me.

In the back of my mind there lies a dream
of good "soul food" and money trees.
In this dream I see me on top makin'
ham hocks, fried chicken
and smothered porkchops.
I am from family roots and blood,
Oh, I forgot to mention love.

I Am From Swingsets and Jungle Gyms

By Debby Gordon

I am from jars for change collections,
cards from Grandma,
and chocolate milk.

I am from swingsets and jungle gyms
rusted metal mounted in dirt
used by many kids,
well broken in.

I am from the cherry tree,
and the pudgy faces climbing out on the branches
for a piece of juicy red fruit.

I am from tattle-tales,
keep-it-froms,
and "shut-up and listen to me."

I am from Rice Crispy Treats,
and pretty rings,
from Melvin and Earline.

I'm from Will and Sharon's long branch,
chunky Peanut-Butter and Jelly,
from the house we lost to fire,
and surgeries we all have had.

I am from the old scrapbooks,
where pictures,
remind me of days that live only in the minds
of those of us who were there.

I am from the people who paved a way for me,
I am from the best that could be,
and I am the best I could be.

An International Proverbs Project

Using telecommunications to investigate folklore

By Jim Cummins and Dennis Sayers

The following describes a project by teachers involved in Orillas, an international learning network whose name is short for the Spanish phrase "De Orilla a Orilla" (From Shore to Shore). Teachers in Orillas usually participate in one of three types of activities: the exchange of cultural packages, using the mail; partner-class projects involving mutually coordinated investigations and usually resulting in a joint product; or group projects involving many teachers and their classes, and usually resulting in an Orillas-wide publication. The group projects are usually based on a theme with global interest, such as the environment, human rights, or the loss of oral traditions. They are particularly suited for themes that benefit from multiple perspectives on a single issue, or in which collective effort can create impressive bodies of information that students can analyze.

In 1989, Orillas announced a group project to collect and analyze proverbs. It is important to note that the categories proposed were simply suggestions, based on the previous experiences of successful team-teaching partnerships. In all Orillas projects, teachers are invited to design and shape the activities according to their local needs. Here we provide a close-up of one particular class in Puerto Rico, and then describe different ways in which other teachers have adapted the project to their own curriculum.

La Escuela Abelardo Diaz Morales, named after a distinguished Puerto Rican educator, is an elementary school in Caguas, Puerto Rico. Its students are proud of their computer lab, the walls of which never fail to catch the eye of the visitor. On these bulletin board walls are photographs of students and their teachers, flags of Mexico and California, illustrated maps, richly colored student artwork, a collection of Yaqui legends from the Southwest, and several

> **Proverbs can't be separated from the inequities of the power relationships within the social fabric, from which they have developed.**

issues of the student-produced newspaper, *Cemi*. The bulletin boards trace the history of this school's participation in Project Orillas.

Each year since 1986, the computer writing teacher, Rosa Hernandez, has engaged in a long-distance team-teaching exchange with a teacher in another part of the world, using a classroom computer, a modem, and a computer network. Networking also has made it possible for Ms.

Hernandez and her students to stay in touch with the wider group of Orillas teachers and to participate in a variety of Orillas group projects, including a survey of endangered species, an international human rights project, and several inter-generational folklore investigations, such as the Proverbs Project, originally presented to Orillas teachers in the following project announcement:

ANNOUNCING: A PROJECT ON INTERNATIONAL PROVERBS, from Kristin Brown, Dennis Sayers, and Enid Figueroa, Orillas Co-Directors.

Orillas is sponsoring a multilingual proverbs contest. We invite your students to participate in one or more of the following categories:

Best Drawing illustrating one of the following proverbs: "Those who live in glass houses should not throw stones" or "It takes all kinds to make the world go around."

Best Original Fable: Students pick a proverb, write an original story illustrating that proverb, then give the proverb at the end of the story as the "punch line."

Largest List of "Animal" Proverbs Submitted by a Single Class: Example, "A barking dog never bites." Helpful hint: Ask the parents and relatives of your students to help out!

Greatest Number of Contradictory Proverbs Submitted by a Single Class: Example, "There's no place like home" contradicts

TOM BOSWELL

"The grass is always greener on the other side of the fence."

Best Original Essay on "What's Wrong With This Proverb": Pick a proverb you don't agree with and write an essay explaining what is wrong with the views it projects. Not all proverbs are wise; some of them say terrible things about others. For example, the sexist proverb "A woman's place is in the home" suggests that women should only do housework. Other proverbs are racist, ageist, or ridicule people with handicaps.

The contest is open to students of all grades and speakers of all languages. Through identifying proverbs whose social, moral, or political views are obsolete, by searching for modern examples to illustrate noble or wise proverbs, and by exploring under what circumstances seemingly contradictory proverbs are true, we can all help define the "collective wis-

dom" of the 20th century, and beyond.

At the end of the semester each participating class will receive a booklet containing selected student essays, photocopies of the drawings, and a list of all the proverbs collected.

During the next few weeks, Ms. Hernandez's class, like many others throughout the Orillas network, gathered proverbs, focusing especially on those containing animals. The list grew as students collected proverbs from parents, older brothers and sisters, grandparents living at home, neighbors, and other nearby relatives. During the school's spring break, the week of *Semana Santa* (the Holy Week preceding Easter), when families travel to other parts of the island to visit friends and relatives, the list grew most dramatically. Just before the vacation, Ms. Hernandez printed out for each student a copy of the animal proverbs collected up to that

point. When the students returned to school the following week, their lists were well worn and much longer. "Nearly a hundred animal proverbs!" they exclaimed when they had finished adding the new proverbs to the old.

The class discovered that the task of categorizing the proverbs they gathered by theme was not as easy as it first appeared. The students debated the meanings of the proverbs and eliminated duplicates while making note of the frequency of use of each proverb. They identified different versions and regional variations, and compared notes with their classmates about the contexts in which their parents and grandparents actually used the proverbs. As they continued to gather and analyze proverbs, they stayed in touch with other classes on the network.

In other classes, teachers and students had integrated the project into their own curriculum in a variety of ways. In Watsonville, California, for example, the proverbs project was used to build parent involvement in the school's bilingual program. A migrant farmer parent at Watsonville and his kindergarten child wrote the following critique of a proverb:

> *"Vale más un pájaro en mano que ver cien volando."*
> *No estamos de acuerdo con este refrán porque las personas no nos debemos conformar con lo que tenemos sino luchar y esforzarnos para vivir mejor cada día.*
> *— Por los padres de Angélica Pérez García, Kinder, Watsonville, California.*

["A bird in the hand is worth two in the bush."

We don't agree with this proverb because people shouldn't be satisfied with what we have but instead should struggle and make an effort to make each day better.

— by the parents of Angelica Perez Garcia, Kindergarten, Watsonville, California.]

In a bilingual fifth/sixth-grade class in Connecticut, students worked on a unit on fables, first reading fables in Spanish and English written by Samaniego, Aesop, and La Fontaine, then writing their own fables that illustrated some proverbs the class in Puerto Rico had collected. In this class, students chose proverbs that reflected their own experiences. Here is one story/fable they wrote illustrating a proverb and tying it to academic learning:

"El mismo perro pero con diferente collar."

Había una vez una maestra llamada Ms. Caraballo. Le estaba enseñando a sus estudiantes de tercer grado como multiplicar. Ella les enseñaba todo lo necesario a sus alumnos.

"Bueno estudiantes," dijo la Sra. Caraballo. "¿Cuánto es 2 x 3?" Solo una estudiante levantó su mano y dijo, "Seis." Todos los estudiantes entendieron eso, menos Pedro.

"Maestra," dijo Pedro, "Yo no sé como hacer eso."

"Bueno Pedro," dijo Ms. Caraballo amablemente. "Esto es como si tu dijeras 3 + 3, pero en otra forma. Como si dijera 3 + 3 + 3 que es lo mismo que 3 x 3, que es igual que 9, pero en otra forma."

"Ahora ya entiendo," dijo Pedro. "Es como mi abuelo me dijo del refrán — el mismo perro pero con diferente collar."

["The same dog but with a different collar".

Once there was a teacher named Ms. Caraballo. She was teaching her third-grade students to multiply. She taught her students everything they needed to know.

"Okay, students," said Ms. Caraballo. "How much is 2 X 3?" Only one student raised her hand and said "six." All the students understood this, except Pedro.

"Teacher," said Pedro. "I don't know how to do that."

"Well, Pedro," said Ms.

JEAN-CLAUDE LEJEUNE

Caraballo in a friendly way, "it is like saying 3 + 3 but in a different form. Just as 3 + 3 + 3, 3 x 3, and 9 are all different ways of saying the same thing."

"Now I understand," said Pedro. "It's just like the proverb my grandfather taught me — the same dog but with a different collar."]

At another school, a sixth-grade class asked students at other grade levels to illustrate familiar proverbs. They then classified the drawings in terms of whether each illustration was based on a literal or figurative interpretation of the proverb. The teacher was excited to note that for the first time in all her years of trying

to get her upper-elementary level students to understand the textbook terms "literal and figurative speech," her students had announced in class, "Now we understand, Sra. Druet. It's like the way you can be talking about the horse's mouth and really it has nothing to do with a horse."

In other classes, this folklore project evolved into a lesson on sophisticated editorial writing. Proverbs are controversial by nature. They cannot be separated from the inequities of power relationships within the social fabric from which they have developed and in which they inextricably exist. In several classes, students wrote about proverbs they could not agree with. In the following exam-

JEAN-CLAUDE LEJEUNE

ples, students from New York drew on their own experiences as they critiqued proverbs that they felt were unfair. The least favorite proverb among students in the United States was "A woman's place is in the home." A New York student explains:

"El lugar de la mujer es en el hogar."

Yo, Martha Prudente, no estoy de acuerdo en que la mujer esté en el hogar. Eso era el pensamiento de los tiempos antiguos. Asi era como mis padres pensaban pero yo no, porque soy rebelde. Si yo voy a tener un hogar pero si quiero trabajar, voy a trabajar. Y pienso ser enfermera antes de casarme y después yo sigo trabajando en mi carrera.

["A woman's place is in the home."

I, Martha Prudente, do not agree that a woman's place is in the home. This kind of thinking is old-fashioned. This is how my parents thought, but not me because I am a rebel. Yes, I will have a home, but if I want to work I will work. I hope to be a nurse before I get married and afterwards continue working in my career.]

Cervantes once referred to proverbs as "short sentences drawn from long experience." The International Orillas Proverbs Project stems from a long-standing and continuing interest on the part of Orillas teachers in exploring folklore in networked classrooms. The teachers involved in the project concluded that proverbs provide an excellent vehicle for students to share cultural and linguistic knowledge for the following reasons:

• Proverbs are universal.
• The families of students are involved, encouraging oral histories.
• Children from families who have immigrated to North America and elsewhere can build links to their (in some cases disappearing) culture, and learn to take pride in their rich proverbial heritage.
• Analyzing proverbs encourages discussion, critical thinking, and a deromanticized appreciation of culture.
• Students studying Spanish as a foreign language gain from the cul-

tural knowledge embodied in proverbs.
• Young students can participate, as the amount of text to be shared is small and easily entered in the computer.
• Proverbs can encourage much longer writings, such as opinion statements or modern fables.
• A database can be used to categorize proverbs by themes in order to facilitate cross-cultural comparisons.
• Collecting proverbs is a provocative yet discrete task resulting in a rich, concrete product.

In this project, telecommunications made it possible for bilingual students from diverse regions to collaborate rapidly in a wide-ranging investigation of proverbs. Moreover, the students created materials that classroom teachers everywhere were able to use to stimulate reading and writing skills, often across two languages. Folklore collections of all kinds can be instrumental in building bridges between schools and families and within the wider community of speakers of a particular language — both among the diaspora of local immigrant communities and their cultures of origin around the world. Yet they also can bring cross-cultural awareness and language skills to students who otherwise would never have access to people from distant lands and other world views. Once again, students from every background stand to benefit from participation in global learning networks. ■

The above is excerpted from Brave New World, *by Jim Cummins and Dennis Sayers.*

The chapter is based on Kristin Brown's "Balancing the Tools of Technology with Our Own Humanity: Team-Teaching Partnerships Between Distant Classes" in Tinajero, J. and Ada, A. (Eds.), The Power of Two Languages, *NY: Macmillan, 1999.*

Race

By Cang Dao

People don't know how
I feel.
"You can't talk like us."
The words hurt me more than
it hurts them to say.

I'm getting an attitude.
Too many jokes,
I cannot accept it.
What's wrong about me
that may not be accepted by them?
Is it the way I look or
the way I talk?

How many languages can you
speak?
I speak four.

Is there something from
me that you want?
My beautiful brown eyes or
my lovely skin?
Don't get jealous.

I'm here to share with you
my knowledge,
but I'm not here for you
to make fun of me.

Like a newspaper that can
show words but not voice,
people just don't know
how I feel.

(Reprinted from *Rites of Passage 1996-1997*, a
literary magazine written and produced at
Jefferson High School in Portland, Oregon.)

For My People

Celebrating community through poetry

By Linda Christensen

"I don't understand how you could walk into that building day after day for twenty-two years," the older woman standing at the copier told me. "I have to go in there once a week, and I fear for my life every time I walk up those stairs. All of those Black boys with their hoodlum clothes — sweatshirt hoods pulled up over their heads, baggy pants — I'm afraid they're going to knock me down the steps and steal my purse."

I look at her and remember Damon and Sekou, young Black men I taught at "that building" — Jefferson High School. I remember their brilliance, imagine their faces — one at law school, one at NASA. I think of Kanaan's huge heart, of Frank's humor. I think of Aaron Wheeler-Kay's poem written after we visited an art museum exhibit of Carrie Mae Weems' work:

> I Went Looking For Jefferson
>   and I found…
> all the nations of the world
>   wrapped in baggy jeans
>   sweatshirts
>   braids.
> Closed minds slowly opening
>   like doors under water.
> Jefferson is our whetstone
>   the blade is our mind.

There was no whetstone to sharpen the mind of the woman at the copy machine. I'd met her before — in countless other closed minds through the years. People — teachers, parents, reporters, students from other schools — who sized up those of us who attended or worked at Jefferson based on stereotyped images and counted us out usually without ever venturing inside to our classrooms.

Their comments disrespected our school, our students, our community. And even when they weren't as blatant in their comments, their looks or their body language spoke bluntly.

Students, particularly students who don't fit the social norm because of their race, language, sexual orientation, weight, or ability to purchase the latest fashions, have plenty of reasons to share their anger and frustration — sometimes at inappropriate times and in inappropriate ways when they feel they've been disrespected. The classroom can be a safe place for students to not only talk back, but to affirm their right to a place in the world. During the years I worked at Jefferson, I found it necessary to develop writing prompts for students that "talk back" to those disrespectful and untrue images that the media and popular opinion formed about my students, my school, and the faculty.

In one assignment, I begin by reading Margaret Walker's powerful poem "For My People." Walker's poem teaches about the hardships that African Americans endured, but she also celebrates the triumphs of her people. She ends the poem with an exhortation — "Let a new earth rise. Let another world be born…Let a race of men now rise and take control!"

We look at how Walker constructs her poem with the repeating phrase "For my people…" She uses the phrase as an introduction to her theme for that stanza and follows it with a list. For example:

> For my people everywhere
> singing their slave songs
>   repeatedly: their dirges and
> their ditties and their blues

and jubilees, praying their prayers nightly to an
> unknown god, bending their knees humbly to an unseen
> power;

I also point out her use repetition and lists as well as the rhythm of her line — "their dirges and their ditties and their blues and jubilees" — and the repetition of sounds — singing slave songs, dirges and ditties, and praying prayers. For beginning poets the format of a repeating line followed by a list as well as repeating sounds is a helpful link into the poem, but in my assignment, I don't require they follow the format.

Then I ask students to create a list of their "people." I tell them to think of all of the communities they belong to. I list mine on the board as a way to stimulate them to think beyond their immediate categories — Jefferson, poor whites, working class, Norwegians, Germans, teachers, women, mothers, overweight people, environmentalists, social justice activists, feminists.

I often use Jefferson as a model because it's the one community we all share. We catalogue reasons to celebrate our school: its diverse student body, the many languages heard in the halls, the Jefferson dancers and the gospel singers, Michele Stemler's Spanish classes, the powerful student-created murals on the walls. Then I ask them to pick one of their communities and list what they could praise about it. I also ask them to think about any common misconceptions people have about any of their "people" and suggest that they might "talk back" to those judgements in their poem.

My student Cang Dao wrote his

poem "Race" (see p. 15) as a way of talking back to those have put him down. When Cang wrote this poem, we discussed how kids made fun of his newcomer English, but we also discussed how he can speak more languages than most of the student body. He embedded pieces of that talk in his poem.

Sophia Farrier takes the opening lines from Walker and uses them to describe her pain in her poem "This is for…" She writes:

This is for the people who
believed I was nothing,
that I would never be special in
anyone's mind.
This is for the people who said
they were my friends,
but always put me down…
This is for the people who took
my self esteem away,
for those who never cared,
who ignored me because I wasn't
"fashionable."

At the end of her poem, she attempts to find strength in herself. She changes the line from "This is for the people" to "This is for me…"

This is for me because I didn't
believe in myself.
For me because I tried too hard to
be who I wasn't and couldn't
be…
And this is for my blood that
rushes thick and thin
that sometimes stands tall,
but sometimes cowers away.

Lori Ann Durbin, a senior in my Writing for Publication class, was a transplanted cowgirl who ended up at Jefferson High School. Her poem celebrates that heritage:

Country Folk

For my folk, two-steppin', shit-
kickin' pioneers.

Blue collar, redneck, bowleggged
horsemen…
This is my song to you.
Moonshiners, horse ranchers, hill-
billy roots,
wild women, bare feet, it's nothin'
or it's boots,
twangy sweet fiddle, songs about
our lives,
maybe sappy to everyone else, but
that's how we survive.
Fishin', singin, ridin' bareback in
the field,
tight cowboy butts and Wranglers.
I love the way they feel.
Tailgate parties, couples in the
barn, hay in our hair.
It's not just music.
It's a way of life.

Justin Morris, another senior, took the stereotypes about Black people and used them in his celebration. His poem demonstrates an in-your-face love for all aspects of his heritage. One night I was at a local copy store making huge posters of these poems to hang around the school. Several African American men were copying on a machine close to my oversize machine. They laughed when they read Justin's poem and took one of the copies to hang in their office.

For My People

This is for my people
who are "colored"
who are proud.

For my people
who cause white women to clutch
their purses
who white men look down on
who drank from different
fountains
who fought prejudice.

For my people
with kinky afros
and gheri curls.

For my people
with big lips
and wide noses.

For my people
with Black power
fingertips drenched with barbecue
sauce.

For the people
with pink hearts
and brown/black skins.
For my people:
Stay strong.

The woman who feared for her life each time she walked Jefferson's halls "confessed" her racism — which is perhaps the first step toward change. I will bring her my students' poems. I want her to see beyond the baggy pants and sweatshirts. I hope that by reading their words, she'll see the "pink hearts" inside the "brown/black" skin; she'll hear the intelligence that ricochets off Jefferson's walls and know that she doesn't have to be afraid.■

Linda Christensen is Language Arts Coordinator for the Portland, Oregon public schools and a Rethinking Schools editor.

Resources

Giovanni, Nikki. "Legacies." *Words with Wings: A Treasury of African-American Poetry and Art.* Ed. Belinda Rochelle. Singapore: HarperCollins, 2001.

Hughes, Langston. "My People." *Words with Wings,* op. cit.

Walker, Alice. "Women." *Words with Wings,* op. cit.

Walker, Margaret, "For My People." *This is My Century: New and Collected Poems.* Athens, GA: University of Georgia Press, 1989.

What Color is Beautiful?

By Alejandro Segura-Mora

Most of my kindergarten students have already been picked up by their parents. Two children still sit on the mat in the cafeteria lobby, waiting. Occasionally, one of them stands to look through the door's opaque windows to see if they can make out a parent coming. Ernesto, the darkest child in my class, unexpectedly shares in Spanish, "*Maestro*, my mom is giving me pills to turn me white."

"Is that right?" I respond, also in Spanish. "And why do you want to be white?"

"Because I don't like my color," he says.

"I think your color is very beautiful and you are beautiful as well," I say. I try to conceal how his comment saddens and alarms me, because I want to encourage his sharing.

"I don't like to be dark," he explains.

His mother, who is slightly darker than he is, walks in the door. Ernesto rushes to take her hand and leaves for home.

An illustration from *Nina Bonita* by Ana María Machado.

ROSANA FARÍA

Childhood Memories

Ernesto's comment takes me back to an incident in my childhood. My mom is holding me by the hand, my baby brother in her other arm, my other three brothers and my sister following along. We are going to church and I am happy. I skip all the way, certain that I have found a solution to end my brothers' insults.

"You're a monkey," they tell me whenever they are mad at me. I am the only one in my family with curly hair. In addition to "monkey," my brothers baptize me with other derogatory names — such as Simio (Ape), Chineca (a twisted and distorted personification of being curly, and even more negative by the feminization with an "a" at the end), and Urco, the captain of all apes in the television program *The Planet of the Apes*.

As we enter the church, my mom walks us to the front of the altar to pray before the white saints, the crucified white Jesus, and his mother. Before that day, I hadn't bought into the God story. After all, why would God give a child curly hair? But that day there is hope. I close my eyes and pray with a conviction that would have brought rain to a desert.

"God, if you really exist, please make my hair straight," I pray. "I hate it curly and you know it's hard. So at the count of three, please take these

curls and make them straight. One, two, three."

With great suspense I open my eyes. I reach for my hair. Anticipating the feel of straight hair, I stroke my head, only to feel my curls. Tears sting my eyes. As I head for one of the benches, I whisper, "I knew God didn't exist."

For Ernesto, the pill was his God; for me, God was my pill. I wonder how Ernesto will deal with the failure of his pill.

A Teachable Moment

I can't help but wonder how other teachers might have dealt with Ernesto's comments. Would they have ignored him? Would they have dismissed him with a, "Stop talking like that!" Would they have felt sorry for him because they agree with him?

As teachers, we are cultural workers, whether we are aware of it or not. If teachers don't question the culture and values being promoted in the classroom, they socialize their students to accept the uneven power relations of our society along lines of race, class, gender, and ability. Yet teachers can — and should — challenge white supremacist values and instead promote values of self-love.

Young students, because of their honesty and willingness to talk about issues, provide many opportunities for teachers to take seemingly minor incidents and turn them into powerful teaching moments. I am grateful for Ernesto's sincerity and trust in sharing with me. Without knowing it, Ernesto opened the door to a lively dialogue in our classroom about white supremacy.

To resurface the dialogue on beauty and skin color, I chose a children's book which deals with resistance to white supremacy (a genre defined, in part, by its scarcity.) The book is *Nina Bonita*, written by Ana María Machado and illustrated by Rosana Fara (1996, available in English from Kane/Miller Book Publishers). The book tells the story of an albino bunny who loves the beauty of a girl's dark skin and wants to find out

how he can get black fur. I knew the title of the book would give away the author's bias, so I covered the title. I wanted to find out, before reading the book, how children perceived the cover illustration of the dark-skinned girl.

"If you think this little girl is pretty, raise your hand," I said. Fourteen hands went up.

"If you think she is ugly, raise your hand," I then asked. Fifteen voted for ugly, among them Ernesto.

I was not surprised that half my students thought the little girl was ugly. Actually, I was expecting a higher number, given the tidal wave of white dolls which make their way into our classroom on Fridays, our Sharing Day, and previous comments by children in which they indicated that dark is ugly.

After asking my students why they thought the girl on the book cover was ugly, one student responded, "Because she has black color and her hair is really curly." Ernesto added, "Because she is black-skinned."

"But you are dark like her," Stephanie quickly rebutted Ernesto, while several students nodded in agreement. "How come you don't like her?"

"Because I don't like black girls," Ernesto quickly responded. Several students affirmed Ernesto's statement with "yes" and "that's right."

"All children are pretty," Stephanie replied in defense.

Carlos then added, "If you behave good, then your skin color can change."

"Are you saying that if you are good, you can turn darker?" I asked, trying to make sure the other students had understood what he meant.

"White!" responded Carlos.

"No, you can't change your color," several students responded. "That can't be done! "

"How do you know that your color can change?" I asked, hoping Carlos would expand on his answer.

"My mom told me," he said.

"And would you like to change your skin color?" I asked.

"No," he said. He smiled shyly as he replied and I wondered if he may have wished he was not dark-skinned but didn't want to say so.

Carlos's mother's statements about changing skin color reminded me of instances in my family and community when a new baby is born. "Oh, look at him, how pretty and blond looking he is," they say if the baby has European features and coloring. And if the babies came out dark, like Ernesto? Then the comments are, "¡Ay! Pobrecito, salió tan prietito" — which translated means, "Poor baby, he came out so dark."

I hear similar comments from co-workers in our school's staff lounge. A typical statement: "Did you see Raul in my class? He has the most beautiful green eyes."

It is no surprise that so many students must fight an uphill battle against white supremacist values; still other students choose not to battle at all.

Challenging the Students

In an attempt to have students explain why they think the black girl in *Nina Bonita* is ugly, I ask them, "If you think she is ugly for having dark skin, why do you think her dark skin makes her ugly?"

"I don't like the color black," volunteers Yvette, "because it looks dark and you can't see in the dark."

"Because when I turn off the light," explains Marco, "everything is dark and I am afraid."

Although most of my kindergarten students could not articulate the social worthlessness of being dark-skinned in this society, I was amazed by their willingness to struggle with an issue that so many adults, teachers included, ignore, avoid, and pretend does not exist. At the same time, it was clear that many of my students had already internalized white supremacist values.

At the end of our discussion, I took another vote to see how students were reacting to *Nina Bonita*; I also wanted to ask individual students

JEAN-CLAUDE LEJEUNE

why they had voted the way they had. This second time, 18 students said the black girl was pretty and only 11 said she was ugly. Ernesto still voted for "ugly."

"Why do you think she is ugly?" I asked, but this time the students didn't volunteer responses. Perhaps they were sensing that I did not value negative answers as much as I did comments by students who fell in love with *Nina Bonita*. In their defense of dark skin, some students offered explanations such as, "Her color is dark and pretty," "All girls are pretty," and, "I like the color black."

Our discussion of *Nina Bonita* may have led four students to modify their values of beauty and ugliness in relation to skin color. Maybe these four students just wanted to please their teacher. What is certain, however, is that the book and our discussion caused some students to look at the issue in a new way.

Equally important, *Nina Bonita* became a powerful tool to initiate discussion on an issue which will affect my students, and myself, for a lifetime. Throughout the school year, the class continued our dialogue on the notions of beauty and ugliness. (One other book that I have found useful to spark discussion is *The Ugly Duckling*. This fairy tale, which is one of the most popular among early elementary teachers and children, is often used uncritically. It tells the story of a little duckling who is "ugly" because his plumage is dark. Happiness comes only when the duckling turns into a beautiful, spotless white swan. I chose to use this book in particular because the plot is a representation of the author's value of beauty as being essentially white. I want my students to understand that they can disagree with and challenge authors of books, and not receive their messages as God-given.)

When I have such discussions with my students, I often feel like instant-ly including my opinion. But I try to allow my students to debate the issue first. After they have spoken, I ask them about their views and push them to clarify their statements. One reason I like working with children is that teaching is always a type of experiment, because the students constantly surprise me with their candid responses. These responses then modify how I will continue the discussion.

I struggle, however, with knowing that as a teacher I am in a position of power in relation to my young stu-

> ## I struggle with how to get my students to begin to look critically at the many unequal power relations in our society.

dents. It is easy to make students stop using the dominant ideology and adopt the ideology of another teacher, in this case my ideology. In this society, in which we have been accustomed to deal with issues in either-or terms, children (like many adults) tend to adopt one ideology in place of another, but not necessarily in a way in which they actually think through the issues involved. I struggle with how to get my students to begin to look critically at the many unequal power relations in our society, relations which, even at the age of five, have already shaped even whether they love or hate their skin color and consequently themselves.

At the end of our reading and discussion of the book, I shared my feelings with my students.

"I agree with the author calling this girl *Nina Bonita* because she is absolutely beautiful," I said. "Her skin color is beautiful."

While I caressed my face and kissed my cinnamon-colored hands several times happily and passionately, so that they could see my love for my skin color, I told them, "My skin color is beautiful, too."

I pointed to one of my light-complexioned students and said, "Gerardo also has beautiful skin color, and so does Ernesto. But Gerardo cannot be out in the sun for a long time because his skin will begin to burn. I can stay out in the sun longer because my darker skin color gives me more protection against sunburn. But Ernesto can stay out in the sun longer than both of us because his beautiful dark skin gives him even more protection."

Despite our several class discussions on beauty, ugliness, and skin color, Ernesto did not appear to change his mind. But hopefully, his mind will not forget our discussions.

Ernesto probably still takes his magic pills, which, his mother later explained, are Flintstones Vitamins. But I hope that every time he pops one into his mouth, he remembers how his classmates challenged the view that to be beautiful one has to be white. I want Ernesto to always remember, as will I, Lorena's comment: "Dark-skinned children are beautiful and I have dark skin, too." ∎

Alejandro Segura-Mora taught kindergarten at a school in La Puente, California, and currently teaches sixth-eighth grade Language Arts in Azusa, California. E-mail: aseguramora@yahoo.com.

The names of the children in this article have been changed.

Ebonics and Culturally Responsive Instruction

What should teachers do?

By Lisa Delpit

The "Ebonics Debate" has created much more heat than light for most of the country. For teachers trying to determine what implications there might be for classroom practice, enlightenment has been a completely nonexistent commodity. I have been asked often enough recently, "What do you think about Ebonics? Are you for it or against it?" My answer must be neither. I can be neither for Ebonics or against Ebonics any more than I can be for or against air. It exists. It is the language spoken by many of our African-American children. It is the language they heard as their mothers nursed them and changed their diapers and played peek-a-boo with them. It is the language through which they first encountered love, nurturance, and joy.

On the other hand, most teachers of those African-American children who have been least well-served by educational systems believe that their students' life chances will be further hampered if they do not learn Standard English. In the stratified society in which we live, they are absolutely correct. While having access to the politically mandated language form will not, by any means, guarantee economic success (witness the growing numbers of unemployed African Americans holding doctorates), not having access will almost certainly guarantee failure.

So what must teachers do? Should they spend their time relentlessly "correcting" their Ebonics-speaking children's language so that it might conform to what we have learned to refer to as Standard English? Despite good intentions, constant correction seldom has the desired effect. Such correction increases cognitive monitoring of speech, thereby making talking difficult. To illustrate, I have frequently taught a relatively simple new "dialect" to classes of preservice teachers. In this dialect, the phonetic element "iz" is added after the first consonant or consonant cluster in each syllable of a word. (*Maybe* becomes miz-ay-biz-ee and *apple*, iz-ap-piz-le.) After a bit of drill and practice, the students are asked to tell a partner in "iz" language why they decided to become teachers. Most only haltingly attempt a few words before lapsing into either silence or into Standard English. During a follow-up discussion, all students invariably speak of the impossibility of attempting to apply rules while trying to formulate and express a thought. Forcing speakers to monitor their language typically produces silence.

Correction may also affect students' attitudes toward their teachers. In a recent research project, middle-school, inner-city students were interviewed about their attitudes toward their teachers and school. One young woman complained bitterly: "Mrs. ___ always be interrupting to make you 'talk correct' and stuff. She be butting into your conversations when you not even talking to her! She need to mind her own business." Clearly this student will be unlikely to either follow the teacher's directives or to want to imitate her speech style.

Group Identity

Issues of group identity may also affect students' oral production of a different dialect. Researcher Sharon Nelson-Barber, in a study of phonologic aspects of Pima Indian language, found that in grades 1-3 the children's English most approximated the standard dialect of their teachers. But surprisingly, by fourth grade, when one might assume growing competence in standard forms, their language moved significantly toward the local dialect. These fourth graders had the *competence* to express themselves in a more standard form, but chose, consciously or unconsciously, to use the language of those in their local environments. The researcher believes that, by ages 8-9, these children became aware of their group membership and its importance to their well-being, and this realization was reflected in their language.[1] They may also have become increasingly aware of the school's negative attitude toward their community and found it necessary — through choice of linguistic form — to decide with which camp to identify.

What should teachers do about

JEAN-CLAUDE LEJEUNE

helping students acquire an additional oral form? First, they should recognize that the linguistic form a student brings to school is intimately connected with loved ones, community, and personal identity. To suggest that this form is "wrong" or, even worse, ignorant, is to suggest that something is wrong with the student and his or her family. To denigrate your language is, then, in African-American terms, to "talk about your mama." Anyone who knows anything about African-American culture knows the consequences of that speech act!

On the other hand, it is equally important to understand that students who do not have access to the politically popular dialect form in this country are less likely to succeed economically than their peers who do. How can both realities be embraced in classroom instruction?

It is possible and desirable to make the actual study of language diversity a part of the curriculum for all students. For younger children, discussions about the differences in the ways television characters from different cultural groups speak can

provide a starting point. A collection of the many children's books written in the dialects of various cultural groups can also provide a wonderful basis for learning about linguistic diversity,[2] as can audiotaped stories narrated by individuals from different cultures, including taping books read by members of the children's home communities. Mrs. Pat, a teacher chronicled by Stanford University researcher Shirley Brice Heath, had her students become language "detectives," interviewing a variety of individuals and listening to the radio and television to discover the differences and similarities in the ways people talked.[3] Children can learn that there are many ways of saying the same thing, and that certain contexts suggest particular kinds of linguistic performances.

Some teachers have groups of students create bilingual dictionaries of their own language form and Standard English. Both the students and the teacher become engaged in identifying terms and deciding upon the best translations. This can be done as generational dictionaries,

too, given the proliferation of "youth culture" terms growing out of the Ebonics-influenced tendency for the continual regeneration of vocabulary. Contrastive grammatical structures can be studied similarly, but, of course, as the Oakland policy suggests, teachers must be aware of the grammatical structure of Ebonics before they can launch into this complex study.

Other teachers have had students become involved with standard forms through various kinds of role play. For example, memorizing parts for drama productions will allow students to practice and "get the feel" of speaking standard English while not under the threat of correction. A master teacher of African-American children in Oakland, Carrie Secret, uses this technique and extends it so that students video their practice performances and self-critique them as to the appropriate use of standard English. (But I must add that Carrie's use of drama and oration goes much beyond acquiring Standard English. She inspires pride and community connections which are truly wondrous to behold.) The use of self-critique of recorded forms may prove even more useful than I initially realized. California State University-Hayward professor Etta Hollins has reported that just by leaving a tape recorder on during an informal class period and playing it back with no comment, students began to code-switch — moving between Standard English and Ebonics — more effectively. It appears that they may have not realized which language form they were using until they heard themselves speak on tape.

Young students can create puppet shows or role play cartoon characters — many "superheroes" speak almost hypercorrect standard English! Playing a role eliminates the possibility of implying that the *child's* language is inadequate and suggests, instead, that different language forms are appropriate in different contexts. Some other teachers in New York City have had their students produce a news show every day for the rest of the school. The students take on the personae of famous newscasters, keeping in character as they develop and read their news reports. Discussions ensue about whether Tom Brokaw would have said it that way, again taking the focus off the child's speech.

Although most educators think of Black Language as primarily differing in grammar and syntax, there are other differences in oral language of which teachers should be aware in a multicultural context, particularly in discourse style and language use. Harvard University researcher Sarah Michaels and other researchers identified differences in children's narratives at "sharing time."[4] They found that there was a tendency among young white children to tell "topic-centered" narratives—stories focused on one event—and a tendency among Black youngsters, especially girls, to tell "episodic" narratives—stories that include shifting scenes and are typically longer. While these differences are interesting in themselves, what is of greater significance is adults' responses to the differences.

C. B. Cazden reports on a subsequent project in which a white adult was taped reading the oral narratives of black and white first graders, with all syntax dialectal markers removed.[5] Adults were asked to listen to the stories and comment about the children's likelihood of success in school. The researchers were surprised by the differential responses given by Black and white adults.

Varying Reactions

In responding to the retelling of a Black child's story, the white adults were uniformly negative, making such comments as "terrible story,

> It is possible and desirable to make the actual study of language diversity a part of the curriculum for all students.

incoherent" and "[n]ot a story at all in the sense of describing something that happened." Asked to judge this child's academic competence, all of the white adults rated her below the children who told "topic-centered" stories. Most of these adults also predicted difficulties for this child's future school career, such as, "This child might have trouble reading," that she exhibited "language problems that affect school achievement," and that "family problems" or "emotional problems" might hamper her academic progress.

The Black adults had very different reactions. They found this child's story "well formed, easy to understand, and interesting, with lots of

detail and description." Even though all five of these adults mentioned the "shifts" and "associations" or "non-linear" quality of the story, they did not find these features distracting. Three of the Black adults selected the story as the best of the five they had heard, and all but one judged the child as exceptionally bright, highly verbal, and successful in school.[6]

This is not a story about racism, but one about cultural familiarity. However, when differences in narrative style produce differences in interpretation of competence, the pedagogical implications are evident. If children who produce stories based in differing discourse styles are expected to have trouble reading, and viewed as having language, family, or emotional problems, as was the case with the informants quoted by Cazden, they are unlikely to be viewed as ready for the same challenging instruction awarded students whose language patterns more closely parallel the teacher's.

Most teachers are particularly concerned about how speaking Ebonics might affect learning to read. There is little evidence that speaking another mutually intelligible language form, per se, negatively affects one's ability to learn to read.[7] For commonsensical proof, one need only reflect on non-standard English-speaking Africans who, though enslaved, not only taught themselves to read English, but did so under threat of severe punishment or death. But children who speak Ebonics do have a more difficult time becoming proficient readers. Why? In part, appropriate instructional methodologies are frequently not adopted. There is ample evidence that children who do not come to school with knowledge about letters, sounds, and symbols need to experience some explicit instruction in these areas in order to become independent readers. Another explanation is that, where teachers' assessments of competence are influenced by the language children speak, teachers may develop low expectations for certain students and subsequently teach them less.[8] A third explanation rests in teachers confusing the teaching of reading with the teaching of a new language form.

Reading researcher Patricia Cunningham found that teachers across the United States were more likely to correct reading miscues that were "dialect" related ("Here go a table" for "Here is a table") than those that were "nondialect" related ("Here is a dog" for "There is a dog").[9] Seventy-eight percent of the former types of miscues were corrected, compared with only 27% of the latter. Cunningham concludes that the teachers were acting out of ignorance, not realizing that "here go" and "here is" represent the same meaning in some Black children's language.

In my observations of many classrooms, however, I have come to conclude that even when teachers recognize the similarity of meaning, they are likely to correct Ebonics-related miscues. Consider a typical example:

Text: Yesterday I washed my brother's clothes.
Student's Rendition: Yesterday I wash my bruvver close.

The subsequent exchange between student and teacher sounds something like this:
　　T: Wait, let's go back. What's that word again? {Points at *washed*.}
　　　S: Wash.
　　　T: No. Look at it again. What letters do you see at the end? You see "e-d." Do you remember what we say when we see those letters on the end of the word?
　　　S: "ed"
　　　T: OK, but in this case we say washed. Can you say that?
　　　S: Wash*ed*.
　　　T: Good. Now read it again.
　　　S: Yesterday I wash*ed* my bruvver...
　　　T: Wait a minute, what's that word again? {Points to *brother*.}
　　　S: Bruvver.
　　　T: No. Look at these letters

JEAN-CLAUDE LEJEUNE

in the middle. {Points to brother.} Remember to read what you see. Do you remember how we say that sound? Put your tongue between your teeth and say "th"....

The lesson continues in such a fashion, the teacher proceeding to correct the student's Ebonics-influenced pronunciations and grammar, while ignoring the fact that the student had to have comprehended the sentence in order to translate it into her own language. Such instruction occurs daily and blocks reading development in a number of ways. First, because children become better readers by having the opportunity to read, the overcorrection exhibited in this lesson means that this child will be less likely to become a fluent reader than other children who are not interrupted so consistently. Second, a complete focus on code and pronunciation blocks children's understanding that reading is essentially a meaning-making process. This child, who understands the text, is led to believe that she is doing something wrong. She is encouraged to think of reading not as something you do to get a message, but something you pronounce. Third, constant corrections by the teacher are likely to cause this student and others like her to resist reading and to resent the teacher.

Language researcher Robert Berdan reports that, after observing the kind of teaching routine described above in a number of settings, he incorporated the teacher behaviors into a reading instruction exercise that he used with students in a college class.[10] He put together sundry rules from a number of American social and regional dialects to create what he called the "language of Atlantis." Students were then called upon to read aloud in this dialect they did not know. When they made errors he interrupted them, using some of the same statements/ comments he had heard elementary school teachers routinely make to their students. He concludes:

The results were rather shocking. By the time these Ph.D candidates in English or linguistics had read 10-20 words, I could make them sound totally illiterate.... The first thing that goes is sentence intonation: They sound like they are reading a list from the telephone book. Comment on their pronunciation a bit more, and they begin to subvocalize, rehearsing pronunciations for themselves before they dare to say them out loud. They begin to guess at pronunciations .... They switch letters around for no reason. They stumble; they repeat. In short, when I attack them for their failure to conform to my demands for

Atlantis English pronunciations, they sound very much like the worst of the second graders in any of the classrooms I have observed.

They also begin to fidget. They wad up their papers, bite their fingernails, whisper, and some finally refuse to continue. They do all the things that children do while they are busily failing to learn to read.

The moral of this story is not to confuse learning a new language form with reading comprehension. To do so will only confuse the child, leading her away from those intuitive understandings about language that will promote reading development, and toward a school career of resistance and a lifetime of avoiding reading.

Unlike unplanned oral language or public reading, writing lends itself to editing. While conversational talk is spontaneous and must be responsive to an immediate context, writing is a mediated process which may be written and rewritten any number of times before being introduced to public scrutiny. Consequently, writing is more amenable to rule application — one may first write freely to get one's thoughts down, and then edit to hone the message and apply specific spelling, syntactical, or punctuation rules. My college students who had such difficulty talking in the "iz" dialect, found writing it, with the rules displayed before them, a relatively easy task.

To conclude, the teacher's job is to provide access to the national "standard" as well as to understand the language the children speak sufficiently to celebrate its beauty. The verbal adroitness, the cogent and quick wit, the brilliant use of metaphor, the facility in rhythm and rhyme, evident in the language of Jesse Jackson, Whoopi Goldberg, Toni Morrison, Henry Louis Gates, Tupac Shakur, and Maya Angelou, as well as in that of many inner-city Black students, may all be drawn upon to facilitate school learning. The teacher must know how to effec-

tively teach reading and writing to students whose culture and language differ from that of the school, and must understand how and why students decide to add another language form to their repertoire. All we can do is provide students with access to additional language forms. Inevitably, each speaker will make his or her own decision about what to say in any context.

But I must end with a caveat that we keep in mind a simple truth: Despite our necessary efforts to provide access to standard English, such access will not make any of our students more intelligent. It will not

> **Where teachers' assessments of competence are influenced by the language children speak, teachers may develop low expectations for certain students and subsequently teach them less.**

teach them math or science or geography — or, for that matter, compassion, courage, or responsibility. Let us not become so overly concerned with the language *form* that we ignore academic and moral *content*. Access to the standard language may be necessary, but it is definitely *not* sufficient to produce intelligent, competent caretakers of the future. ■

©1997 Lisa Delpit

Lisa Delpit is holder of the Benjamin E. Mays Chair of Urban Educational Excellence at Georgia State University in Atlanta. A former MacArthur fellow, her books include Other People's Children *(New Press, 1995) and* The Real Ebonics Debate *(Beacon, 1998).*

Notes

1. Nelson-Barber, S. "Phonologic Variations of Pima English," in R. St. Clair and W. Leap (Eds.), *Language Renewal Among American Indian Tribes: Issues, Problems and Prospects.* Rosslyn, VA: National Clearinghouse for Education, 1982.

2. These books include a series of biographies produced by Yukon-Koyukkuk School District of Alaska and published by Hancock House Publishers in North Vancouver, British Columbia, Canada and the following:
Clifton, Lucille. *All Us Come 'Cross the Water.* New York: Holt, Rinehart, and Winston, 1973.
Green, Paul (aided by Abbott, Abbe). *I Am Eskimo — Aknik My Name.* Juneau, AK: Alaska Northwest Publishing, 1959.
Jacobs, Howard, and Rice, Jim. *Once Upon a Bayou.* New Orleans, LA: Phideaux Publications, 1983.
Elder, Tim. *Santa's Cajun Christmas Adventure.* Baton Rouge, LA: Little Cajun Books, 1981.

3. Heath, Shirley Brice. *Ways with Words.* Cambridge, England: Cambridge University Press, 1983.

4. Michaels, S., and Cazden, C. B. "Teacher-Child Collaboration on Oral Preparation for Literacy," in Schieffer. B. (Ed.), *Acquisition of Literacy: Ethnographic Perspectives.* Norwood, NJ: Ablex, 1986.

5. Cazden, C. B. *Classroom Discourse.* Portsmouth, NH: Heinemann, 1988.

6. *Ibid.*

7. Sims, R. "Dialect and Reading: Toward Redefining the Issues," in Langer, J., and Smith-Burke, M. T. (Eds.), *Reader Meets Author: Bridging the Gap.* Newark, DE: International Reading Asssociation, 1982.

8. *Ibid.*

9. Cunningham, Patricia M. "Teachers' Correction Responses to Black-Dialect Miscues Which Are Nonmeaning-Changing," *Reading Research Quarterly* 12 (1976-77).

10. Berdan, Robert. "Knowledge into Practice: Delivering Research to Teachers," in Whiteman, M. F. (Ed.), *Reactions to Ann Arbor: Vernacular Black English and Education.* Arlington, VA: Center for Applied Linguistics, 1980.

Exploring Black Cultural Issues

By Bakari Chavanu

When I was growing up in Oklahoma in the late 1960s and early 1970s, books or short stories by Black authors were as rare in my classroom as the number of television shows featuring Black characters or performers. Just as my friends and I would phone one another when a Black musical special would air or a famous Black person was being interviewed, we would have probably responded similarly if we had been introduced to a piece of literature by James Baldwin, Richard Wright, Zora Neale Hurston, or Nikki Giovanni.

For my friends and me, Black culture centered on music and archetypes of popular culture such as Richard Pryor. "Back in the day," as my students describe any decade before the '90s, none of my friends or classmates knew about Black authors in the way we knew about the Jackson Five, Aretha Franklin, The Temptations, The Funkadelics, *Superfly*, Richard Pryor, or J. J. Walker of the Black family sitcom *Good Times*. We displayed our Michael Jackson Afros, quoted Pryor's best jokes, and some of us, sadly, sold drugs like our gangsta heroes of Black exploitation films.

Our high school English classes certainly didn't broaden our horizons. All we learned about literature, if we cared to attend class, was Edgar Allan Poe, William Shakespeare, and a few short stories by Ernest Hemingway. If someone had asked us about the racial issues in James Baldwin's *The Fire Next Time*, or what if anything the Harlem Renaissance was about, we would

have blinked our eyes and laughed at such stupid questions. Reading about Black cultural issues just didn't happen unless our parents introduced us to literature beyond the classroom.

Today, literature by Black authors is more widely accepted than ever before. The number of books by Black authors published last year, for instance, far exceeds the number published during my entire four years of high school. And authors like Terri McMillan and Toni Morrison have a strong crossover appeal and rack up weeks and weeks on the best-sellers list. Furthermore, there's a broader diversity in style and genre, from novelists like Alice Walker, to science fiction writers like Octavia Butler, to crime writers like Walter Mosely, to poets like Maya Angelou, to essayists like June Jordan and Lisa Jones.

But while the tradition of Black literature is growing ever stronger, most students are still not provided opportunities to read, discuss, study, and write about the issues and insights these works have to offer. Clearly, people are reading Black literature. But if we wait for school

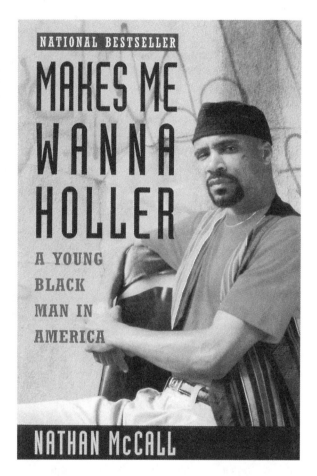

boards and teacher colleagues to approve and introduce these works in the classroom, we will see another generation of students graduate with more knowledge of rap artists and goofy sitcoms than of Black literature and the cultural issues that they address.

Multicultural Literature

I teach in Florin High School, in Sacramento, California, whose 2,500 students are approximately 36% white, 23% Asian, 17% Black, 12% Latino/Latina, and 1% Native-

American. Despite the cultural diversity in my school, many Black and other multicultural books are not taught as whole-class sets or are nonexistent in the English curriculum. In addition to resistance to a multicultural canon, some school boards often don't approve of class sets of books that contain profanity or sexual matter — making sure that many Black books, along with most contemporary books, are not approved for classwide use.

For Black students, the traditional high school canon doesn't come close to confronting topics that affect their personal lives, such as Black identity, Black language, Black interpersonal relationships, pride in culture, confronting white supremacy, criminal injustice, Black music, and overcoming social and economic obstacles. But I also believe that Black literature is of value to all students, especially as it deals with ever-important issues of multicultural diversity, racism, sexism, and poverty.

When I started teaching at Florin High School seven years ago, I was expected to teach the traditional curriculum — *Huckleberry Finn, The Great Gatsby, Of Mice and Men*, and so forth. Over the years, my department has wrestled with the issue of how best to engage students in reading good books, and we have found ways to make changes in our curriculum. Last year, I also had the good fortune to teach a course called African-American Cultural Studies, where I was free to focus exclusively on Black literature. While the class was open to all students in the school, all those who signed up were African-American.

Finding the resources and getting the approval to buy entire class sets of books is still difficult, however. To get around textbook approvals and lack of funding for class sets, I use study groups of about four or five stu-

dents. The groups are arranged either around a particular book or a set of different works addressing a particular theme.

I have found that, in general, thematically based groups are most useful. They allow students to have a choice in what they would like to

A Taste of Power

A BLACK WOMAN'S STORY
ELAINE BROWN

read, providing a richer learning experience. Students learn more when they pose and answer questions as part of a group and hear the insights, understandings, and feedback of other students.

Raising Broad Themes

In my African-American Cultural Studies group, first the entire group read *The Autobiography of Malcolm X*. But I also wanted to introduce my students to a wider range of Black authors and cultural themes, and knew that thematically based groups would make this possible. (For years I had tried a variation of literature discussion groups based on what I had read in *English Journal*. But Harvey Daniels' *Literature Circles*

(1994) provided me with the best methods for managing and sustaining literature groups in my classroom.)

To prepare for this thematically based, four-week unit of the class, I developed a list of classical and contemporary African-American books I had either read or were suggested to me by friends, teachers, and students. I then brainstormed a list of cultural themes I thought would encompass the selected books.

Anticipating four to six students per group, I came up with six topics: "Fighting the Power: Traditions of Resistance," "Growing Up in the Hood," "Ain't I Woman: Struggles of Black Women," "Learning to Love: Black Male/Female Relationships," "Growing Up Black and Overcoming Obstacles," and "In My Opinion: The Black Essay." (See p. 30 for the list.)

After I gave brief summaries of the books and allowed the students to peruse sample copies of the books, the students selected a book and theme. By using the books from my classroom and from the school and community libraries, and because some students wanted to buy certain books, I was able to make sure that every student had their own copy of a book. Themes such as "Learning to Love" and "Growing Up Black" were particularly popular, partly because the students were curious about the contemporary works that were part of that theme — such as April Sinclair's *Coffee Will Make You Black* and Nathan McCall's *Makes Me Wanna Holler*.

Because the students in a particular study group were reading books with different titles, I required members of each group to prepare for their literature discussions by taking on one of the following roles:

• Facilitator — develops a list of questions that focus on the theme.

• Connector — develops a list of examples for his/her book that connect with real life or another book or movie.

• Highlighter — selects three passages from his/her book that connects with the theme.

• Illustrator— draws a symbol or illustration that connects with the theme.

The roles rotate, so that members have a different task each time the group meets. (This strategy is further explained in Daniels' book.)

The groups met twice a week for about 25 minutes during the four weeks. I usually participated in each group for a few minutes each time they met. I also asked that each group provide a minutes-taker for the meeting. I then asked for an oral report from each of the different groups during the last 15 minutes of class — both as a form of accountability and to stimulate whole-class discussions. Students also were required to keep journals and respond to both their books and the discussions in their groups.

Some of the feedback I got from my students was that they appreciated the opportunity to discuss issues raised by the books that are seen as off-limits by some teachers. As one student wrote in her journal: "A lot of the issues that we discussed some teachers probably wouldn't have approved of." Some of these issues included problems dealing with the opposite sex, homosexuality, racism in school, and interracial dating. Some of the liveliest and loudest discussions came from the Black Male/ Female Relationships group, which often spilled over into whole-class discussions. The students discussed problematic issues that were prevalent in their own lives but also in books such as Patrice Gaine's *Laughing in the Dark*, April Sinclair's *Coffee Will Make You Black,* and Terri McMillan's *Mama.*

In response to the memoir *No Disrespect,* by rap artist Sister Souljah, one female student wrote:

The book has a profound effect on the way I look at other Black women. I feel we sometimes attack each other out of insecurities.... I wish we women could have some type of level to come together on and relate to one another. I feel only a Black woman could understand and feel the problems of another Black woman.

As part of the final exam for the unit, each group was required to conduct a 15-minute "fishbowl" discussion — in which the group sits in the middle of a circle in front of the class — and answers a question I had handed out to them a few days in advance. The exam's purpose was to allow the students to demonstrate their oral skills and to lead an effective discussion about their book and theme. The students were evaluated based on how well they answered the prompt question, using examples from the book, their own experiences, and issues related to the theme.

In preparation for one of the exam prompts, for instance, a student who had read Alex Haley's *Queen* reflected in her journal:

Black women are struggling — looking for their role in society. Are we here to help the Black man struggle or should we fight for our own struggle? In that aspect the problems of African-American women are different than that of any other race or gender. Not only are we fighting against racism but we are fighting against sexism too. Black women are struggling with their own jealousies. Black women along with white women did not like Queen because she attracted attention from men of both races. In effect we are truly beating ourselves down. In the future young Black females need to strive for unity. No one understands the Black woman but the Black woman, and if we can not confide and communicate with each other, then our future will be severely limited.

While introducing various works of Black literature in thematic discussion groups doesn't always bring a nice neat closure to a particular topic, I feel it provides students the basis upon which to continue their reading. As one student wrote in an evaluation of the unit, "I never really had the mind to read any books by Black authors but it really surprised me how many there is and how good they are."

As with the units I conduct in my English class, I'm finding that the only way I can get Black and other multicultural books in the classroom is by breaking the mold of tradition and forging a path for change. ■

Bakari Chavanu (e-mail address: BakariC@aol.com) is a teacher at Florin High School in Sacramento, California.

WARRIORS DON'T CRY

A Searing Memoir of the Battle to Integrate Little Rock's Central High

Commemorating the 40th Anniversary

MELBA PATTILLO BEALS

"Riveting...monumentally important....a rare and eloquent behind-the-scenes look at the 1957 integration of Central High...."—Patricia Holt, San Francisco Chronicle

Exploring Black Cultural Issues: Resources

Fight the Power: Traditions of Resistance

Beals, Melba. *Warriors Don't Cry.* New York: Pocket Books, 1995.

Brown, Elaine. *A Taste of Power.* New York: Pantheon, 1992.

Davis, Angela. *Angela Davis: An Autobiography.* New York: Random House, 1974.

Douglass, Frederick. *Narrative of the Life of Frederick Douglass.* New York: Anchor Books, 1963, originally published in 1845.

King, Martin Luther Jr. *Stride Toward Freedom.* San Francisco: Harper & Row, 1986.

Mandela, Nelson. *A Long Walk to Freedom.* New York: Little Brown, 1994.

Mandela, Winnie. *Part of My Soul Went With Him.* New York: Norton, 1985.

Newton, Huey P. *Revolutionary Suicide.* New York: Writers & Readers, 1993.

Nkrumah, Kwame. *The Autobiography of Kwame Nkrumah.* New York: International Publishers, 1957.

Shakur, Assata. *Assata.* Chicago: Lawrence Hill, 1987.

Growing Up In the Hood

Brown, Claude. *Manchild in the Promised Land.* New York: Signet, 1965.

Gaines, Patrice. *Laughing in the Dark.* New York: Anchor Books, 1994.

McCall, Nathan. *Makes Me Wanna Holler: A Young Black Man in America.* New York: Vintage Books, 1994.

Marshall, Joseph Jr. *Street Soldier.* New York: Delacorte Press, 1996.

Shakur, Sanyika (a.k.a. Monster Kody Scott). *Monster: The Autobiography of an L.A. Gang Member.* New York: Atlantic Monthly Press, 1993.

Growing Up Black and Overcoming Obstacles

Campbell, Bebe M. *Sweet Summer: Growing Up With and Without My Dad.* New York: Ballantine Books, 1989.

Gates, Henry Louis, Jr. *Colored People,* New York: Knopf, 1994.

McCall, Nathan. *Makes Me Wanna Holler: A Young Black Man in America.* New York: Vintage Books, 1994.

Shakur, Sanyika (a.k.a. Monster Kody Scott). *Monster: The Autobiography of an L.A. Gang Member.* New York: Atlantic Monthly Press, 1993.

Staples, Brent. *Parallel Time: Growing Up in Black and White.* New York: Pantheon Books, 1994.

Wright, Richard. *Black Boy.* New York: Perennial Library, 1937.

Ain't I A Woman: The Struggles of Black Women

Angelou, Maya. *I Know Why the Caged Bird Sings.* New York: Bantam Books, 1969.

Angelou, Maya. *The Heart of a Woman.* New York: Bantam Books, 1981.

Gaines, Patrice. *Laughing in the Dark.* New York: Anchor Books, 1994.

Naylor, Gloria. *The Women of Brewster Place.* New York: Penguin Books, 1980.

Shakur, Assata. *Assata.* Chicago: Lawrence Hill, 1987.

Souljah, Sister. *No Respect.* New York: Vintage Books, 1994.

Walker, Alice. *The Color Purple,* Alice. New York: Houghton-Mifflin, 1989.

Learning to Love: Black Male/Female Relationships

Baldwin, James. *If Beale Street Could Talk.* New York: Laurel Books, 1974.

Hurston, Zora Neale. *Their Eyes Were Watching God.* New York: HarperPerennial, 1991, originally published in 1937.

McMillan, Terri. *Disappearing Acts.* New York: Pocket Books, 1994.

McMillan, Terri. *Mama.* New York: Washington Square Press, 1989.

Sinclair, April. *Coffee Will Make You Black.* New York: Avon, 1994.

Walker, Alice. *The Color Purple,* Alice. New York: Houghton-Mifflin, 1989.

In My Opinion: The Black Essay

Abu-Jamal, Mumia. *Live from Death Row.* New York: Avon, 1995.

Cleage, Pearl. *Deals With the Devil.* New York: Ballantine Books, 1993.

Davis, Angela Y. *Women, Culture, & Politics.* New York: Random House, 1989.

Hutchinson, Earl Ofari. *The Assassination of the Black Male Image.* New York: Simon and Schuster, 1996.

Jones, Lisa. *Bulletproof Diva.* New York: Anchor Books, 1994.

Jordan, June. *Civil Wars.* New York: Touchstone, 1981.

Jordan, June. *Technical Difficulties: African-American Notes on the State of the Union.* New York: Pantheon Books, 1992.

Madhubuti, Haki R. *Black Men: Obsolete, Single, Dangerous?* Chicago:Third World Press, 1990.

Njeri, Itabari. *Every Good-Bye Ain't Gone.* New York: Vintage Books, 1991.

Tarpley, Natasha (Ed.). *Testimony: Young African-Americans on Self-Discovery and Black Identity.* Boston: Beacon, 1995.

— compiled by Bakari Chavanu

Ode to Writing

By Jessica Rawlins

I screamed
and scribbled
tore words from within
that were never meant to match.
I lived the story,
tortured the page
like life and death.
It was the fear that drove me
somewhere in my stomach
remembering the thought
of spilled words
numbers of them
that didn't make sense.
I yearned to be eloquent,
understood.
Somehow
the writing
bandaged the wounds,
made up for the words
not spoken
on the page.
I became pungent,
invincible,
knowing I could always be better
from the inside.
I spelled out a new name
making myself a face
with paper,
pen, and ink.

(Jessica Rawlins was a senior at Jefferson High School in Portland, Oregon when she wrote this poem. See "Basketball and Portfolios," p. 207, for assignment ideas.)

By Reynaldo

I Am Proud to Be Bilingual

I am very proud to be bilingual and do not agree with the idea of having to give up my first language and culture. I live in a home where I eat different food, listen to different music and speak a different language. I am my grandparents' little angel who talked to them in Hmong everyday when I was young. At age four, I had a fever which affected my language ability. My teacher worried about me pronouncing English wrong. Mommy referred me to speech, and Daddy didn't let me take Hmong class. I was supposed to speak only English.

One night, I had a dream that my eighty-year-old grandmother was dying. I said I loved her, but it was in English. I struggled word by word in Hmong. She was gone before I finished saying I loved her. I cried in my dream. I told Daddy I must go to Hmong class. I was born bilingual from the beginning. My first language and culture give me strength to make up myself. How can I live in two cultures and speak only one language? My life will be more beautiful and interesting if I speak both Hmong and English.

Monica Thao
4th Grade
Hellgate Elementary School
Missoula, MT

A winning essay in a contest sponsored by the National Association for Bilingual Education

THE POWER OF THE PAST

The power of the past shapes school experience in many ways. Examining that influence critically is a key to understanding current social arrangements and a guide to where we might go in the future. In this section, teachers show how they use history as a point of departure to deepen the meaning and purpose of learning in the classroom.

Unsung Heroes

By Howard Zinn

A high school student recently confronted me: "I read in your book *A People's History of the United States* about the massacres of Indians, the long history of racism, the persistence of poverty in the richest country in the world, the senseless wars. How can I keep from being thoroughly alienated and depressed?"

It's a question I've heard many times before. Another question often put to me by students is: Don't we need our national idols? You are taking down all our national heroes — the Founding Fathers, Andrew Jackson, Abraham Lincoln, Theodore Roosevelt, Woodrow Wilson, John F. Kennedy.

Granted, it is good to have historical figures we can admire and emulate. But why hold up as models the 55 rich white men who drafted the Constitution as a way of establishing a government that would protect the interests of their class — slaveholders, merchants, bondholders, land speculators?

Why not recall the humanitarianism of William Penn, an early colonist who made peace with the Delaware Indians instead of warring on them, as other colonial leaders were doing?

Why not John Woolman, who in the years before the Revolution refused to pay taxes to support the British wars, and who spoke out against slavery?

Why not Capt. Daniel Shays, veteran of the Revolutionary War, who led a revolt of poor farmers in Western Massachusetts against the oppressive taxes levied by the rich who controlled the Massachusetts

> **Our country is full of heroic people who are not presidents or military leaders or Wall Street wizards, but who are doing something to keep alive the spirit of resistance to injustice and war.**

Legislature?

Why go along with the hero-worship, so universal in our history textbooks, of Andrew Jackson, the slave-owner, the killer of Indians? Jackson was the architect of the Trail of Tears, which resulted in the deaths of 4,000 of 16,000 Cherokees who were kicked off their land in Georgia and sent into exile in Oklahoma.

Why not replace him as national icon with John Ross, a Cherokee chief who resisted the dispossession of his people, and whose wife died on the Trail of Tears? Or the Seminole leader Osceola, imprisoned and finally killed for leading a guerrilla campaign against the removal of the Indians?

And while we're at it, should not the Lincoln Memorial be joined by a memorial to Frederick Douglass, who better represented the struggle against slavery? It was that crusade of Black and white abolitionists, growing into a great national movement, that pushed a reluctant Lincoln into finally issuing a halfhearted Emancipation Proclamation, and persuaded Congress to pass the Thirteenth, Fourteenth, and Fifteenth amendments.

Take another presidential hero, Theodore Roosevelt, who is always near the top of the tiresome lists of Our Greatest Presidents. There he is on Mount Rushmore, as a permanent reminder of our historical amnesia about his racism, his militarism, his love of war.

Why not replace him as hero — granted, removing him from Mount Rushmore will take some doing — with Mark Twain? Roosevelt, remember, had congratulated an American general who in 1906 ordered the massacre of 600 men, women, and children on a Philippine island. As vice president of the Anti-Imperialist League, Twain denounced this and continued to point out the cruelties committed in the Philippine war under the slogan, "My country, right or wrong."

As for Woodrow Wilson, another honored figure in the pantheon of American liberalism, shouldn't we remind his admirers that he insisted on racial segregation in federal build-

ings, that he bombarded the Mexican coast, sent an occupation army into Haiti and the Dominican Republic, brought our country into the hell of World War I, and put anti-war protesters in prison?

Should we not bring forward as a national hero Emma Goldman, one of those Wilson sent to prison, or Helen Keller, who fearlessly spoke out against the war? (See the article on Helen Keller on p. 42.)

And enough worship of John F. Kennedy, a Cold Warrior who began the covert war in Indochina, went along with the planned invasion of Cuba, and was slow to act against racial segregation in the South.

Should we not replace the portraits of our Presidents, which too often take up all the space on our classroom walls, with the likenesses of grassroots heroes like Fannie Lou Hamer, the Mississippi sharecropper? Mrs. Hamer was evicted from her farm and tortured in prison after she joined the Civil Rights Movement, but she became an eloquent voice for freedom. Or with Ella

Baker, whose wise counsel and support guided the young Black people who joined the Student Nonviolent Coordinating Committee, the militant edge of the Civil Rights Movement in the Deep South?

In the year 1992, the quincentennial of the arrival of Columbus in this hemisphere, there were meetings all over the country to celebrate him, but also, for the first time, to challenge the customary exaltation of the Great Discoverer. I was at a symposium in New Jersey where I pointed to the terrible crimes against the indigenous people of Hispaniola committed by Columbus and his fellow explorers. Afterward, the other man on the platform, who was chairman of the New Jersey Columbus Day celebration, said to me: "You don't understand — we Italian Americans need our heroes." Yes, I understood the desire for heroes, I said, but why choose a murderer and kidnapper for such an honor? Why not choose Joe DiMaggio, or Toscanini, or Fiorello LaGuardia, or Sacco and Vanzetti? (The man was not persuaded.)

The same misguided values that have made slaveholders, Indiankillers, and militarists the heroes of our history books still operate today. We have heard Sen. John McCain, Republican of Arizona, repeatedly referred to as a war hero. Yes, we must sympathize with McCain's ordeal as a war prisoner in Vietnam, where he endured cruelties. But must we call someone a hero who participated in the invasion of a far-off country and dropped bombs on men, women, and children?

I have come across only one voice in the mainstream press daring to dissent from the general admiration for McCain — that of the poet, novelist, and Boston Globe columnist James Carroll. Carroll contrasted the heroism of McCain, the warrior, to that of Philip Berrigan, who has gone to prison dozens of times for protesting the war in Vietnam and the dangerous nuclear arsenal maintained by the U.S. government. Carroll wrote: "Berrigan, in jail, is the truly free man, while McCain remains imprisoned in an unexamined sense of martial honor."

Our country is full of heroic people who are not presidents or military leaders or Wall Street wizards, but who are doing something to keep alive the spirit of resistance to injustice and war.

I think of Kathy Kelly and all those other people from Voices in the Wilderness who, in defiance of federal law, have traveled to Iraq more than a dozen times to bring food and medicine to people suffering under the U.S.-imposed sanctions.

I think also of the thousands of students on more than 100 college campuses across the country who are protesting their universities' connection with sweatshop-produced apparel.

I think of the four McDonald sisters in Minneapolis, all nuns, who have gone to jail repeatedly for protesting against the Alliant Corporation's production of land mines.

I think, too, of the thousands of

> **The same misguided values that have made slaveholders, Indian-killers, and militarists the heroes of our history books still operate today.**

people who have traveled to Fort Benning, Georgia, to demand the closing of the murderous School of the Americas.

I think of the West Coast Longshoremen who participated in an eight-hour work stoppage to protest the death sentence levied against Mumia Abu-Jamal.

And so many more.

We all know individuals — most of them unsung, unrecognized — who have, often in the most modest ways, spoken out or acted on their beliefs for a more egalitarian, more just, peace-loving society.

To ward off alienation and gloom, it is only necessary to remember the unremembered heroes of the past, and to look around us for the unnoticed heroes of the present. ∎

Howard Zinn is author of A People's History of the United States *(HarperCollins, 1980).*

Copyright © 2000 by The Progressive Magazine, Madison, WI.

JEAN-CLAUDE LEJEUNE

Teaching About Unsung Heroes

Encouraging students to appreciate those who fought for social justice

By Bill Bigelow

Schools are identity factories. They teach students who "we" are. And as Howard Zinn points out in his essay "Unsung Heroes" (see p. 34), too often the curricular "we" are the great slaveholders, plunderers, imperialists, and captains of industry of yesteryear.

Thus when we teach about the genocide Columbus launched against the Taínos, or Washington's scorched-earth war on the Iroquois, or even Abraham Lincoln's promise in his first inaugural address to support a constitutional amendment making slavery permanent in Southern states, some students may experience this new information as a personal loss. In part, as Zinn suggests, this is because they've been denied a more honorable past with which to identify — one that acknowledges racism and exploitation, but also highlights courageous initiatives for social equality and justice.

One of the best and most diverse collections of writing I have received from my sophomore U.S. history students was generated from a project aimed to get students to appreciate those "other Americans." From time to time over the years, I've had students do research on people in history who worked for justice. But these were often tedious exercises and, despite my coaxing and pleading, student writing ended up sounding eerily encyclopedia-like.

An idea to revise this assignment came to me while reading Stephen O'Connor's curricular memoir, *Will My Name Be Shouted Out?*, about his experiences teaching writing to jun-

Sequoyah, holding a copy of the Cherokee alphabet he developed.

ior high school students in New York City. O'Connor was captivated by August Wilson's monologues in his play *Fences*. He read some of these aloud to his students and offered them a wide-open prompt: "Write a monologue in which a parent tells his or her life story to a child."

It struck me that I might get much more passionate, imaginative writing about the lives of social justice activists if I offered students a similar assignment. Instead of asking them to stand outside their research subjects and write in the third person, I invited them to attempt to become those

individuals at the end of their lives. Students could construct their papers as meditations about their individuals' accomplishments and possibly their regrets. They might narrate parts of their lives to a child, a younger colleague, or even to a reporter.

Last year I decided to launch this project out of a unit I do that looks at the sometimes tense relationship between the abolitionist movement and the women's rights movement in the years before and right after the Civil War. I framed it as the "Racial and Gender Justice Project: People Who Made Change." Because this would likely be the only time during the year that I would structure an entire research project around the lives of individual social justice activists, I wanted to give students an opportunity to learn about people throughout U.S. history, not simply during the decades between the 1830s and 1860s. I was aware that this presented something of a problem, as students wouldn't yet have the historical context to fully appreciate the work of, say, Dolores Huerta or Emma Goldman. But their reading would alert them to themes and events that we would cover later, and I could fill in some of the blank spots in their knowledge as they completed their research.

I remember one year writing up and assigning a choice-list of activists for students to research. I reviewed them in class one by one, talking briefly about their work and accomplishments. Can you spell b-o-r-i-n-g? This time I decided to write up short first-person roles for students to "try on" in class and to meet each other in character. I wasn't very scientific in the choices of activists that I offered students — in fact, some, like Bessie Smith, fell a bit

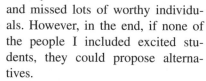

Instead of asking students to stand outside their research subjects and write in the third person, I invited them to attempt to become those individuals.

awkwardly into the "activist" category. I tried for racial and gender diversity; I also tried to mix the famous with the not-so famous, mostly concentrating on people who worked in social movements. (If the activists were too "unsung," students would have difficulty finding out enough about them to complete the writing. See box with complete list on p. 40.) My list was unavoidably idiosyncratic and missed lots of worthy individuals. However, in the end, if none of the people I included excited students, they could propose alternatives.

I wanted the roles I wrote up to be short and provocative. The point was not to do the assignment for students but to lure them into the activists' lives. Because my students are mostly white — and with this group (my only U.S. History class), overwhelmingly male — I wanted to make sure that at least several of the social justice activists were white men. It was important that the young white men in class know that people who look like they do have not only been the slaveowners and land-grabbers, they have also been part of a rainbow of resistance in U.S. history. Here are a couple of typical roles (the entire list is archived on the Rethinking Schools website, located at www.rethinkingschools.org, under Vol. 15 #1):

• John Brown: People have called me crazy because I, a white man, gave up my life in the cause to free Black slaves. I fought in what was

Abolitionist John Brown

called "bloody Kansas" to make sure that Kansas did not enter the United States as a slave state. And it's true, I killed people there. But it was a just cause, and I took no pleasure in killing. I'm most famous for leading the attack on the U.S. arsenal at Harper's Ferry, Virginia. In one sense my mission failed, because we were captured and I was executed. But I am convinced that my actions hastened the day of freedom for Black slaves.

• Fannie Lou Hamer: I was the youngest of 20 children. After I married, I was a sharecropper in Mississippi for 18 years. I risked my life when I registered to vote in 1962. I'd had enough of poverty. I'd had enough of racism. I began to organize for our rights, by working with SNCC, the Student Nonviolent Coordinating Committee. In the summer of 1964, I traveled to the Democratic National Convention where I was a representative of the Mississippi Freedom Democratic Party, which we'd created because the regular Democratic Party wouldn't allow Blacks to participate. I sang "Go Tell It on the Mountain," and asked the now-famous question: "Is this America?"

In class, I briefly described the project and distributed a card with one role description to each student. I gave them a few minutes to trade cards if they felt like it, but I emphasized that ultimately they weren't stuck researching the person on the card they drew; they would be able to choose someone else if they liked. I wanted these students-as-historical-activists to meet each other and learn a bit about each other's life work. Once they'd settled on an individual, I distributed "Hello, My Name Is...." stickers and had them write down and wear their names prominently, so other students would be able to easily see who was who. Finally, I gave each of them a "Racial and Gender Justice Hunt" sheet. The assignment gave students tasks like, "Find someone in the group who has spent time in jail for their activities or beliefs (or would have if they'd been caught). What happened?" I required them to use a different person in their

answers to each question, so they needed to keep circulating among other class members to complete the assignment. This was a delightful activity, filled with laughter and energy.

The following day we circled-up to review some of the questions and talk over what they had learned about the different individuals. Before we headed for the library to begin research, I gave the students an assignment sheet: "Choose an individual who stood up for racial or gender justice. Perhaps this individual worked to end slavery, for women's right to own property or to vote, for farmworkers' rights, or to integrate schools in the South. You needn't agree with everything this person stood for or agree with how he or she went about working for change. The only requirements are that the person tried to make this a better place to live and also significantly affected society. You may choose an individual (or group) who attended the 'getting to know you' gathering we did in class or come up with one of your

own. If you choose one on your own, check with me first."

I told them that they were going to be writing about their individual in the first person, but I didn't want to describe the full assignment until they had read and collected stories.

For their library and outside-of-class research, I gave students written research guidelines: "Find out as much about your individual as you can. Try to answer the following questions — and be sure to look for specific stories from their lives:

1. What significant events in this person's life shaped their social commitment? What happened in their life to make them willing to take the risks they took?

2. What did the person want to accomplish or change?

3. What did they accomplish?

4. What methods did this person use to try to effect change?

5. What, if anything, about their life reminds you of something in your life? Is there anything in their life that you relate to, or that is similar to feelings or experiences you've had?

6. What meaning does this per-

> It's vital that we alert students to currents of generosity, solidarity, democracy, anti-racism, and social equality in the nation's past — and present.

Racial and Gender Justice Hunt

Find someone in the group who:

• Has spent time in jail for their activities or beliefs (or would have if they'd been caught). What happened?

• Worked against slavery or other forms of racism. What exactly did they do?

• Worked for women's rights, workers' rights, or for the rights of gays and lesbians. What did they do?

• Believed it was necessary to use violence to achieve justice. What did they do?

• Worked for justice *nonviolently*. What did they do?

• You had never heard of before. What did they do? Why do you think you'd never heard of them?

• You *had* heard of. What new thing(s) did you learn about this person?

• Was not born in the United States. What did they do? What became of them?

• Is a white person who worked for racial justice. What did they do?

• Find five people here who you might want to research and learn more about. List these people. Tell what they did and why they interest you.

son's life have for today?

7. Find at least three quotes from the individual that you agree with or think are somehow significant."

I told them that they would need to turn in full answers to these questions with their final write-up.

Not surprisingly, some students had an easier time than others. The student doing Elaine Brown, one-time leader of the Black Panther Party, had trouble finding anything on her life and, unfortunately, didn't have the energy to read the entirety of Brown's excellent book, *A Taste of Power,* so moved on to Elizabeth Cady Stanton. But by and large students were able to discover lots about their activists.

Grandma T. and Other Stories

I've found that it's always better to show students what I'm looking for, rather than just tell them. So I save student papers from year to year to use as examples. My student Wakisha Weekly virtually became Sojourner Truth in a paper she had written for me in a previous year. I read it to the class to demonstrate the kind of intimacy, detail, and voice that I hoped students would strive for. She structured it as a conversation between a dying Sojourner Truth and her granddaughter. It opened:

"Grandma T., how are you?"

"Oh, I am fine, baby doll. As fine as you can be in a hospital bed with all of these tubes."

"Are you going to die, Grandma?"

"I'm not going to die, honey. I'm going home like a shooting star."

"Can you tell me a story, Grandma?"

Wakisha's "Grandma T." tells her granddaughter about life as a slave, being sold when her master died and of life with successive owners. She talks of her escape and her conversion:

"Later in my life is when I felt a powerful force. It was God all around me. God gave me the name Sojourner and told me to move to New York and to speak to people. I called it preaching. I often put people in tears. The better educated didn't like me because I was so good at what I did, and I loved speaking out to people. I can't read a book, but I can read the people."

"You don't know how to read, Grandma?"

"No, I was never taught. Slaves didn't go to school or to college to be educated. The masters thought you were there just to work for them."

"But Grandma, I love to read, and I am really good at it."

"That's good, baby. And part of the reason you can read and go to school is because women didn't like to be put down by the men and wanted to work, earn money, and even go to school. So we stood up for ourselves."

"Who is we, Grandma T.?"

Wakisha used the granddaughter's questions to pull her narrative along. In response to questions and comments, Grandma T. continued to tell the history, weaving her personal story with movement history — both the abolitionist and women's rights movements.

After hearing Wakisha's piece, students and I talked about what they liked about it and what made the writing both interesting and informative. We followed by brainstorming ways that we could write about the lives of our racial and gender justice activists. They came up with excellent ideas, including: students going to a nursing home to interview someone for a class project; a letter to a loved one, saying what you never got to say during your life; two lifelong friends walking and talking about the activities they participated in together.

I didn't want students to run simply with the first thing that came into their heads, so for homework I asked them to write two different introductions to their piece. We began these in class and the next day they brought them in and read them to one another in pairs. I asked people to nominate exemplary openings that they heard so that these could be shared with the entire class and broaden our sampling of possible approaches.

What students ultimately pro-

People Who Made Change

Frederick Douglass
Harriet Tubman
John Brown
Soldier of the 54th
    Massachusetts Regiment
Elizabeth Gurley Flynn
César Chávez
Sojourner Truth
Jeannette Rankin
Malcolm X
Elizabeth Cady Stanton
Susan B. Anthony
Carlos Bulosan
William Lloyd Garrison
Sarah and Angelina Grimké
Emma Goldman
Elaine Brown
Marcus Garvey
Black Panther Party for
    Self Defense Member
Jackie Robinson
Rosa Parks
Bessie Smith
Bernice Reagon
Queen Lili'uokalani
Nat Turner
Henry David Thoreau
Melba Pattillo Beals
Mickey Schwerner,
    James Cheney, and
    Andrew Goodman
Fannie Lou Hamer
Harvey Milk
Dolores Huerta
Fred Korematsu
Leonard Peltier

duced sounded nothing like an encyclopedia. Andy wrote a story about "Nicholas," a former member of the Massachusetts 54th, the first regiment of Black soldiers in American history. Drawing largely on letters in the book *A Grand Army of Black Men* (edited by Edwin S. Redkey), Andy set his piece in a facility for seniors, many years after the Civil War. Nicholas is sitting with his regular breakfast companion, Susan, who asks him at long last about the part of his ear that is missing. "To know about my ear, I would have to tell you a story," and launches into a richly detailed tale about his decision to volunteer for the 54th and his experiences fighting in South Carolina.

> Not all activism is equally effective, and some can actually do more harm than good. But the curriculum that demands perfection will be filled with blank pages.

Tyler's Marcus Garvey lies on his death bed wondering whether or not he did enough for racial equality. He flashes back to his impoverished Jamaican childhood: "Though we had close to no money, we had heart, and each other."

Sojourner Truth

Jennifer patterned her story about Rosa Parks on Wakisha's Grandma T. In an interior monologue, Jeff's Malcolm X reflected on how he changed, and what he feared and hoped for, while sitting in a hotel room the day before his final speech at the Audubon Ballroom. Jonathan wrote an unusual and complex piece that began on the day Leonard Peltier was released from prison — a day that is still in the future. His daughter tells the story of how she became an activist for Native-American rights after listening to her father narrate a videotape-letter to her about why he can't be with her as she grows up.

Gina wrote an utterly authentic-feeling story about two young children who visit César Chávez for a class project. In her story, Chávez narrates episodes from La Causa:

> "The fight was not over. In 1968, I fasted — that means I didn't eat anything — for 25 days. A different time I fasted for 24 days, and again I fasted, this time for 36 days. You know how hungry you can get when you miss breakfast or lunch — but imagine missing 36 breakfasts, lunches, and dinners."

> "But Mr. Chávez, didn't you ever fight? Like punch them or anything?" Richard asked.

"No, no! Violence isn't right. Everything can be done without hurting somebody else. You can always show people your side with words or pictures or actions. Hurting somebody to make your point is wrong, and it never needs to be done. We never punched anyone, even if they punched us first. We just stayed at our place and showed them that they couldn't stop us."

"That's really neat, Mr. Chávez! I'm gonna do that," Linda said determinedly.

"I'm Gonna Do That"

In a myth-shattering history curriculum where heroes are regularly yanked from their pedestals, it's vital that we alert students to currents of generosity, solidarity, democracy, anti-racism, and social equality in the nation's past — and present. We don't need to make these up. They are there. Yes, we need to carefully analyze movements for change and acknowledge their shortcomings, the times they manifested those very characteristics that they sought to oppose in the larger society. And yes, we need to engage students in thinking about the relationship between strategies and aims, because not all activism is equally effective, and some can actually be counterproductive. But the curriculum that demands perfection will be filled with blank pages. As Howard Zinn emphasizes, there are countless individuals who have worked "to keep alive the spirit of resistance to injustice and war." Let's work concretely toward a curriculum of hope. Let's give students the opportunity to conclude: "I'm gonna do that." ■

Bill Bigelow (bbpdx@aol.com) teaches at Franklin High School in Portland, Oregon and is a Rethinking Schools editor.

Discovering the Truth About Helen Keller

By James Loewen

Teachers have held up Helen Keller, the blind and deaf girl who overcame her physical handicaps, as an inspiration to generations of schoolchildren. Every fifth-grader knows the scene in which Anne Sullivan spells *water* into young Helen's hand at the pump. At least a dozen movies and filmstrips have been made on Keller's life. Each yields its version of the same cliché. A McGraw-Hill educational film concludes: "The gift of Helen Keller and Anne Sullivan to the world is to constantly remind us of the wonder of the world around us and how much we owe those who taught us what it means, for there is no person that is unworthy or incapable of being helped, and the greatest service any person can make us is to help another reach true potential."[1]

To draw such a bland maxim from the life of Helen Keller, historians and filmmakers have disregarded her actual biography and left out the lessons she specifically asked us to learn from it. Keller, who struggled so valiantly to learn to speak, has been made mute by history. The result is that we really don't know much about her.

Over the past ten years, I have asked dozens of college students who Helen Keller was and what she did. They all know that she was a blind and deaf girl. Most of them know that she was befriended by a teacher, Anne Sullivan, and learned to read and write and even to speak. Some students can recall rather minute details of Keller's early life: that she lived in Alabama, that she was unruly and without manners before Sullivan came along, and so forth. A few know that Keller graduated from college. But about what happened next, about the whole of her adult life, they are ignorant. A few students venture that Keller became a "public figure" or a "humanitarian," perhaps on behalf of

> **Keller learned how the social class system controls people's opportunities in life, sometimes determining even whether they can see or hear.**

the blind or deaf. "She wrote, didn't she?" or "She spoke." — conjectures without content. Keller, who was born in 1880, graduated from Radcliffe in 1904 and died in 1968. To ignore the 64 years of her adult life or to encapsulate them with the single word *humanitarian* is to lie by omission.

The truth is that Helen Keller was a radical socialist. She joined the Socialist Party of Massachusetts in 1909. She had become a social radical even before she graduated from Radcliffe, and *not*, she emphasized, because of any teachings available there. After the Russian Revolution, she sang the praises of the new communist nation:

> In the East a new star is risen! With pain and anguish the old order has given birth to the new, and behold in the East a man-child is born! Onward, comrades, all together! Onward to the campfires of Russia! Onward to the coming dawn![2]

Keller hung a red flag over the desk in her study. Gradually she moved to the left of the Socialist Party and became a Wobbly, a member of the Industrial Workers of the World (IWW), the syndicalist union persecuted by Woodrow Wilson.

Keller's commitment to socialism stemmed from her experience as a disabled person and from her sympathy for others with handicaps. She began by working to simplify the alphabet for the blind, but soon came to realize that to deal solely with blindness was to treat the symptom, not the cause. Through research she learned that blindness was not distributed randomly throughout the population but was concentrated in the lower class. Men who were poor might be blinded in industrial accidents or by inadequate medical care; poor women who became prostitutes faced the additional danger of syphilitic blindness. Thus Keller learned how the social class system

Helen Keller holds a Braille book in this 1955 photo. Schools and media often tell students about Keller's heroic struggles to overcome blindness and deafness, but leave out that she became a radical socialist.

controls people's opportunities in life, sometimes determining even whether they can see. Keller's research was not just book-learning: "I have visited sweatshops, factories, crowded slums. If I could not see it, I could smell it."[3]

At the time Keller became a socialist, she was one of the most famous women on the planet. She soon became the most notorious. Her conversion to socialism caused a new storm of publicity — this time outraged. Newspapers that had extolled her courage and intelligence now emphasized her handicap. Columnists charged that she had no independent sensory input and was in thrall to those who fed her information. Typical was the editor of the Brooklyn *Eagle*, who wrote that Keller's "mistakes spring out of the manifest limitations of her development."

Keller recalled having met this editor:

At that time the compliments he paid me were so generous that I blush to remember them. But now that I have come out for socialism he reminds me and the public that I am blind and deaf and especially liable to error. I must have shrunk in intelligence during the years since I met him.

Oh, ridiculous Brooklyn *Eagle*! Socially blind and deaf, it defends an intolerable system, a system that is the cause of much of the physical blindness and deafness which we are trying to prevent.[4]

Keller, who devoted much of her later life to raising funds for the American Foundation for the Blind, never wavered in her belief that our society needed radical change.

Having herself fought so hard to speak, she helped found the American Civil Liberties Union to fight for the free speech of others. She sent $100 to the NAACP with a letter of support that appeared in its magazine *The Crisis* — a radical act for a white person from Alabama in the 1920s. She supported Eugene V. Debs, the Socialist candidate, in each of his campaigns for the presidency. She composed essays on the women's movement, on politics, on economics. Near the end of her life, she wrote to Elizabeth Gurley Flynn, leader of the American Communist Party, who was then languishing in jail, a victim of the McCarthy era: "Loving birthday greetings, dear Elizabeth Flynn! May the sense of serving mankind bring strength and peace into your brave heart!"[5]

One may not agree with Helen Keller's positions. Her praise of the

U.S.S.R. now seems naive, embarrassing, to some even treasonous. But she *was* a radical — a fact few Americans know, because our schooling and our mass media left it out.[6]

We teach Keller as an ideal, not a real person, to inspire our young people to emulate her. Keller becomes a mythic figure, the "woman who overcame" — but for *what*? There is no content! Just look what *she* accomplished, we're exhorted — yet we haven't a clue as to what that really was.

Keller did not want to be frozen in childhood. She herself stressed that the meaning of her life lay in what she did once she overcame her disability. In 1929, when she was nearing fifty, she wrote a second volume of autobiography, entitled *Midstream*, that described her social philosophy in some detail. Keller wrote about visiting mill towns, mining towns, and packing towns where workers were on strike. She intended that we learn of these experiences and of the conclusions to which they led her. Consistent with our American ideology of individualism, the truncated version of Helen Keller's story sanitizes a hero, leaving only the virtues of self-help and hard work. Keller herself, while scarcely opposing hard work, explicitly rejected this ideology.

I had once believed that we were all masters of our fate — that we could mould our lives into any form we pleased.... I had overcome deafness and blindness sufficiently to be happy, and I supposed that anyone could come out victorious if he threw himself valiantly into life's struggle. But as I went more and more about the country I learned that I had spoken with assurance on a subject I knew little about. I forgot that I owed my success partly to the advantages of my birth and environment.... Now, however, I learned that the power to rise in the world is not within the reach of everyone.[7]

Textbooks don't want to touch this idea. "There are three great taboos in textbook publishing," an editor at one of the biggest houses told me, "sex, religion, and social class." While I had been able to guess the first two, the third floored me. Sociologists know the importance of social class, after all. Reviewing American history textbooks convinced me that this editor was right, however. The notion that opportunity might be unequal in America, that not everyone has "the power to rise in the world," is anathema to textbook authors, and to

> The notion that opportunity might be unequal in America, that not everyone has "the power to rise in the world," is anathema to textbook authors, and to many teachers as well.

many teachers as well. Educators would much rather present Keller as a bland source of encouragement and inspiration to our young — if she can do it, you can do it! So they leave out her adult life and make her entire existence over into a vague "up by the bootstraps" operation. In the process, they make this passionate fighter for the poor into something she never was in life: boring. ■

James Loewen is author of Lies My Teacher Told Me: Everything Your American History Textbook Got Wrong *(New Press, 1995), from which this article is adapted.*

Notes

1. *Helen Keller.* New York: McGraw-Hill Films, 1969.

2. Keller, Helen. "Onward, Comrades," address at the Rand School of Social Science, New York, December 31, 1920, reprinted in Foner, Philip S. (Ed.) *Helen Keller: Her Socialist Years.* New York: International Publishers, 1967, p. 107.

3. Quoted in Kozol, Jonathan. *The Night Is Dark and I Am Far From Home.* New York: Simon and Schuster, 1990 [1975], p. 101.

4. Foner, ed., *Helen Keller: Her Socialist Years*, p. 26.

5. Lash, Joseph P. *Helen and Teacher.* New York: Delacorte, 1980, p. 454; Wepman, Dennis. *Helen Keller.* New York: Chelsea House, 1987, p. 69; Foner, ed., *Helen Keller: Her Socialist Years*, pp. 17-18. The United States did not allow Flynn to receive the letter.

6. Jonathan Kozol brought this suppression to my attention in an address at the University of Wyoming in 1975. Nazi leaders knew her radicalism: in 1933 they burned Keller's books because of their socialist content and banned her from their libraries. We overlook her socialist content, thus learning no more than the German public about her ideas. See Wallace, Irving; Wallechinsky, David; and Wallace, Amy. *Significa.* New York: Dutton, 1983, pp. 1-2.

7. Keller, Helen. *Midstream: My Later Life.* New York: Greenwood, 1968 [1929], p. 156.

On the Road to Cultural Bias

A critique of "The Oregon Trail" CD-ROM

By Bill Bigelow

The critics all agree: *The Oregon Trail* is one of the greatest educational computer games ever produced. In 1992, *Prides' Guide to Educational Software* awarded it five stars for being "a wholesome, absorbing historical simulation," and "multi-ethnic," to boot. The newer version, *Oregon Trail II*, is the "best history simulation we've seen to date," according to a 1994 review by Warren Buckleitner, editor of *Children's Software Review Newsletter*. Susan Schilling, a key developer of *Oregon Trail II* who was later hired by *Star Wars* filmmaker George Lucas to head Lucas Learning Ltd., promised new interactive CD-ROMs targeted at children and concentrated in math and language arts.

Because interactive CD-ROMs like *The Oregon Trail* are encyclopedic in the amount of information they offer, and because they allow students a seemingly endless number of choices, they may appear educationally progressive. CD-ROMs seem tailor-made for the classrooms of tomorrow. They are hands-on and "student-centered." They are generally interdisciplinary — for example, *Oregon Trail II* blends reading, writing, history, geography, math, science, and health. And they are useful in multi-age classrooms because they allow students of various knowledge levels to "play" and learn.

But like the walls of a maze, the

Women played a different kind of role on the cross-country journey than the *Oregon Trail* CDs portray.

Beginning of the Oregon Trail: Independence, Missouri.

choices built into interactive CD-ROMs also channel participants in very definite directions. The CD-ROMs are programmed by people — people with particular cultural biases — and children who play the computer games encounter the biases of the programmers (Bowers, 1988). Just as we would not invite a stranger into our classrooms and then leave the room, teachers need to become aware of the political perspectives of CD-ROMs, and need to equip our students to "read" them critically.

At one level, this article is a critical review of the *Oregon Trail* CD-ROMs. I ask what knowledge is highlighted and what is hidden as students play the game. But I also reflect on the nature of the new electronic curricula, and suggest some questions teachers can ask before choosing to use them with our students. And I offer some classroom activities that might begin to develop students' critical computer literacy.

Playing the Game

In both *Oregon Trail* and *Oregon Trail II*, students become members of families and wagon trains crossing the Plains in the 1840s or 1850s on the way to the Oregon Territory. A player's objective, according to the game guidebook, is to safely reach the Oregon Territory with one's family, thereby "increasing one's options for economic success."

The enormous number of choices offered in any one session — what to buy for the journey; the kind of wagon to take; whether to use horses, oxen, or mules; the size of the wagon train with which to travel; whom to "talk" to along the way; when and where to hunt; when to rest; how fast to travel — is a kind of gentle seduction to students. It invites them to "try on this world view; see how it fits." In an interactive CD-ROM, you don't merely identify with a particular character, you actually adopt his or her frame of reference and act as if

you were that character (Provenzo, 1991). In *Oregon Trail*, a player quickly bonds to the "pioneer" maneuvering through the "wilderness."

In preparation for this article, I've played *Oregon Trail II* until my eyes became blurry. I can see its attraction to teachers. One can't play the game without learning a lot about the geography from Missouri to Oregon. (However, I hope I never have to ford another virtual river ever again.) Reading the trail guide as one plays teaches much about the ailments confronted on the Oregon Trail, and some of the treatments. Students can learn a tremendous amount about the details of life for the trekkers to Oregon: the kinds of wagons required, supplies needed, vegetation encountered along the route, and so forth. And the game has a certain multicultural and gender-fair veneer that, however limited, contrasts favorably with the white male dominated texts of yesteryear.

But as much as the game teaches,

CHIMNEY ROCK, ON THE NORTH PLATTE RIVER.

OREGON HISTORICAL SOCIETY

it *mis*-teaches more. In fundamental respects, *Oregon Trail II* is sexist, racist, culturally insensitive, and contemptuous of the earth. It imparts bad values and wrong history.

They Look Like Women, But...

To its credit, *Oregon Trail II* includes large numbers of women. Although I didn't count, women appear to make up roughly half the people students encounter as they play. But this surface equity is misleading. Women may be present, but gender is not acknowledged as an issue in *Oregon Trail*. In the opening sequences, the game requires students to select a profession, special skills they possess, the kind of wagon to take, the city they'll depart from, etc. Class is recognized as an issue — bankers begin with more money than saddlemakers, for example — but not gender or race — a player cannot choose these.

Without acknowledging it, *Oregon Trail* maneuvers students into thinking and acting as if they were all males — and, as we'll see, *white* males. The game highlights a male lifestyle and poses problems that historically fell within the male domain: whether and where to hunt, which route to take, whether and what to trade, to caulk a wagon or ford a river. However, as I began to read more feminist scholarship on the Oregon Trail, I realized that women and men experienced the Trail very differently. It's clear from reading women's diaries of the period that women played little or no role in deciding whether to embark on the trip, where to camp, which routes to take and the like. In real life, women's decisions revolved around how to maintain a semblance of community under great stress, how "to preserve the home in transit" (Faragher and Stansell, 1992; Schlissel, 1992; Kesselman, 1976).

Women decided where to look for firewood or buffalo chips, how and what to cook using hot rocks, how to care for the children, and how to resolve conflicts between travelers, especially the men.

These were real life decisions, but, with the exception of treating illness, they're missing from *The Oregon Trail*. Students are rarely required to think about the intricacies of preserving "the home in transit" for 2,000 miles. An *Oregon Trail II* information box on the screen informs a player when "morale" is high or low, but other than making better male-oriented decisions, what's a player to do? *Oregon Trail* offers no opportunities to encounter the choices of the Trail as women of the time would have encountered them, and to make decisions that might enhance community, and thus "morale." As Lillian Schlissel concludes in her study, *Women's Diaries of the Westward Journey* (1992): "If ever there was a time when men and women turned their psychic energies toward opposite visions, the overland journey was that time. Sitting side by side on a wagon seat, a man and a woman felt different needs as they stared at the endless road that led into the New Country." (p. 15).

Similarly, *Oregon Trail* fails to represent the *texture* of community life on the Trail. Students confront a seemingly endless stream of problems posed by *Oregon Trail* programmers, but rarely encounter the details of life, especially that of women's lives. By contrast, in an article in the book *America's Working Women* (1976), Amy Kesselman includes a passage from the diary of one female trekker, Catherine Haun, in 1849:

We women folk visited from wagon to wagon or congenial friends spent an hour walking ever westward, and talking over our home life "back in the states" telling of the loved ones left behind; voicing our hopes for the future in the far west and even whispering, a little friendly gossip of pioneer life. High teas were not popular but tatting, knitting, crocheting, exchanging receipts for cooking beans or dried apples or swopping food for the sake of variety kept us in practice of feminine occupations and diversions* (Kesselman, 1976, p. 71).

The male orientation of *Oregon Trail* is brought into sharp relief in the game's handling of Independence Day commemoration. Students as pioneers are asked if they wish to "Celebrate the Fourth!" Click on this option, and one hears loud "Yahoos" and guns firing. Compare this to the communal preparations described in Enoch Conyers' 1852 diary (but not in *The Oregon Trail*):

A little further on is a group of young ladies seated on the grass talking over the problem of manufacturing "Old Glory" to wave

over our festivities. The question arose as to where we are to obtain the material for the flag. One lady brought forth a sheet. This gave the ladies an idea. Quick as thought another brought a skirt for the red stripes... Another lady ran to her tent and brought forth a blue jacket, saying: "Here, take this; it will do for the field." Needles and thread were soon secured and the ladies went at their task with a will, one lady remarking that "necessity is the mother of invention," and the answer came back, "yes, and the ladies of our company are equal to the task" (Hill, 1989, p. 58).

> ## Oregon Trail's treatment of African Americans reflects a very superficial multiculturalism. Black people are present, but their lives aren't.

The contrast between the "yahoos"/gunfire of *Oregon Trail* and the collective female exhilaration described in the diary excerpt is striking. This comparison alerted me to something so obvious that it took me awhile to recognize. In *Oregon Trail*, people don't talk to *each other*, they all talk to you, the player. Everyone in the *Oregon Trail*-constructed world aims her or his conversation at you — underscoring the simulation's individualistic ideology that all the world exists for *you*, controller of the mouse. An *Oregon Trail* more alert to feminist insights and women's experiences would highlight relations

between people, would focus on how the experience affects our feelings about each other, would feature how women worked with one another to survive and weave community, as women's diary entries clearly reveal.

As I indicated, large numbers of women appear throughout the *Oregon Trail* simulation, and they often give good advice, perhaps better advice than the men we encounter. But *Oregon Trail*'s abundance of women, and its apparent effort to be gender-fair, masks an essential problem: The choice-structure of the simulation privileges men's experience and virtually erases women's experience.

African Americans as Tokens

From the game's beginning, when a player starts off in Independence or St. Joseph, Missouri, African Americans dot the *Oregon Trail* landscape. However, by and large they are no more than black-colored white people. Even though Missouri was a slave state throughout the entire Oregon Trail period, I never encountered the term "slavery" while playing the game. I found race explicitly acknowledged in only one exchange, when I "talked" to an African-American woman along the trail: "I'm Isabella. I'm traveling with the Raleighs and their people. My job is to keep after the cows and watch the children. My husband Fred is the ox-driver — best there is." Are they free, are they enslaved? Are we to assume the Raleighs are white? I asked to know more: "I was born in Delaware. My father used to tell me stories of Africa and promised one day we'd find ourselves going home. But I don't know if I'm getting closer or farther away with all this walking." The end. Like Missouri, Delaware was a slave state in antebellum days, but this is not shared with students. Isabella offers provocative details, but they hide more than they reveal about her identity and culture.

Oregon Trail's treatment of African Americans reflects a very superficial multiculturalism. Black people are present, but their lives

*The original spelling and phrasing have been retained in material cited here.

The Dalles on the Columbia River.

aren't. Attending to matters of race requires more than including lots of Black faces, or having little girls "talk Black"—"I think it's time we be moving on now." (This little girl reappears from time to time to repeat these same words. A man who looks Mexican likewise shows up frequently to say, with heavy accent: "Time is a-wasting. Let's head out!")

Even though one's life prospects and worldview in the 1840s and 1850s — as today — were dramatically shaped by one's race, this factor is invisible in *Oregon Trail*. Players know their occupations but not their racial identities, even though this knowledge is vital to decisions participants would make before leaving on the journey as well as along the way.

For example, many of the constitutions of societies that sponsored wagon trains specifically excluded Blacks from making the trip west. Nonetheless, as Elizabeth McLagan points out in her history of Blacks in Oregon, *A Peculiar Paradise* (1980), Blacks did travel the Oregon Trail, some as slaves, some as servants, and at least some, like George Bush, as

well-to-do pioneers. Race may not have seemed important to the *Oregon Trail* programmers, but race mattered a great deal to Bush: Along the Trail, he confided to another emigrant that if he experienced too much prejudice in Oregon, he would travel south to California or New Mexico and seek protection from the Mexican government (ibid, p. 19).

And Bush had reason to be apprehensive: African Americans arriving in Oregon Territory during the 1840s and 1850s were greeted by laws barring Blacks from residency. Black exclusion laws were passed twice in Oregon Territory in the 1840s, and a clause in the Oregon state constitution barring Black residency was ratified in 1857 by a ratio of 8-1— a clause, incidentally, not removed until 1926.

Upon completion of one of my simulated Oregon Trail journeys, I clicked to see how I turned out: "In 1855, Bill built a home on 463 acres of land in the Rogue River Valley of Oregon," experienced only "moderate success" and later moved to Medford, "establishing a small business that proved more stable and sat-

isfying." Although the *Oregon Trail* simulation never acknowledges it, "Bill" must have been white, because in 1850 the U.S. Congress passed the Oregon Donation Land Act granting 640 acres to free white males and their wives — only. It is unlikely that a Black man, much less a Black woman, would have been granted land in 1855 or been allowed to start a business in Medford some years later.

Why were whites so insistent that Blacks not live in Oregon? The preamble of one Black exclusion bill explained that "situated as the people of Oregon are, in the midst of an Indian population, it would be highly dangerous to allow free negroes and mulattoes to reside in the territory or to intermix with the Indians, instilling in their minds feelings of hostility against the white race...." (McLagan, 1980, p. 26). And Samuel Thurston, a delegate to Congress from Oregon Territory explained in 1850 why blacks should not be entitled to homestead in Oregon:

The negroes associate with the Indians and intermarry, and, if their free ingress is encouraged or allowed, there would a relationship spring up between them and the different tribes, and a mixed race would ensue inimical to the whites; and the Indians being led on by the negro who is better acquainted with the customs, language, and manners of the whites, than the Indian, these savages would become much more formidable than they otherwise would, and long and bloody wars would be the fruits of the comingling of the races. It is the principle of self preservation that justifies the action of the Oregon legislature (McLagan, 1980, pp. 30-31).

Thurston's argument carried the day. But *Oregon Trail* programmers have framed the issues so that race seems irrelevant. Thus, once students-as-pioneers arrive in Oregon, most of them will live happily after ever — never considering the impact that race would have on life conditions.

Just Passing Through?

Oregon Trail programmers are careful not to portray Indians as the "enemy" of westward trekkers. However, the simulation's superficial sympathy for Native groups masks a profound insensitivity to Indian cultures and to the earth that sustained these cultures. The simulation guidebook lists numerous Indian nations by name — and respectfully *calls* them "nations." The *Oregon Trail* guidebook explains that emigrants' fear of Indians is "greatly exaggerated:"

Some travelers have been known to cross the entire breadth of the continent from the Missouri River to the Sierra Nevadas without ever laying eye on an Indian, except perhaps for occasional brief sightings from a distance.
This is all well and good, for it is probably best for all parties concerned for emigrants and Indians

to avoid contact with each other. Such meetings are often the source of misunderstandings, sometimes with regrettable consequences.

Emigrants often spread disease, according to the guidebook, which made the Indians "distrust and dislike" the emigrants. The guidebook further warns *Oregon Trail* players not to overhunt game in any one place as "few things will incur the wrath of the Indian peoples more than an overstayed welcome accompanied by the egregious waste of the natural resources upon which they depend."
What orientation is highlighted and what is hidden in the simulation programmed for students to follow? The ideology embedded in *Oregon Trail I and II* is selfish and goal-driven: Care about indigenous people insofar as you need to avoid "misunderstanding" and incurring the wrath of potentially hostile natives. *Oregon Trail* promotes an anthropocentric earth-as-natural resource outlook. Nature is a *thing* to be consumed or overcome as people traverse the country in search of success in a far-away land. The simulation's structure coerces children into identifying with white settlers and dismissing non-white others. It contributes to the broader curricular racialization of identity students absorb — learning who constitutes the normalized "we" and who is excluded.
Oregon Trail players need not take into account the lives of others unless it's necessary to do so in order to accomplish their personal objectives. Thus the cultures of Plains Indians are backgrounded. The game marginalizes their view of the earth. Contrast, for example, the Indians' term "mother earth" with the *Oregon Trail* term "natural resource."
The metaphor of earth as mother suggests humans in a reciprocal relationship with a natural world that is alive, nourishing us, sustaining us. A resource is a thing to be

used. It exists *for* us, outside of us, and we have no obligations in return.
The consequences of the Oregon Trail for the Plains Indians, the Indians of the Northwest and for the earth were devastating. In fairness, as they play *Oregon Trail*, students may hear some of the details of this upheaval. For example, on one trip I encountered a "Pawnee Village." Had I paid attention to the warning in the guidebook to "avoid contact" I would have ignored it and continued on my trip. But I entered and "talked" to the people I encountered there. A Pawnee woman: "Why do you bother me? I don't want to trade. The things that we get from the white travelers don't make up for all that we lose." I click to hear more. "We didn't know the whooping cough, measles, or the smallpox until your people brought them to us. Our medicine cannot cure these strange diseases, and our children are dying." I click on "Do you have any advice?" Angrily, she says, "No. I just want you to leave us alone." The implication is that if I just "leave them alone" and continue on the trail I can pursue my dream without hurting the Indians.
However, this interpretation misses the fact that the Oregon Trail itself, not just contact with the so-called pioneers, devastated Indian cultures and the ecology of which those cultures were an integral part. For example, pioneers — let's begin to call them their Lakota name, *Wasi'chu*, "greedy persons"* — cut down all the cottonwood trees found along the rich bottomlands of plains rivers — trees which "offered crucial protection during winter blizzards as well as concealing a village's smoke from its enemies. In lean seasons, horses fed on its bark, which was surprisingly nourishing" (Davidson and Lytle, 1992, p. 114).
The Oregon Trail created serious wood shortages, which even the *Wasi'chu* acknowledged. "By the Mormon guide we here expected to find the last timber," wrote overlan-

---

* The Lakota "used a metaphor to describe the newcomers. It was *Wasi'chu*, which means 'takes the fat,' or 'greedy person.' Within the modern Indian movement, *Wasi'chu* has come to mean those corporations and individuals, with their governmental accomplices, which continue to covet Indian lives, land, and resources for private profit. *Wasi'chu* does not describe a race; it describes a state of mind" (Johnansen and Maestas, 1979, p. 6).

der A.W. Harlan, describing the Platte River, "but all had been used up by others ahead of us so we must go about 200 miles without any provisions cooked up." A few weeks later, in sight of the Black Hills, Harlan wrote: "[W]e have passed many cottonwood stumps but no timber....." (p. 115)

Wasi'chu rifles also killed tremendous numbers of buffalo that Plains Indians depended upon for survival. One traveler in the 1850s wrote that "the valley of the Platte for 200 miles presents the aspect of the vicinity of a slaughter yard, dotted all over with skeletons of buffaloes" (ibid p 117). Very soon after the beginning of the Oregon Trail the buffalo learned to avoid the Trail, their herds migrating both south and north. Edward Lazarus points out in *Black Hills/White Justice: The Sioux Nation Versus the United States — 1775 to the Present*: "But the Oregon Trail did more than move the buffalo; it destroyed the hunting pattern of the Sioux, forcing them to follow the herds to the fringes of their domain and to expose themselves to the raids of their enemies" (1991, p. 14).

However, wrapped in their cocoons of self-interest, *Oregon Trail* players push on, oblivious to the mayhem and misery they cause in their westward drive. This is surely an unintended, and yet intrinsic, part of the game's message: Pursue your goal as an autonomous individual, ignore the social and ecological consequences. Look out for number one.

No Violence Here

Oregon Trail never suggests to its simulated pioneers that they should seek permission of Indian nations to travel through their territory. And from this key omission flow other omissions. The simulation doesn't inform players that because of the disruptions wrought by the daily intrusions of the westward migration, Plains Indians regularly demanded tribute from the trekkers. As John Unruh, Jr., writes in *The Plains Across*:

The natives explicitly emphasized that the throngs of overlanders were killing and scaring away buffalo and other wild game, overgrazing prairie grasses, exhausting the small quantity of available timber, and depleting water resources. The tribute payments... were demanded mainly by the Sac and Fox, Kickapoo, Pawnee, and Sioux Indians — the tribes closest to the Missouri River frontier and therefore those feeling most keenly the pressures of white men increasingly impinging upon their domains (1993, p. 169).

Wasi'chu travelers resented this Indian-imposed taxation and their

> ## The sanitized, nonviolent Oregon Trail fails to equip students to reflect on the origins of conflicts between whites and Indians.

resentment frequently turned to hostility and violence, especially in the later years of the Trail. The Pawnees were "hateful wretches," wrote Dr. Thomas Wolfe in 1852, for demanding a 25-cent toll at a bridge across Shell Creek near the North Platte River (ibid p. 171). Shell Creek and other crossings became flashpoints that escalated into violent skirmishes resulting in the deaths of settlers and Indians.

Despite the increasing violence along the Oregon Trail, one choice

Oregon Trail programmers don't offer students-as-trekkers is the choice to harm Indians. Doubtless MECC, producer of *Oregon Trail*, is not anxious to promote racism toward Native peoples. However, because simulation players can't hurt or even speak ill of Indians, the game fails to alert students that white hostility was one feature of the westward migration. The omission is significant because the sanitized, nonviolent *Oregon Trail* fails to equip students to reflect on the origins of conflicts between whites and Indians. Nor does it offer students any insights into the racial antagonism that fueled this violence. In all my play of *Oregon Trail* I can't recall any blatant racism directed at Indians. But as John Unruh, Jr., points out: "The callous attitude of cultural and racial superiority so many overlanders exemplified was of considerable significance in producing the volatile milieu in which more and more tragedies occurred" (p. 186).

The End of the Trail

> *Soon there will come from the rising sun a different kind of man from any you have yet seen, who will bring with them a book and will teach you everything, after that the world will fall to pieces.*
>
> — *Spokan Prophet, 1790* (Limerick, 1987, p. 39)

Someone can spend two or three hours — or more — playing one game of *Oregon Trail* before finally reaching Oregon Territory. Once we arrive, the game awards us points and tells us how our life in Oregon turned out. And yet it fails to raise vital questions about our right to be there in the first place, and what happened to the people who were there first.

In its section on the "Destination," the guidebook offers students its wisdom on how they should view life in a new land. It's a passage that underscores the messages students absorb while engaged in the simulation. These comforting words of advice

End of the Trail: Oregon City.

and social vision are worth quoting at length:

Once you reach the end of your journey, you should go to the nearest large town to establish your land claim. If there are no large towns in the area, simply find an unclaimed tract of land and settle down.... As they say, possession is nine-tenths of the law, and if you have settled and worked land that hasn't yet been claimed by anyone else, you should have little or no trouble legally establishing your claim at a later time.

As more and more Americans move into the region, more cities and towns will spring up, further increasing one's options for economic success. Rest assured in the facts that men and women who are willing to work hard will find their labors richly rewarded, and that you, by going west, are helping to spread American civilization from ocean to ocean across this great continent, building a glorious future for generations to come!

The Lakota scholar/activist Vine Deloria, Jr., in his book, *Indians of the Pacific Northwest*, (1977) offers a less sanguine perspective than that included in the CD-ROM guidebook. People coming in on the Oregon Trail "simply arrived on the scene and started building. If there were Indians or previous settlers on the spot they were promptly run off under one pretext or another. Lawlessness and thievery dominated the area" (p. 53). From 1850 on, using provisions of the Oregon Donation Act, thousands of "pioneers" invaded "with impunity."

As Deloria points out, there were some in Congress who were aware that they were encouraging settlers to steal Indian land, and so shortly after, Congress passed the Indian Treaty Act requiring the United States to get formal agreements from Indian tribes. Anson Dart, appointed to secure land concessions, pursued this objective in a despicable fashion. For example, he refused to have the treaties translated into the Indians' languages, instead favoring "Chinook jargon," a non-language of fewer than 300 words good for trading, giving orders, and little else. Dart's mandate was to move all the Indians east of the Cascades, but he decided some tribes, like the Tillamooks and Chinooks, should keep small amounts of land as cheap labor reserves:

Almost without exception, I have found [the Indians] anxious to work at employment at common labor and willing too, to work at prices much below that demanded by the whites. The Indians make all the rails used in fencing, and at this time do the boating upon the rivers: In consideration, therefore, of the usefulness as labourers in the settlements, it was believed to be far better for the Country that they should not be

Settlers in Oregon built their homes on the lands of Native Americans.

removed from the settled portion of Oregon if it were possible to do so (Deloria, 1977, p. 51).

Meanwhile, in southwestern Oregon white vigilantes didn't wait for treaty niceties to be consummated. Between 1852 and 1856 self-proclaimed Volunteers attacked Indians for alleged misdeeds, or simply because they were Indians. In August of 1853, one Martin Angel rode into the Rogue River valley gold mining town of Jacksonville shouting, "Nits breed lice. We have been killing Indians in the valley all day," and "Exterminate the whole race." Minutes later a mob of about 800 white men hanged a seven-year-old Indian boy. In October 1855, a group of whites massacred 23 Indian men, women, and children. This incident began the Rogue Indian war, which lasted until June 1856 (Beckham, 1991, p. 103). Recall that this is the same region and the same year in one *Oregon Trail* session where "Bill" built a home and experienced "moderate success" — but thanks to the *Oregon Trail* programmers, learned nothing of the social conflicts swirling around him.

Nor did Bill learn that, even as a white person, he could protest the outrages committed against the Rogue River Valley Indians as did one anonymous "Volunteer" in a passionate 1853 letter to the *Oregon Statesman* newspaper:

A few years since the whole valley was theirs [the Indians'] alone. No white man's foot had ever trod it. They believed it theirs forever. But the gold digger come, with his pan and his pick and shovel, and hundreds followed. And they saw in astonishment their streams muddied, towns built, their valley fenced and taken. And where their squaws dug camus, their winter food, and their children were wont to gambol, they saw dug and plowed, and their own food sown by the hand of nature, rooted out forever, and the ground it occupied appropriated to the rearing of vegetables for the white man. Perhaps no malice yet entered the Indian breast. But when he was weary of hunting in the mountains without success, and was hungry, and approached the white man's tent for bread; where instead of bread he received curses and kicks, ye treaty kicking men — ye Indian exterminators think of these things. (Applegate and O'Donnell, 1994, p. 34)

Oregon Trail hides the nature of the Euro-American invasion in at least two ways.

In the first place, the *Oregon Trail* CD-ROM simply fails to inform simulation participants what happened between settlers and Indians. To the *Oregon Trail* player, it doesn't feel like an invasion; it doesn't feel wrong. After one of my arrivals, in 1848, "Life in the new land turned out to be happy and successful for Bill, who always cherished bittersweet but proud memories of the months spent on the Oregon Trail." (This struck me as a rather odd account, given that I had lost all three of my children on the trip.)

The only person that matters is the simulation player, in this case Bill. I was never told whether life turned out equally "happy and successful" for the Klamaths, Yakamas, Cayuses, Nez Percés, Wallawallas, and all the others who occupied this land generations before the *Wasi'chu* arrived.

The second way the nature of the white invasion is hidden has to do with the structure of the simulation. For a couple hours or more the player endures substantial doses of frustration, tedium, and difficulty. By the time the Willamette or Rogue Valleys come up on the screen we, the simulated trekkers, feel that we *deserve* the land, that our labors in transit should be "richly rewarded" with the best land we can find.

Data Deception and What to Do About It

In the Beatles' song, all you need is love; in *Oregon Trail*, all you need is data. *Oregon Trail* offers students gobs of information: snake bite remedies, river locations and depths, wagon specifications, ferry costs, daily climate reports. Loaded with facts, it feels comprehensive. Loaded with people voicing contrasting opinions, it feels balanced. Loaded with choices, it feels free. But the simulation begins from no moral or ethical standpoint beyond individual material success. It contains no vision of social/ecological justice, and hence promotes the full litany of sexism, racism, and imperialism, as well as exploitation of the earth. And simultaneously, it hides this bias. The combination is insidious, and makes interactive CD-ROMs like this one more difficult to critique than traditional textbooks or films. The forced

> We need to figure out ways to equip students to recognize and evaluate the deep moral/political messages imparted as they maneuver within various computer software programs.

identification of player with simulation protagonist leaves the student no option but to follow the ideological map laid out by the programmers.

Nonetheless, my critique is not a call to boycott "edutainment" resources. But we need to remember that these CD-ROMs are not teacher substitutes. The teacher's role in analyzing and presenting these devices in a broader ethical context is absolutely vital. Thus teachers across the country must begin a dialogue toward developing a critical computer literacy. We need to figure out ways to equip students to recognize and evaluate the deep moral/political messages imparted as they maneuver within various computer software programs.

Before choosing to use CD-ROMs that involve people and place, like *The Oregon Trail* — or, for example, its newer siblings *The Yukon Trail*, *The Amazon Trail*, and *Africa Trail* — teachers can consider a series of questions. These include:

• **Which social groups are students *not* invited to identify with in the simulation?** For example, Native Americans, African Americans, women, and Latinos are superficially present in *Oregon Trail*, but the stuff of their lives is missing.

• **How might these social groups frame problems differently than they are framed in the simulation?** As we saw in this critique of *Oregon Trail*, women tended to focus more on maintaining community than on hunting. Native Americans had a profoundly different relationship to the earth than did the Euro-American "tamers of the wilderness."

• **What decisions do simulation participants make that may have consequences for social groups not highlighted in the simulation? And what are these consequences?** Even though the very existence of the Oregon Trail contributed to the decimation of Plains and Northwest Indians, simulation participants are never asked to consider the broader effects of their decision making. What may be an ethical individual choice may be unethical when multiplied several hundred thousand times. (In this respect, CD-ROM choice-making both reflects and reinforces conventional notions of "freedom" that justify disastrous social and ecological practices.)

• **What decisions do simulation participants make that may have consequences for the earth and non-human life?** Similarly, a simulation participant's choice to cut down trees for firewood may be "rational" for that individual, but may also have deleterious effects on the ecological balance of a particular bio-region.

• **If the simulation is time-specific, as in the case of *The Oregon Trail*, what were the social and environmental consequences *after* the time period covered in the simulation?** The wars between Indians and U.S. Cavalry in the latter decades of the 19th century are inexplicable without the Oregon Trail as prologue.

• **Can we identify the ideological orientation of a particular CD-ROM?** The question is included here simply to remind us that all computer materials — indeed, all curricula — *have* an ideology. Our first step is becoming aware of the nature of that ideology.

These are hardly exhaustive, but may suggest a useful direction to begin thinking, as CD-ROMs become increasingly available and as they come to cover more and more subjects.

Finally, let me use the example of *Oregon Trail* to sketch out a number of ways that teachers can begin to foster a critical computer literacy:

• Once we've identified some of the social groups that are substantially missing in a CD-ROM activity like *Oregon Trail*, we can make an effort to locate excerpts of their diaries, speeches, or other communications (to the extent that these cultures are print-oriented) and read these together.

• We might then engage students in a role-play where, as a class, students face a number of Oregon Trail problems. For example, class members could portray women on the Oregon Trail and decide how they will attempt to maintain a community in transit. Or they might role-play a possible discussion among Oglala people as they confront the increas-

ingly disruptive presence of *Wasi'chu* crossing their lands.

• Students might be asked to list all the ways that African Americans would experience the Oregon Trail differently than Euro-Americans would — from planning to the trip itself. (It's unlikely, for example, that every white person on the streets of Independence, Missouri said a friendly "Howdy," to blacks encountered, as each of them does to the implied but unacknowledged white male *Oregon Trail* simulation player.)

> *Oregon Trail is sexist, racist, culturally insensitive, and contemptuous of the earth. It imparts bad values and wrong history.*

• In playing the *Oregon Trail* simulation, students could assume a particular racial, cultural, or gender identity, and note whether the choices or experiences described in the simulation make sense from the standpoint of a member of their group. For example, would a typical African American in Missouri in 1850 be allowed to choose which city to begin the trek west?

• As we share with students the social and ecological costs of the Oregon Trail, we could ask them to write critical letters to each of the "pioneers" they portrayed in the simulation. Some could represent Rogue Valley Indians, Shoshoni people, or even Mother Earth. For instance, how does "Mother Earth" respond to the

casual felling of every cottonwood tree along the Platte River?

• A Native-American elder or activist could be invited into the classroom to speak about the concerns that are important to his or her people and about the history of white-Indian relations.

• We could encourage students to think about the politics of naming in the simulation. They could suggest alternative names for the Oregon Trail itself. For example, one historian of the American West, Frederick Merk, aptly calls the Oregon Trail a "path of empire" (1978). Writer Dan Georgakas names it a "march of death" (1973). Other names might be "invasion of the West," or "the 20-year trespass." Just as with Columbus's "discovery" of America, naming shapes understanding, and we need classroom activities to uncover this process.

• Students could write and illustrate alternative children's books describing the Oregon Trail from the standpoint of women, African Americans, Native Americans, or the earth.

• Now have them "play" *The Oregon Trail* again. What do they see this time that they didn't see before? Whose world view is highlighted and whose is hidden? If they choose, students might present their findings to other classes or to teachers who may be considering the use of CD-ROMs.

The Oregon Trail is not necessarily more morally obnoxious than other CD-ROMs or curricular materials with similar ideological biases. My aim here is broader than to merely shake a scolding finger at MECC, producer of the *Oregon Trail* series. I've tried to demonstrate why teachers and students must develop a critical computer literacy. Some of the new CD-ROMs seem more socially aware than the blatantly culturally insensitive materials that still fill school libraries and bookrooms. And the flashy new computer packages also invoke terms long sacred to educators: student empowerment, individual choice, creativity, high interest. It's vital that we remember that

> # Computer programs are not politically neutral in the big moral contests of our time. Inevitably, they take sides.

coincident with the arrival of these new educational toys is a deepening social and ecological crisis. Global and national inequality between "haves" and "have-nots" is increasing. Violence of all kinds is endemic. And the earth is being consumed at a ferocious pace. Computer programs are not politically neutral in the big moral contests of our time. Inevitably, they take sides. Thus, a critical computer literacy, one with a social/ecological conscience, is more than just a good idea — it's a basic skill. ■

Bill Bigelow (bbpdx@aol.com) teaches at Franklin High School in Portland, Oregon and is a Rethinking Schools editor.

References

Applegate, Shannon and O'Donnell, Terrence. *Talking on Paper: An Anthology of Oregon Letters and Diaries.* Corvallis, OR: Oregon State University Press, 1994.

Armstrong, David. (February 23, 1996). "Lucas getting into education via CD-ROM." *The San Francisco Examiner.*

Beckham, Stephen Dow. "Federal-Indian Relations." *The First Oregonians.* Portland, OR: Oregon Council for the Humanities, 1991.

Bowers, C.A. *The Cultural Dimensions of Educational Computing: Understanding the Non-neutrality of Technology.* New York: Teachers College Press, 1988.

Davidson, James West and Lytle, Mark Hamilton. *After the Fact: The Art of Historical Detection.* New York: McGraw-Hill, 1992.

Deloria, Jr., Vine. *Indians of the Pacific Northwest.* Garden City, NY: Doubleday, 1977.

Faragher, Johnny and Stansell, Christine. "Women and Their Families on the Overland Trail to California and Oregon, 1842-1867", in Binder, Frederick & Reimer, David (Eds.), *The Way We Lived: Essays and Documents in American Social History, Vol. I.* Lexington, MA: D.C. Heath.

Georgakas, Dan. *Red Shadows: The History of Native Americans from 1600 to 1900, From the Desert to the Pacific Coast.* Garden City, NY: Zenith, 1973.

Hill, William E. *The Oregon Trail: Yesterday and today.* Caldwell, ID: Caxton, 1989, p. 58.

Johansen, Bruce and Maestas, Roberto. *Wasi'chu: The continuing Indian wars.* New York: Monthly Review, 1979.

Kesselman, Amy. "Diaries and Reminiscences of Women on the Oregon Trail: A Study in Consciousness", in Baxandall, Rosalyn, Gordon, Linda, and Reverby, Susan, *America's Working Women: A Documentary History — 1600 to the Present.* New York: Vintage, 1976.

Lazarus, E. *Black Hills/White Justice: The Sioux Nation Versus the United States — 1775 to the Present. New York*: HarperCollins, 1991.

Limerick, Patricia Nelson. *The Legacy of Conquest: The Unbroken Past of the American West.* New York: W.W. Norton, 1987.

McLagan, Elizabeth. *A Peculiar Paradise: A History of Blacks in Oregon, 1788-1940.* Portland, OR: The Georgian Press, 1980.

MECC. *The Oregon Trail II.* Minneapolis, MN, 1994.

Merk, Frederick. *History of the Westward Movement.* New York: Knopf, 1978.

Pride, Bill and Mary. *Prides' Guide to Educational Software.* Wheaton, IL: Crossway Books, 1992.

Provenzo, Jr., Eugene F. *Video Kids: Making Sense of Nintendo.* Cambridge, MA: Harvard University Press, 1991.

Schlissel, Lillian. *Women's Diaries of the Westward Journey.* New York: Schocken, 1992, p. 15.

Unruh, Jr., John, D. *The Plains Across: The Overland Emigrants and the Trans-Mississippi West, 1840-1860.* Urbana and Chicago, IL: University of Illinois Press, 1993.

Fiction Posing as Truth

A critical review of Ann Rinaldi's *My Heart Is on the Ground: The Diary of Nannie Little Rose, a Sioux Girl*

By Debbie Reese, et al.

(There is a story behind this article and how it came to be. In March 1999, Debbie Reese saw My Heart Is on the Ground, *by Ann Rinaldi, in a local bookstore. She picked it up, put it down in distaste, but then decided it couldn't be ignored. After reading the book, she called Beverly Slapin and read excerpts to her. A day later and equally outraged, Beverly called other colleagues.*

In the meantime, Debbie wrote to Barb Landis. Barb had already read the book and also felt it was an outrageous depiction of a tragic period in Native American history. A series of Internet and telephone discussions followed, and the circle grew to the nine women who are listed alphabetically in the box on p. 61.)

The book *My Heart Is on the Ground: The Diary of Nannie Little Rose, A Sioux Girl* is a historical fiction diary, part of Scholastic's "Dear America" series. Parents, teachers, and librarians have been grabbing up this immensely popular series, which Scholastic markets aggressively to 9- to 12- year-old girls.

Rinaldi's story takes place during the 1879-1880 school year and tells of Nannie Little Rose, a Lakota child sent to the government-run boarding school for Native Americans in Carlisle, Pennsylvania. In the author's note, Rinaldi writes that she visited the Indian burial ground there and saw the "dozens of white headstones bearing the names of Native American children...who had died while at the school. The names...were so lyrical that they leapt out at me and took on instant personalities. Although many of these children attended Carlisle at dates later than that of my story, I used some of their

Dear America

My Heart Is on the Ground

The Diary of Nannie Little Rose, a Sioux Girl

Carlisle Indian School, Pennsylvania, 1880

names for classmates of Nannie Little Rose.... I am sure that in whatever Happy Hunting Ground they now reside, they will forgive this artistic license, and even smile upon it."

We doubt it. In writing this story, Rinaldi has done a tremendous disservice to the memories of the dead children whose names she used, to their families, to Native children today, and to any child who reads and believes this book to be an accurate

or authentic story about boarding school life. She has cast the government boarding school in a positive light as though it were a good thing, when it is not regarded as such by Native and non-Native historians, educators, and sociologists.

Carlisle was founded in 1879 by Captain Richard Henry Pratt, whose stated philosophy was, "Kill the Indian, save the man." Under his administration, the school was set up to break spirits, to destroy traditional extended families and cultures, to obliterate memories and languages, and especially to make the children deny their Indianness, inside and out.

During the period in which the novel takes place, Native people were confined to reservations and not allowed to leave without permission of the government- appointed Indian agent assigned to their reservations. Many parents were coerced into sending their children to these early schools. Many children were kidnapped and sent far away to schools where they were kept for years on end. Children died at the school and died running away from the school, and they were beaten and worse for speaking their Native languages. Physical and emotional abuse is well documented in the stories of survivors of the boarding schools in the United States and Canada.

Appropriation

Appropriation of our lives and literatures is nothing new. Our bodies

Lakota girls and young women arriving at the Carlisle Indian School in 1879.

and bones continue to be displayed in U.S. and Canadian museums. For the last hundred years, our traditional stories have been turned into books for children without permission and with little, if any, respect given to their origins or sacred content. Now Rinaldi has taken appropriation one step further. That she would take the names of real Native children from gravestones and make up experiences to go with them is the coldest kind of appropriation. These were children who died alone, without their parents to comfort them. They were buried without proper ceremony in this lonely and sad place. Native people who visit the cemetery today express a profound sense of sadness.

Rinaldi named this book by appropriating a Cheyenne proverb that goes, "A nation is not conquered until the hearts of its women are on the ground. Then it is done, no matter how brave its warriors nor how strong their weapons." In its original form, this statement is about the strength and courage of Indian women. In its original form, the phrase suggests total defeat, the conquering of a nation, the death of a way of life. Throughout this book, the child protagonist uses the phrase "my heart is on the ground" whenever she happens to feel sad or upset. This trivializes the belief system of a people.

Lack of Historical Accuracy

A basic criterion of historical fiction is that facts about people who actually lived and events that actually happened must be accurate, or, at least, any deviations cleary spelled out. And these deviations cannot change the entire historical record. This is especially important in books for young readers. Factual errors abound here; they are on nearly every page.

Many of these errors are glaring. For instance, Sitting Bull was Hunkpapa Lakota, not "of Cheyenne nation" (p. 14); American Horse was a cousin to Red Cloud, not "chief of the Red Cloud Sioux" (p. 20); and the whites did not "give" the sacred Black

---

Sun Elk, from Taos Pueblo, told of his experiences at Carlisle in 1890:

"They told us that Indian ways were bad. They said we must get civilized. I remember that word, too. It means 'be like the white man.' I am willing to be like the white man, but I did not believe Indian ways were wrong. But they kept teaching us for seven years. And the books told how bad the Indians had been to the white men burning their towns and killing their women and children. But I had seen white men do that to Indians. We all wore white man's clothes and ate white man's food and went to white man's churches and spoke white man's talk. And so after a while we also began to say Indians were bad. We laughed at our own people and their blankets and cooking pots and sacred societies and dances. I tried to learn the lessons and after seven years I came home." (Nabokov, 1991, p. 222.)

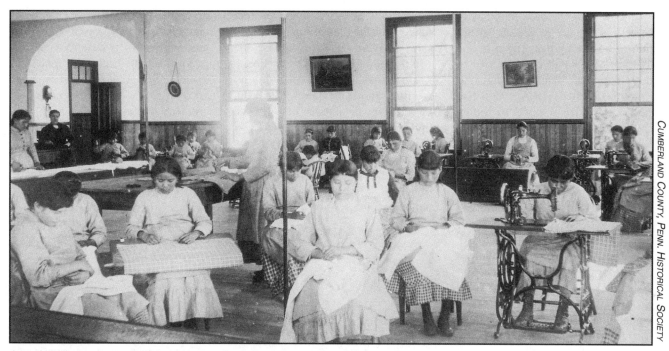

As part of the assimilation process, girls at Carlisle Indian School were assigned to make Victorian dresses.

Hills to the Lakota people (p. 12).

Besides errors, there are out-and-out distortions of history. Although Rinaldi sets her story in 1879-1880, the first full year of the Carlisle School's operation, she admits that she uses events that happened much later to convey her portrait of the school (p. 196). Despite her admission, the book still gives the impression that the school emerged fully equipped and organized in its first year, which was clearly not the case. The first students, who would have attended in the same year as the protagonist, reported no beds and little furniture of any kind, inadequate food, and generally chaotic conditions. The author leads readers to believe that from the beginning the school was a far better place than it actually was.

When Spotted Tail visited Carlisle in 1880 and found his children unhappy, in military uniform, and drilling with rifles, he insisted that they return with him to Rosebud. In Rinaldi's rendition of this episode, Nannie writes (p. 121) that the children did not want to go with Spotted Tail, and that he had to drag one of the children into the wagon. But according to historical accounts, the scene was just the opposite. When Spotted Tail visited

Carlisle, he learned how miserable and homesick the children were and took all his sons to the train with him. Pratt guarded the rest of the children, "as there were indications that a general stampede for the train might take place. As it was, some of the heartbroken children who were being left at the school managed to steal away and hide themselves on the train.... At Harrisburg the train was searched again and a little Oglala girl . . . was

found and dragged screaming back to captivity."

Contrary to Rinaldi's statement in the historical note that "most of the graduates were able to earn a living away from the reservation," and "others went on to higher education," evidence points to the opposite. Earning a living "away from the reservation" meant going into Indian service and working on a reservation or agency or in one of the dozens of off-reservation boarding schools modeled after Carlisle. And very few children graduated. Of the total population of 10,000, only 758 students, or fewer than 10 percent, graduated. More students ran away than graduated — 1,758 runaways are documented.

Lack of Cultural Authenticity

The events in *My Heart Is on the Ground* are not plausible. In 1880, a Lakota child of the protagonist's age would have been well educated by her aunts and grandmothers in Lakota tradition and lore, ways of seeing the world, and behaving in the right relation to it. She would probably have had younger children to care for, as well as older sisters in her extended family, her *tiospaye*, to emulate.

> **Commissioner of Indian Affairs Thomas Jefferson Morgan described his procedure for taking the children from their families:**
>
> "I would...use the Indian police if necessary. I would withhold from [the Native-American adults] rations and supplies... and when every other means was exhausted... I would send a troop of United States soldiers, not to seize them, but simply to be present as an expression of the power of the government. Then I would say to these people, 'Put your children in school;' and they would do it." (Josephy, 1994, p. 432.)

She would not have referred to herself as "Sioux," a French corruption of an enemy-name used by the Ojibwe. She would have referred to herself by her band (Sicangu) or location (Spotted Tail Agency). Nor would she have referred to Sitting Bull by his English name; she would have called him Tatanka Iotanka. If she had been encouraged to write in a diary that would be read by her white teachers, she would not have written disparagingly of them: "Then there is Woman-Who-Screams-A-Lot. She is bad to the eye. Fat and ugly" (p. 13). Nor would she have indicted her own people for the theft of the land: "Our chiefs have made large mistake in giving over our lands" (p. 5). In fact, while some student artworks can be traced to the Carlisle School, no diaries have been found.

Rinaldi's interpretation of Lakota belief is oversimplified and distorted: "A war club has a spirit. A prairie dog has two spirits. Birds, insects, and reptiles have spirits" (p. 81). Nannie's entry about Sun Dance, the most sacred ceremony of Lakota people, is exoticized and reflects the author's lack of understanding of Sun Dance, which is a thank-offering for the good of the community (p. 29).

Similarly, Lakota children of that time period did not engage in the same grieving rituals as adults, and what Nannie describes is not a Lakota grieving ritual (p. 44). And wealth is not, and never has been, measured by the number of poles in a tipi! (p. 41.) Wealth was measured by how much one gave away, not how much one collected.

Rinaldi also distorts familial relationships. The traditional bond between sister and brother is

WE DANCED, WE SANG, UNTIL THE MATRON CAME.

JEAN LaMARR

described as adversarial; the bond between wives (who were often sisters or cousins) is described as torn by jealousy; the "act of bravery" and vision quest that Nannie's father assigns her would have been her brother's responsibility.

Finally, any discussion of authenticity would have to address the story of Lucy Pretty Eagle, Nannie Little Rose's young friend who was possibly "buried alive" during a self-induced trance in the story. A ghost story of a child buried alive circulated at Carlisle over several decades, and there is a gravestone for a Lucy Pretty Eagle, who died at the school at the age of 10 in 1883, after being there only four months. However, there is no documented connection between the two.

Rinaldi's gruesome and sensationalistic presentation of the ghost story, infused with her own interpretation of Lakota cosmology, is both inauthentic and demeaning. In the story Nannie Little Rose knew about Lucy's trancelike states and blames herself for not being able to tell the white people in charge that Lucy wasn't really dead. Here we have Indian children responsible for the death of Indian children when the

---

Lone Wolf, Blackfoot, told this story:

"It was very cold that day when we were loaded into the wagons. None of us wanted to go and our parents didn't want to let us go. Oh, we cried for this was the first time we were to be separated from our parents. I remember looking back at Na-tah-ki and she was crying too. Nobody waved as the wagons, escorted by the soldiers, took us toward the school at Fort Shaw. Once there our belongings were taken from us, even the little medicine bags our mothers had given to us to protect us from harm. Everything was placed in a heap and set afire.

"Next was the long hair, the pride of all the Indians. The boys, one by

one, would break down and cry when they saw their braids thrown on the floor. All of the buckskin clothes had to go and we had to put on the clothes of the White Man.

"If we thought that the days were bad, the nights were much worse. This was the time when real loneliness set in, for it was when we knew that we were all alone. Many boys ran away from the school because the treatment was so bad, but most of them were caught and brought back by the police. We were told never to talk Indian and if we were caught, we got a strapping with a leather belt.

"I remember one evening when we were all lined up in a room and one of the boys said something in Indian to another boy. The man in

charge of us pounced on the boy, caught him by the shirt, and threw him across the room. Later we found out that his collar-bone was broken.

"The boy's father, an old warrior, came to the school. He told the instructor that among his people, children were never punished by striking them. That was no way to teach children; kind words and good examples were much better. Then he added, 'Had I been there when that fellow hit my son, I would have killed him.'

"Before the instructor could stop the old warrior he took his boy and left. The family then beat it to Canada and never came back." (Nabokov, 1991, p. 220.)

real culprits were malnutrition, tuberculosis, pneumonia, smallpox, physical abuse (including sexual abuse), and — no less important — loneliness and broken hearts and spirits. Moreover, the "trance-mistaken-for-death" scenario perpetuates the stereotype that Indians died or were decimated because of their unwillingness to adapt and because they were physically and emotionally different from white people.

Stereotypes

A basic criterion of good children's literature is that it be free of stereotypes. However, they abound in children's books about Native Americans and are usually found in descriptive passages about Native characters. A few authors like Rinaldi go one step further, by placing stereotypical language and images in an Indian child protagonist's own words.

Throughout, Rinaldi uses stereotypical language to express Lakota (or "Indian") speech and thought patterns. These include overemphasis on compound words ("Friend-To-Go-Between-Us," or "Time-That-Was-Before," or "night-middle-made"), romantic-sounding metaphors ("the council fire burns bright," or "his spring is poisoned with anger"), and an obsession with the words "bravery," "honor," and "nobleness." In addition, in the beginning, Nannie writes in the stilted speech pattern we call "early jawbreaker" ("Teacher tells it that I know some English, that she is much proud of me, but wants be more proud").

There is stereotypical nobility as throughout, Nannie "explains" Lakota belief and ritual to the child reader, a transparent literary device we find annoying. And the many derogatory references to girls and women that are peppered throughout this book are outrageous and offensive ("only a stupid girl would say such a thing;" "women's dreams are worth nothing"). They are not — and never have

been — the way in which Lakota women were thought of or treated.

Final Comments

Nowhere in this book are to be found the screaming children, thrown onto horse-drawn wagons, being taken away from their homes. Nowhere to be found are the desperately lonely children, heartbroken, sobbing into the night. Nowhere to be found are the terrified children, stripped naked and beaten for trying to communicate with each other and not understanding what was expected of them. Nowhere to be found is the unrelenting daily humiliation, in word and deed, from the teachers, matrons, and staff. Nowhere to be found are the desperate runaways,

lost, frozen in the snow. Nowhere to be found is the spirit of resistance.

Resistance among the Indian students was deep, subtle, lasting, and valiantly carried on for as long as boarding schools existed. Besides running away, this resistance took many forms — physical, spiritual, intellectual. Children destroyed property and set fires. They refused to speak English. They subverted teachers' and matrons' orders whenever they could. But except for Charles Whiteshield's "war dance," which is presented as a shameful thing, that resistance — and the courage it represents — receives no attention in this book. As in Francis LaFlesche's *The Middle Five* and Basil H. Johnston's *Indian School Days*, an Indian author would have made this resistance a central part of such a story.

Reviewers

• Marlene Atleo (Nuu-chah-nulth) is a mother and grandmother, adult educator, and doctoral candidate at the University of British Columbia investigating transformational learning strategies in First Nations narratives.

• Naomi Caldwell (Ramapough Mountain) is a mother, doctoral candidate at the University of Pittsburgh, and past president of the American Indian Library Association.

• Barbara Landis is a mother and the Carlisle Indian School Research Specialist for the Cumberland County Historical Society in Carlisle, PA.

• Jean Mendoza is a mother and doctoral student in early childhood education at the University of Illinois. She has been teaching children for more than 20 years.

• Deborah Miranda (Ohlone-Coastanoan Esselen/Chumash) is a poet, mother, and doctoral candidate in English at the University of Washington. Her article, "A String of Textbooks: Artifacts of Composition Pedagogy in Indian

Boarding Schools" was scheduled for publication in *The Journal of Teaching Writing*.

• Debbie Reese (Nambé) is a mother and doctoral student at the University of Illinois studying representations of Native Americans in children's literature. She is a regular reviewer for Horn Book, and her articles include "Look Mom, It's George and He's a TV Indian!" and "Teaching Young Children about Native Americans."

• LaVera Rose (Lakota) is a mother and grandmother, an archivist at the South Dakota State Historical Society, and author of *Grandchildren of the Lakota* and *Meet the Lakota People/Oyate Kin*.

• Beverly Slapin is a mother, co-founder and executive director of Oyate, co-editor, with Doris Seale (Santee/Cree), of *Through Indian Eyes: The Native Experience in Books for Children* and co-author of *How to Tell the Difference: A Guide to Evaluating Children's Books for Anti-Indian Bias*.

• Cynthia Smith (Creek) is a reviewer of Native-themed children's books.

Proponents of the Carlisle Indian School circulated these "before and after" photos of Tom Torlino (Navajo), who arrived there in 1882, to demonstrate their "success." Note the dramatic difference in how his skin color is depicted.

To those who would argue that "it is possible" that a Native child might have had Nannie Little Rose's experiences, the overwhelming body of evidence — written and oral — suggests otherwise. The premise of this book — that a Native child would come in and, within a period of 10 months, move from someone who reads and writes limited English and has a totally Indian world view to someone who is totally fluent in a language that is foreign to her and totally assimilated to a foreign culture (and be better for the experience) — is highly unlikely. Brainwashing does not come readily. Brainwashing takes time.

Given the marketing and distribution forces behind *My Heart Is on the Ground,* it will probably be more widely read than any other book about the boarding school experience. This book only adds to the body of misinformation about Native-American life and struggle in the United States and Canada. This one book epitomizes the utter lack of sensitivity and respect that characterizes the vast majority of children's books about Native peoples. Non-

Native readers of *My Heart Is on the Ground* will continue to be validated in whatever feelings of superiority they may have; Native children will continue to be humiliated.

In the author's note, Rinaldi writes, "I am sure that in whatever Happy Hunting Ground they now reside, they will forgive this artistic license, and even smile upon it." That these children might smile on Rinaldi from their "Happy Hunting Ground" is the epitome of white fantasy: that Indian people will forgive and even smile upon white people, no matter the atrocities — past and present. ■

NOTE: This article is excerpted from a more comprehensive review of My Heart is on the Ground *available at the Oyate website, www.oyate.org.*

References/Resources

Harper, Maddie. *"Mush-hole," Memories of a Residential School.* Sister Vision Press, 1993.

Hyer, Sally. *One House, One Voice, One Heart: Native American Education at the Santa Fe Indian School.* Museum of New Mexico Press, 1990.

Johnston, Basil H. *Indian School Days.* University of Oklahoma Press, 1989.

Johnston, Diane Hamm. *Daughter of Suqua,* Albert Whitman, 1997.

Josephy, Alvin M. Jr. *500 Nations.* New York: Alfred A. Knopf, 1994.

LaFlesche, Francis. *The Middle Five: Indian Schoolboys of the Omaha Tribe.* Omaha: University of Nebraska Press, 1900/1978.

Lomawaima, K. Tsianina. *They Called It Prairie Light: The Story of Chilocco Indian School.* University of Nebraska Press, 1994.

Nabokov, Peter. *Native American Testimony.* New York: Viking, 1998.

Sterling, Shirley. *My Name is Seepeetza.* Douglas & McIntyre, 1997.

Teachers may also want to read biographical information of Native children's books authors who went to boarding school. Two of these authors are Shonto Begay and Lucie Tapahonso.

Rethinking the U.S. Constitutional Convention: A Role Play

By Bob Peterson

The Constitution of the United States has been called one of the great documents of human history. In my own schooling, however, I recall the study of the Constitution instead as a source of great boredom. Sterile descriptions of the three branches of government dominated much of the study of that time period each time I was cycled through American history — in 5th, 8th, and 10th grade. U.S. history textbooks gave the Constitution considerable space and probably share blame for the lifeless rendition of what was undoubtedly a very exciting time in our nation's history.

It was only years later when I returned to the classroom as a teacher that I realized the Constitution's importance and its potential as a learning tool. In fact the study of the American Revolution and the struggle over the Constitution in my fifth grade classroom helps set the basis for the rest of the year. I pose questions such as: Who benefited most (and the least) from the American Revolution? Who wrote and ratified the Constitution for the new nation? Who benefited most (and least) from the Constitution? Since the Cons-

Historical paintings, like this famous scene of the signing of the Constitution, can spark discussion about who was represented when this country was founded — and who wasn't.

Howard Chandler Christy

titution was finally ratified in 1787 how have people struggled to expand the democratic impulses of the American Revolution?

This article describes a role play that I use as part of my U.S. history curriculum on the American Revolution and the Constitution. It brings the above questions to life, energizes the class, and helps me assess my students' knowledge and skills. The inspiration for this role play and some of the parts are taken directly from a role play developed by high school teacher Bill Bigelow.

I do this role play after my students have studied early European colonialism in the Americas (using many materials from *Rethinking Columbus*) and also the American Revolution. It could, however, be part of a government class, or just a stand alone lesson, depending on the background knowledge of the students. Students like this role play of the Constitutional Convention because it is done with a twist — we invite many groups who were not invited to the original one in Philadelphia in 1787. The basic components of the role play are the dividing of the class into seven distinct social groups, having them focus on the key issues of slavery and suffrage, negotiate among themselves to get other groups to support their positions, and then have debate and a final vote at a mock Constitutional Convention. The issues that I have students address in the role play are:

• Should slavery and slave trade be abolished, and should escaped slaves be returned to their owners?

• Who should be allowed to vote in our new nation, especially what role should gender, race, and property ownership play in such a decision?

I have several objectives for students:

• To learn about the social forces active during and immediately following the American Revolution.

• To explore two burning questions that confronted the new American nation: slavery and suffrage.

• To develop strong oral presentation skills, including both persuasive and argumentative skills.

• To develop critical skills of examining arguments and social reality.

Setting the Stage

I start this mini-unit by showing an overhead or poster of a painting that depicts the Constitutional Convention (the one by Howard Chandler Christy on the previous page works well, and in a pinch "The Signing of the Declaration of Independence" by John Trumball is a passable substitute, given that the same types of people are represented). We then make a composite list of our observations. Students observe everything from the men's long hair, to "funny" pants, to most of them looking old, to the participants being white and male. I ask why they think only those people were involved in the writing of the Constitution.

I explain the importance and the difficulty of the task of writing a set of laws that would govern a new nation, especially considering that this was the first time in human history that a revolution had been won with the express purpose of having the governed — or at least some of them — involved in determining how they were to be governed. I explain that these people were wrestling with the difficult issues of slavery, taxation, suffrage, and how much power the federal government should have compared to the states.

I tell students that we are going to have our own constitutional convention to discuss some of these issues, but that we are going to invite groups of people who weren't invited to the real convention. I tell them that in addition to the southern slave owners and the northern merchants who attended the first Constitutional Convention, we will invite white indentured servants, women of all nationalities and social classes, free African Americans, enslaved African Americans, and Iroquois. I explain the two issues we will focus on — slavery and suffrage.

I also explain that there are key vocabulary words for the role play. I go through the list and then have students, working in groups, write out individual definitions. For homework that night they are to finish their vocabulary sheets and practice the words. (The words include: unfair, just, justice, wealthy, property, merchant, trader, suffrage, Constitution, abolitionist, fugitive, convention, Bill of Rights, taxes, abolish, prohibit, resolve, indentured servant, slavery, Iroquois, and plantation owner.)

Explaining Each Group

The following day I review the words by having kids first in pairs and then in foursomes explain the words to each other. I observe how well the kids do and then as a whole group go over a few words that seem the most confusing.

I then give mini-lectures on each of the seven groups and encourage students to take notes. I use the handouts and other materials as background. We discuss these roles drawing on what they've learned in our previous study of the American Revolution. At the end of the lesson I explain the role play format. I show a short video clip of one from a previous year (a three minute segment is part of the excellent video on multicultural education, *Many Voices, Many Lives*, available from NCREL in Chicago: 800-356-2735). I then re-list the seven groups on the overhead and ask students to write down their top three choices.

Then I divide the class into seven groups, trying to balance each group with strong readers, speakers, thinkers, and a racial and gender diversity. (In my classroom I also mix children by language dominance.) I attempt to places students in one of their top three choices.

Brainstorming in Groups

I post the categories in the morning so that if any changes need to occur, they can be negotiated by that afternoon. In the afternoon I review the format and explain what the groups will have to do to prepare for the role play. Each group is to read over the explanation of their positions (see pp. 66-69) and then decide how they are going to argue their case on slavery and suffrage. I explain that my expectation is for each group to brainstorm a list of arguments they can use during the role play. I give them a manila folder with enough copies of the "position" paper for each group member, one copy of a brainstorming sheet, and additional reading materials. I explain that one person should write down the group's ideas, but that soon each person will have to write his or her own speech. I encourage them to use other sources to find additional background information about their group. If there is time I bring the students back together as a whole group and ask for an argument that they think can be used either to support or oppose slavery or the right to vote for a certain group. I write that argument down on the overhead and ask if anyone can think of a counter-argument. I then ask for a counter-counter argument. In this way I try to get children to think more critically about their positions and anticipate opposing arguments. For example, in the past students have argued that slavery is necessary to produce cotton and tobacco, two items essential to the well-being of the nation. Countering this, students have argued the "well-being" should include everyone; and that even if the nation as a whole benefits it doesn't warrant enslaving a whole race of people. At the end of the lesson I collect the manila folders.

Alliance Building

As a prelude to the role play I have the students engage in an "alliance building" session in which they make arguments and try to win groups over to their positions. I explain that the purpose of this session is to sharpen their arguments and thinking skills and to seek alliances with other groups. One or two designated "negotiators" from each group travel to other groups to seek alliances around the issues that will be debated at the convention. The negotiators wear 4-by-6 cards identifying their group and their role as a negotiator. The other students sit grouped together with signs identifying their group. This exchange of ideas whets the appetite of students and further encourages them to start thinking about arguments and counter arguments. It should also help them become clearer as to what they want to put in their speeches. The length of this alliance-building session varies according to each class. Sometimes I bring people together and we briefly discuss how the session went. Other times I go immediately into the next activity of creating speeches.

Preparing Individual Speeches

I review what we did previously and tell the students that in their groups they will each write a speech about one or both of the two key questions: "Should slavery be abol-ished?" and "Who should have the right to vote?" I explain that they must first introduce themselves (as either a fictitious or real historical figure), tell a little about who they are, and then present their arguments. I prepare a formatted sheet with headings for each student to help facilitate this process. I model writing one speech for one individual in the class (usually one with weak English language skills so he or she can get a jump start on the task). (A prototype of the blank speech form I use is available on line at www.rethinkingschools.org/roc2.) I encourage them, when possible, to choose real people who fit the category of their group, reminding them that examples (both fictitious and real) are contained in the original statements that they received earlier. Students then work in groups writing their individual speeches. I circulate to help where needed.

After about a half hour I have one or two people present their speeches in front of the class. We give positive feedback and constructive suggestions. For homework that night the students are to finish writing their speeches, rehearse them and ask an adult for feedback and suggestions.

Practicing Speeches and Final Preparations

I usually have the students practice their speeches in pairs or in their entire group once or twice before the final role play. Sometimes I have students make signs or posters for their group, highlighting their main concerns. I ask them to develop questions to counter arguments that they anticipate will be made against their positions.

At the end of this session I call the groups together and have a few people present at least part of their opening statement. I also pull out my drama box and show some possible hats and vests that students might wear, which usually animates kids to think of what they might bring from home to dress the part. (I find the use of props in role plays to be a tricky matter — on the one hand it can stimulate genuine student interest, on the other hand it can detract them from the real purpose of the project.) I explain how the class will be rearranged so that delegations will sit together. I also tell students that I will assess their work by the content of what they say in their opening statements, their interactions, and their behavior. I explain that I won't permit any put downs or insults of individuals or groups, but that one can be very critical of the ideas of individuals or groups. Homework is to practice their presentations and to think up two arguments and counter arguments for at least one of the two issues.

The Role Play

During lunch time the day of the role play I have some students rearrange and decorate the room (with red, white and blue crepe paper). We group the desks according to the number of students in each delegation and affix the group's sign. We decorate the school podium and hang a banner "Constitutional Convention — Philadelphia, 1787."

I have students go to their places and put on their costumes if they have something to wear.

I introduce the role play and act as chair. I start by thanking everyone for attending this historic convention, quickly introduce the delegations and then repeat the two burning questions:

• Should slavery, as well as the entire slave trade, be abolished, and should escaped slaves be returned to their owners?

• Who should be allowed to vote in our new nation, and especially, what role should gender, race, and property ownership play in such a decision?

I explain that the meeting will consider each question separately. We will debate one after another. I restate the first question and then ask for commentary on it. Once a representative has spoken I immediately allow feedback in the form of questions and counter statements. When I feel the students have thoroughly debated the slavery question, I cut it off and ask for a group to make a formal proposal what our constitution should say about the issue. Sometimes we vote on the issue then, other times I wait for all the voting to take place at the end of the convention.

I then pose the second question. At the end I ask for another formal proposal. I allow for closing arguments. During the role play I make some observational notes — including a tally of who speaks and key arguments and rebuttals. At the end I distribute written ballots for everyone to vote. While two people count the ballots in the hall, the rest of the students reflect on the experience by filling out a sheet with open-ended questions such as: What did you learn from your participation in the role play and the preparation? Given the different social groups in United States at the time what do you think might have happened if other people were really given a voice at the convention? In what ways did the arguments at the mock convention remind you of controversies in our community/nation/world today? (for a sample visit the Rethinking Schools website: www.rethinkingschools.org/publication/roc2/roc2links.shtml). I also encourage them to write additional reflections in their journal during the next journal time.

Follow-up

Sometimes I have a students videotape the role play. This makes the role play seem all the more special and occasionally helps them realize why only one person should speak at a time. However, it has the disadvantage of requiring time on my part to edit or choose sections of the role play to show — as I have found re-showing the whole thing not a valuable use of class time.

On the day following the role play I have students reflect in groups and as a whole class. We focus on two aspects: content and process. In terms of content we compare our convention with what really happened in 1787. Students naturally think it is not fair that such an exclusive group of people crafted the Constitution. (See the handout written by Bill Bigelow, available online at www.rethinkingschools.org/publication/roc2/roc2links.shtml, for a listing of who actually attended the Constitutional Convention and their social positions.) I point out that it has been precisely these conflicts of exclusion and power that make studying U.S. history and learning from the past so important. I explain that throughout the rest of the year we are going to examine other exciting conflicts in which those who have been excluded and oppressed throughout history — working people, women, enslaved African Americans, Native Americans and others — fought, sometimes to the death, for their freedom in subsequent centuries.

In terms of process we talk about how such role plays could be improved; how we can encourage broader participation; how arguments can be more effective. ■

Bob Peterson (repmilw@aol.com) teaches fifth grade at La Escuela Fratney in Milwaukee, Wisconsin and is a Rethinking Schools editor. He would like to thank Bill Bigelow for many of these ideas and his feedback on earlier drafts of the article.

White Workers/Indentured Servants

You are shoemakers in the city of Boston, Massachusetts. Before this you were indentured servants for seven years. (At the beginning of the Revolution there were 200,000 indentured servants in the colonies.)

You had come over to the 13 colonies from England because you were promised a good life. In order to pay for your boat trip over here, you had to agree to work for some wealthy person for seven years for no pay. It was a hard seven years. You were almost slaves, although your white skin allowed you freedom. Because of your experience with being indentured servants, you understand more what it must be like to be a slave. You don't think anyone should have to be a slave or servant to anyone else.

You have families with small children. You barely make enough money to live. You want the right to vote so that you can make sure that the government represents people like you, and not just rich people.

The rich are the ones who should pay more taxes, not poor and working people.

You fought in the Revolutionary Army, unlike the rich plantation owners or the bankers who either sent their son or paid someone else to take their place. You didn't do it for the money. In fact the government didn't pay you in money. They gave you some IOUs which weren't worth anything.

Now that there is talk about writing a new constitution, you're concerned about how the new government will deal with people like you who are poor and own no property. You've also heard that some people at the Constitutional Convention don't even want to allow people like you to be able to vote in elections. No property, no vote, they say. Who do they think they are? When people were dying in the war, it was the farmers and workers who did most of the bleeding, not the rich plantation owners, bankers and merchants.

Questions for Thought:

1. How do you make your living?

2. What are some of the similarities between being an indentured servant and being a slave? What are the differences?

3. If a runaway slave appeared at your home, what would you do? What is your position on slavery?

4. Who should be allowed the right to vote?

Possible Historical Figures:

Very few have been recorded in historical records. Please make up your own name.

Additional Reading:

Hansen, Joyce. *The Captive.* Scholastic, 1994. In this fictionalized account inspired by the capture and enslavement of Olaudah Equiano, Olaudah befriends a white indentured servant and they escape together.

Enslaved African Americans

The year is 1787. Eleven years ago the Declaration of Independence stated that "all men are created equal." And yet because your skin is black, and you were born a slave, you still remain a slave. Obviously the American Revolution didn't mean freedom for everyone. In fact the man who wrote those words in the Declaration of Independence, Thomas Jefferson, is himself a Virginia slave owner. And the man who led the Continental Army, George Washington, is a slave owner as well. There are about 700,000 enslaved Africans in the new United States.

Your life as a slave is harsh. Up at dawn when the sun rises, you must work until it is dark at night. Then there are more chores when you return from the fields. You are under constant control by your master, though with your family you have tried to make the best out of your life. However, you know the owner could sell you to South Carolina or wherever he wanted, away from your family, if he felt like it.

With the Constitutional Convention is raised the possibility of freedom. Slavery might be outlawed. A number of states in the North have already abolished slavery, and there is much talk about abolishing the slave *trade* — the bringing of new enslaved Africans into the country. Thousands of slaves have been allowed to buy or earn their freedom in Virginia in recent years. Maybe slavery will not be outlawed in every state, but perhaps slaves would be allowed to keep their freedom if they escaped into a free state. True, the Revolution didn't really free you, but the talk of liberty and justice makes you want your fair share.

Questions for Thought:

1. What things worry you?
2. What do you hope the Constitution will do for you?
3. Who do you think should have the right to vote?

Possible Historical Figures:

Slaves who fought for the Americans became free after the war, so there are few records of slaves in 1787. Please make up your own name.

Additional Reading:

American Revolution (Voices in African American History series) by Sharon Harley and Steven Middleton, Modern Curriculum Press, 1994.

"What to the Slave is the Fourth of July?" (speech by Frederick Douglass, July 5, 1852). Available online at: http://douglass.speech.nwu.edu/doug _a10.htm.

Black Heroes of the American Revolution, by Burke Davis. New York: Harcourt Brace Jovanovich, 1976.

(For teacher reference: *Chronology on the History of Slavery,* by Eddie Becker, 1999. Includes hundreds of websites: http://innercity.org/holt/slavechron.html.)

Free African Americans

You are free African Americans. There are over 59,000 of you in the 13 colonies. (Unfortunately, there are nearly 700,000 enslaved African Americans!) You know that African Americans — both free and enslaved — make up 20% of all the non-Native American people in the colonies. And yet you have virtually no rights:

• You are not allowed to own property in many of the 13 colonies.
• You are not allowed to vote.
• You are not allowed to speak in court.
• You are not allowed to serve on a jury of any kind.
• You are not allowed to attend most schools.

Even though you are free, if a slave catcher catches you and takes you back to the South or sends you to the Caribbean, it would be very difficult for you to prove that you are free.

Some are arguing that the Constitution should allow slave owners to come into Northern states where there is no slavery and take runaways back south. The "runaway" may be you — even though you are free. If slavery exists anywhere in the

United States, it is a threat to free African Americans, such as yourselves.

Over 5,000 African American men fought in the Revolution. They were promised their freedom if they fought. Some of them, after the war, were not given their freedom and had to fight their former owners to get it.

Remember that the first American killed by the British in the War was Crispus Attucks — whose father was African and whose mother a member of the Massachuset (Indian) tribe. He was killed in the Boston Massacre in 1770. African Americans have petitioned the government to end slavery. And between 1780 and 1786, the states of Pennsylvania, Massachusetts, Connecticut, Rhode Island, New York, and New Jersey passed laws against slavery.

Questions for Thought:

1. Did most Africans want to be brought to the United States?
2. What role did Africans — enslaved and free — have in creating the wealth of the 13 colonies?
3. What are arguments you can use to convince people to oppose slavery?

4. Who do you think should have the right to vote? Why?

Possible Historical Figures:

Phyllis Wheatley, Peter Salem (fought at Bunker Hill), William Lee (aide to General Washington), Oliver Cromwell (with Washington at Delaware).

Additional Reading:.

Black Heroes of the American Revolution, by Burke Davis. New York: Harcourt Brace Jovanovich, 1976.

"Essay on Slavery," by Caesar Sarter, August 17, 1774. From *The Essex Journal and Merrimack Packet*, available on the Rethinking Schools website: www.rethinkingschools.org/publication/ roc2/roc2links.shtml.

"What to the Slave is the Fourth of July?" (speech by Frederick Douglass, July 5, 1852). Available online at: http://douglass.speech.nwu.edu/doug _a10.htm.

Excerpts from *Walker's Appeal*, by David Walker, September 28, 1829, online at www.pbs.org/wgbh/aia/part4 /4h2931t.html.

White Women

You live in Boston. Some of you are married to men who fought in the Revolution. Some of you are widows because your husbands were killed in the war. You and your women friends organized in favor of the American Revolution. Women built the organization "Daughters of Liberty" which organized campaigns to refuse to buy British products. Abigail Adams was the leader of such activities. During the war many women continued their support of the Revolution through "Ladies Associations." They donated clothing and medical supplies to the Continental Army of George Washington. In Philadelphia alone, the Ladies Association collected about $300,000 in Continental money. The money was used to buy shirts for the soldiers. The women organized sewing circles throughout the colonies to spin, weave cloth, and make clothing for troops. They also passed resolutions supporting the rebel cause and pledged not to do business with merchants who imported British goods or didn't support the Patriots' cause. On one occasion 500 Boston women held a protest against a merchant found to be hoarding coffee.

The women also kept the country going. While their husbands were off fighting the war the women kept small businesses open, kept the farms running, and took care of the children.

You know that some women actually fought in the Revolution. Deborah Sampson and Molly Pitcher fought in the army. Others like Lydia Darragh acted as spies. Why shouldn't women benefit from the Revolution if they helped with it?

You also know that you pay taxes when you buy certain things. Wasn't one of the main issues of the Revolution, "no taxation without representation"?

Right now in many ways you are little more than the property of your husbands or fathers. Even a decade after the Declaration of Independence you don't have the right to do the following things, just because you are a woman:

• You do not have the right to vote.
• You do not have the right to own property.
• You do not have the right to speak in court.
• You do not have the right to be a member of a jury in court.
• You do not have the right to be a government official.
• You do not have the right to go to most high schools and colleges.

In 1776, Abigail Adams wrote the following to her husband, John Adams:

"Remember the Ladies and be more generous and favorable to them than your ancestors. Do not put such unlimited power into the hands of the husbands. Remember all men would be tyrants if they could. If particular care and attention is not paid to the Ladies, we are determined to foment a rebellion, and will not hold ourselves bound by any laws in which we have no voice, no representation."

Questions for Thought:

1. Should you have the right to vote? Why?

2. How is the position of women in our nation similar to that of a slave? How does it differ?

3. What do you think of slavery and the slave trade?

Possible Historical Figures:

Abigail Adams, Deborah Sampson, Lydia Darragh, Molly Pitcher.

Additional Reading:

Hoobler, Dorothy and Thomas. *The Sign Painter's Secret: The Story of a Revolutionary Girl.* Englewood Cliffs, NJ: Silver Burdett Press, 1991. [The story of Annie Laurie MacDougal.]

McGovern, Ann. *Secret Soldier: The Story of Deborah Sampson.* New York: Scholastic, 1975.

Silcox-Garrett, Diane. *Heroines of the American Revolution.* Chapel Hill, NC: Green Angel Press, 1998.

Terrana, Joan Barton. "Remember the Ladies: Abigail Adams," in *Cobblestone Magazine.* November 1993.

Male Southern Plantation Owners

You live in Virginia and are tobacco planters. Your family owns about thirty black slaves and you are quite wealthy. Your wealth, however, depends on your slaves. Slaves do all the hardest work. They plant, harvest, dry, pack, and load the tobacco to get it off for sale. You wouldn't know where you'd get people to do the work if you had no slaves.

From time to time a slave will run away. You hire a slave catcher and usually the runaway is brought back. Sometimes the slaves get up into the North before they're caught. But slaves are your property, and fortunately you usually get them back.

The American colonies defeated Great Britain in the Revolution but there are still lots of problems. One problem is that there is a lot of protest from the common people, the "rabble" — the poor farmers, unemployed and workers in the towns and cities. Up in the state of Massachusetts, Daniel Shays led a rebellion against the government and large property owners. As property owners yourselves, when these people talk about "equality" you wonder if they mean to take away *your* property so you're equal to them! These people scare you. In some places they're even allowed to vote and run for office. Sometimes they make laws which threaten the safety of private property: your property.

Questions for Thought:

1. How do you make your money?
2. How do you feel about slavery?
3. Do you think that you should have the right to go to northern states and get your property (slaves) if they try to run away?
4. How do you feel about common people?

Possible Historical Figures:

George Washington, Thomas Jefferson, James Madison.

Additional Reading:

Olds, Bruce. "Slave Owner's Lament" in *Raising Holy Hell, A Novel of John Brown.* New York: Penguin, 1995, pp. 61-62.

Dudley, William (Ed.). *Slavery: Opposing Viewpoints.* San Diego, CA: Greenhaven Press, 1992.

Currie, Stephen. *Slavery.* San Diego, CA: Greenhaven Press, 1999.

Northern Merchants and Bankers

You are rich. Some of you own ships, some own mills, and some own banks. You were strong supporters of the Revolution because the British didn't let you trade and make deals with countries other than Britain. Now you can trade with the French, the Dutch, the Spanish and Portuguese. You are getting richer and richer. While you didn't fight directly in the battles, your son served as a leader in the Continental Army (George Washington's army).

While you are not as set in your ways as the Southern Plantation owners, you still have many questions regarding who should vote and how slavery should be handled. While it may not be OK in Boston, the South is different. The slaves in the South harvest the tobacco you smoke and the cotton that comes to your mills. If it wasn't for them you wouldn't be so well off.

Very upsetting things have been happening recently. Many state legislatures have passed laws allowing "debtors" — people who owe money — to pay their debts "in kind" with corn, tobacco, or other products whether or not they may be of any value. In other words, a banker might loan out $100 and get paid back two cows and a bushel of corn! That's outrageous! There is very little respect for property anymore. The state legislatures have entirely too much power. Maybe if all those poor people didn't vote, this stuff wouldn't happen.

You were educated in school and speak English and French. You believe in democracy and the right to vote, but really only for those who have the schooling and money that give them the knowledge and time to understand the issues.

Questions for Thought:
1. How do you make your money?
2. Why might it be against your interests if lots of people could vote?
3. How do you benefit from slavery and slave trade?

Possible Historical Figure: John Hancock.

Native Americans • Iroquois Nation

You are members of the great Iroquois League of Nations. You live with your families in a Seneca village on the Genesee River in New York. You live in a longhouse with your families and grandparents. You have attended the Grand Council — the meeting of leaders from the original Five — now Six Nations of the Iroquois. At that council the leaders tried to solve their differences peacefully.

The American War of Independence changed all that. Some of the Iroquois — the Oneida and Tuscarora Nations — generally supported the Americans. But many Iroquois — under the leadership of Mohawk Chief Joseph Bryant and Seneca Chief Red Jacket — fought on the side of the British. They were so angry at the Americans taking their land that they hoped a defeat of the settlers would mean the settlers would no longer take their lands. Even though you fought on the British side, you feel people at the Constitutional Convention should listen to you and your ideas for several reasons:

• Some members of the Iroquois Nation met Benjamin Franklin many years ago when Franklin was a young journalist who made a study of the Iroquois governmental system. Franklin was impressed with the fine workings of democracy among the Iroquois — with its checks and balances among different "branches" of government. Franklin was so impressed that he drew up a similar plan for the thirteen colonies (called the Albany Plan) but few people paid attention to it. The Iroquois' "League of Nations" has six tribes or nations. The government of the Iroquois includes three parts — executive, an assembly, and a judicial system. (That's the same as the proposal by Ben Franklin that the new United States government have a President (executive), a Congress (an assembly) and a court system (the judicial system). A key difference is that the Iroquois allow *all* people to vote, and in fact, women are the ones who run your court system — the ones who make the final decision when there is a disagreement.

• The American settlers have taken much of your land. They have paid you almost nothing. They keep breaking treaties. They say they won't take any more land and then a few years later settlers start moving in. You need the right to vote in order to get laws passed to protect Native Americans.

• You have suffered under the armies of George Washington. During the War of Independence Washington was angry at Iroquois support for the British and so he ordered an army into Iroquois lands specifying that it should "not merely be overrun, but destroyed." The American army was to scorch the earth, and they did — burning towns, stealing things, uprooting crops, chopping down orchards, slaughtering cattle, and destroying grain supplies. He ordered the destruction of your villages and the killings of women and children.

• You know that your Native American relatives have suffered as slaves ever since the time Columbus came to this part of the world. The Europeans eventually decided not to use Indians for slaves because you could run away so easily — you knew the land. Plus, by using Africans, their black skin was a way to identify them as property.

Questions for Thought:
Whose land is this?
Why should you have rights even though you fought against the Americans in the War of Independence?
Who should be allowed to vote and why?

Possible Historical Figures:
Red Jacket, Joseph Bryant.

Additional Reading:
"George Washington: An American Hero?" in *Rethinking Columbus*, 2nd edition, pp. 56-57.
(For teacher reference: Johansen, Bruce E. *Forgotten Founders: How the American Indian Helped Shape Democracy*. Boston: Harvard Common Press, 1982.)

A New U.S. Bill of Rights

By Larry Miller

As Bob Peterson's role play shows (see p. 63), rights are not granted, they are won — often through years-long struggle. Frederick Douglass pointed this out almost 150 years ago: "Power concedes nothing without a demand. It never has and it never will."

In this activity, students reflect on the rights that they believe should be universal, and create a new U.S. Bill of Rights. They do this through discussion, and examination of the United Nations Universal Declaration of Human Rights, as well as the U.S. and South African Bill of Rights — two remarkable but substantially different documents. The aim is to alert students to rights that they have, and to provoke them to consider rights that may still need to be fought for.

1. Ask students to brainstorm a list of 20 rights that should be guaranteed to every person in every country.

2. Give students a copy of the UN Universal Declaration of Human Rights, which was agreed to at a world meeting following World War II. (Available at www.rethinking schools.org/publication/roc2/roc2links.shtml)

3. Have students compare their list of rights with the articles of the Universal Declaration.

4. Ask: Does the Universal Declaration include rights that you didn't think of? How do you explain the differences between your lists and the Universal Declaration? Are there any rights in the Universal Declaration that you feel should not be there?

5. Ask students: Does the Universal Declaration protect against dis-

---

Excerpts from the South African Bill of Rights

Here are selected articles from South Africa's Bill of Rights. (An abbreviated version of the complete South African Bill of Rights is available on the Rethinking Schools website: www.rethinkingschools.org/publication/roc2/roc2links.shtml)

The state may not unfairly discriminate directly or indirectly against anyone on one or more grounds, including race, gender, sex, pregnancy, marital status, ethnic or social origin, color, sexual orientation, age, disability, religion, conscience, belief, culture, language and birth.

Everyone has the right:
a. to an environment that is not harmful to their health or well-being.
b. to have the environment protected, for the benefit of present and future generations, through reasonable legislative and other measures that:
i. prevent pollution and ecological degradation.
ii. promote conservation.
iii. secure ecologically sustainable development and use of natural resources while promoting justifiable economic and social development.

Every child has the right:
a. to a name and a nationality from birth.

b. to family care or parental care, or to appropriate alternative care when removed from the family environment.
c. to basic nutrition, shelter, basic health care services and social services.
d. to be protected from maltreatment, neglect, abuse or degradation.
e. to be protected from exploitative labor practices;
f. not to be required or permitted to perform work or provide services that:
i. are inappropriate for a person of that child's age;
ii. place at risk the child's well-being, education, physical or mental health, or spiritual, moral, or social development.

Everyone has the right to receive education in the official language or languages of their choice in public educational institutions where that education is reasonably practicable. In order to ensure the effective access to, and implementation of, this right, the state must consider all reasonable educational alternatives, including single medium institutions, taking into account:
a. equity.
b. practicability.
c. the need to redress the results of past racially discriminatory laws and practices.

crimination against people of color, women, and gays and lesbians? Does it provide for protection against racism, male chauvinism, and homophobia? What does it include about the right to live in a clean environment?

6. Explain to students that they will now compare the bills of rights of two countries — the United States and South Africa — in order to write a new U.S. Bill of Rights.

7. Read the U.S. Bill of Rights (the first ten Amendments) and also read Amendments 13, 14, 15, and 19, which expand rights included in the original Bill of Rights (available on the Rethinking Schools website: www.rethinkingschools.org/publication/roc2/roc2links.shtml). Students should summarize the differences and similarities between the Universal Declaration of Human Rights and the U.S. Bill of Rights and later amendments. Does the U.S. Bill of Rights offer protection against racism, male chauvinism, and homophobia? Which of these documents comes closest to the list that students brainstormed earlier?

8. Read and discuss an abbreviated version of South Africa's Bill of Rights. (The text of an abbreviated version is available on the Rethinking Schools website: www.rethinking schools.org/publication/roc2/roc2 links.shtml) Read and discuss each section, comparing to see if each right is also guaranteed in the U.S. Bill of Rights or U.S. law, other amendments, or in the U.N. Declaration of Human Rights. Discuss the following questions:

• Do we in the United States have the same protections as the South African Bill of Rights?

• Does our Bill of Rights have the same environmental guarantees as those stated in the South African Bill of Rights?

• Are the rights stated in the South African Bill of Rights for children comparable to children's rights in the United States?

• Article 24 of the abbreviated South African Bill of Rights states that education in South African needs

to "redress the results of past racially discriminatory laws and practices." Does education in the United States redress past racially discriminatory laws and practices?

• Does the U.S. Bill of Rights deal with past discrimination ?

• Ask students if they know the conditions under which each of these bills of rights were written.

9. Raise with students issues of employment and income. Do the U.S. and South African bills of rights guarantee the right to a job and a living wage?

10. Have students, in groups, write a new U.S. Bill of Rights for the American people. They should pay attention to each of the 29 areas of rights presented in the abbreviated South African Bill of Rights, even if they decide not to include these, along with other areas they wish to address.

11. When students have finished their Bill of Rights they should present to the class the rights they guaranteed and the rights they did not include. Each of the following rights should be considered, with students explaining why certain rights are left out of their Bill of Rights:

Equality
Human Dignity
Freedom and Security of the Person
Slavery, Servitude and Forced Labor
Privacy
Freedom of Religion, Belief and Opinion
Freedom of Expression
Assembly, Demonstration, Picket and Petition
Freedom of Association
Political Rights
Citizenship
Freedom of Movement and Residence
Freedom of Trade, Occupation and Profession
Labor Relations
Environment
Property
Housing
Health Care, Food, Water and Social Security

Children
Education
Language and Culture
Cultural, Religious, and Linguistic Communities
Access to Information
Just Administrative Action
Access to Courts
Arrested, Detained, and Accused Persons

12. Encourage students to show how a society would interact having the Bill of Rights they have constructed. They should be encouraged to do this in creative ways (including skits, holding court sessions showing the protection of rights, "street interviews" of citizens living in the society protected by the new Bill of Rights, etc.)

13. After students finish their presentations, ask them to list which rights appeared on most people's lists. Are any of these not presently in the U.S. Bill of Rights?

Follow up discussion questions for the class:

• What in the South African Bill of Rights do you think should be stated in the U.S. Bill of Rights?

• How do you compare the rights for women stated in the South African Bill of Rights with those stated in the U.S. Bill of Rights?

• If there are rights that we believe are important but which we do not yet have, how can we go about trying to gain them?

• Ask students how the statement by Frederick Douglass, "Power concedes nothing without a demand. It never has and it never will," applies to this activity. How should the fight for rights be organized in our time?

(You can read and download the complete South African Constitution via links on the Rethinking Schools website: www.rethinkingschools.org/publication/roc2/roc2links.shtml.) ∎

Larry Miller teaches social studies at Metropolitan High School in Milwaukee, Wisconsin and is a Rethinking Schools editor.

Waiting at the Railroad Cafe

All the white kids are eating.
"Let's go, Dad," I say.
"Let's get out of this place."
But Dad doesn't move.
He's going to prove
the Asian race
is equal. We stay
and take our silent beating.

He folds his arms
across his chest
glaring at the waitresses who
pass by like cattle
ready for a western battle.
They will not look, they refuse to
surrender even to my best
wishing on bracelet charms.

"Consider this part of your education,"
Dad says. I wonder how long
we'll be ignored, like hungry ghosts
of Chinese men who laid this track,
never making their journeys back
but leaving milestones and signposts
to follow. "Why do they treat us so wrong?"
I wonder. "Don't they know we're on vacation?"

A drunk shouts at us and
gets louder and redder
in the face
when we pay
him no mind. I say
"Let's get out of this place.
We're not equal. We're better,"
as I pull Dad by the hand.

— Janet Wong

(Teaching Ideas, p. 240)

A Lesson on the Japanese-American Internment

By Mark Sweeting

World War II, like so many other issues in history, presents the classroom teacher with an overwhelming range of topics. The rise of Nazism and fascism in Europe, the Holocaust, the military history and diplomacy of the war, the attack on Pearl Harbor and the war in the Pacific, the Nuremberg Trials, the dropping of atomic bombs, the beginnings of the Cold War — there is no way to cover all these events in a typical month-long unit.

One event that invariably gets neglected is the war-time internment of Japanese Americans from the West Coast of the United States. The reasons are numerous. But I suspect the main reason is that serious investigation of the internment would contradict the traditional presentation of the American role in the war — how American ingenuity and power turned back Hitler, liberated the concentration camps, halted Japanese expansionism, and generally fought the good fight. Such an interpretation does not leave much room for aberrations, particularly one as anti-democratic as the Japanese internment.

However, I have covered the internment in my American History classes in some detail. One reason is that I teach in Oregon, which along with California and Washington was one of the states most affected by Executive Order 9066, which initiated the internment.

Executive Order 9066, signed by President Roosevelt on Feb. 19, 1942, empowered the Secretary of War to force Japanese Americans (two-thirds of whom were U.S. citizens) on the coast into hastily built prisons in the desert regions of the American West. For the war's duration, 120,000 inno-

"My Papa" by Henry Sugimoto (1943) depicts a farmer's forced internment.

JAPANESE AMERICAN NATIONAL MUSEUM

cent and un-accused Japanese Americans were imprisoned. The order is perhaps the single largest collective civil rights violation in post-Civil War America. Even an abbreviated list of the constitutional rights violated by the executive order is distressing: freedom of speech, freedom from unreasonable searches and seizures, the right to be informed of charges, the right to a speedy and public trial, the right to legal counsel, the right to a trial by jury, and the right to equal protection under the law.

Fortunately, I was able to gather a lot of information and firsthand accounts of Japanese Americans' experiences in the internment camps. We read primary documents and did role plays, simulations, and interior monologues concerning the internment. (An interior monologue is when a student attempts to write from the point of view of a historical or literary figure.) My students were genuinely surprised by the cruelty and illegality of the act.

Textbooks and the Internment

One of my students missed most of the topic due to illness. When he asked me about make-up work, I felt a bit trapped, because so much of what we do in class is interactive and participatory. I told him I would come up with a list of assignments. Desperate, I turned to the district-adopted textbook for the class: *The Americans* (Jordan, Greenblatt, Bowes, 1985). In looking for information on the internment, I found only two paragraphs conveniently buried at the end of a chapter on the initial stages of World War II. The heading for the paragraphs read: "Nation Relocates Japanese Americans."

Relocates! I did not expect to see this term still used to describe Executive Order 9066. I doubted whether anyone who had endured the internment would describe it as merely being "relocated."

From that heading I came up with the following activity, which I carried out the next day.

'Mark Relocates Jimmy'

When the students settled into their seats, I told them we were going to practice writing newspaper articles and headlines. I told them they were to write headlines for what happened in class that day. As I was describing what was to be done, I interrupted myself in mid-sentence to "yell" at Jimmy, a student. (I had told Jimmy earlier that at some point during class I was going to get very mad at him, berate him, and then move his seat. I asked that he keep this secret and he was more than happy to go along.) As part of my "yelling" I said very angrily and very loudly: "Wait a moment. Jimmy! I've had enough of that. I want you to leave your books and your jacket and come up here and sit at my desk where I can keep an eye on you! Right now! Move it!"

"What did I do?" Jimmy protested.

"I don't have to tell you anything Jimmy," I answered. "Now move it!"

The class sat in bewilderment. Although they hadn't necessarily been watching Jimmy, they also hadn't heard him fooling around or distracting anyone. They also had never seen me lose my temper in class. I could see their uneasiness.

At this point I announced: "OK, assume you are a reporter for the school paper and you are going to write a headline to explain what just happened."

I gave them a few minutes and then asked them to read their headlines out loud as I wrote them on the board. Here is a sample:

"Teacher Forces Student Up Front!"

"Mark Screams and Humiliates Jimmy in Social Studies!"

"Mark Forgets His Medication and Slams Jimmy!"

Each student read aloud his/her headline and most of them were along the same line — that I had gotten angry and made Jimmy move despite his pleas of innocence.

I then said, "Well, here's my headline, what do you think of it: 'Mark Relocates Jimmy.'"

Cries of "No!" came from the class.

"What's wrong with my headline?" I asked. "Isn't that what I did?"

More cries of "No!" "Relocates is so weak," they said. "Relocates, that word's not right, it just doesn't fit."

"Why?" I asked. "Why do you think 'relocates' is a weak word choice?"

The students and I then began a discussion on the word "relocates" and used it in various sentences. One student remarked that sometimes people say they relocated for a new job. I offered that newlyweds often will "relocate" to begin their lives together. Through the discussion, we came to agree that the word "relocates" implies voluntary action or compliance by the person or persons doing the actual relocating.

I asked again if Jimmy was "relocated."

"No!" they cried. He was forced to move by me, the teacher. I had not merely relocated Jimmy, but had in fact screamed at him, humiliated him for no reason, and then made him sit at my desk.

I then asked students to open their textbooks, *The Americans*, to p. 742 and read the heading in the middle of the page: "Nation Relocates Japanese Americans." There was spontaneous laughter.

"Based on what we have seen and read and experienced about Executive Order 9066, would you say this was a fair headline?" I asked. The students immediately recognized the headline's inappropriateness.

"'Arrests them' is more like it," one student said. "The authors are just trying to make it sound better, more polite."

In fact, the headline is worse than sleazy or polite. It is wrong. Japanese-Americans were arrested and detained without charge or provocation or probable cause. Fifty years ago the term used to describe the internment was "relocation." That it is still used in text-

books to characterize the internment is discouraging.

The word "Nation" in the headline is equally offensive. "Nation Relocates Japanese Americans" implies that Japanese Americans were not part of the nation, that they were somehow separate. Two-thirds of those imprisoned were U.S. citizens, and many first-generation Japanese were forbidden to become citizens by laws never applied to Europeans. Even those who were not yet citizens were still entitled to equal protection under the law. Furthermore, the American "nation" did not imprison the Japanese; this was a decision by the ruling powers, carried out by presidential order.

As a result of this exercise, I appreciated anew the power of words. And I became even more aware of how the teaching of history is shaped by the materials we use in our classrooms. American history textbooks, unfortunately, are filled with euphemisms and sanitized language for many indefensible acts. The internment is presented as an aberration, an unfortunate government reaction made during a stressful time. In fact, the removal of Japanese Americans from the West Coast was lobbied for, and beneficial to, certain groups of people, among them white farmers looking for a greater share of the thriving fruit industry. When something like Executive Order 9066 is still presented as a "relocation," the event simply does not sound all that bad — or even wrong.

Far too often, oppressive events, if included in textbooks at all, are packaged and phrased in such a way as to take away any blame or to remove any hint of ill-intent. Passive voice and vague language are two favorite techniques used by textbook writers trying to avoid controversy.

Even though newer textbooks present a greater number of controversial acts from our nation's past, that is not enough. If we are going to use textbooks, we must examine how they present such controversies and analyze both what is, and isn't, included. ■

Mark Sweeting teaches at Reynolds High School in Troutdale, Oregon.

In Response to Executive Order 9066:

All Americans of Japanese Descent Must Report to Relocation Centers

During World War II President Roosevelt signed Executive Order 9066, which mandated people of Japanese ancestry on the West Coast be confined in internment camps. Dwight Okita's parents were among the 120,000 Japanese-American citizens forced to go to such camps. His father was released to fight in Europe with the Japanese-American 442nd regiment, the most decorated Army brigade in U.S. history, while Okita's mother remained in the camp.

Dear Sirs:

Of course I'll come. I've packed my galoshes
and three packets of tomato seeds. Denise calls them
"love apples." My father says where we're going
they won't grow.

I am a fourteen-year-old girl with bad spelling
and a messy room. If it helps any, I will tell you
I have always felt funny using chopsticks
and my favorite food is hot dogs.
My best friend is a white girl named Denise —
we look at boys together. She sat in front of me
all through grade school because of our names:
O'Connor, Ozawa. I know the back of Denise's head very well.
I tell her she's going bald. She tells me I copy on tests.
We're best friends.

I saw Denise today in Geography class.
She was sitting on the other side of the room.
"You're trying to start a war," she said, "giving secrets away
to the Enemy. Why can't you keep your big mouth shut?"
I didn't know what to say.

— Dwight Okita

(Teaching Ideas, p. 240)

What the Tour Guide Didn't Tell Me

Tourism, colonialism, and resistance in Hawai'i

By Wayne Wah Kwai Au

"Sex, *hula*, and naked ladies!" I had just asked a class of eleventh-grade U.S. literature and history students in Portland, Oregon, what images come to mind when I say the word "Hawai'i." I received a volley of fairly stereotypical responses: blue water, beaches, coconuts, sun, surf, *luau*, hotels, paradise, pineapple, palm trees, vacation, Waikiki, volcanoes, and of course, "sex, *hula*, and naked ladies."

This particular answer, given by an enthusiastic young man, was different than most because of its honesty about the sexual overtones the mystique of Hawai'i holds in the "American" mind. To me, what was most significant about his remark was not just its honesty, but that it shows the need for a more critical examination of the history, politics, and culture of Hawai'i in our classrooms.

The Hawai'i most of my students know is the "paradise" construct of tourist Hawai'i, a conception that hinges on the marketing of a hyper-sexualized version of the islands and the indigenous Hawaiian culture. As Native Hawaiian sovereignty activists Haunani-Kay Trask and Mililani Trask put it: "It is our culture tourists come to see. It is our land the tourists come to pollute."

Many advocates of tourism say Native Hawaiian culture "naturally" lends itself to the tourist industry, touting that "aloha spirit" — based on sharing and love — has welcomed tourists with open arms. In fact, tourism has nothing to do with the Native Hawaiian concept of aloha,

King Kalakaua, the last reigning king of Hawai'i, ruled from 1874 to 1891.

HAWAI'I HISTORICAL SOCIETY

and what must be made clear is that tourism is not a natural outcome of Native Hawaiian culture.

Fantasy Islands

The year 1998 marked an important centennial for Hawai'i. (I use "Hawai'i" instead of "Hawaii" because it reflects a more culturally and linguistically correct spelling and acknowledges the glottal stop com-

mon in the Hawai'ian language.) In 1898, the United States formally annexed the islands (see the sidebar on p. 78). The centennial provided a window of opportunity for teachers to explode the idealized notions of Hawai'i and its beaches, sun, and *hula*.

When I teach about Hawai'i, I use these fantastic images of the islands as an entry point into studying the politics and history of Hawai'i in general. Historically, tourism has never based its marketing on reality, mainly because it seeks to commodify real, living people, complex cultures, and environments into "sellable" products. I ask the students to analyze tourist brochures. They make an ideal text because they represent the epitome of advertising — shallow, glossy, and chock full of stereotypes. Because tourist propaganda is so holistic in its depiction of Hawai'i, its total impact culminates in the creation of a "paradise" that obscures the reality of Hawai'i.

I usually ask the students to write creative descriptions of a place called "Tourist Hawai'i," based solely on the images and information in the brochures. The key question for the students is: "What kind of Hawai'i has the tourist brochure defined *for* you?" I encourage them to include aspects like climate, geography, culture, food, architecture, people, and attitude of the Hawai'i found in the brochures.

Students pick up on a number of visible trends in the brochures — for instance, that all the people are fit and trim and all the women are hourglass-shaped. The students also see a "land filled with hotels," where it is "sunny and warm 24 hours a day" and "you never have to sleep." The most telling comment was from one group of students who noticed how the Native Hawaiians are depicted: "always smiling and friendly," and obviously there for the pleasure, entertainment, and excitement of the tourists.

After they've looked at what the tourist industry has to say, I ask the students to read excerpts from Haunani-Kay Trask's book, *From A Native Daughter: Colonialism & Sovereignty in Hawai'i.* From the reading, students get a taste of one Native Hawaiian woman's perspective on the colonization of the islands and the subsequent effects of capitalism and tourism. Some of the realities Trask points out:

• More than 30 years ago, at statehood, Hawai'i residents outnumbered tourists by more than 2 to 1. Today,

Queen Lili'uokalani, last ruler of the sovereign Hawai'ian kingdom.

tourists outnumber residents by 6 to 1; they outnumber Native Hawaiians by 30 to 1.

• More plants and animals from Hawai'i are now extinct or on the endangered species list than in the rest of the United States.

• Nearly one-fifth of Hawai'i residents are considered "near homeless" — and just one missed paycheck will result in missing the rent or mortgage.

• Groundwater supplies on O'ahu are being used up more quickly than they can be replenished.

At the end of the excerpt I give students, Trask makes a request: "Now that you have heard a Native view, let me just leave this thought behind. If you are thinking of visiting my homeland, please don't. We don't want or need any more tourists, and we certainly don't like them. If you want to help our cause, pass this message on to your friends."

Student Response

Trask's view alienates some students. A classroom conversation that stays in my mind was centered around one young woman's reaction to Trask's request that tourists stay away. This young woman was held up by the idea that she should relinquish her individual right to go anywhere, regardless of the consequences. After all, she had already vacationed in Hawai'i, had a great time with her family, and would love to go back. Who's to tell her where she can and cannot go?

Although I did not agree with the student, I could see why she was having a hard time swallowing Trask's request. Trask forces readers to challenge themselves, to think about what kinds of privileges they may have as "Americans." The annual pilgrimage to blissful paradise is something many have learned to see as the pay-off for trudging to work every day.

What lurks behind this reasoning is a deeper, more political, and historical argument. In the canon of American history, Hawai'i is *supposed* to be a U.S. property, justly acquired and

The Price of Paradise

By Wayne Au

Lost in all the glamour and glitz of tourist advertising is any acknowledgment that the Hawai'i we know today has come at a steep price.

Before Western contact, Hawai'i maintained a richly complex, thriving culture, including an overall population estimated by some to have been one million people. However by the 1840s, a little over 60 years after Captain Cook's arrival in 1778, the Hawaiians faced near extinction from foreign diseases, and only about 100,000 Native Hawaiians were still alive. Native Hawaiian conversions to Calvinism flourished amid this scene of mass death and desperation, and consequently the Western missionaries garnered enough influence in the Hawaiian government to begin changing traditional Native land tenure and economic systems to the foreigners' advantage.

The foreigners' power grab culminated in the *Mahele* of 1848, which was a division of Hawaiian land granted by King Kamehameha III under the influence of foreign advisors. Under the division, foreigners were allowed to own land in the Hawaiian kingdom, resulting in the massive dispossession of Native Hawaiians from their traditional lands. By 1888, three-quarters of all farmable land was under non-Hawaiian control. In this same era, U.S. President John Tyler issued the Tyler Doctrine, declaring to the other imperialist powers of the world that Hawai'i was in the U.S. "sphere of influence."

In 1893, a group of foreign businessmen — led by U.S. Minister to Hawai'i John L. Stevens and supported by the Marines of the U.S.S. Boston — led a military coup and illegally overthrew the sovereign Native Hawaiian government. Sanford B. Dole, a descendant of missionaries, was selected president of the newly established provisional government. A little over a year later the independent Republic of Hawai'i was proclaimed. A Native rebellion ensued in 1895, and subsequently the leader of the Hawaiian Kingdom, Queen Lili'uokalani, was imprisoned by Dole's provisional government. Finally, in 1898, the United States government officially annexed the Hawaiian islands. This effectively took away — for the meantime at least — the Native Hawaiians' right to self-determination.

Resistance in Paradise: 1898-1998

The United States annexed Hawai'i during a time of imperialist expansion. During the same year, following its victory in the Spanish-American War, it made other key acquisitions in the Pacific and the Caribbean and took control of the Philippines, Guam, Samoa, Cuba, and Puerto Rico. In all of these places, the American military played a prominent role — both in the immediate sense of direct military support and coercion, and in the sense of fulfilling long-term goals of establishing naval stations in strategic positions throughout the Atlantic and Pacific oceans.

As part of the occupations, the indigenous peoples of these areas were dispossessed of massive amounts of land. In Hawai'i alone, it has been estimated that 95% of all state-controlled lands were ceded to the United States by the illegally established government of Sanford Dole, including nearly 30% of the island of O'ahu, which belongs to the military.

During the centennial in 1998, a number of protests and projects were organized to mark these events. Among the many projects, at least one was aimed at classroom educators: The Asia Pacific Program of the American Friends Service Committee assembled a resource guide entitled *Resistance in Paradise: Rethinking 100 Years of U.S. Involvement in the Caribbean and the Pacific*. This guide, co-written and edited by a wide range of classroom educators and community activists, is made up of source materials, historical essays, lesson plans, and various perspectives surrounding the U.S. annexation and control of these islands in the Pacific and Caribbean. Among other topics, the guide examines issues of indigenous resistance and sovereignty, the fight against continual U.S. militarization of indigenous lands, and the environmental and cultural impacts of U.S. imperialism on the land and people in their respective settings. ∎

For information on how to order Resistance in Paradise, *see the Resources list, p. 229.*

owned — hands down, no questions asked. It is *our* paradise to use at *our* leisure, and traveling there is supposed to be one of *our* quintessential, "American," middle-class rights.

At first, I was disheartened by this type of student response. But I have also come to realize that history is complex, and when it is taught from the perspective of education-as-liberation, it will inevitably clash with some traditional American values. Learning to develop our own perspectives on the world takes time, and students need to be able to process their own feelings of social justice for themselves.

Resistance

Eventually, with a lot more work, students move themselves to a deeper understanding of the islands. As a response to a mini-unit I taught on Hawai'i, one of my students, Wi-Moto, wrote the following poem:

Can we go on vacation?
Can we see the clear blue waters
And bathe in the sun rays?
Can I marvel at the green
and sip the coconut juice?

Should I play on the golf courses?
Should I swim in the pools?
Or should I turn my head
To see what's over my shoulder?

Standing there are the people of
Hawaii.
The homeless, poor. The dying
race,
The slowly fading culture.

Images of death and destruction,
Ghosts of the weak and suffering.
They're being pushed out;
The forgotten natives.

I don't want to vacation anymore.

While such a poem shows how the mini-unit led to an increased understanding about Hawai'i and tourism — and for Wi-Moto, a willingness to take a personal stand on the issue — I also felt less than satisfied when I read it. My dissatisfaction, however, was not with Wi-Moto's poem but

with my curriculum. In my attempt to expose the atrocities of colonization and tourism in Hawai'i, I had not focused enough on Native Hawaiian resistance and survival. This is painfully obvious in the 3rd and 4th stanzas where Wi-Moto refers to the "dying race," "fading culture," and the "weak and suffering...forgotten natives."

Hawaiians, however, are far from weak. During the last 220 years they have more than proven that they won't let themselves be forgotten. Hawaiians have resisted the

> Lost in all the glamour and glitz of tourist advertising is any acknowledgment that the Hawai'i we know today has come at a steep price.

onslaught of colonizing forces since before they killed Captain Cook in 1779 on the beaches of Hawai'i after he had desecrated a sacred temple (see sidebar on p. 78). In 1893, Queen Lili'uokalani ardently protested the overthrow of her government — and 100 years later, 20,000 Native Hawaiians and supporters marched in downtown Honolulu to commemorate the Queen and express their outrage at her overthrow. Today, Hawaiians are involved in cultural revivals and land occupations, and have re-opened demands for Native Hawaiian sovereignty.

In 1998, during the centennial of Hawai'i's occupation by the United States, a number of protests and proj-

ects were organized. One resource, *Resistance in Paradise*, is aimed specifically at classroom educators, giving them a chance to commemorate the last 100 years of resistance to the U.S. occupation (see Resources list).

Hopefully the next time I ask a group of students what images come to mind when I say the word "Hawai'i," I'll get more substantial answers than "sex, *hula*, and naked ladies." ∎

Wayne Au (wayne.wk.au@gmail.com), a Rethinking Schools editor, is an assistant professor of secondary social studies at the University of Washington-Bothell.

Resources on Hawai'i

Curriculum/Resource Guide

Resistance in Paradise: Rethinking 100 Years of U.S. Involvement in the Caribbean and the Pacific, Asia Pacific Program of the American Friends Service Committee (1998), Quaker Books of Friends, 1216 Arch Street, #2B, Philadelphia, PA 19107. 800-966-4556 (U.S.), 215-561-1700 (int'l.), www.Quakerbooks.org. . Cost: $6.50. Limited quantity. Source materials, historical essays, lessons plans, and various perspectives surrounding the U.S. annexation of Pacific and Caribbean lands seized in 1898. Especially geared toward educators and activists.

Books/Articles

He Alo A He Alo: Hawaiian Voices on Sovereignty - Face to Face, American Friends Service Committee, Hawai'i area office (1993). AFSC-Hawai'i, 2426 O'ahu Avenue, Honolulu, HI 96822. 808-988-6266, www.afschawaii.org. A collection of interviews, poetry, essays, and artwork reflecting the diverse views of Native Hawaiians and the sovereignty movement in Hawai'i.

Bamboo Ridge Press, P.O. Box 61781, Honolulu, HI 96839. 808-626-1481. www.BambooRidge.com. Publisher of a literary journal of poetry and fiction, and books, all portraying a wide cross-section of Native Hawaiian experience in Hawai'i.

"Hawai'i: Stirrings in the Colony," by José Luis Morín, (1997, Nov./Dec.) *NACLA Report on the Americas. Vol. XXXI, No. 3.* 10-14 (1997). NACLA, 38 Greene St., 4th Floor, New York, NY 10113. 646-613-1440, nacla@nacla.org, www.nacla.org. A concise and updated look at the sovereignty movement in Hawai'i, including an analysis of the controversial sovereignty plebiscite sponsored by the State of Hawai'i in 1997. Also contains a good, brief history of Hawai'i.

From A Native Daughter: Colonialism & Sovereignty in Hawai'i, by Haunani-Kay Trask, Monroe, ME: Common Courage Press (1993). An insightful collection of essays and speeches from one of Hawai'i's most fiery sovereignty activists and Native Hawaiian academics.

Light in the Crevice Never Seen, by Haunani-Kay Trask. Corvallis, OR: Calyx Books (1994). Considered the first book of poetry by an indigenous Hawaiian to be published in North America, this collection of original poetry by the renowned Hawaiian scholar and activist deals with her love for the land and outrage over its dispossession and destruction.

Videos

Na Maka O Ka Aina - P.O. Box 29, Na'alehu, HI 96772-0029. 808-929-9659, Namaka@interpac.net, www.namaka.com. An outstanding list of videos, including topics such as Environment, Teaching/Learning, Spirit of the Land, History/Independence/Sovereignty, Language, Culture, and Art/Music/Dance.

Internet

Rebuilding a Nation. www.oha.org. Outlines several models of Native Hawaiian sovereignty and includes a sovereignty Q&A section.

Hawai'i - Independent and Sovereign Nation-State. www.hawaii-nation.org. Covers a range of issues on Native Hawaiian sovereignty.

JEAN-CLAUDE LEJEUNE

THE POWER OF CRITIQUE

Critical teachers breathe life, purpose and passion into classroom lives (including their own) by making connections across the boundaries between subject areas, between "real life" and "school life," between the personal and the political. In this section teachers offer ideas, models, and strategies they have used to challenge themselves and their students to reach new levels of educational performance, personal growth, and social insight.

Ten Chairs of Inequality

A simulation on the distribution of wealth

By Polly Kellogg

Inequalities of wealth are becoming more extreme in the United States. While billionaires double their wealth every 3 to 5 years, we have by far the highest poverty rate in the industrialized world. No industrialized country has a more skewed distribution of wealth. Students need information about this concentration of wealth — and the power that accompanies it — in order to become critical thinkers and aware citizens.

A Boston-based group, United for a Fair Economy, has developed a simulation activity to dramatize the increasingly unequal distribution of wealth. I describe here how my college human relations classes respond to the exercise. It can easily be adapted for younger students.

To begin the simulation, I ask 10 students to volunteer to line up at the front of the room, seated in their chairs and facing the rest of the class. I explain that each chair represents 10% of the wealth in the United States and each occupant represents 10% of the population; thus when each chair is occupied by one student, the wealth is evenly distributed. I explain that wealth is what you own: your stereo, the part of your house and car that are paid off, savings like stocks and bonds, vacation homes, any companies you own, your yachts, villas on the Riviera, private jet airplanes, etc. Then I ask students to estimate how much wealth each family would have if the wealth were equally distributed. Students usually guess about $50,000 and are surprised to

hear that the answer is $250,000.

I ask them what it would feel like if every family could have a $100,000 home, a $10,000 car paid for and $140,000 in savings. Some make comments like, "It'd be wonderful. I wouldn't have to work two

> **Students need information about this concentration of wealth — and the power that accompanies it — in order to become critical thinkers and aware citizens.**

jobs and take out a loan to go to college." But many can't imagine such a society. Others express concern that the incentive to work would be taken away: "It sounds like socialism."

I tell those worried about socialism, that they have nothing to fear. We have nowhere near an equal dis-

tribution of wealth in this country. The poorest 20% of the population is in debt, and the next 30% averages only $5,000 in wealth (primarily in home equity).

I ask students at either end of the lineup which one of them wants to represent the richest 10% and experience being rich. Some students volunteer happily and others express distaste at the idea. When asked about their motives, they say, "I'll never be rich, so I'd like to see what it feels like," or "I don't want to oppress other people, and rich people exploit their workers." Sometimes a student, often female, will say, "I don't like to be above other people."

I invite the class to speculate how many chairs belong to the richest student, whom I will call Sue. In 1998, the richest 10% owned 71% of the wealth — thus Sue controls about seven chairs. I tell the six students sitting nearest to Sue to give up their chairs to her and move to the poorer end of the lineup. I provoke them by telling them that the standing students can sit on the laps of the three students seated at the end, and I invite Sue to sit in the middle of her seven chairs, to stretch out, relax, or even lie down across the chairs.

I then announce that Sue's arm represents the wealthiest 1% of families and that her arm's share of the wealth doubled from 2 chairs (22% of the wealth) to 4 chairs (38%) during the years from 1979 to 1998. I solicitously help Sue find a comfortable position with one arm stretched over four chairs. To engage Sue in clowning and playing up her role, I offer her food or drink.

I ask the other nine students crowded around three chairs what life is like at their end of the line. "We're pissed and tired of working all the time," is a typical comment. Another is, "I want a revolution." I ask students if, in real life, they or people they know are crowded into the bottom one or two chairs, and what that's like. Working-class students tell stories of financial stress they have experienced, such as, "My mother had to work at two jobs to support us." "My family was really poor when my dad was laid off. We lived on macaroni and cheese." Often one student, usually a white male, says he has hopes that he can work hard and join Sue.

Students' knowledge of how inequality is rationalized erupts when I ask, "What do those in power tell us to justify this dramatic inequality?" Typical student answers are: "They work harder than we do." "They create jobs." "The U.S. stands for equality and justice for all." "It's our fault if we don't make it." If students do not mention scapegoating, I bring it up. I may select one student to represent the poorest 10% and ask, "Wouldn't there be more money for the rest of you if he or she weren't ripping off the system for welfare?" I also ask, "Who does Sue want you to blame for your tough economic conditions?" Answers range from welfare moms and immigrants to gays and lesbians, and bad schools.

When I ask the nine students grouped around the three chairs why they don't get organized to force a redistribution of the wealth, they offer a variety of answers. "We're too busy working to organize." "We are told we can't change things." "We don't get along with each other." "They'd call out the army to stop us."

At some point I ask the class to describe the "super rich" — the 1%, Sue's arm. College students share examples from their experiences. A junior high coach described a local billionaire who offered to write the coach's school a check of any amount in order to get his child on the baseball team. Another student worked as a waiter in an elite club where "you had to be elected to be able to have lunch there." The club was all white and only recently began allowing women on the premises; some of the older men refused to let her serve them because they resented her presence. Another student described doing carpentry in a mansion of the DuPonts, "The faucet in the kid's bathroom cost $3,000."

The athletes and entertainers whose salaries are hyped in the media and newly rich entrepreneurs like Donald Trump and Bill Gates are always mentioned. I point out that these are the upwardly mobile people, who moved from the three chairs up to Sue's chair. How often does this happen? Why do we hear so much about them? I want students to understand that the exaggerated publicity about these rags-to-riches icons perpetuates the myth that anyone who tries can make it.

Most texts and teachers stop after they have taught about the unequal distribution of wealth, but that is only a piece of the picture. We need to go on to ask why wealth is so unequally distributed. Where does wealth come from? Why does our system concentrate wealth in the hands of so few? And what can ordinary people do to effect change? The simulation creates a foundation for these later lessons. ∎

Polly Kellogg is an assistant professor in the Human Relations and Multicultural Education Department at St. Cloud State Universty, St. Cloud, Minnesota.

More teaching resources are available from United for a Fair Economy. See Resources, p. 238.

Teaching Math Across the Curriculum

A fifth-grade teacher battles 'number numbness'

By Bob Peterson

I recently read a proposal for an innovative school and it set me thinking about math. It wasn't the proposal's numbers that got my mind going, but rather the approach to structuring math into the curriculum. I disagreed with it.

The plan called for the curriculum to be divided into three areas — math/science, the arts (including fine arts and language arts), and history/philosophy. Blocks of time were set aside for a unified approach in each area. As I mulled over the proposal and thought of my experience in a self-contained fifth-grade classroom, I realized I was uneasy with the proposed curricular divisions, specifically the assumption that science and math belong together as an unified block. It reminded me of how some elementary teachers integrate the curriculum by lumping language arts and social studies together in one strand, and math and science in another.

It also raised several questions for me. Why place math and science together, and not math and social studies? What are the political and pedagogical assumptions behind such an approach? Why shouldn't reformers advocate math in all subject areas? Why not have "math across the curriculum," comparable to "writing across the curriculum?"

One reason reformers have advocated changes in how math is structured is because of the historic problems with math instruction itself: rote calculations, drill and practice ad nauseum, endless reams of worksheets, and a fetish for "the right

SUSAN LINA RUGGLES

answer." These have contributed to "number numbness" among students, and ultimately among the general population when students become adults.

But the problem is deeper than a sterile teacher-centered and text-driven approach. "Number numbness" also has its roots in how math is segregated in schools and kept separate from the issues that confront students in their daily lives. Most students don't want to

do abstract exercises with numbers or plod through text-based story problems that have them forever making change in some make-believe store. The curriculum rarely encourages students to link math and history, math and politics, math and literature — math and people.

There are unfortunate consequences when math is isolated. First, the not-so-subtle message is that math is basically irrelevant except for success in future math classes, or if you want to be a scientist or mathematician, or in commercial transactions. Second, students learn that math is not connected to social reality in any substantive way. Thus students approach math in the abstract and never are encouraged to seriously consider the social and ethical consequences of how math is sometimes used in society. Third, if students are not taught how math can be applied in their lives, they are robbed of an important tool to help them fully participate in society. An understanding of math and how numbers and statistics can be interpreted is essential to effectively enter most debates on public issues such as welfare, unemployment, and the federal budget. For example, even though the minimum wage is higher than it has ever been, in constant dollars it is the lowest in 40 years. But you need math to understand that.

When I first began teaching more than 18 years ago, I was dissatisfied with "number numbness," but wasn't sure what to do about it. My growth as a teacher first came in the area of language arts and reading. I increasingly stressed that students should write for meaningful purposes, and read books and stories that were connected to their lives. Thus I had children read and discuss whole books, conducted writing workshops, and had students read and write in science and social studies. My math, however, remained noticeably segregated from the rest of the curriculum, even though I increasingly emphasized problem-solving and the use of manipulatives.

More recently, with the help of my teaching colleague Celín Arce and publications from the National Council of Teachers of Mathematics, I have begun to view math as akin to language. I believe that math, like language, is both a discipline unto itself and a tool to understand and interact with the world and other academic disciplines. Just as written and oral language helps children understand their community, so can written and oral mathematics. Just as teach-

ers stress the need for "writing across the curriculum," I believe it is important to advocate "math across the curriculum." Just as students are expected to write for meaningful purposes, they should do math for meaningful purposes.

Plans to integrate math into science are a step in the right direction. And assuming that the science curriculum is "meaningful," the teaching of mathematics will improve. But linking math with science is only a beginning, and should be followed with integration of math across the curriculum. I have found that my fifth graders, for instance, are particularly interested in social issues. Thus integrating math with social studies is an effective way to bring math alive for the students.

Before I go any further, I want to make two important clarifications. First, I don't mean to imply that distinct math "mini-lessons" aren't important. They are, just as such lessons are necessary in reading and writing. I also want to make clear that integrating math with social studies does not necessarily make the teaching more student-centered or the content more concerned with issues of social justice. Those important components depend on the teacher's philosophical and pedagogical beliefs.

In the past few years I have tried in a variety of ways to integrate mathematics — from the simplest understanding of number concepts to more complex problem solving — with social studies. In the interests of clarity (my classroom life is never so neatly ordered), I outline these approaches as: Connecting Math to Students' Lives; Linking Math and Issues of Equality; Using Math to Uncover Stereotypes; Using Math to Understand History.

Connecting to Students

The starting point of many teachers is to build on what students bring into the classroom, and to connect curriculum to students' lives. Math is

a great way to do this. I usually start the year with kids exploring, in small groups, how math is used in their homes and communities. They scour newspapers for numbers, cut them out, put them on poster paper and try to give sense to their meanings, which at times is difficult. They interview family members about how they use math and write up their discoveries. As part of a beginning-of-the-

year autobiography, they write an essay, "Numeric Me," tying in all the numbers that connect to their lives, from height and weight, to the number of brothers and sisters they have, to addresses, phone numbers, and so forth. I also ask them to write a history of their experiences in math classes, what they think about math, and why.

This process starts a year long conversation on what we mean by mathematics and why it is important in our lives. As the class increasingly becomes sensitive to the use of numbers and math in news articles, literature, and in everyday events, our discussions help them realize that math is more than computation and definitions, but includes a range of concepts and topics — from geometry and measurements to ratios, percentages, and probability.

As part of the autobiography project we also do a timeline. We start by putting the students' birthdates and those of their parents and grandparents on a class timeline that circles the outer perimeter of my classroom (and which is used throughout the year to integrate dates that we come across in all subject areas). The students also make their own time lines — first of a typical day and then of their life. In these activities, students use reasoning skills to figure out relations between numbers, distance, time, fractions and decimals.

I also use another beginning-of-the-year activity that not only builds math skills but fosters community and friendship. The whole class discusses what a survey or poll is and brainstorms questions that they would like to ask each other. After I model one survey, each student surveys their classmates about a different topic. Kids, for example, have surveyed classmates on their national origin, their favorite fast food restaurant, music group, or football team, or what they think of our school's peer mediation program. Each student tabulates his or her survey data, makes a bar graph displaying the results, and reflects in writing on what they have learned. Later in the year they convert the data into fractions and percentages and make cir-

cle graphs. I encourage the students to draw conclusions from their data, and hypothesize about why the results are the way they are. They then present these conclusions orally and in writing.

This activity is particularly popular with my students, and often they will want to do more extensive surveys with broader groups of people. The activity lays the basis for more in-depth study of polling and statistics around issues such as sampling, randomness, bias, and error. For extensive curricular ideas on the use of polls and statistics in social studies, see *The Power of Numbers* curriculum published by the Educators for Social Responsibility.

Math and Inequality

To help my students understand that mathematics is a powerful and useful tool, I flood my classroom with examples of how math is used in major controversies in their community and in society at large. I also integrate math with social studies lessons to show how math can help us better understand the nature of social inequality. Kids are inherently interested in what is "fair," and using math to explore what is and isn't "fair" is a great way to get kids interested in all types of math concepts, from compu-

tation to fractions, percentages, ratios, averages, and graphing.

For example, during October and November, there is often lots of discussion of poverty and hunger in my classroom, related either to the UNICEF activities around Halloween or issues raised by the Thanksgiving holiday. This is a good time to use simulation exercises to help children understand the disparity of wealth in the United States and around the world. In one lesson (explained in detail in "World Poverty and World Resources", on p. 92 of *Rethinking Our Classrooms, Volume 1*) I provide information on the distribution of population and wealth in the six continents, and then have children represent that information using different sets of colored chips. After working with students so they understand the data, we do a class simulation using a map of the world painted on our playground. Instead of chips to represent data we use the children themselves. I tell them to divide themselves around the playground map in order to represent the world's population distribution. I then use chocolate chip cookies, instead of chips, to represent the distribution of wealth, and hand out chocolate chip cookies accordingly. As you can imagine, some kids get far more chocolate chip cookies than others, and lively discussions ensue. Afterwards, we discuss the simulation and write about the activity.

Not only does such a lesson connect math to human beings and social reality, it does so in a way that goes beyond paper and pencil exercises; it truly brings math alive. I could just tell my students about the world's unequal distribution of wealth. But that wouldn't have the same emotional impact as when they see classmates in the North American and European sections of the map get so many more cookies even though they have so many fewer people.

I also use resources such as news articles on various social issues to help students analyze inequality. In small groups, students examine data such as unemployment or job trends, convert the data into percentages,

SUSAN LINA RUGGLES

make comparisons, draw conclusions, and make graphs. This is a great way to help students understand the power of percentages. Because they also use a computerized graph-making program, they realize how the computer can be a valuable tool.

One group, for example, looked at news stories summarizing a university report on the 10,000 new jobs created in downtown Milwaukee due to commercial development. According to the report, African Americans held fewer than 8% of the new jobs, even though they lived in close proximity to downtown and accounted for 30% of the city's population. In terms of the higher-paying managerial jobs, Latinos and African Americans combined held only 1%, while white residents who are overwhelmingly from the suburbs took almost 80% of the new managerial jobs. Using these data, students made bar and pie graphs of the racial breakdown of people in different jobs and in the city population. They compared the graphs and drew conclusions.

They then did a role play, with some students pretending to be representatives of community organizations trying to convince the mayor and major corporations to change their hiring practices. What began as a math lesson quickly turned into a heated discussion of social policy. At one point, for example, a student argued that the new jobs should be split 1/3 Black, 1/3 Latino and 1/3 white, because those are the three principal ethnic groups in Milwaukee. Others, however, disagreed. Needless to say, this led to an extensive discussion of what is "fair," of reasons why minorities had so few of the jobs created downtown, and what it would take for things to be different.

Math, Stereotypes, and Voice

It is important for students to be aware of whose voices they hear as they read history books or the newspaper, or watch a movie. Who gets to narrate history matters greatly, because it fundamentally shapes the

SUSAN LINA RUGGLES

readers' or viewers' perspective. We can analyze these things with kids and help them become more critical readers of books and other media. In this process math plays an important role.

I usually start with something fairly easy. I have students analyze children's books on Columbus, tabulating whose views are represented. For instance, how many times do Columbus and his men present their perspective, versus the number of times the views of the Taíno Indians are presented? The students, using fractions and percentages, make large graphs to demonstrate their findings and draw potential conclusions. Large visual displays — bar graphs made with sticky tape, for instance — are good points of reference to discuss and analyze. Math concepts of percentages, proportions, and comparisons can be used to help kids discuss the statistics they've uncovered and the graphs they've made.

A similar tabulation and use of percentages can be used to analyze popular TV shows for the number of "put-downs" versus "put-ups," who is quoted or pictured in newspapers, stereotypes of females in popular cartoons, who is included in textbooks, and who is represented in the biography section of the school library. (For further information see "Math and Media," which can be found in Volume 1 of *Rethinking Our Classrooms.*)

Numbers and History

As we study history, we pay particular attention to dates and data. I try to highlight numbers that relate to social movements for equity and justice. For example, as we look at women's struggle for equality we try to imagine what it was like for Susan B. Anthony to go to work as a teacher and get paid $2.50 a week, exactly half the salary of the previous male teacher. Lots can be done with such a statistic — from figuring out and graphing the difference on an annual or lifetime basis, to looking for wage differentials in other occupations and time periods, including the present. I have found children particularly interested in looking at wages paid to child workers — whether it be in coal mines or textile mills. We compare such wages to the price of commodities at the time, to wages of adult workers, and to wealth that was accumulated by owners of industry. Such historical connections can be easily linked to present-day concerns over U.S. child labor and minimum wage laws or to international concerns over multinational corporations exploiting child labor in Asia or Latin America to make consumer goods for worldwide markets.

One math/history connection that can range in sophistication depending on the level of the students is to look at who is represented in different occupations and areas of power in our society, and how that has changed over time. For example, students can figure out what percentage of the signers of the Constitution were slave holders, common working people, women, wealthy individuals who held bonds, and so forth. A similar exercise would be to analyze U.S. Presidents, or the people our country has chosen to honor by putting their faces on currency and coins. Such historical number-crunching can take a contemporary turn if the students analyze the gender and racial breakdown of the U.S. House and Senate, the editors of major newspapers, or the CEOs of the Fortune 500.

It's important for students to understand that such numbers are not permanent fixtures of our social structure, but have changed as result of social movements such as the Civil Rights or women's movements. To demonstrate this, a teacher might have students tally the current percentage of African Americans or women in selected professional occupations and compare it to the 1960s, before the rise of affirmative action.

Another area is to teach the history of math, pointing out the contributions of various non-European cultures and civilizations to mathematical thought. Greek mathematicians, for instance, were heavily influenced by their predecessors and counterparts in Africa and Asia. Arab mathematicians inspired European Renaissance scholars. The Mayans were one of the first peoples to develop the concept of zero and make sophisticated mathematical calculations. I have used a unit on the Mayan counting system of a base 20 with my fifth-graders to demonstrate such sophistication and to help students expand their understanding of place value.

Conclusion

The level of sophistication and complexity of the math we use in our classrooms naturally depends on the developmental level of our students. Teachers, however, too often underestimate what students are capable of doing. To the degree that I provide quality instruction, clear modeling, and purposeful activities, I am usually pleased with the enthusiasm with which my kids take on such math-based projects, and the success they have in doing them.

> Kids need every tool they can get to make this world — their world — a better place. Mathematics is one such important tool.

I have found that as a result of trying to implement "math across the curriculum" — and in particular, integrating math and social studies — my students' interest and skill in math have increased, in terms both of their understanding of basic concepts and of their ability to solve problems. Furthermore, they can better clarify social issues, understand the structures of society, and offer options for better social policies.

Kids need every tool they can get to make this world — their world — a better place. Mathematics is one such important tool. ■

Bob Peterson (repmilw@aol.com) teaches fifth grade at La Escuela Fratney in Milwaukee, Wisconsin and is a Rethinking Schools editor.

Resources

Bigelow, Bill, et al. (Eds.). *Rethinking Our Classrooms: Teaching for Equity and Justice.* Milwaukee: Rethinking Schools, Ltd., 1994.

Frankenstein, Marilyn. *Relearning Mathematics: A Different Third R - Radical Maths.* London: Free Association Books, 1989.

Folbre, Nancy and The Center for Popular Economics. *The New Field Guide to the U.S. Economy.* New York: New Press, 1995.

Gross, Fred, et al. *The Power of Numbers: A Teacher's Guide to Mathematics in a Social Studies Context.* Cambridge, MA: Educators for Social Responsibility, 1993. (Available from ESR, 23 Garden St., Cambridge, MA 02138. 800-370-2515.)

Leiva, Miriam A. (Ed.). *Curriculum and Evaluation Standards for School Mathematics Addenda Series, Grade K-6.* Reston, VA: National Council of Teachers of Mathematics, 1991.

National Council of Teachers of Mathematics. *Curriculum and Evaluation Standards for School Mathematics.* Reston, VA: Author, 1989.

Nelson, David; Gheverghese, Joseph; and Williams, Julian. *Multicultural Mathematics: Teaching Mathematics from a Global Perspective.* New York: Oxford University Press, 1993.

Rose, Stephen J. "Social Stratification in the United States" poster. New York: New Press, 1992.

U.S. Department of Labor. *By the Sweat and Toil of Children: The Use of Child Labor in American Imports.* Washington, DC: The Department of Labor, 1994.

Zaslavsky, J. *Multicultural Mathematics,* Portland. ME: Weston Walch, 1993.

Percent as a Tool for Social Justice

By Bob Peterson

JEAN-CLAUDE LEJEUNE

An understanding of percentages is essential to know what's going on in the world. Unfortunately in some math programs the concept is not even introduced in elementary school, and even when it is taught, textbooks and teachers tend to downplay its social and political significance.

Whether one wants to learn about issues of wealth, power, gender, culture, race, or discrimination it's very difficult without the basic understanding of percent and the ability to understand and manipulate certain types of data.

Helping Kids with the Basic Idea

It makes sense to teach percent along with fractions and decimals, as they are all ways to describe parts of a whole or part of a set of things. I start by having my 5th grade students list all they know about how people use fractions, decimals, and percent. For an initial homework assignment they find examples of the three things at home in newspapers, magazines, and household items. (I stress they must bring in enough information so that we know the context of the number.) I provide newspapers for those students who don't have them at home. I also encourage them to ask an adult member of their household why they think percent is important. We make a bulletin board focusing on the power and omnipresence of these kinds of numbers.

I start by noting that the word "percent" comes from the Latin "per centum," meaning "per hundred." We talk about how many cents are in a dollar and I put 100 pennies in a plastic jar and keep it handy for percentage activities. I talk about "one hundred" being that "special percent number" that allows us to easily compare one thing to another. I usually start out with something in the students' lives — like how many of them have a pet in their household, or how many homes have computers and then ask them how we might be able to compare whether our class is similar to kids across the nation or world. Eventually I explain that the math concept of percent allows us to do that. We use that "special" number 100 and think, for every one hundred kids, a certain number have whatever thing we are talking about. I then explain that if our class had 100 kids we could make an easy comparison by just counting the number of kids who had a certain thing. But since we don't have 100 kids in our classroom, I ask, how can we make it seem like — or more accurately, equivalent to — 100? I remind the kids we have my special jar of 100 pennies and with minimal discussion soon someone suggested that we divide the 100 pennies among us to see how much each of us is "worth." We pass out the pennies and each student usually is worth about four pennies — or four percentage points. We write this as an equation and see that 100 divided by the number of students in my class is about 4. Each student is equivalent to 4%. Thus if 9 kids have a grandmother or an elderly relative living with them, we multiply 9 by 4% and we

JEAN-CLAUDE LEJEUNE

realize 36% of the students in the class have an elderly relative in their household, compared to 25% of households nationwide. After several more polls of the class and group calculations most of the students have a rudimentary understanding of this aspect of percent. Through a variety of exercises we compare these values to fractions and decimals, attempting to get the students to understand the meaning behind the concepts and not just a rote algorithm of how to figure out percent.

To deepen students' understanding of these math concepts and their social significance I encourage kids to continue to find news articles and write about what the percent numbers mean to them — and put all that up on the bulletin board. Here are a few examples of "facts" that have spurred thinking, writing, and discussion:

1) During our school's annual "No-TV Week" my students survey the students in our school and use percentage and pie graphs to show among other things the number of kids who have TVs in their bedrooms, have cable, who can watch TV whenever they want, and who would rather spend time with parents than watching TV.

2) We use information from UNICEF (www.unicef.org) to compare our lives with those of children from around the world. For example, 20% of the children in "developing" countries are not enrolled in primary school, 71% of households in developing countries have access to safe water, and 42% have access to adequate sanitation. Like any other description of poverty, it is important for students to look at root causes and to ask the hard questions of why affluent governments, corporations, and people aren't doing what is necessary to change such situations.

3) In looking at discrimination and prejudice percent is key. As explained in the Number Numbness article (p. 84), I have used local reports on discriminatory hiring practices as a way to bring math alive and delve into this difficult issue. After the students graphically portray such issues on circle or bar graphs, I set up impromptu dramatizations where some students are advocates for those being discriminated against and others are those in authority.

4) Look at online news services as quick sources of this kind of information (wire stories from several services are available via the Web at http://dailynews.yahoo.com). As an example, an AP story in spring of 1997 reported that the Geneva based Inter-Parliamentary Union reported that of all the parliamentary representatives in the world, only 12% are women, and only 7% of the parliaments are headed by women.

Of course the bottom line is what students do with this information that they discover. How can we best help them use that information to pose problems for further study, and share what they learn with others, and ultimately work with others to make the work a more equitable and just place?

∎

Bob Peterson (repmilw@aol.com) teaches fifth grade at La Escuela Fratney in Milwaukee, Wisconsin and is a Rethinking Schools editor.

The Human Lives Behind the Labels

The global sweatshop, Nike, and the race to the bottom

By Bill Bigelow

I began the lesson with a beat-up soccer ball. The ball sat balanced in a plastic container on a stool in the middle of the circle of student desks. "I'd like you to write a description of this soccer ball," I told my high school Global Studies class. "Feel free to get up and look at it. There is no right or wrong. Just describe the ball however you'd like."

Looks of puzzlement and annoyance greeted me. "It's just a soccer ball," someone said.

Students must have wondered what this had to do with Global Studies. "I'm not asking for an essay," I said, "just a paragraph or two."

As I'd anticipated, their accounts were straightforward — accurate if uninspired. Few students accepted the offer to examine the ball up close. A soccer ball is a soccer ball. They sat and wrote. Afterwards, a few students read their descriptions aloud. Brian's is typical:

> The ball is a sphere which has white hexagons and black pentagons. The black pentagons contain red stars, sloppily outlined in silver.... One of the hexagons contains a green rabbit wearing a soccer uniform with "Euro 88" written parallel to the rabbit's body. This hexagon seems to be cracking. Another hexagon has the number 32 in green, standing for the number of patches that the ball contains.

But something was missing. There was a deeper social reality associated with this ball — a reality that advertising and the consumption-oriented

> The importance of making visible the invisible, of looking behind the masks presented by everyday consumer goods, became a central theme in my first-time effort to teach about the "global sweatshop" and child labor in poor countries.

rhythms of U.S. daily life discouraged students from considering.

"Made in Pakistan" was stenciled in small print on the ball, but very few students thought that significant enough to include in their descriptions. However, these three tiny words offered the most important clue to the human lives hidden in "just a soccer ball" — a clue to the

invisible Pakistanis whose hands crafted the ball sitting in the middle of the classroom.

I distributed and read aloud Bertolt Brecht's poem "Questions from a Worker Who Reads"* as a tool to pry behind the soccer-ball-as-thing:

> Who built the seven gates of
> Thebes?
> The books are filled with names
> of kings.
> Was it kings who hauled the crag-
> gy blocks of stone?...
> In the evening when the Chinese
> wall was finished
> Where did the masons go?
> Imperial Rome
> Is full of arcs of triumph. Who
> reared them up?...
>
> Young Alexander conquered
> India.
> He alone?
> Caesar beat the Gauls.
> Was there not even a cook in his
> army?...
>
> Each page a victory.
> At whose expense the victory
> ball?
> Every ten years a great man,
> Who paid the piper?...

"Keeping Brecht's questions in mind," I said, after reading the poem, "I want you to re-see this soccer ball. If you like, you can write from the point of view of the ball, you can ask the ball questions, but I want you to look at it deeply. What did we miss the first time around? It's not 'just a soccer ball.'" With not much more than these words for guidance —

*Included in full in *Rethinking Our Classrooms, Volume 1*, p. 91.

although students had some familiarity with working conditions in poor countries — they drew a line beneath their original descriptions and began again.

Versions one and two were night and day. With Brecht's prompting, Pakistan as the country of origin became more important. Tim wrote in part: "Who built this soccer ball? The ball answers with Pakistan. There are no real names, just labels. Where did the real people go after it was made?" Nicole also posed questions: "If this ball could talk, what kinds of things would it be able to tell you? It would tell you about the lives of the people who made it in Pakistan.... But if it could talk, would you listen?" Maisha played with its colors and the "32" stamped on the ball: "Who painted the entrapped black, the brilliant bloody red, and the shimmering silver? Was it made for the existence of a family of 32?" And Sarah imagined herself as the soccer ball worker:

I sew together these shapes of leather. I stab my finger with my needle. I feel a small pain, but nothing much, because my fingers are so calloused. Everyday I sew these soccer balls together for 5 cents, but I've never once had a chance to play soccer with my friends. I sew and sew all day long to have these balls shipped to another place where they represent fun. Here, they represent the hard work of everyday life.

When students began to consider the human lives behind the ball-as-object, their writing also came alive.

Geoffrey, an aspiring actor, singer, and writer, wrote his as a conversation between himself and the ball:

"So who was he?" I asked.
"A young boy, Wacim, I think," it seemed to reply.
I got up to take a closer look. Even though the soccer ball looked old and its hexagons and other geometric patterns were cracked, the sturdy and intricate

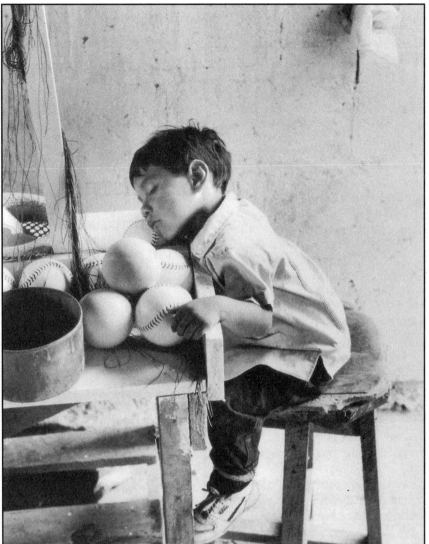

A Honduran boy making softballs falls asleep at his workbench.

stitching still held together.
"What that child must've gone through," I said.
"His father was killed and his mother was working. Wacim died so young.... It's just too hard. I can't contain these memories any longer." The soccer ball let out a cry and leaked his air out and lay there, crumpled on the stool. Like his master, lying on the floor, uncared for, and somehow overlooked and forgotten.

Students had begun to imagine the humanity inside the ball; their pieces were vivid and curious. The importance of making visible the invisible, of looking behind the masks presented by everyday consumer goods,

became a central theme in my first-time effort to teach about the "global sweatshop" and child labor in poor countries. [I did an abbreviated version of this unit with my U.S. history classes. Some of the student writing here is theirs.]

Teaching About the Global Sweatshop

The paired soccer ball writing assignment was a spur-of-the-moment classroom introduction to Sydney Schanberg's June 1996 *Life* magazine article, "Six Cents an Hour." Schanberg, best known for his *New York Times* investigations of Cambodia's "killing fields," had traveled to Pakistan and posed as a soccer ball exporter. There, he was offered children for $150 to $180 who would labor for him as virtual slaves. As Schanberg reports, in Pakistan, children as young as six are "sold and resold like furniture, branded, beaten, blinded as punishment for wanting to go home, rendered speechless by the trauma of their enslavement." For pennies an hour, these children work in dank sheds stitching soccer balls with the familiar Nike swoosh and logos of other transnational athletic equipment companies.

Nike spokesperson Donna Gibbs, defended her company's failure to eliminate child labor in the manufacture of soccer balls: "It's an ages-old practice," she was quoted as saying in Schanberg's article, "and the process of change is going to take time." But as Max White, an activist with the "Justice. Do It NIKE!" coalition, said when he visited my global studies class: "Nike knew exactly what it was doing when it went to Pakistan. That's why they located there. They went because they knew child labor was an 'ages-old practice.'"

My initial impulse had been to teach a unit on child labor. I thought that my students would empathize with young people around the globe, whose play and education had been forcibly replaced with the drudgery of repetitive work — and that the unit would engage them in thinking about inequities in the global division of labor. Perhaps it might provoke them to take action on behalf of child workers in poor countries.

But I was also concerned that we shouldn't reduce the growing inequalities between rich and poor countries to the issue of child labor. Child labor could be entirely elimi-

Nike CEO Phil Knight sits before a portrait of Michael Jordan.

Associated Press

nated and that wouldn't affect the miserably low wages paid to adult workers, the repression of trade unions and democratic movements, the increasing environmental degradation, and the resulting Third World squalor sanitized by terms like "globalization" and "free trade." Child labor is one spoke on the wheel of global capitalism, and I wanted to present students with a broader framework to reflect on its here-and-now dynamics. What I share here is a sketch of my unit's first draft — an invitation to reflect on how best to engage students in these issues.

The Transnational Capital Auction

It seemed to me that the central metaphor for economic globalization was the auction: governments beckoning transnational corporations to come hither — in competition with one another — by establishing attractive investment climates (e.g., by maintaining low-wage/weak union havens and not pressing environmen-

tal concerns.) So I wrote what I called "The Transnational Capital Auction: A Game of Survival." I divided students into seven different "countries," each of which would compete with all the others to accumulate "Friendly-to-Capital points" — the more points earned, the more likely Capital would locate in that country. In five silent auction rounds, each group would submit bids for minimum wage, child labor laws, environmental regulations, conditions for worker organizing, and corporate tax rates. For example, a corporate tax rate of 75% won no points for the round, but a zero tax rate won 100 points. (There were penalty points for "racing to the bottom" too quickly, risking popular rebellion, and thus "instability" in the corporate lexicon.)

I played Capital and egged them on: "Come on group three, you think I'm going to locate in your country with a ridiculous minimum wage like $5 an hour? I might as well locate in the United States. Next round, let's not see any more sorry bids like that one." A bit crass, but so is the real-world downward spiral simulated in the activity.

At the game's conclusion, every country's bids hovered near the bottom: no corporate taxes, no child labor laws, no environmental regulations, pennies an hour minimum wage rates, union organizers jailed, and the military used to crush strikes. As I'd anticipated, students had breathed life into the expressions "downward leveling" and "race to the bottom." In the frenzied competition of the auction, they'd created some pretty nasty conditions, because the game rewarded those who lost sight of the human and environmental consequences of their actions. I asked them to step back from the activity and to write on the kind of place their country would become should transnational Capital decide to accept their bids and locate there. I also wanted them to reflect on the glib premise that underlies so much contemporary economic discussion: that foreign investment in poor countries is automatically a good thing. And finally I hoped that they would consider the impact that the race to the bottom has on their lives, especially their future work prospects. (That week's *Oregonian* carried articles about the Pendleton Co.'s decision to pull much of its production from Oregon and relocate to Mexico.) I gave them several quotes to reflect on as they responded:

"It is not that foreigners are stealing our jobs, it is that we are all facing one another's competition."
William Baumol,
Princeton University economist

"Downward leveling is like a cancer that is destroying its host organism — the earth and its people."
Jeremy Brecher
and Tim Costello,
authors of *Global Village
or Global Pillage*

"Globalization has depressed the wage growth of low-wage workers [in the United States]. It's been a reason for the increasing wage gap between high-wage and low-wage workers."
Laura Tyson, former Chair, U.S. Council of Economic Advisers

Many global issues courses are structured as "area studies," with units focusing on South America, sub-Saharan Africa, or the Middle East. There are obvious advantages to this region-by-region progression, but I worried that if I organized my global studies curriculum this way, students might miss how countries

> **Child labor is one spoke on the wheel of global capitalism, and I wanted to present students with a broader framework to reflect on its here-and-now dynamics.**

oceans apart, such as Indonesia and Haiti, are affected by the same economic processes. I wanted students to see globalization as, well, global — that there were myriad and far-flung runners in the race to the bottom.

This auction among poor countries to attract Capital was the essential context my students needed in order to recognize patterns in such seemingly diverse phenomena as child labor and increased immigration to the world's so-called developed nations. However, I worried that the simulation might be too convincing, corporate power depicted as too overwhelming. The auction metaphor was accurate but inexorable: Students could conclude that if transnational Capital is as effective an "auctioneer" as I was in the simulation, the situation for poor countries must be hopeless. In the follow-up writing assignment, I asked what if anything people in these countries could do to stop the race to the bottom, the "downward leveling."

By and large, students' responses weren't as bleak as I feared. Kara wrote: "Maybe if all the countries come together and raise the standard of living or become 'Capital unfriendly,' then Capital would have no choice but to take what they receive. Although it wouldn't be easy, it would be dramatically better." Adrian suggested that "people could go on an area-wide strike against downward leveling and stand firm to let Capital know that they won't go for it." And Matt wrote simply, "Revolt, strike." Tessa proposed that people here could "boycott products made in countries or by companies that exploit workers."

But others were less hopeful. Lisa wrote: "I can't see where there is much the people in poor countries can do to stop this 'race to the bottom.' If the people refuse to work under those conditions the companies will go elsewhere. The people have so little and could starve if they didn't accept the conditions they have to work under." Sara wrote, "I don't think a country can get themselves out of this because companies aren't generous enough to help them because they wouldn't get anything out of it."

What I should have done is obvious to me now. After discussing their thoughts on the auction, I should have regrouped students and started the auction all over again. Having considered various alternative responses to the downward spiral of economic and environmental conditions, students could have practiced organizing with each other instead of competing against each other, could have tested the potential for solidarity across borders. At the least, replaying the auction would have suggested that people in Third World countries aren't purely victims; there are possible routes for action, albeit enormously difficult ones.

T-shirts, Barbie Dolls, and Baseballs

We followed the auction with a "global clothes hunt." I asked students to: "Find at least ten items of clothing or toys at home. These can be anything: T-shirts, pants, skirts, dress shirts, shoes, Barbie dolls, baseballs, soccer balls, etc.," and to list each item and country of manufacture. In addition, I wanted them to attach geographic location to the place names, some of which many students had never heard of (for example, Sri Lanka, Macau, El Salvador, and Bangladesh). So in class they made collages of drawings or magazine clippings of the objects they'd found, and with the assistance of an atlas, drew lines on a world map connecting these images with the countries where the items were produced.

We posted their collage/maps around the classroom, and I asked students to wander around looking at these to search for patterns for which kinds of goods were produced in which kind of countries. Some students noticed that electronic toys tended to be produced in Taiwan and Korea; that more expensive shoes, like Doc Martens, were manufactured in Great Britain or Italy; athletic shoes were made mostly in Indonesia or China. On their "finding patterns" write-up, just about everyone commented that China was the country that appeared most frequently on people's lists. A few kids noted that most of the people in the manufacturing countries were not white.

As Sandee wrote, "The more expensive products seem to be manufactured in countries with a higher number of white people. Cheaper products are often from places with other races than white." People in countries with concentrations of people of color "tend to be poorer so they work for less." We'd spent the early part of the year studying European colonialism, and some students noticed that many of the manufacturing countries were former colonies. I wanted students to see that every time they put on clothes or kick a soccer ball they are making a connection, if hidden, with people around the world — especially in Third World countries — and that these connections are rooted in historic patterns of global inequality.

From here on, I saturated students with articles and videos that explored the working conditions and life choices confronting workers in poor

> I wanted students to see that every time they put on clothes or kick a soccer ball they are making a connection, if hidden, with people around the world.

countries. Some of the resources I found most helpful included: *Mickey Mouse Goes to Haiti*, a video critiquing the Walt Disney Co.'s exploitation of workers in Haiti's garment industry (workers there, mostly women, made 28 cents an hour; Disney claimed it couldn't afford the 58 cents an hour workers said they could live on); a CBS *48 Hours* exposé of conditions for women workers in Nike factories in Vietnam, reported by Roberta Baskin; several Bob Herbert "In America" *New York Times* columns; a Nov. 3, 1996, *Washington Post* article, "Boot Camp at the Shoe Factory: Where Taiwanese Bosses Drill Chinese Workers to Make Sneakers for American Joggers," by Anita Chan; *Tomorrow We Will Finish*, a UNICEF-produced video about the anguish and solidarity of girls forced into the rug-weaving industry in Nepal and India; and an invaluable collection of articles called a "Production Primer," collected by "Justice. Do it NIKE!," a coalition of Oregon labor, peace, and justice groups. (See Resources, p. 225, for an updated list of materials on teaching about globalization.)

I indicated above that the advantage of this curricular globe-trotting was that students could see that issues of transnational corporate investment, child labor, worker exploitation, poverty, etc. were not isolated in one particular geographic region. The disadvantage was that students didn't get much appreciation for the peculiar conditions in each country we touched on. And I'm afraid that after awhile, people in different societies began to appear as generic global victims. This was not entirely the fault of my decision to bounce from country to country, but was also a reflection of the narrow victim orientation of many of the materials available.

I was somewhat unaware of the limits of these resources until I previewed a 25-minute video produced by Global Exchange, *Indonesia: Islands on Fire*. One segment features Sadisah, an Indonesian ex-Nike worker, who with dignity and defiance describes conditions for workers there and what she wants done about them. I found her presence, however brief, a stark contrast to most of the videos I'd shown in class that feature white commentators with Third World workers presented as objects of sympathy. Although students generated excellent writing during the unit, much of it tended to miss the humor and determination suggested in the *Islands on Fire* segment and concentrated on workers' victimization.

Critique Without Caricature

Two concerns flirted uncomfortably throughout the unit. On the one hand, I had no desire to feign neutrality — to hide my conviction that people here need to care about, and to act in solidarity with, workers around the world in their struggles for better lives. To pretend that I was a mere dispenser of information would be dishonest, but worse, it would imply that being a spectator is an ethical response to injustice. It would model a stance of moral apathy. I wanted students to know these issues were important to me, that I cared enough to do something about them.

On the other hand, I never want my social concerns to suffocate student inquiry or to prevent students from thoughtfully considering opposing views. I wanted to present the positions of transnational corporations critically, but without caricature.

Here, too, it might have been useful to focus on one country in order for students to evaluate corporate claims — e.g., "Nike's production can help build thriving economies in developing nations." I'd considered writing a role play about foreign investment in Indonesia with roles for Nike management as well as Korean and Taiwanese subcontractors. (Nike itself owns none of its own production facilities in poor countries.) This would have provoked a classroom debate on corporate statements, where students could have assessed how terms like "thriving economies" may have different meanings for different social groups.

Instead, I tried in vain to get a spokesperson from Nike, in nearby Beaverton, to address the class; I hoped that at least the company might send me a video allowing students to glean the corporate perspective. No luck. They sent me a PR packet of Phil Knight speeches, and their "Code of Conduct," but stopped returning my phone calls requesting a speaker. I copied the Nike materials for students, and they read with special care the Nike Code of Conduct and did a "loophole search" — discovering, among other things, that Nike promises to abide by local minimum wage laws, but never promises to pay a living wage; they promise to obey "local environmental regulations" without acknowledging how inadequate these often are. Having raced themselves to the bottom in the transnational capital auction, students were especially alert to the frequent appearance of the term "local government regulations" in the Nike materials. Each mention might as well have carried a sticker reading "WEASEL WORDS."

I reminded students of our soccer ball exercise, how we'd missed the humanity in the object until we read Bertolt Brecht's poem. I asked them to write a "work poem" that captured some aspect of the human lives connected to the products we use everyday. They could draw on any situation, product, individual, or relationship we'd encountered in the unit. As prompts, I gave them other work poems that my students had produced over the years. Students brainstormed ways they might complete the assignment: from the point of view of one of the objects produced, or that of one of the workers; a dialogue poem from the point of view of worker and owner, or worker and consumer (see "Two Women" in volume 1 of *Rethinking Our Classrooms*, p. 112); a letter to one of the products, or to one of the owners (like Oregon-based Phil Knight, CEO of Nike).

Cameron Robinson's poem, below, expressed the essence of what I was driving at with the assignment:

Masks

Michael Jordan soars
through the air,
on shoes of unpaid labor.

A boy kicks a soccer ball,
the bloody hands are forgotten.

An excited girl combs
the hair of her Barbie,
an overworked girl makes it.

A child receives a teddy bear,
"Made in China" has no meaning.

The words "hand made"
are printed,
whose hands were used
to make them?

A six year old in America starts
his first day of school,
A six year old in Pakistan starts
his first day of work.

They want us to see the ball,
not to see the millions
of ball stitchers.

The world is full of many masks,
the hard part
is seeing beneath them.

As we read our pieces aloud (I wrote one too), I asked students to record lines or images that they found particularly striking and to note themes that recurred. They also gave positive feedback to one another after each person read. Sandee wrote: "I liked the line in Maisha's paper that said, 'My life left me the day I stitched the first stitch....' I like Antoinette's paper because of the voice. It showed more than just pain, it also reflected a dream" — an ironic dream of a sweatshop worker who wants to flee her country for the "freedom" of the United States.

Dirk had written a harshly worded piece from the point of view of a worker for a transnational company; it drew comments from just about everyone. Elizabeth appreciated it because "he used real language to express the feelings of the workers. As he put it, I doubt that the only thing going through their minds is 'I hate this job.'"

As a whole the writings were a lot angrier than they were hopeful; if I'd missed it in their pieces, this came across loud and clear in students' "common themes" remarks. As Jessica

Mauritanian girls weaving a straw rug.

UNITED NATIONS PHOTO 148.040/JEAN PIERRE LAFFONT

wrote: "One of the things I noticed was that none of the [papers] had a solution to the situation they were writing about." Maisha agreed: "Each paper only showed animosity...."

I expected the unit to generate anger, but I hoped to push beyond it. From the very beginning, I told students that it was not my intention merely to expose the world's abuse and exploitation. A broader aim was to make a positive difference. For their final project, I wanted students to do something with their knowledge — I wanted to give them the opportunity to act on behalf of the invisible others whose lives are intertwined in so many ways with their own. I wasn't trying to push a particular organization, or even a particular form of "action." I wanted them simply to feel some social efficacy, to sense that no matter how overwhelming a global injustice, there's always something to be done.

The assignment sheet (see "Child Labor/Global Sweatshop: Making a Difference Project") required students to take their learning "outside the walls of the classroom and into the real world." They could write letters to Phil Knight, Michael Jordan, or then-President Clinton. They could write news articles or design presentations to other classes. I didn't want them to urge a particular posi-

tion if they didn't feel comfortable with that kind of advocacy; so in a letter they might simply ask questions of an individual.

They responded with an explosion of creativity: Three groups of students designed presentations for elementary school kids or for other classes at the school; one student wrote an article on child labor to submit to the *Franklin Post,* the school newspaper; four students wrote Phil Knight, two wrote Michael Jordan, and one each wrote the Disney Co., President Clinton, and local activist Max White.

Jonathan Parker borrowed an idea from an editorial cartoon included in the "Justice. Do It NIKE!" reader. He found an old Nike shoe and painstakingly constructed a wooden house snuggled inside, complete with painted shingles and stairway. He accompanied it with a poem that reads in part:

There is a young girl
who lives in a shoe.
Phil Knight makes six million
she makes just two.

When Nike says "just do it"
she springs to her feet,
stringing her needle
and stitching their sneaks.
With Nike on the tongue,

The swoosh on the side,
the sole to the bottom,
she's done for the night....

When will it stop?
When will it end?
Must I, she says,
toil for Nike again?

The "sculpture" and poem have been displayed in my classroom, and have sparked curiosity and discussion in other classes, but Jonathan hopes also to have it featured in the display case outside the school library.

Cameron, a multi-sport athlete, was inspired by a *Los Angeles Times* article by Lucille Renwick, "Teens' Efforts Give Soccer Balls the Boot," about Monroe High School students in L.A. who became incensed that all of their school's soccer balls came from Pakistan, a child labor haven. The Monroe kids got the L.A. school board there to agree to a policy to purchase soccer balls only from countries that enforce a prohibition on child labor.

Cameron decided to do a little detective work of his own, and discovered that at the five Portland schools he checked, 60% of the soccer balls were made in Pakistan. He wrote a letter to the school district's athletic director alerting him to his findings, describing conditions under which the balls are made, and asking him what he intended to do about it. Cameron enclosed copies of Sydney Schanberg's "Six Cents an Hour" article, as well as the one describing the students' organizing in Los Angeles — hinting further action if school officials didn't rethink their purchasing policies.

One student, Daneeka, bristled at the assignment, and felt that regardless of what the project sheet said, I was actually forcing them to take a position. She boycotted the assignment and enlisted her mother to come in during parent conferences to support her complaint. Her mother talked with me, read the assignment sheet, and — to her daughter's chagrin — told her to do the project. Daneeka and I held further negotiations and agreed that she could take her learning "outside the walls of the classroom" by "visiting" online chat rooms where she could discuss global sweatshop issues, and describe these conversations in a paper. But after letting the assignment steep a bit longer, she found a more personal connection to the issues. Daneeka decided to write Nike about their use of child labor in Pakistan as described in the Schanberg article. "When I was first confronted with this assignment," she wrote in her letter, "it really didn't disturb me. But as I have thought about it for several weeks, child labor is a form of slavery. As a young Black person, slavery is a disturbing issue, and to know that Nike could participate in slavery is even more disturbing." Later in her letter, Daneeka acknowledges that she is a "kid" and wants to stay in fashion. "Even I will continue to wear your shoes, but will you gain a conscience?"

"Just Go With the Flow"

At the end of the global sweatshop unit, I added a brief curricular parenthesis on the role of advertising in U.S. society. Throughout the unit, I returned again and again to Cameron Robinson's "masks" metaphor:

The world is full of many masks,
the hard part
is seeing beneath them.

I'd received a wonderful video earlier in the year, *The Ad and the Ego*, that, among other things, examines the "masking" role of advertising — how ads hide the reality of where a product comes from and the environmental consequences of mass consumption. The video's narrative is dense, but because of its subject matter, humor, and MTV-like format, students were able to follow its argument as long as I frequently stopped the VCR. At the end of part one, I asked students to comment on

Child Labor/Global Sweatshop: Making a Difference Project

This is the handout given to students for the global sweatshop final project.

The project you choose is up to you. The major requirement is that you take your learning — about Nike; the "global sweatshop;" child labor; conditions for workers in Indonesia, China, Vietnam, Haiti, etc. — outside the walls of the classroom and into the real world. Some examples:

• Write a detailed letter of opinion or inquiry to someone connected with these issues — for example, Phil Knight, Michael Jordan, the president of the United States, U.S. labor unions, the Disney Co., the governments of China, Vietnam, or Indonesia, etc. In this letter, you can either make a strong point and back it up with evidence from class and your own research, or you can raise important questions. However, if you choose to raise questions, you still need to indicate lots of information that you know about the issue.

• Write an article for the *Franklin Post*, [the school newspaper], *The Oregonian*, or some other journal or newsletter.
• Prepare testimony for the Portland School Board, or some other agency or office.
• Design a presentation for classes at Franklin or one of our feeder schools (Kellogg, Mt. Tabor, et al.) to teach others about these issues.
• Become involved with a group that is trying to make a difference around these issues. Write up your reasons for choosing this group and what you hope to accomplish.
• Produce a rap, audio tape, video, or visual display on these issues. (You would also need to accompany this with an essay explaining and defending your point of view.) Write a skit to perform or a story to share.
• An original idea that my teacher-brain was too dull to come up with.

Other Considerations:

• You may work in a group if required by the nature of your project — for example, presenting to other classes or giving testimony before the school board. But I will need to see evidence that each member of the group has participated.
• You must use at least five different sources in your project. At least two of these must be sources you found on your own.
• The final draft of your project must demonstrate clear ideas and support, and it needs to be "correct." No spelling, grammatical, or other errors on the final draft. (People outside of schools are always looking for ways to make students look ignorant; let's not give them any ammunition.)
• Remember to go deep with this. Point out specific conditions that need changing, but also remember to talk about the deeper causes of these problems. ■

any of the quotes from the video and to write other thoughts they felt were relevant. One young woman I'll call Marie wrote in part: "I am actually tired of analyzing everything that goes on around me. I am tired of looking at things at a deeper level. I want to just go with the flow and relax."

I'd like to think that Marie's frustration grew from intellectual exhaustion, from my continually exhorting students to "think deep," to look beneath the surface — in other words, from my academic rigor. But from speaking with her outside of class, my sense is that the truer cause of her weariness came from constantly seeing people around the world as victims, from Haiti to Pakistan to Nepal to China. By and large, the materials I was able to locate (and chose to use) too frequently presented people as stick figures, mere symbols of a relationship of domination and subordination between rich and poor countries. I couldn't locate resources — letters, diary entries, short stories, etc. — that presented people's work lives in the context of their families and societies. And I wasn't able to show adequately how people in those societies struggle in

big and little ways for better lives. The overall impression my students may have been left with was that the unit was an invitation to pity and help unfortunate others, rather than as an invitation to join with diverse groups and individuals in a global movement for social justice — a movement already underway.

Another wish-I'd-done-better, that may also be linked to Marie's comment, is the tendency for a unit like this to drift toward good guys and bad guys. In my view, Nike is a "bad guy," insofar as it reaps enormous profits as it pays workers wages that it knows full-well cannot provide a decent standard of living. They're shameless and they're arrogant. As one top Nike executive in Vietnam told Portland's *Business Journal*: "Sure we're chasing cheap labor, but that's business and that's the way it's going to be" — a comment that lends ominous meaning to the Nike slogan, "There is no finish line." My students' writing often angrily targeted billionaire Nike CEO Phil Knight and paired corporate luxury with Third World poverty. But corporations are players in an economic "game" with rules to maximize profits, and rewards and punishments for

how well those rules are obeyed. I hoped that students would come to see the "bad guys" less as the individual players in the game than as the structure, profit imperatives, and ideological justifications of the game itself. Opening with the Transnational Capital Auction was a good start, but the unit didn't consistently build on this essential systemic framework.

Finally, there is a current of self-righteousness in U.S. social discourse that insists that "we" have it good and "they" have it bad. A unit like this can settle too comfortably into that wrongheaded dichotomy and even reinforce it. Teaching about injustice and poverty "over there" in Third World countries may implicitly establish U.S. society as the standard of justice and affluence. There is poverty and exploitation of workers here, too. And both "we" and "they" are stratified based especially on race, class, and gender. "We" here benefit very unequally from today's frantic pace of globalization. As well, there are elites in the Third World with lots more wealth and power than most people in this society. Over the year, my global studies curriculum attempted to confront these complexities of inequality. But it's a crucial postscript that I want to emphasize as I edit my "race to the bottom" curriculum for future classes.

Enough doubt and self criticism. By and large, students worked hard, wrote with insight and empathy, and took action for justice — however small. They were poets, artists, essayists, political analysts, and teachers. And next time around, we'll all do better. ■

Bill Bigelow (bbpdx@aol.com) teaches at Franklin High School in Portland, Oregon and is a Rethinking Schools editor. Some of the students' names in this article have been changed.

The Stitching Shed

By Tho Dong

Day by day
Sit in the stitching shed.
Stitch by stitch.
Hope I could do faster,
Do faster to earn money,
Do faster so my brother
won't cry because of hunger,
Do faster so my family can
survive.

Stitch by stitch.
One by one.
I want to cry out,
But can't do that.
Family still there.
I want to give up.
But can't do that.
My family needs food!!
Can't do it faster.
My hands hurt.
I hear the voices through the winds.
They tell me to let go of the pain.
Oh, god! I am too young to give up.
The hope eases my pain.
Hope tomorrow will be better.

(Tho Dong was an eleventh-grade student at Franklin High
School in Portland, Oregon when she wrote this poem.)

Bias and CD-ROM Encyclopedias

Integrating math and social studies to analyze bias

By Bob Peterson

When our elementary school library got its CD-ROMs, I hoped my fifth graders would use them for social studies research projects. Little did I know that they would become the basis of a broader project using math to explore racial and gender bias in educational materials.

As in many fifth grades, my students do a major research project on a famous American. Perhaps less typically, it has to be an American who has fought for justice, and "American" is defined to include people from Mexico and Puerto Rico (as many of my students are from those two places). This past year, I told my students that in addition to biographies and encyclopedias, they'd be able to use the library's CD-ROM encyclopedia. They were excited. I was skeptical. I feared that the new technology would add just one more source of information to be copied and plagiarized by uncritical and inexperienced researchers.

During writing workshop, the students went in pairs to the library to look up information on their famous person, and to get a printout of the CD-ROM entry to be used as one of the sources for their report.

When the first two girls, Jade and Lafayette, returned from the library, they raised an issue that I hadn't thought about. Jade, who had chosen to write about Harriet Tubman, was upset that Lafayette's printout on Thomas Edison was 4 or 5 times longer than hers. (My immediate reaction was to question how Lafayette had concluded that Thomas Edison fit the criterion of a famous

person who fought for justice, but she was determined to report on him so I let that matter drop.) When I asked Jade why she thought there was this difference her response was, "I don't know."

> **The students saw that the "white males got the most information" and "Puerto Rican females got nothing."**

I asked Jade and Lafayette to quantify the difference somehow and to tell the rest of the class about their research during sharing time at the end of writing workshop. They reported that while there was less than 2 inches of information on Harriet Tubman, there was more than 10 inches on Thomas Edison. Some students thought this wasn't fair, but there were no profound insights as to the cause of the inequity. When I asked the class how we might find out why there was this disparity, a popular response was to ask the librarian. So we postponed further discussion until our next library visit a few days later.

During the next library visit, the

librarian, Maggie Melvin, and I led a discussion that tried to get students to think more deeply about the nature of the information in the CD-ROM encyclopedia and other educational materials. We used Jade's concern as a jumping off point. We taped to the wall the printouts on Harriet Tubman and Thomas Edison and asked the kids what they noticed and what they knew about the two individuals. The students agreed that both Edison and Tubman were dead and famous; that Edison was a white man who invented things, while Tubman was an African-American woman abolitionist who fought for freedom.

Children came up with a variety of hypotheses to explain the length difference. Some thought that the CD-ROM makers "didn't know much about Harriet Tubman;" "didn't get much information about Harriet Tubman when they were little;" "had to meet a deadline and didn't have time to put Harriet Tubman in;" or that "maybe they were racist, so first they put in white inventors and then they added a little extra." Another student disagreed that the disparity was due to racism and suggested that it was because "Thomas Edison was a man and Harriet Tubman was a woman and maybe it was men who did the CD-ROM."

When one student suggested that perhaps inventors were more important than other people, a Puerto Rican girl disagreed. She argued that abolishing slavery "was more important than the light bulb." Another boy said that the disparity wasn't fair because "Harriet Tubman had to risk her life and did work that was more dangerous" than Edison's.

We then began a conversation about what criteria one should use to put people into the encyclopedia and how much should be written about them. Some kids thought "everybody should get treated the same" while others argued that those who helped people should get more space.

To broaden the discussion we taped on the wall two additional print-outs — bibliographies of books in our library on Thomas Edison and Harriet Tubman. Our school library had three or four times more books on Tubman than Edison. One student concluded from this that "the CD-ROM people are just making up for the difference in the amount of books we have at our school." This in turn led to a lengthy conversation about who makes decisions about educational resources. At our school, I told the kids, teachers have tried to make up for the lack of information about women and people of color in the mainstream libraries and encyclope-dias by buying more books about those people. In fact, the availability of such biographies in the the school library was the way many of the kids came to choose their famous person in the first place.

We ended our conversation by asking students how we might find out if the accusations of racism or sexism were accurate. One student thought we should write to the CD-ROM makers and ask them, but most thought the company wouldn't be honest. Finally, it was agreed that two examples weren't enough, and that as a class we would chart the length of the printouts on all the famous people that we were studying, as well as the person's race and gender.

Over the next two weeks students recorded the length of entries for 30 different individuals on large chart paper on the classroom wall. Students were surprised to find that Felisa Rincón de Gautir, the first woman mayor of San Juan and a famous Puerto Rican leader, was not listed, nor were the 19th century African-American journalist Ida B. Wells, Mexican-American farm-worker organizer Dolores Huerta, the first female chief of the Cherokee Nation Wilma P. Mankiller, or Puerto Rican scientist Maria Cordero Hardy. Two presidents, Abraham Lincoln and George Washington, had the longest entries, and others varied from 2 to 13 inches. (A complete list of people studied is at the end of the article.)

Analyzing the Data

I realized that a key tool in analyzing the data would be the concept of averages. So I worked with my student teacher Susan Hersh and math teacher Celín Perez to develop a mini-unit on averages. We built on the students' existing knowledge of averages — mainly involving sports and grades — and deepened their understanding by having them use counters and other physical objects. We also discussed and practiced

Bob Peterson working with fifth-grade students at La Escuela Fratney in Milwaukee, Wisconsin.

SUSANN LINA RUGGLES

using the formula for figuring out an average.

The students were ready to analyze the data. We prepared a sheet that helped students organize their work, then pairs of students chose different categories of people (white females, Mexican females, etc.) and found the average length of the entries in inches. They each calculated a number of groups and recorded their answers on chart paper in the front of the room. When pairs came up with different averages, they rechecked their work until they agreed.

After all the conceivable categories were calculated, we gathered as a group. I asked for observations. The students saw that the "white males got the most information" and "Puerto Rican females got nothing." Other observations included more specific comparisons: for example, that the information for males was "three times as long as information for females" and that "information for whites was three times as long as information for nonwhites."

We asked the children how they felt about what they had discovered. Some of the comments: "I feel very bad because the Puerto Ricans don't have much information;" "I hate it because it's not fair;" "Other kids might think that women don't do very many important things."

Other students weren't as upset and said: "We should not blame them [CD-ROM makers] for what they did. If we don't like it, just don't buy it and get a book." Others countered that the disparities were important because younger students would use the CD-ROM and not get sufficient information.

I asked how the students might present the information to other children in the school. They decided to make large wall graphs using sticky tape, which the children did in groups of four. The construction of the large graphs was difficult, as the average lengths ranged from 0 inches for Puerto Rican females to 28 inches for white males. The vibrant colors of

the sticky tape made the finished products show quite clearly the bias that we had discovered in the CD-ROM.

Some students wanted to do more than just show other kids the results of their research. A couple suggested we visit the CD-ROM makers and tell them to change their encyclopedia. When the kids found that the company was based in California, that put a damper on that idea. Instead students role-played what they would have said and wrote letters to the company. The students wrote from the heart: "My name is Alfonso and you made me and kids in my classroom mad. You discriminat-

> **Students need to find multiple sources of information, and read everything with a healthy dose of skepticism.**

ed against people that are ladies and nonwhites;" "I am a Puerto Rican student at Fratney Street School and I did not like what you gave Puerto Rican people on the CD-ROM encyclopedia." Some wrote in Spanish: *No es justo que haiga mas información sobre hombres que mujeres.* [It is not just that you had more on men than on women]; "Women and men of all cultures should be treated fairly!" wrote another. One student threatened, "You better do something about it before I take you to court."

One student who didn't think writing to the company would do much good wrote to the superintendent of the school district instead, informing him of our investigation. He wrote:

"The purpose of this letter is to try to get the people who buy or make this program to either stop making it or to change the information. This might not matter to me cause I'm going to sixth grade next year and my new school doesn't have a CD-ROM system in their computers. But this matters to the kids who are going to get the information from this encyclopedia in the future." He went on to suggest that "the school system not buy any more CD-ROM encyclopedias from this company."

Problems and Lessons

The whole project took several weeks and involved a great deal of discussion. It was not part of my pre-planned curriculum. The fact that the project was initiated by students' concerns about the learning materials in the school was positive and provided important motivation. It fit well into our school district's K-12 Learning Goal #1, that "students will project anti-racist, anti-biased attitudes" and "analyze, critique, and assess bias in all forms of communication." It also gave the students a chance to act on their concerns.

In retrospect the project had some serious shortcomings. First, while we were looking at one aspect of bias in the CD-ROM encyclopedia, we barely approached the larger, more important issue: the content of the information itself. While I encouraged children to look out for stereotypes or misinformation in the text, with a limited knowledge base this type of critique is difficult at the elementary school level. Students found some incongruities with other sources of information — for example, with the dates given for the births of Nat Turner and Harriet Tubman. But it was usually only when I pointed out that the encyclopedia selection omitted something that the students became aware of potential content problems.

Earlier in the year we had spent time analyzing children's books that dealt with Christopher Columbus —

whose voice was being heard and whose was being silenced, what was being omitted in books, etc. While that experience might have helped spur Jade and Lafayette into questioning the new learning materials they encountered, it did little to prepare kids to critique encyclopedia sections, or even come up with ways of thinking about the issue beyond the question of omission and voice.

Another problem was that our statistical approach was far from accurate. Our sampling was limited, and the inclusion of the two presidents weighted the statistics in favor of white men. Nonetheless, the students gained experience in collecting data, manipulating it, and looking at it through the lens of race and gender, something that isn't readily encouraged in most texts and curricula. Similar projects could be done by looking at traditional encyclopedias, or by analyzing the racial and gender composition of the biographical books in a school library.

Finally, the project raised several questions that we didn't fully answer: Who makes the decisions for CD-ROM encyclopedias? What criteria are used for the inclusion or exclusion of people? What criteria *should* be used?

Because this project was started near the end of the school year, such questions were raised, but left unanswered. With more time I could have had students develop their own criteria for inclusion in encyclopedias. Then they might have tried to use such criteria to rank the famous people they had studied. We might have organized a debate or role play, with students representing different groups of people arguing for their inclusion.

But even with these shortcomings, lessons were learned. One was that even something as sophisticated and flashy as a CD-ROM encyclopedia cannot always be trusted as an "objective" source of information. Students need to find multiple sources of information, and read everything with a healthy dose of skepticism.

A second important lesson was that mathematics can be an effective tool, like written and oral language, in the fight against injustice and discrimination. Knowing how to figure out things like averages and percentages, being able to use mathematical data in arguments, and making clear graphs became more than just preparation for next year's math class, but a means by which one can help figure out and change the world. ∎

Bob Peterson (repmilw@aol.com) teaches fifth grade at La Escuela Fratney in Milwaukee, Wisconsin and is a Rethinking Schools editor. He would like to thank the colleagues who helped him with this project: Maggie Melvin, Celín Perez, and Susan Hersh.

Author's Note:

The famous people chosen for study by the students included: Harriet Tubman, Thomas Edison, Felisa Rincón de Gautir, Abraham Lincoln, Langston Hughes, César Chávez, George Washington, Jackie Robinson, Roberto Clemente, Nat Turner, Helen Keller, Wilma Mankiller, Ida B. Wells, Emiliano Zapata, the Wright Brothers, Martin Luther King, Jr., Malcolm X, Sitting Bull, General Custer, Frederick Douglass, Juana Ines de la Cruz, Susan B. Anthony, Amelia Earhart, John Brown, Mariá Cordero Hardy, Dolores Huerta, Benito Juarez, Marie Curie, Sojourner Truth, Diego Rivera, and Miguel Hidalgo.

The CD-ROM encyclopedia analyzed by my class is the Multimedia Encyclopedia, published by Software Toolworks, of Novato, California. Since my students looked at this encyclopedia, I have looked at the even-flashier Grolier's *Multimedia Encyclopedia* and Microsoft's *Encarta*. While I have not had time to review these encyclopedias, I did repeat the original activity that led to the classroom project described above. In both cases Edison has about five times more text than Tubman, and neither encyclopedia had articles on Ida B. Wells, Felisa Rincón de Gautir, Dolores Huerta, or María Cordero Hardy.

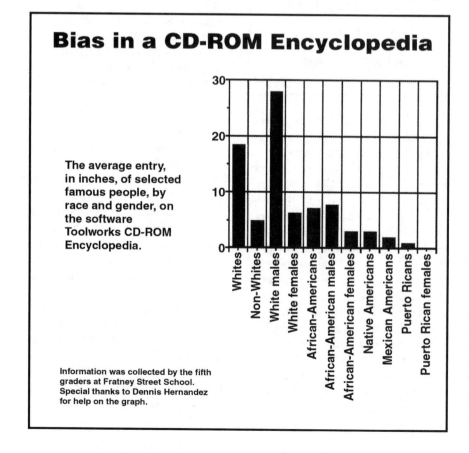

Bias in a CD-ROM Encyclopedia

The average entry, in inches, of selected famous people, by race and gender, on the software Toolworks CD-ROM Encyclopedia.

Categories (x-axis): Whites, Non-Whites, White males, White females, African-Americans, African-American males, African-American females, Native Americans, Mexican Americans, Puerto Ricans, Puerto Rican females

Information was collected by the fifth graders at Fratney Street School. Special thanks to Dennis Hernandez for help on the graph.

Where's the R-Word?

Speaking out on textbook silences

By Bob Peterson

President Clinton called for national conversation about it. Students talk about it. Even the media have become more willing to explore it. But school textbooks ignore it.

The "it," of course, is race.

I was recently a member of a district committee adopting social studies textbooks for kindergarten through fifth grade. I found only one oblique reference to race or racism in the four U.S. history textbooks under consideration for fifth grade. Each book is more than 650 pages long and professes to cover U.S. history from the arrival of Native peoples through the 1990s.

Fifth grade is when students get their first sustained instruction in U.S. history. Every major textbook company and most of the nation's school districts focus fifth-grade social studies on U.S. history, usually followed by another year of U.S. history in eighth and then tenth grade.

The four major textbook companies — Houghton Mifflin, Silver Burdett Ginn, Harcourt Brace, and Macmillan — offer brightly colored texts, with accompanying guides, supplements, and technological bells and whistles such as CD-ROMs, cassette tapes, and websites. Over the years, the companies have made some progress in including people of different races in their books' photos and text. They also proudly advertise

the names of well-known multicultural educators as their advisors.

Nonetheless, the r-word is noticeably absent — except perhaps to those writing the texts. When I mentioned to one textbook company representative that there was no reference to race or racism in their U.S. history textbook, he responded: "Darn, that's interesting. I hadn't noticed that before."

Another textbook representative was more to the point. She responded that the word "racism" had a "negative connotation" and so it really wasn't appropriate to put in a U.S. history textbook. Hmm, I thought. "War" has a negative connotation too. Perhaps we shouldn't mention

JEAN-CLAUDE LEJEUNE

the Revolutionary War or the Civil War in our history textbooks. Or "death" — what could be more negative? Perhaps we should pretend that George Washington is still alive?

A representative from a third company was the most up-front. She explained that their company had tried to align their texts with the emerging state standards and that "racism" was not in those standards. Unfortunately, this explanation was all too real. I had recently testified on the proposed Wisconsin state standards and had raised the concern that in the history standards for elementary and secondary students, the word "racism" didn't appear even once.

Regardless of one's political orientation, such an omission is absurd. Do people think one can even minimally understand U.S. history without mentioning racism? Was the dispossession of Native Americans from their lands devoid of racial overtones? Did slavery and lynchings have nothing to do with race? What of the anti-Chinese riots at the turn of the century in which hundreds were killed?

Repercussions

The issue involves more than acknowledging the stain of racism on our country's past. By omitting the "r" word, texts help to obscure racism's relationship to economic exploitation — whether in the case of slavery, the theft of Indian and Mexican land, the underpayment and mistreatment of Chinese railroad workers in the mid-19th century, or the use of Third World sweatshop workers today. Furthermore, if textbooks and educators can't even discuss past racism, it makes it incredibly difficult to examine current problems of racism.

Finally, when texts don't talk about racism, they automatically eliminate any discussion of anti-racism. As a result, kids rarely learn of moments in U.S. history when people worked across racial lines for equality — as in the Black/Indian unity in the Seminole Wars and Black/white collaboration in the abolitionist and Civil Rights movements.

Whites have a particular responsibility to combat racism, and yet few kids know of whites in U.S. history who have dedicated their lives to such a struggle: abolitionists such as John Brown, William Lloyd Garrison, Wendell Phillips, Prudence Crandall, Theodore Weld, Lydia Maria Child, Lucretia Mott, and Elijah Lovejoy, or Civil Rights leaders such as Anne Braden, Father James Groppi, and Myles Horton.

As we enter a new century, it's worth recalling the words of historian W. E. B. Du Bois nearly 100 years ago: "The problem of the 20th century is the problem of the color line." If educators continue to ignore the issue of race, Du Bois' prophetic words will ring as true for the 21st century as they have for the past. ∎

Bob Peterson (repmilw@aol.com) teaches fifth grade at La Escuela Fratney in Milwaukee, Wisconsin and is a Rethinking Schools editor.

Girls, Worms, and Body Image

A teacher deals with gender stereotypes among second- and third-graders

by Kate Lyman

"I need to lose weight," Kayla was saying. Another second-grade girl chimed in, "So do I. I'm way too fat."

My students' conversation shocked me. Distracted from my hallway responsibility of monitoring the noise level at the water fountains, I listened in more closely. Linda, a third-grade girl who is thin to the point of looking unhealthy, grabbed a piece of paper from Kayla. "I'm the one who needs this." "No, I need it!" insisted Rhonda.

The hotly contested paper turned out to contain the name of an exercise video that my second- and third-grade class had seen in gym class. The gym teacher later assured me that the student teacher had stressed that the exercises were for health and fitness, not weight loss. However, the girls were convinced that the video would help them lose weight and were frantic to get ahold of it.

Issues of women and body image are certainly not new to me. I thought back to when I was a teenager struggling to make my body match the proportions of the models in *Seventeen* magazine. I had learned that the average model was 5'9" and 110 pounds. I was the ideal 5'9", but even on a close-to-starvation diet of 900 calories a day I could not get my weight down to 110 pounds.

But that was in the 1960s. Hadn't girls liberated themselves from such regimens? I asked myself. And even back in the 1960s, it wasn't until high school that I remembered my classmates living on coffee and oranges. Seven-and eight-year-olds ate all the

> I asked them why the toy manufacturers might make a doll for girls to play with that looked so different from real girls and women. The consensus was that girls want to look like her so that men would like them better.

cake and candy and potato chips that they could get their hands on.

I wondered how I could enlighten my seven- and eight-year-old girls who were so concerned about their body image. What follows are ways, sometimes successful, sometimes not, in which I struggled with the issue throughout a recent year of teaching.

At the time of the incident with the gym video, I had been teaching a unit on women's history, and the class had shown an interest in learning about women's struggle to get the vote. I realized the unit needed to take a new turn. It was time to move on to the gender issues they face as girls and women today.

Facts and Stereotypes

I decided to start by learning more about the students' knowledge and perceptions about gender. I divided the students into two groups and asked the girls to decide on 10 facts about boys/men, and asked the boys to do the same in regard to girls/women. Before the activity, I tried to clarify the difference between opinions and facts, but the lists of "facts" revealed the futility of my attempts:

Facts about Boys/Men
(written by the girls)

1. Boys are selfish.
2. Boys are different than girls because of their body parts.
3. Men make their wives take care of the children and house.
4. Dads make the moms do the shopping.
5. Men get paid more than women.
6. Men get women just for their looks.
7. Men are mean and lazy and jealous.
8. Men are picky eaters and like their dinners when they get home.
9. Men and boys are bossy.

Facts about Girls/Women
(written by the boys)

1. They always complain.
2. They are too loud and picky.
3. They are sensitive.
4. Girls and women are better bakers than boys and men.
5. They are bossy.
6. Girls are always talking about boys and men.
7. Girls and women aren't as smart as boys and men.
8. Girls are more jealous than boys.
9. Girls and women spend a long time getting ready and want to look pretty.

We discussed the "facts" as a group and tried to come to an agreement about which statements were indeed facts and which were stereotypes, generalizations, or opinions. The girls protested vehemently the idea that boys and men were smarter than girls and women. They insisted, in fact, that the opposite was true.

Many students were reluctant to concede the veracity of some of the other statements. One student, Yer, for instance, argued: "I know for a fact that women are better bakers than men!" Anna countered that not only was her dad a good cook, but he also helped with the shopping and didn't insist on his dinner on time.

The other students saw Anna's dad as a single exception to the rule, but were willing to add the qualifier "most" to the statements about men and household tasks.

It occurred to me that a short story, "X," would be a good vehicle for further discussions on gender stereotypes. In "X," written by Lois Gould (1982), a couple agrees to let their baby be part of a scientific experiment in which no one is allowed to know the baby's gender except the parents and the baby him/herself.

At first, students responded to the dilemmas posed by X's situation with their own gender blinders. In the story, X's relatives cannot figure out what kind of presents to buy X — "a tiny football helmet" or "a pink-flow-

MARILYN NOLT

ered romper suit." The students in my class were equally confounded.

"Maybe they could buy an outfit that was split down the middle, half blue and half pink," said one student. Another suggested that X "could wear a baseball top and pink lacy bottoms."

I asked them to look around the room at each other's clothes. To a child, they were wearing unisex outfits — mainly jeans and T-shirts. But it still didn't occur to them that there might be baby clothes that would be suitable for either a boy or girl.

After my frustrating attempts to define fact vs. stereotypes about gender and my less than successful attempts at discussion around the story "X," I again thought back to my childhood. A photo taken of me at about my students' ages shows me in a lacy dress, cuffed white socks, and patent leather "Mary Jane" shoes, my hair tightly braided and tied in ribbons. I am sitting on a bench in my yard, surrounded by my dolls. My head is turned to the side and I am smiling shyly. What would I have said about men's and women's roles? Would the story of X have made any sense to me? I'm not sure how that '50s girl would have fit into the gender discussion, but I do remember that under the neat, frilly dress was a girl whose heroes were TV cowboys, a girl who daydreamed about being a boy so she, too, could have adventures on horseback.

I was trapped in the much more

rigid gender expectations of the 1950s, and yet I wondered if my girls in their jeans and sweats really had that many more options than I'd had. The girls in my class were right. Most women do have the major responsibility for taking care of the children and house. Most men do still get higher pay in their jobs. And the stereotypes still abound.

I was stuck in this examination of gender roles. Stuck in the classroom and stuck with my own personal history. I did not know where I was going with the unit.

A Saving Rain

But then, just as lesson plans were failing me as often as not, nature cooperated with a heavy rain that forced hundreds of worms up from the soil onto the playground. At recess the boys picked the worms up and dangled them at the girls while the girls ran screaming. Kayla, Stephanie, and Melissa, who will take on any drama, were leading the group with their screaming. Linda, Mandy, and other more shy, usually passive girls were joining in, follow-

ing their lead.

Kayla came running up to me, "Help, help, Tony's got a bunch of worms and he's chasing me with them. The worms are going to bite me!"

Reasoning was useless. Boys and girls were too engrossed in their drama. I picked up a worm and demonstrated that it did no harm, but my attempts to educate the girls failed. The chasing and screaming continued. I was successful at stopping Tony from coming into the school with worms in his shoes and pockets, but the screaming continued into the halls and music class.

I felt defeated. Times had not changed. This playground scene could have occurred in my elementary school in the 1950s. I decided that before I moved on to more subtle aspects of gender stereotyping, I needed to deal with girls and worms.

Then, after recess, Stephanie and Kayla took a brave step forward. They came back to the classroom with rubber gloves that they had gotten from the "lunch lady" so that they could touch the worms. I suggested to the class that we could collect

worms for our classroom, but that the rubber gloves were not necessary.

I put Kayla in charge of the terrarium and gave Stephanie the spoon. A group of 10 or 12 girls followed them outside to collect worms for the classroom. "Can't boys help get the worms? Only girls?" asked David dejectedly. I assured him that he could help, and several other boys joined the project, but the ringleaders were still the girls. They quickly got over their squeamishness.

"I'm not scared of worms anymore!" Anna proudly announced.

Soon we had about two dozen large, fat earthworms and several cups of dirt. The worm center was so noisily enthusiastic that I could barely hear the principal's announcement over the intercom. I think it had something to do with keeping the halls clean by not tracking the mud in from the playground.

The girls had conquered their fears of worms, but I still heard conversations — and, even worse, insults — about body image. One girl told another student that he should think about going to Jenny Craig.

Toys and Media

I decided to lead a critique on two sources of stereotypical images of women: toys and the media. I wanted to give the students an opportunity to analyze images of women that they see every day, to have some understanding how those images influence their self concepts.

I began with a lesson focused on a Barbie doll. Most girls in my class said that they owned Barbies, but none remembered to bring one in, so I borrowed one from another classroom. I started with an open-ended question: "Tell me what you notice about Barbie."

I was somewhat nervous because there was a university student visiting my classroom and I had little confidence in what my probing would bring about. Quickly, however, the observations poured out. Kayla, who is of stocky build herself, as is her mom, was quick to point out that Barbie has a very skinny waist.

"But she has big boobs," added Stephanie. I asked Stephanie if she knew a respectful way to refer to that part of a woman's body and she nodded. "Breasts," she corrected. "She has huge breasts."

"Barbie has tiny feet," someone said. "They are made for high heels."

"She has a cute, turned up nose."

"She has a very long, skinny neck."

"She has very skinny arms and legs."

Students agreed that Barbie looked very different from the women they knew — their moms, grandmas and teachers. The students didn't bring up Barbie's ethnicity, so I asked them to look around the circle and see how else she was different from many of them.

They looked around at each other, more than half with dark or various shades of brown faces, and only one blonde-haired child among them.

"She's white!" yelled out Shantee. "She has yellow hair and blue eyes."

"My mom will only let my sister play with Black Barbies," added Steven.

"Do the Black Barbies look like real-life African-American girls?" I asked.

"No, they have hair like white people," concluded Shantee. "Only it's colored black."

I asked them why the toy manufacturers might make a doll for girls to play with that looked so different from real girls and women. The consensus was that girls want to look like her so that men would like them better. The only dissenting voice was Kayla, who said that her mom's partner liked his women big.

Other comments were that women wanted to look beautiful, like Barbie, all skinny and pretty, with hair down to their waist. To further probe why that might be, I moved to the part of my lesson dealing with women in advertisements.

I hoped my students could grasp the concept that advertisers create an illusion that their product will transform a woman into a younger, prettier, more appealing self. I also wanted my students to practice looking at advertisements more critically — to analyze the hidden messages and to begin to see how women are objectified and minimized. I didn't expect them to understand all these concepts; I saw the lesson as an introduction.

I had torn out dozens of ads from women's magazines, general magazines such as *Ebony*, and other sources, showing women using products from cigarettes to weight-loss formulas to cosmetics. We discussed several ads as a group. I asked my students to look at how the woman was shown, what product the advertiser was trying to sell, and what the advertiser was telling women about what would happen if they bought the product. Then I sent them on their own to choose one of the ads and write about it. After they typed and edited their writing, they made the ads and script into posters that I hung in the hall.

Stephanie chose a cigarette ad with the message "A Taste for the Elegant" and the picture of a thin, sophisticated woman in a white pantsuit and high heels. Her commentary noted in part:

"'A taste for the elegant' is what it says on my poster, but it can't be a taste for the elegant because cigarettes don't taste good. Cigarettes are bad for your lungs."

Anna wrote that her ad for a perfume product was saying that "women have to be skinny and have a dress with no sleeves and if she uses this perfume then she gets a man."

Kayla wrote: "I think she's trying to get people to get the Oil of Olay to look young when they just look fine the way they are. I mean they don't have to listen to a woman that wants people to look young. That's stupid. The people look fine the way they are!!"

Rhonda interpreted the message in a shampoo ad as: "You should be cute and be skinny. The ad says that you should use Redken Shampoo, and wear a lot of makeup, and wear cute clothes so you can look like a Barbie doll."

Nathan saw some humor in his ad about a weight-loss product: "It is telling women that they have to be skinny, wear lipstick, and wear high heels. And from the picture of what she used to look like, I think she looks so different [now] that she should get a new [driver's] license."

Afterwards, I thought of many things I should have done differently with the lesson. More background on advertising. More time for discussion and sharing. Perhaps a follow-up action project. The visiting university student, however, was impressed that elementary students could handle such a complex topic so well.

Maybe I was on the right track.

An Old-Fashioned Day

But just to make sure, I wanted to provide an opportunity for the class to experience gender discrimination firsthand, in an exaggerated yet playful setting. For the last day of our unit, I decided to have a role play of an old-fashioned school day, with an emphasis on how girls and boys were treated differently.

I sent home interview sheets in which kids questioned their parents on what school was like when they

went to school, including how boys and girls were treated differently. The students shared their findings (one student noted, "My mom got hit with a PADDLE!"). My student teacher shared some old books and a slate that her grandfather had saved. Students read a book, *Early Schools*, and, using information from it, wrote first-person accounts about a day in an old-fashioned school.

Not concerned with strict historical accuracy (also knowing that schools varied regionally), we planned the morning based on the parent interviews, the book on early schools, and our own experiences. We sent home a note preparing the families for this experiment. Girls were to come dressed in dresses (not above the knees) and boys in slacks and shirts with collars. We pushed back the tables, moved the chairs into rows and set up an "old-fashioned" schedule of handwriting, spelling bees, rote math, and textbook science. We used a variety of discipline techniques: children got sent to the corner, they had to write 100 sentences, they had to wear the dunce cap — anything short of physical punishment.

We also incorporated differential treatment for boys and girls in everything we did, from having a boys' line and a girls' line, to calling on the boys more often than the girls, to chastising the girls more for messy handwriting. The experiment went on for two-and-a-half hours, with the participation of the gym teacher and principal. The latter came in sporting a white wig and a paddle.

After gym class, we gathered back in our circle to discuss how the kids felt about the morning. I was especially interested to hear if they noticed the differential gender treatment, which was not as obvious as the differences in the set-up of the room, work, and punishments. Not only did they notice the bias, but the girls were indignant, while the boys were gleeful.

"You were paying more attention to the boys!" was the first comment. "Boys were called on more and they were getting all the answers."

My students noted that there were different rules for boys than girls. A boy had been allowed to whistle. A girl had been reprimanded for the same behavior.

"I didn't like how you said,

'That's not ladylike,'" said Stephanie.

"I liked how you didn't make us do it over when we smudged our handwriting," noted Henry.

"Yeah, you tore mine up and made me start over," said Melissa.

"And I hate wearing dresses," added Rhonda.

Girls were upset about how they had to play with hula hoops while the boys played dodge ball in gym and how in science, boys did hands-on experimentation with worms while girls filled out glossary definitions from their science book.

"I know why you did this," said Anna, her face lighting up with a sudden realization. "You wanted us to know what prejudice feels like!"

Well, Anna was close. I thought that if I exaggerated the effect of gender discrimination, maybe then they would be better able to recognize the more subtle forms that they encountered within and outside of themselves. Certainly, my experience growing up had made me sensitive to gender stereotyping. But, at the same time, the cynical side of me knew that experiences with gender discussions, worms, and media critiquing paled in the light of Barbies, television, and Jenny Craig.

As I was packing up to go home after a long day, one especially exhausting due to our old-fashioned school experiment, Stephanie and Rhonda ran through the classroom to cut through the back door. As they stepped out to head for home, I heard Stephanie ask Rhonda, "So if I come over to your house, will you still be on your diet?" "Oh, no," answered Rhonda flippantly. "I don't do that on the weekend." ∎

Kate Lyman teaches in Madison, Wisconsin. She can be reached via e-mail at clyman@madison.k12.wi.us. The names of the children in this article have been changed.

Math, Maps, and Misrepresentation

By Eric Gutstein

What happens when students begin to question what they have been taught in school? What other questions does this help them raise, and how does it help them to better understand the world? How can teachers create these kinds of experiences?

I considered such questions as I taught my eighth-grade mathematics class at Rivera, a public school in a Mexican immigrant community in Chicago. As part of my job as a faculty member at DePaul University (where I teach several sections a year of Teaching and Learning Elementary Mathematics), I have taught one middle-school math class at Rivera on a daily basis for the past few years. My goal as a teacher has been influenced by the work of Paulo Freire and other critical educators. I want to help my students learn to *read* (i.e., understand) the world — through learning and using mathematics — as a way for them to begin to *write* (i.e., change) the world.

Going Beyond Mathematics

As the basis of my curriculum, I used *Mathematics in Context* (*MiC*) a new, innovative mathematics curriculum developed in accordance with the National Council of Teachers of Mathematics Standards. I found that *MiC* helped students learn to use mathematics to understand the world, as it developed many critical mathematical reasoning skills, but by itself, it was not enough. Therefore, I developed 17 real-world mathematics projects (for details, visit the Rethinking Schools website: www.rethinkingschools.org/publication/roc2/roc2links.shtml) that my

WORLD MAP — MERCATOR PROJECTION

WORLD MAP — PETERS PROJECTION

seventh- and eighth-grade students completed over the almost two years I was their teacher. (I moved up to eighth grade with my class.) This story, from the spring of 1999 when they were in eighth grade, is about one of those projects.

One significant lesson I learned is that going *beyond* mathematics is important in helping middle-school students read the world *with* mathematics. Teachers need to develop a classroom culture that incorporates reading the world and examining injustice and oppression. An important part of going beyond mathematics is to try to *normalize politically*

taboo topics. For example, my students and I had many conversations about race and racism, and they were central to a number of our classroom projects. I found that such an orientation is vital for students to appreciate and be more interested in mathematics, because they begin to see that mathematics can help them make sense out of their surroundings.

Analyzing Map Projections

The project I describe here was called *Analyzing Map Projections— What Do They Really Show?* Maps are two-dimensional representations of the earth that we often take for granted. Few of us think that our standard maps might be woefully inaccurate, and we do not often consider how the images students see everyday on classroom walls shape their perceptions of the world. Mathematics is central to map making, and different mathematical ways of representing the world produce very distinct maps. A goal of the map project was for students to use mathematics to analyze diverse map projections and to raise questions about what the various maps showed — and why. A larger goal of this project was to help students develop a more critical outlook towards knowledge in general.

I used two very different projections: the Mercator projection (developed in 1569 in Germany), the traditional map in U.S. schools (including Rivera); and the Peters projection (developed in 1974 by Arno Peters). The sizes, shapes of land masses, and coloring schemes of the maps are quite distinct. The Mercator map was developed during European expansion when colonial exploitation required that maps be used to navigate accurately (so as not to repeat Columbus' blunder) and was used successfully to find new territories. All maps unfortunately are misleading because they are two-dimensional projections of a sphere — and the Mercator suffers from serious visual distortion by altering the relative size of land masses. This is because the scale changes as you move away from the equator. Thus countries far from the equator (e.g., Greenland) appear much larger than they are. (Some Mercator maps have, in fine print, an explanation of this distortion and the mathematical information necessary to find the actual areas.)

For example, Mexico is about 760,000 square miles, Alaska is about 590,000, but Alaska looks two to three times larger because it is farther from the equator. The representations of Greenland and Africa are more distorted. Greenland, at 840,000 square miles, appears rough-

ly comparable to Africa, which, at 11,700,000 square miles, is about 14 times larger. In addition, Germany is near the center of the map, which may have made sense from the perspective of European expansionism. However, since Germany is in the northern quadrant of the earth (Berlin is 52° north), the only way to make it the center is to push the equator approximately two thirds of the way down the map. This compresses the Southern Hemisphere and enlarges the Northern.

These distortions remain true of today's Mercator maps, even though we now have better navigational means than the Mercator to sail across the Atlantic. Whether or not Mercator meant consciously to diminish the South, it is worthwhile to focus on the effect of its widespread use today.

In contrast, the Peters projection was developed to fairly and accurately portray the earth. As Ward Kaiser writes in an explanation of the Peters projection, "Peters is ... clearly focused on justice for all peoples, recognizing the values and contributions that all nations and all cultures can bring to the emerging world civilization."

The Peters map distorts shapes somewhat, but unlike the Mercator, it accurately presents the relative size of land masses.

As part of our project, I gave each group of three students a large Mercator map, borrowed from classrooms in the building. I gave them Mexico's size to use as a unit of measure and turned them loose to measure and compare several areas on their Mercator map (like Greenland and Africa; Mexico and Alaska). They used a variety of mathematical means to estimate the areas. For example, some traced Mexico and estimated how many Mexicos fit into other countries. They then multiplied the area of Mexico by the number (of Mexicos) that fit into other countries. Others overlaid centimeter grids on top of Mexico to determine the area per square centimeter, then measured other countries and found their areas. And some students used a

combination of methods, including reallocating areas to make rectangular shapes whose sizes were easier to estimate. Afterwards, they dug through our almanacs to find the real areas of the places they had measured and compared those to their estimates. Finally, I had students respond in writing to several questions, both in their groups and individually.

Questioning Past Learning

My students determined for themselves that the Mercator map did not show equal areas equally. This was further confirmed when they examined the Peters map. They were astonished and upset to discover the Mercator's visual distortions, and the majority felt they had been "lied to." Many were quite concerned about the implications of this misinformation, and some questioned other sources of knowledge and things they had learned.

In particular, many wanted to know why they had been mistaught. As one of my students, Rosa, commented, "The questions raised in my mind are why teachers never told us how wrong the map was."

Another student, Lupe, took a position of advocacy: "I think it's sad that we've all been taught this way. We should make our analysis public and let it be known. I just want to understand what [is] the point exactly of Mercator's map. What did he want us to believe, to see?"

One of the questions I had asked was, "Knowing we were all raised on the Mercator Map, how does that make you feel?" In response, Marisol commented that it "makes me think what other wrong information we have been given since childhood. It makes you doubt your social studies book, history written by the white people." And Gloria summed up the feeling of many. "Thinking that we were all raised with the Mercator map makes me feel kind of miseducated," she said, "because all these years we've been using the wrong map."

Race as a Central Issue

As politically taboo topics became normalized in our class, race and racism became central discussion topics. Students talked and wrote about race and racism as easily as about field trips and homework. A number of my projects focused more closely than this one on race. However, because race was an ordinary topic of conversation and a political issue about which students were concerned, and because I asked which races (in general) lived in the North and the South, students also analyzed the project using race as a point of inquiry.

Several found the shrinking of the South relative to the North and the skewing of the relative sizes of Alaska and Mexico particularly troublesome. Sandra had a particularly cogent analysis. "Doing this project has opened my eyes in different ways," she wrote. "I am learning how small details like maps, etc., have a lot to do with racism and power. Even though these kinds of things are small it can make a big difference in a person's view after learning what's really going on."

I also asked students to reflect on why the Mercator map is used so much in schools. One student, Elena, wrote, "I guess that's so because they wanted to teach [that] all Americans [are] superior and that all whites (that color and race) are better and superior than us (brown or lightly toasted, hardly white and Mexican). We were always taught that we were a minority and didn't deserve anything."

Issues of race and racism also surfaced in students' responses when I asked: "In your opinion, is this in any way connected to anything else we've studied over the last two years?" Among those who answered affirmatively, Javier wrote, "It all has to do with white being the superior ... because the map maker was from Europe, he put Europe in the 'middle of the world' and on top of other countries. But as we know, there is no such thing as a middle of the world."

Marisol also commented on the issue of race. "I think this is connected to what we studied over the past two years about equality, minorities, etc.," she wrote. "These maps seem to make minority-filled countries smaller than white-filled countries. To make us smaller and more insignificant? Yes, definitely."

Reflections

A principal purpose of this and other projects was to get my students to think deeply about their educational experiences and what they had learned both in and out of school. I wanted my students to discover for themselves that "what you see is not always what you get." I did not want my students to take my word, nor anyone else's, without questioning. I wanted them to both use mathematics to read their worlds and to see the value of doing so — that is, to also develop a particular disposition towards using mathematics for social analysis.

My students did begin to read their world with mathematics, but clearly they were still developing in this area; for a variety of reasons, their development was uneven. They were still struggling to form their ideas about the world, and their contradictory beliefs often surfaced. Some at times tried to explain away certain things, for example, hypothesizing that we still used the Mercator because perhaps the earth had changed since 1569 and mapmaking was just catching up. This type of accommodation repeatedly appeared in class, sometimes even from students who at other times took strong positions against various forms of injustice.

It is important to note that beyond beginning to analyze society using mathematics, my students also succeeded in mathematics on conventional academic measures. All passed their standardized tests and graduated eighth grade on time, and several made it to academic magnet high schools. Although these are neces-

sary accomplishments under the current high stakes testing policies, they are not enough. Educator Gloria Ladson-Billings' perspective on educating African-American students also applies to working-class Latinos and other marginalized students. In her 1994 book *The Dreamkeepers,* she writes that "parents, teachers, and neighbors need to help arm African-American children with the knowledge, skills, and attitude needed to struggle successfully against oppression. These, more than test scores, more than high grade-point averages, are the critical features of education for African Americans. If students are to be equipped to struggle against racism, they need excellent skills from the basics of reading, writing, and math, to understanding history, thinking critically, solving problems, and making decisions."

A broader definition of educational success incorporates the vision of working for social justice. Mathematics can be an appropriate tool to realize this vision. The words of my student Lupe exhibit the sense of purpose needed in this struggle. In commenting on our map project she wrote: "This is definitely connected to all we've done during the past two years. This goes back to why South America is so small in the Mercator's Projection Map, to injustice and some sort of propaganda with false information. This relates to not just accepting what we have, but to search for answers to our questions. You have taught us to do that in many ways, and that only makes us grow. Who knows? Maybe *we* can someday prove things wrong and show the right way!" ■

Eric Gutstein teaches in the School of Education at DePaul University in Chicago and at Rivera Middle School.

A New View of the World: A Handbook to the World Map: Peters Projection, *by W. L. Kaiser (Amherst MA: Friendship Press, 1987). Call 800-889-5733 to order.*

THE POWER OF SOCIAL ACTION

In a sense, all teaching is ultimately about promoting change — change in the ability of our students to achieve and understand, change in the capacity of our schools to inspire and support excellence, and change in the world around us to create a more just and enlightened society. Here teachers discuss lessons to be learned from movements for social justice, and some of the challenges of moving beyond the classroom to action.

"We Had Set Ourselves Free"

Lessons on the Civil Rights Movement

By Doug Sherman

"I was fifteen years old when I began to hate people. I hated the white men who murdered Emmett Till and I hated all the other whites who were responsible for the countless murders Mrs. Rice had told me about and those I vaguely remembered from child-hood."

— Anne Moody on the murder of fourteen-year-old Emmett Till in 1955 in *Coming of Age in Mississippi*, (1968).

"What happened in Selma was more than getting the right to vote. We first had to set ourselves free. After 300 years, we had to set our-selves free. That's what Dr. King was telling us, when he said we couldn't stay on the sidelines, that we had to get out and march. In Selma, getting the right to vote didn't set us free. No sir. In Selma, we got the right to vote because we had set ourselves free."

— Rachel West Nelson, describ-ing the victory in Selma in 1965, when she was nine years old in *Selma, Lord, Selma: Girlhood Memories of the Civil-Rights Days*, (1981).

The Civil Rights Movement lies at the margins of my memory. For today's high school stu-dents, it is a generation or more dis-tant. In spite of good intentions, when the new year brings the anniversary of the Rev. Martin Luther King, Jr.'s birthday and Black History Month, school activities often reduce the Civil Rights Movement to a scenario of "heroic leader and brave followers." Less

> **Unless we accept the reality of the choices students face, we can't credibly invite them to consider the reality of the choices those in different circumstances of history, gender, class, race, and culture have faced.**

often explored is the experience of those whose everyday lives intersect-ed with the struggle, and who responded with the kind of life-changing decisions that formed the heart of the movement.

The autobiographical narratives from which the above quotations are drawn move from headlines and text-book accounts to particular choices young people made during the Civil

Rights Movement. Anne Moody describes herself in 1955 as a girl who "didn't know what was going on all around." Through fear, anger, and pride, she learned and she changed: "Before Emmett Till's murder, I had known the fear of hunger, hell and the Devil. But now there was a new fear known to me — the fear of being killed just because I was Black."

My high school students learn about the murder of young Emmett Till as I tell his story: that he was from Chicago, visiting relatives in Mississippi; that he was taken from his uncle's house in the middle of the night and killed for saying "Bye, baby" to a white woman in a store; that his killers were acquitted.

As a class we then begin reading Chapter 10 of *Coming of Age in Mississippi*, Moody's account of the impact Till's death had in her com-munity. Her friends talk among them-selves: "What I mean is these god-damned white folks is gonna start some shit here you just watch!" Her mother warns her to play dumb with the white woman she works for: "You go on to work now before you is late. And don't you let on like you know nothing about that boy being killed before Miss Burke them. Just do your work like you don't know nothing." Mrs. Burke tells Anne the lesson she should learn from Till's murder: "He was killed because he got out of his place with a white woman."

As a class we discuss the themes in Moody's story. I then ask students to write for 15 minutes about an experience that reflects one of those themes in their own lives. The stories in their writing are powerful and var-ied: Many of my students relate to the fear of physical violence; many have experiences of degradation because of race, class, and gender, or because of age; many sense that they possess "dangerous" knowledge and attitudes, and have to "play dumb" much of the time. As we write and then tell each other our own stories, we compare them to identify common experiences, and see the ways that what is felt as private or individual experience has a social context that can be explored and understood.

The 1955 Till murder occurred at the beginning of the grassroots "civil rights" period of the larger struggle for racial equality, and it is dealt with extensively in the first episode of the television series *Eyes on the Prize - America's Civil Rights Years, 1954-1965,* titled "Awakenings 1954-56." Viewing this segment after reading Anne Moody's account, the documentary perspective of *Eyes on the Prize* puts the Till murder in a wider perspective.

Myrlie Evers of the Mississippi NAACP office, and widow of murdered Medgar Evers, recalls: "The Emmett Till case was one that shook the foundations of Mississippi, both Black and white. With the white community because of the fact that it had become nationally publicized, with us Blacks because it said that even a child was not safe from racism, bigotry and death." (Hampton and Fayer, 1990; p. 6)

Rachel West Nelson was not yet born when Emmett Till was killed, but at age nine she and her eight year-old friend Sheyann Webb found themselves drawn to the movement in Selma. On her way to school one morning in early 1965, Sheyann was passing the Brown Chapel AME Church. Although she saw a gathering there, she went on:

I started to cross the street, headed for school. A car went by and I waited. Then for reasons I can't explain, I just turned and went down the sidewalk to the church. I knew it was probably wrong. But it didn't feel wrong. Something inside me just told me

Martin Luther King, Jr., Ralph Abernathy (center), and Malcolm X.

I belonged in there, that what was going on inside there was more important than school.

Sheyann skipped school for most of the next three months; she became a "regular" in the Selma voting rights movement.

Perhaps the idea that there are more important things than school is itself "dangerous knowledge," but it is certainly a truth most of my students accept. Webb's decision offers a chance to discuss that truth in her life and in theirs. In deciding whether to skip class or to do their homework, for example, my students balance doing what's "officially" right against staying with a friend who is upset, a suicidal friend, a friend in trouble; against making spending money, helping support their families; against attending a county commission meeting on homeless youth.

Not all decisions involve what adults might consider "constructive" alternatives, but they are part of students' lives. Unless we accept the reality of the choices students face, we can't credibly invite them to consider the reality of the choices those in different circumstances of history, gender, class, race, and culture have faced. The magnitude of the decisions do not have to be equivalent for students to find in their own experience a foundation for a broader perspective on history and the social world and their relationship to them.

Among the many other issues *Selma, Lord, Selma* makes available for the classroom, one of the most riveting is the courage those in the movement showed in the face of violence. Different incidents and different sources can be used to develop this. The shooting of Jimmie Lee Jackson by a state trooper in neigh-

KATHY SLOANE

can feel overwhelming. The courage and determination of those who resist, and of those whose form of resistance must be endurance, nourish our hopes. At the same time, identifying real victories, large and small, is important, and the Civil Rights Movement for equality under law did achieve major victories. From our vantage point now, seeing such progress in racial justice under attack, we can look at the odds activists faced then, at their courageous decisions, and take inspiration. Fourteen years after Selma, Sheyann reflects: "I'm just so happy that I could be a part of a thing that touched our souls. I am so proud of the people who did something in 1965 that was truly amazing. We were just people, ordinary people, and we did it." ■

Doug Sherman is an associate professor in the Graduate School of Education at Portland State University. He was a high school teacher for 17 years. A version of this article first appeared in the Fall 1990 issue of Oregon English.

Resources

Hampton, Henry and Fayer, Steve. *Voices of Freedom: An Oral History of the Civil Rights Movement from the 1950s Through the 1980s.* New York: Bantam Books, 1990.

Moody, Anne. *Coming of Age in Mississippi.* New York: Dial, 1968.

Teaching Tolerance. *America's Civil Rights Movement.* Includes a 38-minute video, the publication *Free At Last,* and a teacher's guide. Free to educators, one package per school, if the request is on school letterhead. Contact: Teaching Tolerance, 400 Washington Ave., Montgomery, AL 36104.

Webb, Sheyann and Nelson, Rachel West. *Selma, Lord, Selma: Girlhood Memories of the Civil Rights Days.* New York: William Morrow, 1981.

Williams, Juan. *Eyes on the Prize: America's Civil Rights Years, 1954-1965.* New York: Penguin Books, 1987.

boring Marion, Alabama brought the danger home to Rachel much as Emmett Till's death had to Anne Moody. "'Shey,' I said, 'This is real bad. If they can shoot somebody over there, then they can shoot somebody here.'" (p. 77.)

While most of those martyred were Black, some were white. Soon after the first Selma march was turned back, The Rev. James Reeb from Boston was viciously beaten; he died a few days later. Sheyann writes about hearing the news:

> I knelt down beside Rachel and we prayed to ourselves for awhile. I didn't cry. I just kept thinking how even though he had been white, he had been one of us, too. I kept thinking that he had come to help us, just because he was a good man who couldn't stand by and watch injustice continue. (p. 115.)

Both these incidents are detailed in "Bridge to Freedom 1965," the final episode of the *Eyes on the Prize* television series. (It also includes footage of Rachel and Sheyann from both 1965 and the mid-1980s.) After viewing parts of this episode, and reading excerpts from *Selma, Lord, Selma,* students are well-prepared to write their way into an imaginative world of historical fiction. As an introduction to their writing assignment, I suggest some possibilities: As the sister or brother of Jimmie Jackson, the son or daughter of James Reeb, what might you write in a letter to your favorite cousin in Detroit? What might relatives of each write together in a two-voice poem about the meaning of the deaths? How might those deaths have been covered in a Black newspaper in Philadelphia? A white newspaper in Jackson, Mississippi?

Forces of unjust authority, greed, violence, and hatred are powerful and

From Snarling Dogs To Bloody Sunday

Teaching past the platitudes of the Civil Rights Movement

By Kate Lyman

"**I**'m not teaching about civil rights this year," my colleague asserted.

"Not teaching about civil rights?" I responded. My teaching buddy and partner had teamed with me in tackling "controversial issues" at the second/third-grade level — AIDS, the "discovery" of America, and homophobia, to name a few. I couldn't believe that she was not going to join me in planning the civil rights unit.

My partner explained that a parent of a child who was continuing in her second/third-grade combination class had objected to the unit on civil rights the previous year. "There was too much violence," she had said. Her daughter had been frightened.

Knowing that I would miss our joint planning sessions and sharing of materials and ideas, I nevertheless decided to go ahead with the unit.

My own experience growing up in an exclusively white and economically privileged suburb of Milwaukee had isolated me from the issues of the Civil Rights Movement. When, as a high school student in the 1960s, I finally became informed in a U.S. history class about the events in the South and the segregation and discrimination in my own city, I was appalled. I started on the long road to try to better understand issues of racism and to do what I could to act on the inequities in our society.

Unlike the suburb I grew up in, my school attendance area is culturally, politically, and socially diverse. More than 50% of the students come from families of color, most of them low-income. There are also low-income and working-class white families, and a smattering of middle-class

A police dog attacks a civil rights demonstrator in Birmingham in 1963.

AP/WIDE WORLD PHOTOS

families from a new development.

I had previously received a generally positive response to the civil rights unit. Parents had shared resources, such as a battered but prized painting of Rosa Parks. One

grandmother came in to teach us freedom songs and talk about her efforts in the 1960s to organize an NAACP chapter in Oklahoma.

My former principal and a few teachers had disapproved of teaching such deep and heavy issues to young children. However, I could recall only one negative comment from a parent: "Why are you still teaching Black History when it's past February?" In fact, even though I generally started the unit on or around the observance of Martin Luther King, Jr.'s birthday, related activities integrated into all subject areas extended past January and February and, depending on student interest and the depth of the projects, into the first few weeks of March.

I planned the civil rights unit within the context of a discussion of human rights and children's rights, in honor of the upcoming anniversary of the United Nations Universal Declaration of Human Rights, signed on Dec. 11, 1949. It was during that discussion that my students had agreed that among basic rights for children is the right "to not be judged by the color of our skin." This idea was a logical lead-in to the Civil Rights Movement.

We began by reading biographies about Martin Luther King, Jr. and gave him his due as a strong and gifted leader. But I also wanted to go beyond the platitudes often taught in elementary classes. I discarded worksheets in my files that summed up the Civil Rights Movement in simplistic language, such as: "Dr. King decided to help the Black people and white people get along better."

One especially useful book was *I Have a Dream*, by Margaret Davidson, (1986), and for 14 days we read a chapter a day from the book. While written in clear and fairly simple language, the book goes way beyond others in its genre in the complexity of its coverage of the Civil Rights Movement.

We used a variety of books, videos, poetry, and music to follow the history of racial discrimination and segregation. We studied not only King but many other people who worked together to overturn unfair laws and practices, especially the children: Ruby Bridges, the Little Rock Nine, the children in the Birmingham children's march, the

students in the sit-ins, and Sheyann Webb, the eight-year-old voting rights activist in Selma.

Sections from the PBS documentary series *Eyes on the Prize* were invaluable in helping my students witness history. They were entranced by the 1957 footage of the nine Little Rock high school students who faced angry mobs as they desegregated Central High. They cheered when one of the students, Minniejean Brown, got so infuriated with the daily intimidation that she finally poured a bowl of chili on her harasser's head. They watched with awe as the children in Birmingham, Alabama, in 1963 joined the protests against segregated facilities and then stood their ground even as they were being slammed against the wall by the power of the hoses held by Bull Connor's fire-fighters.

My students were especially captivated by the story of the Birmingham children's crusade. The class participated in a role play about how these high school students helped desegregate public facilities in the city.

Jerome, an African-American student with a gift for the dramatic, made a remarkable Martin Luther King, Jr. Imitating King's style for oratory, Jerome addressed his classmates who were playing the children gathered in the church after their first encounter with police brutality. Repeating the lines I gave him from the book *I Have a Dream*, he challenged the crowd, "Don't get bitter. Don't get tired. Are we tired?"

The students role-playing the Birmingham children responded before I had a chance to give them their lines. "NO!" they shouted, standing up and shaking their fists.

A Parent's Concern

I was halfway through the unit, feeling good about how the kids were conceptualizing the conviction of the civil rights activists — as well as how their enthusiasm was extending into reading, writing, and math activities — when Joanne, one of the eight African Americans in the class, hand-

ed me a letter from her mom. The letter expressed opposition to the civil rights unit, pointing out that Joanne had never witnessed hatred and brutality toward Blacks. Joanne, she said, had "no experience with police and guns, snarling dogs, hatred, people who spit and/or throw soup at others." Joanne felt afraid at bedtime because of the "true stories" she remembered from the books and movies.

I had anticipated that such issues might come up, and had tried to take steps to deal with the children's reaction to the violence of racism. For example, before we began the Emmett Till section in *Eyes on the Prize*, we had discussed how scary some of these historical events were. Third-grade students, who had been exposed to some of the content the year before, shared some feelings of fear, but also affirmed that they wanted to learn more about what they had been introduced to in second grade. I assured the class that acts that the Ku Klux Klan and others had committed with impunity 30 years ago could not go unpunished today.

I also knew I couldn't pretend that racial hatred is a thing of the past, however. I knew that many of my students were aware of the racist acts of violence reported in the national news. I also knew that many encounter racist name-calling or other biased acts in school and in their neighborhoods.

I hadn't seen signs that Joanne had been upset; in fact, her contributions to class discussions revealed a fascination with the topic. However, I was glad that Joanne's mom had communicated to me a problem that I might have missed.

As Joanne's mom had suggested, and in fact, as I would have done anyway, I took Joanne aside to talk with her. She said that the story of Emmett Till had bothered her, but that the rest had been okay. Cheerful and positive, as usual, Joanne dismissed my concern, and said she wanted to learn more.

I asked her to let me know if something was troubling her. I decid-

Marchers cross the Edmund Pettus Bridge from Selma to Montgomery, Alabama in 1965.

ed to watch her closely for signs of distress or withdrawal and to ask her frequently if she was doing all right. I also said she had the option to leave if the content disturbed her. But then I received another communication from her parents that she was to be excused from all books, movies, and poems that showed hatred toward Blacks.

I thought back to my teaching partner's reason for not teaching about the Civil Rights Movement. I thought of a few other parents and one other teacher (all middle-class African Americans, like Joanne's mom) who had told me that they didn't want slavery or racism taught about in schools because that was all behind them and they didn't want it dredged up. It was too painful. It was over. It made them out to be victims. Joanne's mom said that she wanted her daughter to know only the positive parts of the movement — the love and the happiness — not the snarling dogs and hatred toward Blacks.

I was in a quandary. Was it possible to teach in any depth about the Civil Rights Movement without including the violence and the racism? On the other hand, as a white

teacher, was it presumptuous of me to decide to teach something that offended an African-American parent? I knew that I couldn't put myself in her or Joanne's shoes. I can't know what it is like to be a racial minority in this country. And as a parent of three children, I know that parents have insight into their children that a teacher might lack.

I respect the right of parents to communicate their concerns and, if possible, I try to address them by altering what I do in the classroom. However, I knew that my obligation went beyond Joanne and her parents. I needed to think about what was best for all my students.

Assessing the Reactions of the Students

I watched my students carefully. It soon became apparent that my African-American and biracial students (9 out of 25) were gaining strength and self-confidence during the unit. They were participating more frequently in class, sharing information that they had learned from the many books available in the class, and relating what they were learning about the Civil Rights

Movement to their own lives.

I knew I had to think of Joanne. But I also had to think of Keisha, Jasmine, Monique, and Jerome.

Take Keisha, who had often drifted off to sleep through our other units and when called on would ramble. During the unit, she suddenly found her voice. In preparation for our enactment of the Birmingham children's march, for example, I talked to the class about what it meant to be "in character" in a drama. I told them to think about how they would feel if they were the people marching for their rights.

"I know," broke in Keisha, "You would be serious. You wouldn't be acting silly or nothing, because this is about getting your freedom. And you are marching for your mother or your father or your sister or your brother or for your children or your grandchildren, not just for yourself."

The next morning, Keisha brought in a friend from another class. "I have something to share," Keisha said. "Yesterday, at the Community Center, LaToya and me made up a speech, like Martin Luther King."

Her friend pulled out a rumpled sheet of paper and they proceeded to present their speech to the class:

Members of the Little Rock Nine at Central High School in 1957.

AP/WIDE WORLD PHOTOS

"Martin Luther King, Jr. and Me." Martin had a dream that Black people would be treated equally. But I have a dream that we would hold hands and study together, read together, and play together. I have a dream that we would go to the mall together, come to school together, and learn together as one. One day Rosa Parks refused to give up her seat on the bus to a white person. Things have gotten better now. Thank you.

Keisha later chose to do her human rights biography project on Harriet Tubman. She read all the books she could find on the topic and wrote the longest, most coherent piece in her journal on Tubman. And once, when the class was having a particularly difficult time settling down, Keisha yelled out, "Hey, would you all be acting like this if Martin Luther King was here?"

Jasmine, a biracial girl with a long history of discipline problems at the school, took to heart the story of six-year-old Ruby Bridges. (See the biographies that begin on p. 125.) Jasmine surprised me one morning with a life-sized portrait of Ruby Bridges that she had made in the after-school program by taping

together smaller pieces of paper. She wrote about Ruby Bridges in her journal and in a letter to then-Wisconsin governor Tommy Thompson on another topic, she asked: "Have you heard of Ruby Bridges?"

One day, Jasmine approached me in confidence. "Kate, you might not know this, because it's a secret, but I'll tell you something I've been doing."

"I'd like to know, Jasmine," I responded, expecting a confession of some wrongdoing.

"Well, Kate, sometimes, when I'm sitting at my table, I just pretend I'm Ruby Bridges. I pretend that the other kids sitting at my table are those people yelling at me because I'm Black and they don't want me in their school. And, just like Ruby, I ignore them and just go on doing my work. I do it real good, just like Ruby. I was doing it just before at math time."

And then there were Monique and Jerome. Previously two of my biggest troublemakers, during this unit they became the two I could count on to be on task for reading, writing, and other activities. Monique, who had previously disrupted numerous group discussions or cooperative projects, suddenly became the model student. "Shhhhh, everybody!" she'd admonish. "I want

to hear this!"

Jerome found a connection from home. "My mom told me that we all need to learn about this because it could happen again," he said. He told the class about when the people next door to his apartment house had put up a sign to prevent kids from cutting through their yard on their way to school. The sign had said: "Private. Stay out of our yard. No niggers."

Many of the other students talked about how they, too, would have been discriminated against if they had lived in the South during Jim Crow. (I also had four Hmong students, one Cambodian American, two Filipino Americans, two born in Mexico, and one with a Mexican-Indian grandparent.) "I would have had to use the 'colored only' drinking fountain because I'm part Filipino," Anita would remind the class. At the drawing table I heard one girl say, "You know, we would all have been discriminated against, because I'm part Mexican, you are Hmong, and you are both Black."

I also watched the reactions of the European-American students. There were fewer white kids than children of color in the class and, although we had learned about many brave white activists, the whites were definitely not shown in a positive light in most of the material. I watched to see if the European Americans were engaged in our discussions and if they showed any signs of discomfort. Chris was tentative at first, hanging back, sometimes fooling around with another white boy. But then he started to participate more and more in the discussions and role plays. As we were watching a video, *My Past Is My Own*, in which a white teenage gang assaults the Black students at a lunch counter sit-in, Chris moved close to where I was sitting.

"I don't like this part," he confided in me. "If those kids were friends of mine, I'd tell them, 'Hey leave them alone. What you're doing isn't right.'"

The next day, Chris decided to write a letter to Rosa Parks relating his admiration for her courage.

Chris and many of the other white kids in our school come with attitudes that are the products of the racism that divides our neighborhood. I came to the conclusion that they, as much as, or even more than, the children of color, needed to hear the story of the racial hatred and the saving power of a nonviolent movement. There may come a time when they find the courage to say, "What you're doing isn't right."

Despite the positive changes I witnessed in many of my students, the opposition of Joanne's parents kept nagging at me. We kept in touch through notes and conversations. I heard, on the one hand, that they supported what I was doing; yet Joanne was still to be kept out of all activities related to the unit. I talked over the situation with colleagues and friends, including the principal, who encouraged me to go on with the unit. (In the first grade, a parent had complained to the principal that the teacher had not gone into enough depth in presenting the history of civil rights.)

I also spoke with an African-American man, the grandfather of a student, who had presented to my class several years ago. He had proudly brought in a huge photograph of the Edmund Pettus Bridge in Alabama and had told how he joined the voting rights march on "Bloody Sunday," March 7, 1965, and crossed that bridge only to be attacked by local and Alabama state police officers armed with weapons and tear gas.

I invited him back to speak to the class and also asked his opinion on my dilemma, sketching out the objections to the civil rights unit. His voice, heretofore somewhat soft and distant, became strident.

"Hey, that's what we were all marching for!" he said. "We were marching for the right for our kids and all kids to learn about the history of Black folks. And it's not like it's over and done with. They might try to keep their kid from knowing about it now, but sooner or later they will find out and then it will be a shock. Better

to learn now what we were all fighting for!"

I decided to also ask the opinion of my students. I was finding it hard to put off questions of why Joanne was dismissed to work in the library each time we worked on the unit. Even though I assigned different work for Joanne, some members of the class were protesting that she was playing on the computers while they were

> **Joanne's mom said that she wanted her daughter to know only the positive parts of the movement — the love and the happiness — not the snarling dogs and hatred toward Blacks.**

working on their writing and reading. One day, when Joanne was out of the room, I told the class that Joanne's parents objected to her learning about the Civil Rights Movement.

I also asked the class if they thought it was an important topic. The consensus was that it was "very, very important." The reasons came out faster than I could record them: "So if that stuff happened again, we could calm down and be strong."…. "It might happen again and then we'd have to go and march."…. "The KKK is still alive and they don't like Blacks and Filipinos."…. "It makes us smarter to learn about this, and then

if we have kids and they wanted to learn about it, we could teach them."…. "When we go to another grade, we will know not to call people names like Darkie."…. "If you learn about it, you get to go to higher grades and get to go to college."…. "Dr. King, he was trying to tell us that we could have a better life."…. "We want no more segregation, no more fights, no more KKK burning down houses."…. "So it don't happen no more."

We went on with our work. At this point in the unit, the focus was on presenting a student-written screenplay of *Selma, Lord, Selma* (1980), (which in turn was based on the Disney television special). Not wanting Joanne to miss what was becoming an even more central part of our curriculum, I suggested to Joanne's parents that they watch the tape of the television special. Since it was shown on *Wonderful World of Disney*, I figured I couldn't go wrong there. I also gave them copies to read of the screenplay that the class had written. I again was told that Joanne could not participate.

The rest of the students, however, immersed themselves in the drama. Jasmine transformed herself into the role of Sheyann Webb, the brave eight-year-old participant in the Selma voting rights movement. She held her head high and sang *Ain't Gonna Let Nobody Turn Me 'Round* with a voice pure in tone, perfect in pitch, and strong in conviction. Monique turned all her energies into not only acting the part of Rachel West, Sheyann's friend, but also keeping the rest of the class on task and in role. Jerome continued as Martin Luther King, Jr., changing the words of his speech for every practice but never failing to perform the part of the orator and leader of the people. It was clear that the play was cementing the history of the Civil Rights Movement in the minds and hearts of every student.

Several days before the final performance, Joanne's parents approached me in the hall. They wanted her to participate, although they were concerned

Children seek shelter from high-pressure fire hoses during a civil rights demonstration in Birmingham in 1963.

it might be too late. They never explained what had led them to change their minds. I knew that Joanne was feeling left out, especially since the class had also been working on their play in their music and movement classes.

Despite my earnest efforts to excuse Joanne to the library whenever we read or discussed material related to civil rights, Joanne, a very bright and curious girl, had not only managed to pick up a lot of information, but had also learned the songs in the play. Joanne took on her role as a voting rights activist in *Selma, Lord, Selma* as smoothly as if she had been practicing it for three weeks with the rest of the class. She not only marched to the courthouse, singing *Kumbaya* and demanding the right to vote, but she also participated in a slow-motion pantomime of the "Bloody Sunday" confrontation, as marchers attempting to cross the Edmund Pettus Bridge were met with the troopers' sticks, cattle prods, and tear gas.

After Joanne and the others recover from the violent attack and rise to the occasion of singing *Ain't Gonna Let Nobody Turn Me 'Round*, this time with added significance to the words, Jasmine (Sheyann) narrates: "We were singing and telling the world that we hadn't been whipped, that we had won. We had really won. After all, we had won."

The Lessons of Selma

The Selma story instructs us that out of unspeakable violence and defeat can come resolution and victory. Out of Bloody Sunday came renewed participation and power in the Civil Rights Movement, resulting in the Voting Rights Act of 1965 and the success of the second Selma to Montgomery march.

Can the Civil Rights Movement be taught without teaching about segregation, racial hatred, and violence? I don't think so. It is against the backdrop of the firehoses and the snarling dogs that the Birmingham children found their strength to sing, even as they were hauled off to jail. When Martin Luther King, Jr. was denied the right to sit in the front of a shoe store or to play with his white friends, the seeds of his leadership were planted. It does not make sense to teach the Civil Rights Movement without teaching about the separate bathrooms and KKK. Furthermore, to do so wouldn't be history. It would be a lie.

Despite the controversy my unit engendered, I did not regret my decision to proceed. Even though the behavior and academic focus of students like Keisha, Jasmine, Jerome, and Monique did not remain at that peak, they still remembered those weeks as the best part of the school year. And as we moved into learning about the struggles of other groups of people for equal rights, or as we talked about issues of justice and tolerance in the classroom, we always had the Civil Rights Movement to look back to for inspiration.

As Keisha said in her end-of-the-year evaluation: "I liked giving my speech in class about Martin Luther King and Rosa Parks, too. They fought for freedom and the right to vote. They are so cool to do that and march and give us freedom. [If they hadn't done that,] me and you would not be together today and be learning." ■

Kate Lyman teaches in Madison, Wisconsin. She can be reached via e-mail at clyman@madison.k12.wi.us. The names of students in this article were changed.

Children Who Made a Difference

The following are just a few of the many children and youth involved in the Civil Rights Movement.

Emmett Till

Emmett Till's death is referred to as the "spark that set the movement on fire." Emmett was 14 when he traveled from Chicago to Mississippi in 1955 to visit his cousin. Ignorant of the social protocol of the South, he made an off-hand comment to a white woman working in a store owned by her husband. Till's body was found three days later. An all-white jury acquitted the husband and his brother, who later admitted to a reporter that they beat Till, shot him in the head, and threw his body in the river. Emmett's mother, Mamie Till, held an open-casket funeral to alert the nation to the racial violence in the South, and the media extensively covered his death.

The Little Rock Nine

Following the 1954 U.S. Supreme Court decision declaring "separate but equal" schools unconstitutional, school officials at Central High School in Little Rock, Arkansas, decided to integrate, admitting a small number of Black students in 1957. The nine students who enrolled faced angry mobs, as well as the National Guard, who had been appointed by Governor Orval Faubus to keep the students out. Federal troops were sent to safeguard the students' entry into the school, but still the students faced continued harassment from their white classmates.

Ruby Bridges

In 1960, New Orleans schools were ordered to follow the U.S. Supreme Court mandate and desegregate. One Black six-year-old girl, Ruby Bridges, was sent on her own to desegregate William Frantz Elementary School. She faced angry mobs and had no help from city and state police. As in Little Rock, Federal marshals were sent to protect her. She was taught alone in an empty classroom, since white parents had pulled their children out of the school to protest integration. Later in the year, two children came back to the school. Slowly, through Ruby's bravery and persistence, the school became integrated.

Sheyann Webb

Eight-year-old Sheyann Webb and her friend Rachel West became the youngest participants in the voting rights movement in Selma, Alabama, in 1965. In Selma, fewer than 200 of 15,000 Black people were registered to vote because of physical intimidation or discriminatory tests given at the voter registration site. Despite her parents' fears, Sheyann participated in marches and rallies held to increase voter registration. One such march included teachers, junior high school students, and some younger students.

These actions were met with violence, including the murder of Jimmie Lee Jackson. To protest Jackson's death, and to further promote voting rights, the leaders planned a march from Selma to Montgomery on March 7, 1965. At the Edmund Pettus Bridge heading out of Selma, the marchers, including Sheyann, were met by local and state police officers with sticks, electric cattle prods, and tear gas. This day became known as "Bloody Sunday." Beaten and temporarily defeated, the marchers retreated. A second march of about 4,000 people, successfully reached Montgomery.

The Children's Crusade

Since 1960, Civil Rights activists had been working to end segregation in public facilities in Birmingham, Alabama. Their gatherings were regularly disrupted by the Ku Klux Klan, who used beatings and bombings to discourage organizing. In May of 1963, James Bevel, an organizer with the Southern Christian Leadership Conference, decided on the controversial plan of involving high school students in the protests and training them in nonviolent direct action.

The high school students were soon joined by younger children, thousands of whom marched in the streets of Birmingham. Bull Connor, the Birmingham Commissioner of Public Safety, responded to the children by sending in officers brandishing clubs, police dogs, and fire hoses. The violence toward the children was shown on national news.

Selected Resources

The following books are recommended for children from about second grade up to middle school:

Bullard, Sara. *Free at Last: A History of the Civil Rights Movement and Those Who Died in the Struggle.* New York: Oxford University Press, 1989.

Coles, Robert. *The Story of Ruby Bridges.* New York: Scholastic, 1995.

Davidson, Margaret. *I Have a Dream: The Story of Martin Luther King.* New York: Scholastic, 1986.

Duncan, Alice Faye. *The National Civil Rights Museum Celebrates Everyday People.* New York: Troll Medallion, 1995.

Levine, Ellen. *If You Lived at the Time of Martin Luther King.* New York: Scholastic, 1990.

Rochelle, Belinda. *Witnesses to Freedom: Young People Who Fought for Civil Rights.* New York: Puffin Books, 1993.

Webb, Sheyann and West, Rachel as told to Frank Sikora. *Selma, Lord, Selma: Girlhood Memories of the Civil Rights Days.* Tuscaloosa, AL: University of Alabama, 1980.

Williams, Juan. *Eyes on the Prize: America's Civil Rights Years, 1954-1965.* New York, Penguin, 1987. Available from Public Broadcasting Service, 800-328-7271. ■

Mississippi Freedom Schools

A project from the past suggests a lesson for the future

By David Levine

In 1964, 20-year-old Allen Gould took a break from his studies at Wayne State University in Detroit to become a teacher in the Mississippi Freedom Summer project. In rural Harmony, Mississippi, he introduced his teenage students to Wright, Baldwin, Cummings, Frost, and Sandburg. Near the start of the summer he gathered his class outside to try their hand at poetry writing. Thirteen-year-old Ida Ruth Griffin stood and slowly read her poem:

> I am Mississippi-fed,
> I am Mississippi-bred,
> Nothing but a poor, Black boy.
>
> I am a Mississippi slave,
> I shall be buried
> in a Mississippi grave,
> Nothing but a poor, dead boy.

Her classmates responded with angry silence, finally broken by voices denying Black inferiority. A student insisted, "We're not Black slaves!" But another retorted, "She's right. We certainly are. Can your poppa vote? Can mine? Can our folks eat anywhere they want to?" Soon the class plunged into animated discussion, trying to puzzle out what it meant to be young and Black at a time when the first big cracks were appearing in the segregated society they had known all their lives.

This episode captures much of the spirit of the Mississippi Freedom Schools: an informal setting, an idealistic college student with no teaching experience, an animated group of Black adolescents, a pedagogy which nurtured student voices, and a discus-

> **The Mississippi Freedom Schools suggest that while personal success is a valid goal of education, our schools are enriched when they also engage young people in collaborative quests for social justice.**

sion through which literature sparked consideration of daily oppression.

The heart of the Freedom School endeavor, the source of its vivid and creative energy, was the insistence of its planners and teachers that learning could (and should) be shaped to serve a liberation struggle. Today, educational goals are more likely to focus on how students can best be turned into "human capital," what modes of control steer children clear of sex, drugs, and violence, and whether the dismantling of a common education through vouchers is the best way to salvage education. Schooling is thus reduced to a privatized journey toward personal prosperity and prestige. The 1964 Mississippi Freedom Schools offer a compelling counter-vision which suggests that while personal success is a valid goal of education, our schools are enriched when they also engage young people in collaborative quests for social justice. I believe that the Freedom Schools demonstrated that education can both help transform society and inspire young people to attack intellectual tasks with a vigor and emotional intensity which deepens learning.

Freedom Summer was coordinated by a Mississippi organization called the Coalition of Federated Organizations (COFO), which included the NAACP, SNCC (the Student Nonviolent Coordinating Committee), SCLC (Southern Christian Leadership Conference), and CORE (Congress On Racial Equality). SNCC provided most of the staff, running the project in four congressional districts, with CORE taking responsibility for the remaining district. The project included three main initiatives: Freedom Schools and community centers, voter registration, and a freedom registration plan designed to elect to the 1964 Democratic National Convention a slate of delegates which would challenge the credentials of the segregated Mississippi Democratic Party delegation.

Before the summer program began, its architects worried about the cultural mismatch between teachers and students. Would privileged,

Northern white college students have the empathy to connect with poor, Southern Black students growing up under the shadow of Mississippi segregation? Widely exceeding the expectations of Freedom Summer planners, Freedom Schools were created in 50 locations during July and August of 1964. Working under constant threat of violence in church basements or ramshackle community centers, 250 volunteers taught between 3,000 and 3,500 students, ranging in age from pre-teens to adults in their sixties. Despite fundamental differences in life circumstances, Freedom School teachers and students were able to build a strong sense of community and achieve substantive personal growth.

In making education a prominent part of Freedom Summer plans, SNCC was acting on the intuition that the new generation of Blacks in Mississippi was ready to take a crucial role in the Civil Rights Movement. In the words of SNCC staffer Charles Cobb:

> There is hope and there is dissatisfaction — feebly articulated — both born out of desperation of needed alternatives not given. This is the generation that has silently made the vow of no more raped mothers — no more castrated fathers; that looks for an alternative to a lifetime of bent, burnt, and broken backs, minds and souls. Where creativity must be molded from the rhythm of a muttered "white son-of-a-bitch," from the roar of a hunger-bloated belly.... What they must see is the link between a rotting shack and a rotting America.

The idea of bringing 1,000 mostly white, Northern, middle-class students into Mississippi was the product of SNCC frustration with the notably vicious and intransigent system of white supremacy which governed the state's race relations from the end of Reconstruction into the early 1960s. Emmet Till's unpunished murder in 1955 typified a pat-

A class at a Mississippi Freedom School in the summer of 1964.

tern of terror employed to ensure the economic and political subordination of the Magnolia State's Black population. Between 1882 and 1952, 534 lynchings occurred in Mississippi — more than in any other state. In 1960, the median income of Black Mississippians was $1,444, the lowest in the United States and one-third lower than the income of the state's white citizens. Black communities suffered from high infant mortality, and two-thirds of Black homes lacked flush toilets.

The separate education provided white and Black students was patently unequal. The 1964 average state expenditure per pupil was $21.77 for Blacks and $81.86 for whites. Freedom School teacher Gary

DeMoss commented on the Ruleville Negro public school:

> Whole classes go out and pick cotton, though they're never given any accounting where the money goes. A freshman algebra class has 72 students, they sit two to a desk, and have only one teacher. Sometimes three and four classes meet at the same time in the gym and the entire library is a couple of incomplete sets of encyclopedias.

SNCC staff member Charles Cobb wrote a prospectus for the Freedom Schools which served as a guiding document. Describing Mississippi classrooms as "intellectual wastelands," Cobb criticized the state's segregated schools for giving Blacks an inferior education and punishing them for challenging the status quo. He suggested that Freedom Schools could provide the effective academic instruction which African-American students weren't getting in regular schools, encourage them to articulate their own aspirations and to question authority, and recruit students to SNCC organizing efforts, thus laying the groundwork for a statewide student movement.

Cobb suggested a curriculum which emphasized political and social studies, cultural programs, and communication skills. A curriculum packet for volunteer teachers included a Citizenship Guide with lessons on the Civil Rights Movement, the Mississippi power structure, and COFO's program. A section entitled "Material Things and Soul Things" was designed to help students question the materialistic orientation of American culture and explore what values could animate a new society which put a higher priority on human relationships. The introduction to the Citizenship Guide urged teachers to help students focus on three questions which reflected SNCC's concern with Black identity and the dangers of uncritical assimilation:

• What does the majority culture have that we want?

• What does the majority have that we don't want?

• What do we want to keep?

Freedom School planners stressed that the project should deliberately reject the teacher-dominated, lecture-centered procedures which characterized most regular schools. Volunteer teachers were urged to ask questions, listen carefully to the answers, and encourage discussions in which students could reach into their own experience to produce knowledge and articulate their own perspectives. Planners warned teachers to avoid traditional school practices which inhibited students. Testing, grades, and formality were discouraged. In regard to writing activities, a memo on teaching suggestions urged volunteers to concentrate on content and clear expression rather than grammar, spelling, and academic jargon. The project organizers hoped that many students would participate in voter registration canvassing and other organizing activities. The idea was that the academic program would simultaneously support and build from this work by focusing on leaflet writing, effective oral communication, the creation of posters, and sociological investigations of the community.

Each Freedom School functioned autonomously. Intensive supervision would have been difficult, since the only staff support consisted of program coordinator Staughton Lynd. In any case, the curriculum's designers realized that the success of the program depended on the capacity of the teachers to function independently and flexibly. They were encouraged to tailor their teaching to the needs of the students and communities they were working with. According to Lynd, teachers were told: "If you want to begin the summer by burning the curriculum we have given you, go ahead!"

This deliberately anti-bureaucratic stance was a natural expression of SNCC's egalitarian ethos. SNCC values also shaped the program through the insistence that the relationships between students and teachers were just as important as the curriculum. This reflected the early SNCC propensity to believe that meaningful change had more to do with forging genuine and loving relationships between people than with elaborate programs or ideology. The volunteers were told that their rapport with students depended on their ability to be honest, to be "real" and "trustworthy," and to admit when they didn't know something. Expressions of feelings were to be explored rather than repressed, even if doing so made students and teachers uncomfortable. By participating in political work with students, teachers would build up a fund of shared experience out of

A picture of a sharecropper, from a Freedom Summer recruiting poster.

which classroom work could grow. When Lynd and SNCC planners admonished teachers to ask questions more readily than they gave answers, they were expressing a pedagogical preference, but more deeply, their desire that the volunteers open their lives to the summer experience and be willing to learn from the communities they were entering.

In the aftermath of the victories of the Civil Rights Movement, it is easy to forget the massive quantity of white resistance to equality in Mississippi. The summer project operated in the context of continual threats and physical attacks. By the end of the summer the movement had endured 35 shooting incidents, the bombing of 30 homes and other buildings, the burning of 35 churches, and 1,000 arrests. This litany of attacks leaves out the constant strain of harassing phone calls, threatening cars driving by, and interaction with hostile law enforcement officials who were sometimes in collusion with vigilantes.

Even before the end of the second Freedom Summer orientation for volunteers in Oxford, Ohio, the participants learned about the disappearance of Andrew Goodman, Mickey Schwerner, and James Chaney. The three civil rights workers had vanished while returning from inspecting a church which had been burned down after its congregation had agreed to let it be used as the site for a Freedom School. In August their bodies would finally be discovered buried beneath an earthen dam in rural Mississippi.

In the face of this repression, the Black communities which hosted the project generally extended the volunteers a cordial welcome. Black families housed and fed volunteers, often at considerable risk. The dialectic of white repression and Black support sometimes played out around the Freedom Schools. In McComb, teachers held class for 75 students on the lawn in front of the second church to be bombed in two days. When the Freedom School staff arrived in Carthage they were greeted by a wel-

> **By participating in political work with students, teachers would build up a fund of shared experience out of which classroom work could grow.**

coming committee of 40 residents who had been waiting for their arrival for nearly four hours. Community members worked with the teachers to clean out and refurbish an old abandoned school building which the Black community had built in the 1930s.

When they finished, the sheriff evicted them from the school under the pretext that the building was the property of the county school system.

Residents moved the school library to a temporary new site in pickup trucks. When a legal challenge to the eviction failed, community members and staff worked long hours in the hot Mississippi sun to build a new community center to house the school and posted an armed guard at night to protect the new building.

Soon after the building was completed, school district authorities moved up the fall starting date of the Black schools by three weeks to block attendance at the Freedom School and to make Black students available to chop cotton in October. The Black community responded with a school boycott which demanded several improvements in the Blacks schools.

Not bound by a standardized curriculum, each Freedom School

evolved its own schedule, topics, and activities, and there was considerable variety across the state. Most of the schools offered three categories of instruction: academic subjects, politically oriented social studies, and recreational and cultural activities.

A glance at the Holly Springs Freedom School daily routine offers a good sample of the range of activities in many of the schools. The school served about 60 students, ranging in age from 4 to 25. Activities began at 9:00 a.m. with civil rights songs, followed by an hour of instruction for all students in Citizenship and Negro History. The morning ended with electives: dance, drama, art, auto mechanics, guitar, games, and sports.

After a long lunch break, classes were offered in play writing, debate, journalism, French, religion, and nonviolence. An evening session offered voter education, sewing, and health classes. A record player and records and a library were also available for community use. Although volunteers lectured and provided individualized instruction, they preferred to teach through small group discussion.

Typical descriptions of classes convey enthusiasm and intellectual engagement. Pam Allen taught a group of 15 women ranging in age from 15 to 25. She reported:

> The atmosphere in class is unbelievable. It is what every teacher dreams about — real, honest enthusiasm and desire to learn anything and everything. The girls come to class of their own free will. They respond to everything that is said. They are excited about learning. They drain me of everything that I have to offer so that I go home at night completely exhausted but very happy....

Staff members often commented on the disparity between the poor academic preparation of many of their students and their sophisticated social and intellectual skills.

Much of the curriculum centered on student writing, with young authors producing short essays, poems, and letters. Their themes included critiques of housing and working conditions experienced by Blacks, exhortations to register to vote, and accounts of personal encounters with discrimination. Several schools produced mimeographed newspapers of four to six pages with names like *The Freedom Fighter*, *The Freedom Flame*, and *The Benton County Freedom Train*. An August issue of *The Freedom Echo*, produced by students at the Mount Nebo School, contained an account of a parents' night, a report on a guest speaker from Ireland, an article on the Democratic National Convention, an excerpt from a speech by the student editor, and a page of comments about the school by students titled "What We Liked and Learned."

Freedom School students in Palmer's Crossing collaborated on a manifesto which detailed several pro-equality demands and concluded: "We, therefore, the Negroes of Mississippi assembled, appeal to the government of the state, that no man is free until all men are free. We do hereby declare independence from the unjust laws of Mississippi which conflict with the United States Constitution."

Class activities often challenged students to understand and articulate varied points of view. One teacher listed Barry Goldwater's reasons for opposing the civil rights bill on the board. His class reviewed the arguments, with one student portraying Goldwater and another trying to counter his reasoning. In Palmer's Crossing, two Freedom Schools held a debate on the proposition that violence was necessary to win civil rights. An impressed visitor described effective arguments and rebuttals presented by the 12- to 16-year-olds, and regretfully reported that the affirmative side won.

Teachers used improvisational acting to help their classes understand social roles. Student role plays

included: a Congressional committee debating better wages for Blacks; three generations of a family interacting at home; convincing a reluctant community member to register to vote; desegregating a restaurant; demonstrating at a courthouse; and Senator and Mrs. Eastland discussing "uppity niggers" over cocktails with Senator Stennis and his wife. A few schools staged dramatic projects. The Mileston students composed "The American Negro," a series of vignettes portraying Black Southern life during slavery, the Civil War,

> True to one of the prime hopes of their organizers, Freedom Schools began to mobilize students as a distinct political force.

segregation, and the contemporary civil rights struggle. In Holly Springs, New York public school teacher Deborah Flynn helped students use improvisation to script a play entitled *Seeds of Freedom*, which chronicled the life and assassination of Mississippi NAACP head Medgar Evers. At the end of the summer, the students performed the play at the Freedom School Convention.

Teachers sparked lively discussions by fashioning their curriculum out of the historical drama unfolding all around the schools. A teacher interrupted his outdoor class so students could interview three women angrily returning from the courthouse, where they had just learned

their registration applications had been rejected. One of the Jackson teachers read to his class a newspaper editorial criticizing civil rights workers for encouraging people to break the law, and asked students to write a response to the editor. Their efforts introduced the issue of civil disobedience and an opportunity to discuss the differences between statutory law, constitutional law, and "natural" law. On another occasion this teacher told his students about his visit to the Neshoba County Annual Fair, near where the bodies of Chaney, Schwerner, and Goodman had just been discovered. He quoted a John Birch Society speaker at the fair: "I am for the Constitution, for freedom, for the Open Bible." He asked students to compare this credo to their own beliefs. In the following discussion students tried to carefully define how their interpretation of constitutional law probably differed from that of the Birch Society representative.

At several schools, students became directly involved in political organizing, most often by helping Freedom Summer volunteers try to convince Black citizens to register to vote. Novice student organizers sometimes reported their experiences in school newspapers. In Holly Springs, the young canvassers found that trying to convince intimidated citizens to register was often a discouraging task, which demanded effective persuasion and helped them understand their neighbors. In an article for *The Freedom News*, Gary Faulkner argued that voting could help Blacks obtain better roads, sewerage, jobs, housing, and schools. After unsuccessfully trying to convince a woman to register, Edna Mary Echols wrote: "It really made me mad. But then I thought awhile and tried to understand her. Probably she was accustomed to letting other people think or talk for her, and if she did register to vote she could lose what she had."

True to one of the prime hopes of their organizers, Freedom Schools began to mobilize students as a distinct political force. This trend was facilitated by the decision to hold a Freedom School Convention in Meridian. Students prepared by electing delegates and putting together planks for a political platform which would be discussed at the convention. The three-day August convention was hosted by the Meridian Freedom School students, who took responsibility for the logistical arrangements. Convened under a large banner declaring "Freedom Is A Struggle," the 75 delegates representing 41 schools divided into workshops on voter registration, medical care, housing, education, jobs, federal aid, and foreign affairs. Workshop proposals were discussed and voted on in plenary sessions. The meeting was addressed by Jim Forman, A. Philip Randolph, and Bob Moses.

The delegates hammered out final planks which indicated a serious focus on state and national issues, sometimes engaging in heated debate. A foreign affairs workshop draft declared support for the Monroe Doctrine and urged the United States to pressure the Latin American countries not to accept aid from communist countries. The plenary session jettisoned this section after a student declared: "As a permanent member of the Negro race I'm sick and tired of anything that smacks of paternalism." A proposal in favor of land reform was voted down as "too socialistic." In the education workshops, students complained about the lack of vocational and language classes and kindergartens. The education platform demanded better school facilities, a school year of nine consecutive months, integration, academic freedom for teachers and students, and permission for teachers to join civil rights groups without being fired.

The convention also considered how to protest inferior conditions in Black schools and revived a Mississippi Student Union (MSU) which COFO had helped start the previous spring. Freedom School discussions throughout the summer had often focused on students' discontent with their regular schools. Besides criticizing the lack of resources and limited curricula of their public schools, students complained of political repression. They were not allowed to form student governments or discuss controversial issues in class. Their teachers were too scared to register to vote, and principals were impelled to carry out the orders of white superintendents.

In Ruleville, young people attending the Freedom School organized a Student Action Group. They handed each teacher at their regular school a letter asking for an accounting for money earned when students picked cotton during school, demanding the right to form clubs and a student government, and asking teachers to take the lead in fighting for improved and integrated education. At the school's compulsory chapel meeting, two students used the time for student announcements to launch into speeches. Bobby Cameron declared that there was "a new day coming," and that teachers should help lead the way. The other students responded with applause as the teachers watched silently. Reaction from the administration was swift. That same day each student received a letter from the superintendent indicating that any student who participated in a demonstration at school would be suspended.

When M. C. Perry protested, he was immediately sent home. He kept trying to return to school, even after being marched out of the building at gunpoint by a policeman and reprimanded by the mayor. On his final attempt he was arrested and sentenced to 30 days in jail. By the time of the Meridian convention, the students and civil rights leader Fannie Lou Hamer had conducted separate meetings with the teachers to resolve the issues. When the

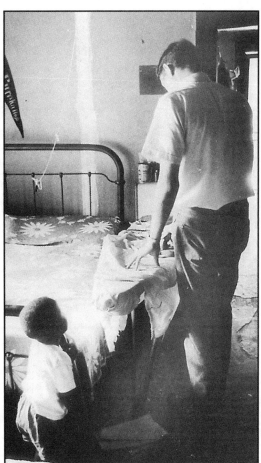

A child watches a Freedom Summer volunteer iron a shirt in Hattiesburg, Mississippi.

Ruleville students told their story to the other convention participants, plans began to be discussed for a statewide school boycott.

We have no comprehensive record of the long-term impact of the Mississippi Freedom Schools. But many young participants testified that the summer experience put them on a path to personal transformation, and later anecdotal reports suggest that alumnae often considered the experience an important influence on their adult lives. Although they did not survive as long-term institutions in Mississippi, the schools did inspire similar educational initiatives within the Civil Rights Movement and helped proponents of liberatory educational reform articulate their own visions. Sociologist Doug McAdam reports that many leaders of the antiwar and women's liberation movements began their political transfor-

RADICAL TEACHER

The word "freedom" appears in white paint on a cross burned outside a Freedom School in Pascalouga, Mississippi.

mations as Freedom Summer volunteers. According to Freedom School teacher Liz Aaronsohn:

It may be true that everyone who participated for a significant period of time in the Mississippi Freedom Summer of 1964 was profoundly changed by that experience. I have met many white "veterans" of that time whose lives seem to me to have been redirected by what they learned in the South. I know that is so for me. My two years in Mississippi taught me first what being fired a few times, and then reading Paulo Freire, later confirmed: all education is political. Traditional education serves the status quo. You risk your job when you encourage students to find their own voices, to engage in dialogue with you and with each other around the issues that affect their lives; but you risk their lives if you do not.

The Freedom Schools do not provide a magic recipe for educating young people today. As a limited, counter-institutional experiment, they offered more favorable terrain

for innovation than large, bureaucratically bound school systems. They also derived optimistic energy from a movement which, despite bitter disappointments, still believed that political mobilization could transform a morally flawed society. Freedom Summer activists and students gained hope, dedication, and camaraderie from being part of a crusade for justice, qualities that have been hard to generate during the conservative swing of the past three decades. But if we respect the contextual differences which separate the 1960s from today, we can gain realistic insights into educational renewal from the Freedom School experience.

First, the Freedom Schools affirmed John Dewey's idea that effective teaching uses the student's own experiences to launch into intellectual engagement with the world. This engagement is best served not by the passive accumulation of inert bodies of knowledge, but by practical activities through which the students pursue purposes they find intrinsically meaningful. Freedom School teachers tried to listen more than lecture and to find active modes of learning which embodied genuine

social tasks — producing alternative papers, writing and rehearsing a drama for a conference, preparing a political platform, convincing disenfranchised citizens to vote. Carefully implemented, this type of instrumentalist approach can be more rigorous than traditional "banking" modes of teaching, because it is fueled by student curiosity and desire to acquire skills which have an impact on reality outside the classroom door. This pedagogical orientation can enliven school for all students but is especially helpful to those who lack the cultural capital necessary to endure and master the passive, teacher-centered modes of instruction which still dominate many secondary schools.

Second, the Freedom Schools impelled young volunteers to view learning as an activity which should transform the teacher as well as the student. Part of being appreciative of the skills, resources, and knowledge of the students and communities they encountered meant taking a critical look at the limitations of their own preconceptions and privileged backgrounds. Some volunteers started the summer with a sense of missionary superiority and arrogance they were not able to shed, but those more capable of self-reflection were able to learn in ways which changed their values and made them more capable teachers.

Ellen Lake's letter to her parents illustrated the new insights many volunteers gained:

Perhaps for the first time, the people who have always appeared

---

> The Freedom Schools impelled young volunteers to view learning as an activity which should transform the teacher as well as the student.

---

to me as servants are becoming people. They are dropping out of their roles and are individuals. One lady said to me today, "I guess there's nothing for poor folks but work; we can't rest till we die." I'd never before come upon such an attitude, expressed to me; and I think it's extremely important that now I have. It makes me so much more aware of people and their sufferings than I have ever before had to be.

Teachers, struggling to challenge their own preconceptions and values, became more capable of building on the cultural strengths and community heritages of their students.

Finally, the Freedom Schools suggest the powerful benefits of education that encourages quests for social justice. In discussing the sources of their own oppression and working together to enter the world of political struggle, Freedom School students gained tools for overcoming their own feelings of inferiority and hopelessness. In contrast, the moral environment of our contemporary schools is often dominated by competition for the private acquisition of prestige and affluence. Such schools generate despair in those the system and the teachers have designated as losers. They weaken the empathy of high achievers and inhibit the cultivation of a practical solidarity which would enrich all students. Even though the depoliticized and cynical ambience of today creates an unsympathetic environment for teaching youngsters civic responsibility, the Freedom School experience suggests that when schools are linked to struggles for social justice, they help students connect with their communities in ways that heighten their intellectual powers and ethical sensibilities. The potential of such education was suggested in 1964 by Freedom School student Verna Mannie:

Education is a medicine which takes hold. It is the whole set of changes produced in a person by learning. The difference between an educated person and an uneducated one is he knows how each little piece of knowledge is connected with every other piece. The world needs freedom, and the only way we can get it is through education. The ideas of the spirit of humanism are carried not in pamphlets or proclamations but in minds and hearts.... ∎

David Levine teaches social foundations at Otterbein College in Westerville, Ohio, and is a Rethinking Schools editor.

Notes

For a longer, fully referenced version of this article, please contact David Levine. He can be reached via e-mail at dlevine@otterbein.edu.

Here are some resources on the Freedom Schools, Freedom Summer, and the civil rights struggle in Mississippi:

Holt, L. *The Summer That Didn't End.* London: Heinemann, 1965.

Howe, F. "Mississippi Freedom Schools: The Politics of Education" in *Harvard Educational Review*, 35, (2), 1965, pp. 144-160.

McAdam, D. *Freedom Summer.* New York: Oxford University Press, 1988.

Payne, C.M. *I've Got the Light of Freedom: The Organizing Tradition and the Mississippi Freedom Struggle.* Berkeley: University of California Press, 1995.

Perlstein, D. "Teaching Freedom: SNCC and the Creation of the Mississippi Freedom Schools" in *History of Education Quarterly*, 30 (3), 1990, pp. 297-321.

Rothschild, M. A. "The Volunteers and the Freedom Schools: Education for Social Change in Mississippi" in *History of Education Quarterly*, Winter 1982, pp. 401-420.

Sutherland, E. (Ed.). *Letters from Mississippi.* New York: McGraw-Hill, 1965.

Improvs and Civil Rights

By Bill Bigelow

As David Levine points out in the preceding article, teachers in the Mississippi Free-dom Schools engaged students in improvisational role plays. Some of these were historical, some were developed by teachers and students in response to events that they took part in.

Our own teaching can benefit from similar pedagogy. We can invite students to "try on" the personas of people in different social circumstances, at different points in history, and to confront actual situations that these individuals faced. Such "first-person" activities allow students to think through the implications of choices made by real people.

Below are some improvisation possibilities drawn from Levine's article and other materials on the "Mississippi Freedom Summer." The more background students have on these issues, the better; the improvs could be incorporated into a broader unit on the Civil Rights Movement.

Divide students into small groups, have them decide who will play which part, and explore the general direction of the improv. Remind them that it is not a play, so they needn't fully script anything. Allow them to perform these for the class and then use the performances as the basis for discussion and writing. Afterwards, students could complete "interior monologues" from the standpoint of a character in one of the improvisations. (See the article "Promoting Social Imagination through Interior Monologues," pp. 110-111 in *Rethinking Our Classrooms, Volume 1*.)

> We can invite students to "try on" the personas of people in different social circumstances and at different points in history.

Improvs

1. In one town, a group of students organized a Student Action Group. Several students approach a number of teachers with a letter demanding that they be able to form clubs and a student government. They also ask teachers to take the lead in fighting for improved and integrated education. Students and teachers discuss the demands.

2. At one required school meeting, two students made civil rights announcements and speeches about racial equality. One student said that there was "a new day coming," and that teachers should help lead the way. Students applauded; teachers watched silently. Administrators sent every student a letter saying that anyone who participated in a demonstration would be suspended. A group of students meets to discuss how to respond.

3. One teacher at this school sympathizes with the students and agrees with the issues they raise. However, s/he worries that s/he will be fired if s/he says anything. The teacher discusses the school situation with her/his family.

4. A group of white students is at an orientation session in Oxford, Ohio, about to travel to Mississippi to register people to vote and to teach in a Freedom School. They have just learned that three civil rights workers — James Chaney, Andrew Goodman, and Mickey Schwerner, one African American and two whites — have disappeared in Neshoba County, Mississippi. They fear the three have been killed. At least one member of the group is thinking about not going to Mississippi. The students discuss the situation.

5. Some civil rights workers try to convince an older African-American man and woman to join the Mississippi Freedom Democratic Party.

6. A white plantation owner goes to an African-American family to warn them that if they attempt to register to vote, he will have them evicted from his property. The family is sharecropping on his land. ∎

Bill Bigelow (bbpdx@aol.com) teaches at Franklin High School in Portland, Oregon and is a Rethinking Schools editor.

Jorge the Church Janitor Finally Quits

No one asks
where I am from,
I must be
from the country of janitors,
I have always mopped this floor.
Honduras, you are a squatter's camp
outside the city
of their understanding.

No one can speak
my name,
I host the fiesta
of the bathroom,
stirring the toilet
like a punchbowl.
The Spanish music of my name
is lost
when the guests complain
about toilet paper.

What they say
must be true:
I am smart,
but I have a bad attitude.

No one knows
that I quit tonight,
maybe the mop
push on without me,
ng along the floor
crazy squid
tringy gray tentacles.
call it Jorge.

Por fin renuncia Jorge el Conserje de la iglesia

Nadie me pregunta
de dónde soy,
tendré que ser
de la patria de los conserjes,
siempre he trapeado este piso.
Honduras, eres un campamento
de desamparados
afuera de la ciudad
de su comprensión.

Nadie puede decir
mi nombre,
yo soy el amenizador
de la fiesta en el baño,
meneando el agua en el inodoro
como si fuera una ponchera.
La música española de mi nombre
se pierde
cuando los invitados se quejan
del papel higiénico.

Será verdad
lo que dicen:
soy listo,
pero tengo una mala actitud.

Nadie sabe
que esta noche renuncié al puesto,
quizá el trapero
seguirá adelante sin mí,
husmeando el piso
como un calamar enloquecido
con fibrosos tentáculos grises.
Lo llamarán Jorge.

— Martín Espada
(translated by Camilo Pérez-Bustillo
and the author)

The Poetry of Protest

By Linda Christensen

Tony tossed the Tootsie Roll paper over his shoulder as he entered my room. "I'm not your mama, Tony. Pick up that mess."

"Ms. Christensen, the custodians are paid to clean up. If I didn't leave anything on the floor, they'd lose their jobs."

Ruthie Griffin, the custodian, would disagree. But Ruthie, like Marlene Grieves, the cafeteria worker who serves them lunch, is largely invisible to students. Their brooms or spatulas might as well be held by robots. That's one reason why I teach the poetry of Martín Espada in my classroom.

Martín Espada's poetry is a weapon for justice in a society that oppresses people who aren't white, who don't speak English, whose work as janitors and migrant laborers is exploited. His poetry teaches students about the power of language — both Spanish and English — and he makes "invisible" workers visible. What Espada writes about Pablo Neruda's poetry is also true for his own: "[T]he poet demanded dignity for the commonplace subject, commanding respect for things and people normally denied such respect."

I want to introduce students to writers, like Espada, whose art speaks out against injustice, as well as give them the tools to write their own poems of empathy and outrage.

A while back, Espada refused Nike's offer to produce a poem for them for TV commercials they planned to air during the 1998 Winter Olympics. *The Progressive* magazine published Espada's letter to an ad agency listing the reasons he refused Nike's poet-for-hire offer:

I could reject your offer based on the fact that your deadline is ludicrous.... A poem is not a pop tart.

I could reject your offer based on the fact that, to make this offer to me in the first place, you must be totally and insultingly ignorant of my work as a poet, which strives to stand against all that you and your client represent. Whoever referred me to you did you a grave disservice.

I could reject your offer based on the fact that your client Nike has — through commercials such as these — outrageously manipulated the youth market, so that even low-income adolescents are compelled to buy products they do not need at prices they cannot afford.

Ultimately, however, I ⸁ rejecting your offer as a pr⸁ against the brutal labor pr⸁ of Nike. I will not associa⸁ with a company that e⸁ the well-documented ⸁ of workers in sweat⸁

Espada's public⸁ yet-another-artis⸁ enough to pr⸁ dents. In m⸁ highlight writ⸁ at the service of ⸁ its. Espada is right: ⸁

ignorant of his work, but my students shouldn't be.

I use Espada's poetry, in English and Spanish, to teach students how to use metaphors and how to write ⸁ "persona poem," but I also ⸁ Espada's poetry because he s⸁ how to make visible the w⸁ those who toil in physical la⸁

In the first volume of ⸁ *Our Classrooms*, the ⸁ about the need to gr⸁ ing in our students'⸁ dents to "talk ba⸁ pose essential q⸁ tural, anti-raci⸁ ticipatory, j⸁ cally rigor⸁ tive: "A⸁ must s⸁ thos⸁ m⸁ T⸁

did he make his letter public?

2. Ask students to read the poem in both languages. (This validates students who speak Spanish and also locates writing in the broader linguistic world. I encourage students who speak more than one language to write in either or both languages.)

3. Discuss the poem: Who is the narrator? How do people treat Jorge? What evidence in the poem tells us that? What does he compare the mop to? What does Espada want us to know about Jorge? How do we learn that?

4. After reading and discussing, return to Espada's letter. He wrote, "I could reject your offer based on the fact that you must be totally and insultingly ignorant of my work as a poet, which strives to stand against all that you and your client represent." Ask students to identify evidence in this poem that might indicate why Espada would turn down Nike's money.

5. Ask students to make a list of "invisible workers" they know whom they could make visible: for example, hotel maids, strawberry harvesters, the seamstress who sewed their shirt or blouse. A few students might share their lists to help stumped classmates find a topic. (For younger students, I sometimes begin by asking them to write a paragraph or two about the worker or situation. Later, they can underline details and language to arrange into a poem.)

6. Direct students to write for 15 to 20 minutes. I demand silence, so we can all write, but I do allow students to move to more comfortable places in the room.

7. Then we share. I tell students to consider their classmates as teachers and to learn techniques from each other that make powerful writing. So while every student reads, I expect them to listen and take notes on what they like in the piece — specifically, the incident/story, the use of metaphor, the illumination of injus-tice or a person who is invisible, the use of language, a particular line. I also speak about the importance of positive feedback: We want people to keep writing. If we criticized them instead of praising them, they might not want to write or share again.

We live in a society where it appears that everything is for sale — including movements for social justice. Students need stories about people who work for change, people who refuse to allow their work to be commodified. They need models of people whose work is animated by social justice. They need to know about poets like Martín Espada. ∎

Linda Christensen is Language Arts Coordinator for the Portland, Oregon public schools and is a Rethinking Schools editor. This article is adapted from her book Reading, Writing, and Rising Up: Teaching About Social Justice and the Power of the Written Word, *available from Rethinking Schools.*

A Bill of Rights for Girls

By Mary Blalock

What's Wrong with Girls: If you look around at our world, it is not hard to find something that tries to tell you that as a girl, something is wrong with you. Girls are always told there's something wrong with them. TV and magazines seem to say that girls aren't any good unless they're thin and beautiful. It's hard to feel good about ourselves with these demands around us.

Recent studies show how adolescent boys differ from adolescent girls. They found that around the age of eleven (when puberty usually hits) girls begin feeling more insecure. Two thousand six hundred girls were asked how many of them agreed with the statement: "I'm happy with the way I am." In elementary school 60% of the girls agreed, but only 29% of the high school girls did. While boys are getting more confident, a lot of girls begin feeling bad about themselves and end up making bad choices.

I wish that I had known about this when I was younger, but I had to go through a lot before getting on the right track again. There are a lot of things I wish I could have learned before. So I've created a list of rights girls deserve to help you on your way to womanhood with confidence. There's already been a woman's movement, now it's time for girls to get some respect.

The Right to Like Yourself. If you get into something that interests you, it helps you feel good about yourself. I like to draw and write, so when I'm feeling bad, I go into my room and draw a picture. There are lots of things that you can get involved in that can become a part of you. It will help you create a personality that you can be proud of.

Also think of things that you like and things that gross you out. What foods are yummy? What music is cool to you? What clothes do you like to wear? All this becomes part of you. Don't be ashamed if other people don't like your taste, or it isn't "cool." Like things because you like them, not because everyone else does. A lot of people like things because they have a name brand. All these names say is that it was expensive. There's nothing wrong with buying something just because you like it, not because it will impress other people.

The Right to Like Your Body. This is a big subject with girls. It's almost impossible to avoid all those ads that try to tell us we need to be pencil thin and look like Cindy Crawford if we want to like ourselves. They are totally wrong! A woman's body is supposed to have fat on it so it can make babies, produce the right hormones, and just work right. The models in these ads have little girl bodies, even though they're women. It's rare for females past puberty to look like this, and it's not healthy to try. It's good for you to realize that while these models are supposedly what we want to be, there are all different ways that people can look and they can all be okay. Take a look around you and compare what you see to what the media shows. You'll find that the world has a lot of different ways people can be beautiful.

The Right to Have Your Cake and Eat It Too. Because of the idea that we're supposed to be skinny, there are a lot of girls dieting and getting involved in eating disorders. An eating disorder is when someone starts looking at food not only as just something we need, and something that tastes good, but as something bad. Though dieting is popular, I say, "No way!" Food is something we all need so we can live and function like a normal person. When we start dieting, we look at food in a bad way. I know from experience because when I started dieting, I got an eating disorder, lost too much weight, and had to go to the hospital. It wasn't fun and I missed out on a lot of things. When you worry about dieting, you don't have time for fun. Dieting can even cause you to want food more. Many people who try to diet end up getting

hungry or craving sweets, and they eat more than they would have usually. My advice to you is: Accept your body the way it is and accept food as necessary. Don't try to diet, no matter what people say.

The Right to Get Angry. I'm not saying that you should yell at people all the time, or get in fights, but there's nothing wrong with just getting mad. Usually when you feel this way, it's for a good reason and it's a signal that something isn't right. I'm sure a lot of people have told you, "Don't get mad," or "Nice girls don't get mad," when you were really angry and you couldn't stop. But it's okay to get mad as long as you use words and express what you feel in a way that won't hurt anyone. It's okay to tell someone you're angry at them and try to work it out. If you just keep it to yourself, nothing will get resolved and you'll end up feeling bad. Don't turn the anger in on yourself either. That makes you feel even worse.

The Right to Feel Protected. When we are little, we don't have to look out for ourselves, because our parents do the job. But as we grow older we need to protect ourselves from dangerous things. Sometimes things may make you feel scared and weak. If someone is bothering you, it's good to know how to defend yourself. Community centers offer classes in self-defense and martial arts. These classes teach you how to feel strong and fight back if someone is trying to hurt you. Find someone you can talk to about things that don't seem right and make sure they get worked out. It's hard to feel confident if you don't feel safe.

The Right to Develop Your Brain. Don't be a stupid-head; make sure you keep getting smarter. Sometimes we're afraid people will think we're nerds if we know a lot of stuff. There's nothing wrong with being smart; it makes you a more interesting person. Don't accept things that people tell you — think about *your* opinion about what you hear. Read lots of books instead of watching TV. It's better for your

brain and can be a lot cooler than some of the boring shows and commercials. You don't have to be a dweeb, just don't be dull when it comes to your brain. Tests and grades have nothing to do with how smart you are. I'm talking about learning how things work and how life works. You may not be very good in school, but that doesn't mean you're not smart in other ways.

The Right to Be Yourself Around Boys. It's fun to flirt and get into relationships, but there's a lot of confusing things that go along with it. Just be sure that you don't get too dependent on boys to tell you that you're a good person. Never change yourself just so a guy will like you. If you change yourself, then they won't be liking the real you, only the show you put on. It's better to wait for a guy who will like you for who you are than to stay with one who doesn't. It's important to feel good about yourself, even if you don't have a boyfriend. Besides, boys aren't the only thing in the world, and I'm sure you've heard the expression, "There's other fish in the sea."

The Right to Your Own Role Models. When we grow up, we get all these ideas about what a woman should be like. These aren't always positive ideas, so sometimes we have to find new places to show us what a woman is. Look around for women whom you admire and ask them about their lives, how they became who they are. Take parts that you like about them and use them to create who you want to be. Don't try and be them; be yourself and walk along their paths. ■

Mary Blalock was a senior at Jefferson High School in Portland, Oregon when she wrote this for Linda Christensen's Contemporary Literature and Society class. Students were assigned to create a proposal for something they saw as a problem at school. Blalock created this as a pamphlet to distribute to middle-school girls.

The Trial

How one teacher explores issues of homelessness

By Kate Lyman

"Hey, what would you do?" Brandon asked. "They are innocent. Their mom was only trying to find a safe place for the family to sleep for the night. Hey, what would you do if you was homeless?"

Brandon was passionate in his plea to his fellow jury members — part of a mock jury trial that culminated a two-month unit on shelter. The students in my 2nd/3rd grade classroom were role-playing the parts of the judge, lawyers, bailiffs, witnesses, and jury members in a trial of a homeless family arrested for vagrancy.

I had done mock trials with my students before, but last year there was a new tone of urgency in the voices of Brandon and the other jurors.

Brandon was one of 7 students in my class (out of 24) who had been in and out of shelters and/or homes of friends and relatives while his family's desperate search for housing continued. Some 75% of my students last year were at the poverty level, as defined by qualifying for free or reduced-price lunch. Many of their families, if not homeless, were just a missed paycheck away. Even the more financially secure students had talked about seeing homeless people in the streets of Madison, Milwaukee, or Chicago. During the year, in fact, students had encountered a homeless man sleeping in the underground bypass that crosses under the highway on the way to our school.

Developing the Unit

Our shelter unit began with a discussion of basic animal and human needs. We then explored concepts commonly studied in the primary grades: the variety and ways that wild animals

> I wanted to support the experiences of the students who had been homeless, as well as to promote empathy and compassion among the others.

find or create shelter, and the proper care of domesticated animals. We learned about the plight of abandoned or abused animals in our city and raised money to sponsor a "crate" at the local Humane Society. Even before we moved away from a focus on animals, my students' empathy with the homeless dogs and cats that we sponsored or read about indicated to me that they were personally invested in the topic.

When we did our initial activity of talking about what the kids already knew about homelessness and drawing a visual "web" that listed and linked their knowledge, just about everyone contributed.

"I saw a homeless person when I was coming to school with my mom," Stephanie said. "She had a sign that said, 'No job, no food.' I asked my

mom if I could give her a dollar from my allowance."

Jamel, who was living in a foster home, said he became homeless when neither his mom nor dad could take care of him. Robert related that his family had lived in a city shelter before moving to the school's neighborhood.

Students also talked about difficulties of life on the streets: getting food, keeping clean, being safe, and finding protection from threatening weather. They spoke with indignation about ways that people could become homeless. Typical comments were, "Landlords kick you out for no good reason," or, "Your boss doesn't like you and he fires you. Then you can't pay the rent." One student shared that her mother had become homeless as a child when her family's house had burned down.

I looked at the student-generated "web" and pondered how to go on. Interest was high. The children had a lot of knowledge. And students like Jamel and Robert, who were as often shooting rubber bands as raising their hands to volunteer information, had been leaders in the discussion.

I was concerned, however, about the very thing that made this topic so compelling — we weren't talking about a distant "other" such as endangered Rainforest animals or the heroic travelers on the Underground Railroad. We were talking about the students and their families. I knew that I had to be very careful not to create a dichotomy of "us" (the lucky ones who have housing) vs. "them" (those homeless people). I wanted to support the experiences of the students who had been homeless, as well as to promote empathy and compassion among the others. I wanted to encourage all the students

the class, seized the opportunity to be the tour guide. Our official guide quickly stepped back as Robert showed the class the laundry room, explained the rules of the dining and TV areas, and showed us the drawers where he had kept his toys. Robert's way of prefacing his comments with, "Hey, guys, you'd like this," or, "But this ain't so good," gave the students a balanced view of life in a shelter.

The Trial

After the visit to the Salvation Army came the culmination of the unit — the mock trial. My partner, a legal services attorney, came to explain what an advocate does and to share work he has done in protecting the rights of the homeless. After straightening out some terms and clarifying how our legal system works (many students had knowledge from television as well as experience in court), I asked why a homeless family might need legal representation. One student who had paid close attention to a presentation about the rules governing our city's shelter system had a suggestion.

"They might need a lawyer because their 30 days are up at the shelter," Melanie said. "They might have no place to go, and what if they had a sick kid and didn't want to be out on the streets?"

I used Melanie's idea, along with the incident that had occurred the previous year, to create the scenario for the trial. I asked if any students remembered encountering the homeless person in the tunnel. Several did. For the sake of the drama, we altered the story so that it was about a family who had reached their 30-day limit, and then were arrested for vagrancy when found sleeping in the tunnel.

The students were very excited to be able to play out a "real trial." However, we reminded them that although their role play would have aspects of a real trial, the legal system was much more complicated than we could explain in a short time.

Students volunteered to take parts in the role play and with some prompting carried out the drama. The "judge,"

to speak up about issues generated by the topic.

I decided to use a book on the United Nations' Children's Bill of Rights to spark a discussion on basic human rights. Then I planned to use books with photos, drawings, stories, and poetry by homeless children to facilitate discussions and writing. I also used our district's Transitional Education Program to find speakers and books written by homeless children in our district. Most of the fictional stories that I selected for use were written from the point of view of the homeless character; I wanted to avoid books that conveyed a "they need our

help" attitude. (See the Resources list on p. 143).

The students responded to the stories, poems, and guest speakers with their own writing. After reading a poem in an anthology that began "If I were President ...," students wrote their own versions. Some students decided to address their concerns directly to the President.

We also visited a Salvation Army shelter — a trip that immediately took on a personal note when Keisha saw her aunt waiting in the lobby. Then Robert, who had been living at the shelter before coming to our school and who was always ready to take charge of played by a student who often has to be reminded to listen to others, took every opportunity to pound the gavel (a hammer) and demand, "Order in the court!" The defense and prosecuting attorneys questioned the witnesses. After the closing statements, the trial participants went out for recess, leaving the jury members in the classroom.

The Jury Deliberation

Turning their chairs — placed in double rows of six — to face each other, the members of the jury solemnly began their task. Jeremy, the foreperson, took charge and asked for initial verdicts.

"The homeless people are guilty — no!" said Keisha, who was passionate about her ideas, but couldn't always find the right words to express herself. "What's that word that means they didn't do it? Yeah, that's right, innocent!"

Ten others proceeded with "innocent" verdicts. Melanie, a sly smile revealing her willingness to stand out on her own, asserted, "Guilty!"

"But Melanie, what if they are thrown into jail?" asked Brandon, a quiet, thoughtful boy. "The whole family will be sleeping on hard, cold floors. And they might get beaten up."

"Yeah," agreed Greg. "I know about that. My dad got beaten up in jail."

"Give them a chance," said Jamie, a student whose voice is rarely heard in group discussions, but whose family I know had been homeless for months. "They just need a roof over their heads."

"What was they supposed to do?" agreed Tasha. "They wasn't hurting nobody. They was just minding they own business."

Silent, with arms crossed against her chest, Melanie held her ground. "Still guilty," was all she said.

Greg, normally quiet and unassertive in class, became vehement: "You've got to have a good reason. You can't just do this to this family. What did they do to you?"

Then, two other students joined in

on the guilty charge, saying that the homeless family was scaring the kids walking to school.

"What?" said Brandon, now shouting, "Did they have weapons — a knife or anything? Did they try to hurt the kids? They were just taking care of themselves."

After several more minutes of debate, Jeremy took a final vote: Eleven said "innocent" and only one (still Melanie) voted "guilty."

As the rest of the class filed in from recess, the judge took his seat. "Order in the court," he demanded, pounding the hammer on his desk. The jury's foreperson announced the verdict: 11-1, "not guilty." The class cheered.

Epilogue

The trial was over, but not the tribulations of the families in my class. Some found housing; for one family of seven, it amounted to one room in a transitional housing shelter. The family of Keisha, who was finally beginning to make some progress in school after two years of absenteeism and "attitude problems," had been evicted from their apartment and was living in the YWCA. Her family joined the ranks of the homeless, moving back and forth from the YWCA to relatives' apartments, finally to transitional housing. The district paid for Keisha to be taxied to our school for 30 days; then, still without permanent housing, she was forced to bid our school — the only place of permanency for her over the last month — a tearful farewell. Brandon also moved to another school, his fifth within the last two years.

Several months ago I heard a voice call out my name in the parking lot of a shopping mall. I looked around, but before I could locate the voice, a body bounded into my arms.

"Keisha! How have you been doing?" I asked as we hugged.

Keisha said she was now living

in an apartment and going to another new school. "I miss you," she said, still hanging on to me. "I miss the class."

I missed her, too, and didn't even let myself wonder about how many steps backwards she had taken academically and behaviorally in her journey from school to school. I could only hope that our trial and related activities had removed some of the stigma of being homeless, and that our classroom had become a place where the homeless were not viewed as criminals and where housing was seen as a basic right. ■

Kate Lyman teaches in Madison, Wisconsin. She can be reached via e-mail at clyman@madison.k12.wi.us. The names of the children in this article were changed.

RICK REINHARD

Resources on Homelessness

Nonfiction

A Children's Chorus: Celebrating the 30th Anniversary of the Universal Declaration of the Rights of the Child, presentation and illustrations by Lemniscaat b.v. Rotterdaam. New York: E. P. Dutton, 1989.

Home: A Collaboration of Thirty Distinguished Authors and Illustrators of Children's Books to Aid the Homeless, by Michael J. Rosen (Ed.). New York: HarperCollins, 1992.

Home Is Where We Live: Life in a Shelter through a Young Girl's Eyes, by Kimiko, photographs by B. L. Groth. Chicago: Cornerstone, 1995.

Lives Turned Upside Down: Homeless Children in Their Own Words and Photographs, by Jim Hubbard. New York: Simon and Shuster Books for Young Readers, 1996.

No Place to Be: Voices of Homeless Children, by Judith Berck. New York: Houghton Mifflin, 1992.

Poems, Pictures, and Other Great Stuff: A Collection of Poetry and Artwork, by Homeless Children and Youth, Homeless Children and Families Program. Salem-Keizer Public Schools. Salem, Oregon, 1996.

Shooting Back: A Photographic View of Life by Homeless Children, by Jim Hubbard. New York: Chronicle Books, 1991.

Fiction

A Chance to Grow, by E. Sandy Powell. Minneapolis: Carol Rhoda Books: 1992.

Fly Away Home, by Eve Bunting. New York: Clarion Books, 1991.

The Homeless Hibernating Bear, by Kids Livin' Life (a group of homeless, post-homeless and low-income children changing the images of homelessness and of poverty). Placerville, CA: Gold Leaf Press, 1993.

A Safe Place, by Maxine Trotter. Morton Grove, IL: Albet Whitman, 1997.

Sam and the Moon Queen, by Alison Cragin Herzig and Jane Lawrence Mali. New York: Clarion Books, 1990.

Sidewalk Story, by Sharon Bell Mathis. New York: Puffin Books, 1971.

Someplace to Go, by Maria Testa. Morton Grove, Illinois: Albert Whitman and Co., 1996.

Space Travellers, by Margaret Wild. New York: Scholastic, 1994.

This Home We Have Made/ Esta Casa Que Hemos Hecho, by Anna Hammond and Joe Matunis. New York: Crown Publishers, 1993.

Uncle Willie and the Soup Kitchen, by Dyanne Disalvo-Ryan. New York: Morrow Junior Books, 1991.

Way Home, by Libby Hathorn. New York: Crown Publishers, Inc., 1994.

Videos

Fly Away Home. A Reading Rainbow Video, 1996.

Kalinga. Unicef Stories for Kids. New York: PDR Productions, 1993.

Facts on Homelessness

• Families with children are the fastest growing segment of the homeless.

• Over 20 million people were homeless in the United States in 1995. In that year alone, the demand for shelter increased by 11%.

• The homeless population is diverse: 25-40% work; 37% are families with children; 25% are children; 30% are veterans; 25-30% are mentally disabled; 40% are drug or alcohol dependent.

• In 1997, 27% of all requests for emergency shelter went unmet due to a lack of resources, according to a recent study of 29 U.S. cities. A review of homelessness in 50 cities found that in virtually every city, the official estimated number of homeless people greatly exceeded the number of emergency shelter and transitional housing spaces.

• Homelessness severely impacts the health and well-being of all family members. Compared with other poor children, homeless children experience worse health; more developmental delays; more anxiety, depression and behavioral problems; and lower educational achievement.

Sources: National Law Center on Homelessness and Poverty (www.nlchp.org), and the National Coalition for the Homeless, Web Page Fact Sheets, May 1998 (online at www.nationalhomeless.org).

Students Blow the Whistle On Toxic Oil Contamination

By Larry Miller and Danah Opland-Dobs

"**M**r. Miller, Mr. Miller, you've got to see what we've found!" demanded Carl and Ken. The two students rushed into class, eager to share their findings from an assignment in civics class to investigate areas named in a local environmental group's listing of toxic sites. They continued their haranguing until several teachers agreed to visit what Carl and Ken described as "a real mess."

When we got to the site, five blocks away from our school, it was clear that Carl and Ken were not exaggerating. Before us was a field that literally stunk, covered with pools of ooze. What was worse, the contamination had spread to an adjacent playground. We didn't have to look far to find the likely source of the ooze: the Moore Oil Company, whose building overshadowed the field.

Thus began a lesson in environmental activism that, before it was over, would have students videotaping toxic sites, collecting soil samples, preparing presentations for parents, engaging in discussions with the president of the Moore Oil Company, addressing hearings before the School Board, and meeting with a newspaper reporter who helped the students blow the whistle on a community health hazard.

Unlike some whistle-blowing incidents, this one had a happy ending. The students' activism prompted an agreement on a timetable for the cleanup, which the students continue to monitor. Equally important, from our perspective as teachers, the students learned invaluable lessons in how civics involves far more than simply memorizing facts about the governmental separation of powers.

Leading Up to the Discovery

The civics class was part of the Career Certificate Program at Custer High School in Milwaukee, an interdisciplinary school-to-work program that also involved English, science, math, and technical classes.

In recent years teachers in the program have used the environment as a beginning theme, in part because there is an almost universal interest among freshmen in the topic. In previous years the environmental unit ended with field trips to a nature center, a sewage processing plant, and a landfill. This particular year, based on student input, we focused on issues closer to home. For example, students took part in science labs and field trips that included testing the water quality of a local creek in the Milwaukee River basin for turbidity, fungi growth, organism population, and oxygen content.

In English classes, students corresponded with national and local environmental groups. They studied articles on citizen activism on environmental issues, and then gave group presentations. The main lesson they learned was that they could make a difference. In civics classes, students contrasted different perspectives on environmental issues. For example, students compared Exxon's view of the 1989 Alaska oil spill cleanup with the views of environmentalists.

The specific topic that led to discovering the pools of ooze involved an interdisciplinary look at the concept of density. This concept is traditionally studied in physical science, and students compare mass and volume to distinguish different materials. Our students, likewise, did this in Jill Crowder's class. And more. In David Caruso's algebra class, they mapped students' homes and figured out the density ratio of students per block within a mile of Custer. In Miller's civics classes, they studied the density of toxic sites in Milwaukee County, using an environmental map of 400 sites developed by the local group Mobilization for Survival. The overall goal, for all the teachers, was to show students the complexity of a concept such as density, and show how it might be applied to different situations.

In Miller's class, students studied the issue of toxic waste for about a month before they were given the assignment to investigate sites near their homes. (Every one of the 120 students in the program lived within eight blocks of an identified site.) Most of the sites didn't have a lot that could be observed: they consisted of underground storage tanks or hidden contamination. Carl and Ken made their find when scouting an area that was near a shortcut they took to school every day.

Looking for Answers

After that initial visit with Carl and Ken, we organized a formal field

Students and staff at Custer High School in Milwaukee helped expose a toxic mess in their neighborhood.

LARRY MILLER

trip with eight students. We video-taped the site, snapped photographs to be developed by the school camera club, and took samples of the soil and liquid ooze. Back at school, students edited the video, developed the photographs, and tested our samples.

Next we invited in a representative of the Wisconsin Department of Natural Resources. Scott Ferguson, a hydrogeologist, gave presentations to all 120 of our students on the history of Moore Oil and problems with getting companies to comply with governmental cleanup regulations. He also brought samples of the groundwater from the site, explaining that toxins like benzene, vinyl chloride, and cadmium were abundant in the groundwater. Always curious, our students asked how long it would take for the groundwater to clean itself naturally. The kids were shocked at Ferguson's reply: Three generations.

It wasn't just the time frame that bothered the students. This park was in the neighborhood where many Custer students live, and they said that their nephews, nieces, brothers, sisters, and cousins played at the park. The health hazard was directly affecting them and they made it clear they wanted to take action.

Through our investigation we learned that the playground was owned by the Milwaukee Public Schools. While the District had been aware of the problem — to the extent that it had prohibited baseball games from being played in the park — it had been slow to push for a cleanup. Following a brainstorming session, students decided we should educate parents and students living in the area, go to the media to talk about our concerns, and ask the School Board about their plan to get the park cleaned up. In hindsight, we realized that we made a mistake in not immediately contacting the management of Moore Oil, in the interest of fairness, to get their version of events.

At the next parent-teacher organi-zation meeting, Opland-Dobs accompanied two students, Malicka Hunt and Ken Post, who gave a presentation on the oil spill. Two days later, at parent-teacher conferences, students wrote a leaflet asking parents to stop by a display where they showed a 3-minute videotape of the toxic site. One couple who stopped by lived across the street from the spill. They could not thank the students enough for pursuing the issue.

Students were concerned that it was taking so long to start the cleanup at the site. To pressure all the parties involved, they decided to contact the media. The result was a front-page article in the metro news section of *The Milwaukee Journal* entitled, "Ooze and ahhs: Students find oil at playground." The students also told the reporter, Jack Norman, how the experience had been an eye-opener. "I didn't know anything about these types of experiences until I got involved in this program," said Samantha Piggee. Darius Bunch

Garbage

Words by Bill Steele, Mike Agranoff and Pete Seeger.

Mister Thompson calls the waiter,
orders steak and baked potatoes,
but he leaves the bone and gristle
and he never eats the skin.
The busboy comes and takes it,
with a cough, contaminates it
and puts it in a can
with coffee grounds and sardine tins.
And the truck comes by on Friday
and carts it all away,
a thousand trucks just like it
are converging on the bay, oh

Garbage! (garbage, garbage, garbage) Garbage!
We're filling up the seas with garbage.
(garbage, garbage, garbage)
What will we do
when there's no place left to put all the garbage?
(garbage, garbage, garbage)

Mister Thompson starts his Cadillac,
winds it down the freeway track,
leaving friends and neighbors in a hydrocarbon haze.
He's joined by lots of smaller cars
all sending gases to the stars,
there to form a seething cloud
that hangs for thirty days.
And the sun licks down into it
with an ultraviolet tongue,
turns it into smog,
then it settles in our lungs, oh

Garbage! (garbage, garbage, garbage) Garbage!
We're filling up the sky with garbage.
(garbage, garbage, garbage)
What will we do
when there's nothing left to breathe but garbage? ·
(garbage, garbage, garbage)

Getting home and taking off his shoes,
he settles with the evening news
while the kids do their homework
with the TV in one ear.
(garbage, garbage, garbage)
While Superman for the thousandth time
sells talking dolls and conquers crime,
dutifully they learn the date-of-birth of Paul Revere.
In the papers there's a piece
about the Mayor's middle name

He gets it read in time
to watch the all-Star bingo game, oh

Garbage! (garbage, garbage, garbage) Garbage!
We're filling up our minds with garbage
(garbage, garbage, garbage)

What will we do when there's nothing left to read
and there's nothing left to need
and there's nothing left to watch
and there's nothing left to touch
and there's nothing left to walk upon,
nothing left to talk upon,
nothing left to see,
and nothing left to be
but Garbage? (garbage, garbage, garbage)

In Mister Thompson's factory
they're making plastic Christmas trees
complete with silver tinsel and a geodesic stand.
The plastic's mixed in giant vats
from some conglomeration that's
been piped from deep within the earth
or strip-mined from the land.
And if you question anything
they say, "Why don't you see?
It's absolutely needed for the economy," oh

Garbage! (garbage, garbage garbage)
Garbage! (garbage, garbage garbage)

Their stocks and their bonds all garbage.
What will they do
when their system goes to smash,
there's no value to their cash,
there's no money to be made,
but there's a world to be repaid?
Their kids will read in history books
about financiers and other crooks
and feudalism and slavery
and Nukes and all their knavery.
To history's dustbin they're consigned
along with many other kinds of
Garbage. (garbage, garbage, garbage)

(This song is available on the album *Pete* by Pete Seeger and Friends, Living Music Records, 1996.)

added: "Changes need to be made in our communities, and we are learning that we can do something about them."

Five days before the article was published, Norman had contacted the president of Moore Oil, Scott Haag, to ask for his view on our students' work. Haag, who was unaware of the students' investigation, was outraged. He immediately came to Custer and met not only with three teachers, but also the principal. Haag was concerned that we were not fulfilling our "educational duty" by talking with him before going to the press. We acknowledged that it would have been better to talk with him first, and arranged a more extensive meeting for the following week.

Teachers and seven students went to the meeting with Moore Oil. Haag made a presentation, as did the hydrogeologist representing the company Haag had hired to clean up the spill. The students took detailed notes on the hydrogeologist's explanation of cleanup plans and asked many questions. We were proud of our students and their ability to debate business-savvy adults. The students were articulate and bold, and asked even tougher questions than we did. One student, Morgan Lampkin, demanded

of Haag: "How could you know about the spill for so many years without making any real steps to clean it up?" As a result of her questioning it became clear that the company had known for years of the problem but no action had been taken on cleaning up the mess due to legal wrangling over responsibility.

Going to the School Board

The next step in our campaign involved the School Board and a request to meet with the committee that oversaw district facilities. As the meeting approached, teachers and students alike got nervous. What exactly would we say to the committee? What would be our demand?

At the meeting, one student, Darius Bunch, made it clear he was skeptical that the bureaucracy would take action before winter, when freezing weather would make the cleanup impossible. School Board members responded that the cleanup would start immediately. We later learned that city of Milwaukee officials, Moore Oil and the School Board had come to an agreement that day on the timetable for a clean-up. It was clear that action had been taken because of our pressure. The students

were proud: because of us the cleanup was starting. We had helped cut through the red tape.

Moore Oil Company ended up paying the state of Wisconsin $133,000 in penalties for violating wastewater and hazardous waste laws at its two sites in the Milwaukee area.

The company that did the cleanup, the U.S. Environmental Corporation, met with students to keep them informed of the progress of the cleanup. We took another field trip as the cleanup continued into the spring.

Some students involved in the project started an environmental club at school, became involved in a recycling project, worked on a science project doing cleanup of Milwaukee's streams, and helped rebuild a greenhouse at the school.

The most important lesson for the students, however, was that they saw they could make a change. They saw the connection between school and their lives and became excited about what they were being taught. ■

Larry Miller teaches social studies at Metropolitan High School in Milwaukee, Wisconsin and is a Rethinking Schools editor. Danah Opland-Dobs is an English teacher at Metropolitan High School.

Toxics/Environmental Justice Bibliography

Books

Shiva, Vandana (Ed.). *Close to Home: Women Reconnect Ecology, Health, and Development Worldwide.* Philadelphia: New Society Publishers, 1994. $12.95 paperback. Twelve activist essays, mostly by Asian women around the world working to make connections between women's health and environmental well-being. Includes reflections on projects in Thailand, the Philippines, and Bhopal, India.

Schwab, Jim. *Deeper Shades of Green: The Rise of Blue-Collar and Minority Environmentalism in America.* San Francisco: Sierra Club Books, 1994. 479 pp. $30 paperback. Documents the struggles of low-income and minority community activists to save their neighborhoods and their health through grassroots environmental action.

Bullard, Robert D. (Ed.) *Confronting Environmental Racism: Voices from the Grassroots.* Boston: South End Press, 1993. 260 pp. $16 paperback. An introduction to the breadth of concerns in the environmental justice framework: toxic sites in low-income neighborhoods, Chicano land rights, migrant workers' occupational hazards, and the export of toxics to the Third World.

Gedicks, Al. *The New Resource Wars: Native and Environmental Struggles Against Multinational Corporations.* Boston: South End Press, 1993. 270 pp. $15 paperback. A critical documentation of Native resistance to corporate takeover of natural resources on Native lands. Particular focus on the mining struggles in Wisconsin.

McIvor, Kirsten (translator). *Exposure: Victims of Radiation Speak Out.* Kodansha International, 1992. 327 pp. Victims of the effects of the nuclear power industry speak out. Articles cover the American Southwest, Three Mile Island, Chernobyl, Polynesia, India, Malaysia, Namibia, and other sites of nuclear mining, testing, production, and accidents.

Moyers, Bill. *Global Dumping Ground: The International Traffic in Hazardous Waste*, with the Center for Investigative Reporting. Washington, DC: Seven Locks, 1990. 152 pp. $11.95 paperback. An engaging companion volume to the *Frontline* documentary of the same name, this book introduces the global toxics trade in lay terms. Includes resources and photographs.

General Reference

Lean, Geoffery, Hinrichsen, Don, and Markham, Adam. *Atlas of the Environment.* New York: Prentice Hall, 1990. 192 pp. More than 200 full-color maps and diagrams providing at-a-glance information on most major environmental problems, including disappearing forests, acid rain, climate change, pollution, and desertification.

Pick, Maritza. *How to Save Your Neighborhood, City, or Town: The Sierra Club Guide to Community Organizing.* San Francisco: Sierra Club Books, 1993. 214 pp. $12 paperback. Practical guide on how to organize your community to solve environmental problems, including how to use the media, do fundraising, and run public information and political campaigns.

Periodical

Green Teacher Magazine
This bimonthly Canadian magazine focuses on issues of environmental and global education. It provides classroom-ready materials for teachers, theoretical articles about teaching and the environment, and reviews of English and French language resources. Subscriptions are $27 (Canadian). Make checks payable to Green Teacher, 95 Robert St., Toronto, Canada M5S 2K5. www.greenteacher.com

Sources for Videos

The Video Project offers 45 environmental videos in its "Eco-Video Collection for Schools" for students in grades 1 through 12. The videos cover issues of wildlife conservation, recycling, nuclear power, food, toxic waste, population growth, and others, and are reasonably priced. Discounts are available on multiple purchases. Environmental films for other age groups are offered as well. Contact The Video Project, P.O. Box 411376, San Francisco, CA 94141-1376. 800-475-2638. www.videoproject.com

Bullfrog Films offers hundreds of environmental videos, films, and videodiscs for all ages. Discounts on rentals and purchases are available for teachers and community groups. Call them at Bullfrog Films, P.O. Box 149, Oley, PA 19547. 800-543-3764. www.bullfrogfilms.com

Umbrella Organizations for Environmental Education

North American Association for Environmental Education (NAAEE), 2000 P Street NW, Suite 540, Washington, DC 20036. 202-419-0412. www.naaee.org For U.S., Canadian, and Mexican teachers and environmental educators.

Canadian Network for Environmental Education and Communication (EECOM), 336 Rosedale Ave., Winnepeg, MB R3L 1L8. 204-221-2007. www.eecom.org ∎

AIDS — "You Can Die from It"

Teaching young children about a difficult subject

By Kate Lyman

"This is poison ivy," indicated our guide on a walk through a nature preserve. "Now, don't touch it. It can give you a painful, itchy rash if it brushes against your skin."

"Wait a minute," interrupted Henry, a new second grader in my class. "You can get AIDS from it, right?"

This year, as in the previous several years of teaching various grade levels from kindergarten through third grade, I had heard the topic of AIDS brought up with increasing frequency. "OOOO, don't let her kiss you!" I would hear on the playground, "You'll get AIDS!" At sharing time, I'd hear about television programs that children had seen about AIDS. Occasionally, a child or a parent would tell me that a relative or friend of the family was in the hospital with AIDS-related symptoms. By first grade, most children at our school had heard about AIDS, whether from the "streets," the media, or their families. When questions arose in the classroom, I would deal with them as with any "controversial" issue, by responding in an open, direct manner, and then returning to the lesson at hand.

I had recently decided to use AIDS Awareness Week as an opportunity to expand the bits and pieces of discussions into a unit on AIDS. I was hoping not only to clear up misconceptions about AIDS and to raise the level of awareness in my combined first/second grade classroom, but also to enhance students' learning in all areas by focusing on a topic of high interest and relevance to their lives.

The unit on birth and reproduction that I had done with half the class the year before had provided something of a knowledge base, as well as a precedent for an AIDS unit. I also felt assured that the second graders, whom I'd had the year before, could be counted on to hold the giggles to a minimum. (At this point I had been teaching in the public schools in Madison, Wisconsin, for 19 years, and had been at Hawthorne School for 7 years. About 50% of the students qualified for free or reduced lunch, and about 38% of the students were minority students, the biggest percentage being African American. About a quarter of the students lived outside the school's neighborhood boundaries, and chose Hawthorne because of its emphasis on the integration of the arts, multicultural education, and open classroom strategies.)

After calling Madison AIDS Support Network (MASN) for ideas and resources, and asking our school librarian and nurse to help me locate developmentally appropriate literature, I was ready to begin the unit. I had decided to start with a group "web," a technique I typically use when beginning a unit to access students' interest, knowledge, and questions on a topic. I felt confident about my resources. I was quite certain that the students' web would help guide my plan.

But what about the parents? I knew that some, especially those with whom I had worked the previous year, would support this unit. But there were many families I didn't know as well. Would they go running to the principal, concerned that it was inappropriate for their children to learn about such matters? AIDS, I knew, is an especially "sensitive" topic. Learning about AIDS means dealing with those life issues that are usually avoided in early elementary school and by our society at large — sex, death, homosexuality, drugs.

I decided to alert parents by inserting a few lines in the weekly newsletter. I informed the parents:

Next week is AIDS Awareness Week. December 1 is World AIDS Day. Next week we will be discussing myths and facts about AIDS. We will be reading related children's books, seeing a video, and having our school nurse visit our classroom to address concerns and questions, and share information appropriate to 1-2 grade students, as outlined in the MMSD Health Curriculum.

Monday, Nov. 28 started as a normal day. No pink phone message slips awaited me in my mailbox. Even though I had given the principal a copy of the newsletter, she greeted me cheerfully in the hall. I was uneasy, but eager to start.

"AIDS," I wrote with thick black marker on the purple roll paper. "AIDS — you can die from it," was the first contribution. "You get it from kissing," offered another student. "No, you don't," said Nathan, with the authority that comes from being one of the youngest of 10 siblings, "You get it from sex." Undaunted by several giggles, he continued, "Hey, it's nothing to laugh about. It's serious. Sex is how we all got here!"

I wrote quickly as the kids shared

their knowledge. Soon the purple paper was filled up with lines and words that radiated from the word, "AIDS." "AIDS is a disease of the blood.".... "It can't jump from one person to another." .... "You can get it from a cut, if you touch someone's blood.".... "You can get it from needles. Don't pick up needles.".... "Magic Johnson got AIDS.".... "You can't get AIDS if you wear a condom.".... "What's a condom?".... "You want to know what a condom is? I'll tell you." Tonisha, who has two teenage sisters, answered the query quickly and accurately. She added, "They stop people from getting pregnant and from getting AIDS."

"I know," suggested Emily. Her contribution to the web had been that her uncle had died of AIDS. "Let's study about AIDS."

Taking Emily's cue, I told the class that I had thought that AIDS could be our next unit, and had contacted a group called Madison AIDS Support Network (MASN) to get ideas about how we could learn more about the subject. At that point I showed a 3-2-1 Contact video on Ryan White. The group sat absolutely still for 30 minutes, a rare occurrence. The video's portrayal of Ryan White's battle with the ignorance and prejudice surrounding his disease was followed by a moment of shocked silence.

Kendra was the first to speak. She stood up, demanding, "Hey, I have asthma. That's a disease. What if Hawthorne School would kick me out because of my disease? Would that be fair?" Her comment sparked a discussion in which students argued that students at Hawthorne would never be as cruel or as ignorant as those who ostracized Ryan White. Their indignation called for some action. I told them that MASN had suggested that they make posters to publicize AIDS Awareness Week in our school, and red ribbons to symbolize support for people with AIDS.

"Why red ribbons?" someone asked. "It's for support," explained Cassie. "It's like the yellow ribbons

that my family had on our tree to show that they supported the soldiers." "But why red?" came the persistent questions. "Are they red for *blood*?" That idea was popular, but inaccurate, so I shared an explanation of the red ribbon that I had seen at the local university's AIDS Awareness display:

The red ribbon demonstrates compassion for people with AIDS and their caretakers; and support for education and research for effective treatment or a cure, the many voices seeking a meaningful response to the AIDS epidemic. It is a symbol of hope; the hope that one day the AIDS epidemic will be over, that the sick will be healed, that the stress on our society will be healed. It serves as a constant reminder of the many ways people are suffering as a result of this disease, and of the many people working toward a cure — a day without AIDS.

"I know," said Jeremy, who listens carefully but rarely contributes to class discussions. "We could sell the red ribbons." That idea was an instant hit. "But whom would you give the money to?" I asked.

"My church," said two of the students. "Homeless people," suggested Nathan. "Poor people," said someone else.

Caleb looked disgusted. "You guys," he said impatiently, "We're selling the ribbons for AIDS. We have to give the money to someone who will help people with AIDS." Caleb's suggestion was accepted by the class.

I was excited, yet unsure. Yes, it was an excellent idea, a meaningful way for the students to work for a cause about which they had some knowledge and felt strongly. And I was glad that the students were not seeing themselves in the role of passive recipients of knowledge, but rather as activists. But, again, what would the parents think?

That next afternoon, Steven's par-

ents had arranged to come in to visit the classroom. Not knowing them well, I worried about how they would react to the giant AIDS web that I had tacked up on the board. I was hoping they wouldn't notice it. Also, kids were planning to start putting together the red ribbons during their free time. Would they think I had put them up to the project? Would they feel that it was inappropriate for first and second graders? Steven led his mom and dad into the classroom after recess.

"Look, it's AIDS Awareness Week," he announced to them, pointing to the sign on the blackboard. "We're going to study about AIDS and make red ribbons to support people with AIDS." After being introduced to the class and showing family photos and pictures of their motorcycles, and fielding questions about their Harleys, Steven's parents approached me.

"It's great, what you're doing," said Steven's mom. "Steven told me all about it. It's so important he is learning about AIDS. I'll help them make the ribbons." Later that day I received a message to call Steven's mom at work. "She's had second thoughts," I worried, as I dialed the number. "Hi, Kate," said Steven's mom, "I told the people at work about the red ribbons and they would like to buy some from the class. Tell Steven to make ten extra ribbons, and I'll send $5.00 with him tomorrow."

Several other parents asked for extra red ribbons to sell at work. One mom brought in some ribbons she had made at home. "Sarah and I had trouble getting them just right, " she said apologetically, "But I think they'll do." I was thrilled. We had trouble keeping up with the demand for ribbons to sell to teachers, custodians, family members, parents' co-workers, and neighbors. Even the principal was seen wearing one.

That week, our classroom exploded with AIDS learning experiences and projects. The school nurse did a presentation on AIDS. She read a book written about AIDS for young

you cant get AIDS by holding hands.

ZACH

children, *Come Sit By Me*. She explained how the immune system works to protect our bodies from most viruses; in the case of AIDS, however, the virus attacks the immune system itself. Students listened carefully and asked questions, which she answered calmly and directly.

Suddenly, the presentation took on a different tenor when the nurse shared: "My brother had AIDS." The class was stunned. "Is he alive?"

"No, he died. It was hard for him and for all of his family, but the hardest part was how he was treated by some people while he was alive." She explained how badly her family felt when a neighbor wouldn't let her children use their pool any more because of a fear that her children could get AIDS from swimming in a pool that he had used. I was grateful that the nurse had shared her personal story with the class. Her presentation, good as it was, had twice the power with the added personal perspective.

Another guest speaker was a friend of Cassie's family who came in to talk about his role as an actor in *Parting Glances*, one of the first

movies made about AIDS. Cassie mentioned to me and other classmates that he was gay, information that was accepted in a matter-of-fact fashion, partly, I think because Jordan's moms had openly identified themselves as lesbians. Neither the class nor the parents appeared to perceive AIDS solely as a gay issue, perhaps because it is also of particular concern to low-income and minority communities.

I showed the class a section of the movie in which our guest was visiting his best friend and they were both struggling with the anger and frustration they felt. The students watched as the friends unleashed their feelings by breaking dish after dish. We discussed why the characters might be compelled to act so violently. Our guest shared how it felt to act out that scene, and why he felt it important to act in a movie about AIDS, including because, as a gay man, many of his friends had been affected by the disease. Children took turns role-playing the character of the friend, exhibiting feelings of sadness, helplessness and frustration in their mini-dramas.

The students read every age-

appropriate book on AIDS that I could provide. Cody, usually a reluctant reader, preferring activities like etching swear words into the woodwork to independent reading, grabbed a book called *Alex, the Kid with AIDS* and guarded it religiously, taking every available moment to read another few words. Kids filled up pages in their journals with stories, questions, facts and feelings about AIDS. Jordan published his own book about Ryan White, who had become a class hero. Some students also made posters about AIDS Awareness Week, which they put up all around the school.

We had compiled a class book about AIDS, containing a statement and drawing from each student in the class. Someone had the idea of reading the book to another class; soon the kids were signing up to go in pairs to read to the second through fifth graders. I felt some trepidation about sending off these pairs of vulnerable first and second-graders to present their information to older children. But my students' confidence in their knowledge and dedication to the task enabled them to rise above the embarrassment and presumed superiority of the older students. Rarely stumped by questions (except in one classroom, where the teacher had to help to clear up confusion about whether or not it was the spread of AIDS that had wiped out so many Native Americans in Columbus' time), and undaunted by the whispering and taunting, the first- and second-graders impressed students and teachers alike.

Meanwhile, the red ribbon sales continued and the coffee cans decorated with construction paper filled up with pennies, nickels and dimes. The delight and pride that the kids displayed in being able to raise money for the AIDS cause appeared to offset, yet not overshadow, the gravity of the life and death issues we were dealing with every day. The function of the red ribbon as a symbol of hope was inspiring children, staff and parents to work toward a common goal. Jeremy, the originator of the idea, was usually the first to say, after each new contribution, "Can we count the money again?" Kids sorted money, counted by fives and tens, made piles of coins equaling a dollar, used the chalkboard, unifex cubs and calculators; individually and in small groups they worked out strategies for counting and recounting the money.

When Larry Davis, the MASN representative, came in to receive our donation, the class was adding on the nickels and dimes donated that morning: "It's almost one hundred dollars . . . It's $96.91!" the kids shouted out. After learning that Larry's job as an MASN volunteer is to work with children whose moms have AIDS while the moms attend a support group, the class voted to give the money to the kids. Everyone was attentive to the drawings that Larry had brought, drawings in which the children had represented AIDS as a demon-like monster or had written words such as, "I hate AIDS but I love Mom." The pictures that Larry brought, and his stories of how the children he worked with struggle with their situations, inspired empathy. Students in the class, many from single-parent families, tried to grapple with the idea of a parent having a terminal disease. "What will happen to the kids when their moms die?" was asked more than once. Larry left with a promise that he would let us know how the kids had decided to spend the money. A few days later we received a note from him. "We are using the money for supplies for the children's group, food, as well as a special trip. We're going roller skating next week. Thanks very much for everything!!"

"$96.91" stayed up on the chalk-board for the rest of the school year, along with the quotation about the meaning of the red ribbon and Larry's kids' drawings. As the school year progressed, we moved to other units, skills, and projects. However, nothing else had the power, the total involvement, the sense of community spirit of our AIDS unit. On the last day of school, several parents came in to say goodbye.

"You won't believe this, Kate" said Kendra's mom, "But learning about AIDS meant so much to Kendra that every night before she goes to sleep, she pins her red ribbon on her pajamas."

Caleb's mom told me that her son was worried about going to a different school in Chicago, where they were moving. "Caleb, you'll like your new school. You'll soon make friends, and I'm sure you will have fun things to do in your new classroom," she pointed out. "But Mom," protested Caleb. "I just *know* they won't learn about AIDS and sell red ribbons like we did!"

Caleb's mom and I exchanged glances. Caleb was probably right, yet I can only hope that primary classrooms in his new school, and in other schools around the country, will open up their classrooms to the study of AIDS.

I now realize that learning and teaching about AIDS will be a continual process. A year after that first unit on AIDS, a teacher came into my room to give me money that he had pledged for the AIDS Walk in Milwaukee. "Why is he giving you money?" asked a student. He told them that, along with thousands of other people, I had walked six miles to raise money for AIDS support, education, and research in Wisconsin. "What's AIDS?" asked a student new to my class. The answers to her question came quickly from students who had been in my class the previous year. I realized, however, that their statements were much more sophisticated than those in our original web. "AIDS," explained Emily, "is a virus, but it's different from other viruses. The white blood cells that

protect you from most viruses can't protect you from AIDS, because AIDS attacks *them!*" The students from the previous year's class expanded on her definition and also talked about the videos, the guest speakers, and the money we'd earned from selling red ribbons to give to the kids whose moms had AIDS. "We made a book. We should read it to them," somebody suggested.

Any questions I had in my mind about doing another AIDS unit were obliterated by the focused, enthusiastic attention of my class. And besides, Henry needed to learn that you can't get AIDS from poison ivy. ■

Kate Lyman teaches in Madison, Wisconsin. She can be reached via e-mail at clyman@madison.k12.wi.us. The names of the children in this story were changed.

Resources

Armstrong, Ewan. *The Impact of AIDS.* New York: Gloucester Press, 1990. This factual book on AIDS is rather com-

plex, but it could be a good resource for teachers and older children.

Fassler, David. *What's a Virus, Anyway? The Kids' Book About AIDS.* Burlington, VT: Waterfront Books, 1990). This book uses children's drawings and writings to present basic facts about AIDS.

Girard, Linda Walvoord. *Alex, the Kid with AIDS.* Morton Grove, IL: Albert Whitman and Company, 1991. A photo essay book that explores the daily life of a fourth-grade boy with AIDS.

Jordan, MaryKate. *Losing Uncle Tim.* Morton Grove, IL: Albert Whitman and Company, 1989. A boy struggles with the experience of his favorite uncle dying of AIDS.

Merrifield, Margaret. *Come Sit by Me.* Toronto: Women's Press, 1990. A girl in a primary classroom wonders why some children are afraid to play with a classmate who has AIDS. Misconceptions about AIDS are cleared up. A video of the story also is available.

Moutoussamy-Ashe, Jeanne. *Daddy and Me.* New York: Alfred A. Knopf, 1993. In photo essay form, Arthur Ashe's daughter describes her relationship with him and her understanding of AIDS.

Sanders, Pete. *The Problem of AIDS* New York: Gloucester Press, 1989. This book contains information about HIV and

AIDS that is suitable for older children.

Schilling, Sharon and Swain, Jonathan. *My Name is Jonathan (and I Have AIDS).* Denver: Prickly Pair Publishing Co., 1989. This a photo essay book that uses the words and drawings of preschool age boy to describe how he lives with AIDS and how he explains it to his classmates.

Starkman, Neal. *Z's Gift.* Seattle: Comprehensive Health Education Foundation, 1988. A fictitious classroom story about AIDS.

Verniero, Joan C. *You Can Call Me Willy: A Story for Children about AIDS.* New York: Magination Press, 1995. An 8-year-old girl who has AIDS deals with discrimination when she joins a baseball team.

Weeks, Sarah. *Red Ribbon.* Hong Kong: HarperCollins, 1995. An 8-year-old girl wears a red ribbon to show her concern for a neighbor who has AIDS.

Weiner, Lori S., Best, Aprille, and Pizzo, Philip A. (Eds.). *Be a Friend: Children who Live with HIV Speak.* Morton Grove, IL: Albert Whitman and Company, 1994.

White, Ryan. *I Have AIDS: A Teenager's Story.* 3-2-1 Contact Extra, 1988. Often available for local AIDS support organizations, such as the Madison AIDS Support Network.

at the cemetery,
walnut grove plantation, south carolina, 1989

among the rocks
at walnut grove
your silence drumming
in my bones,
tell me your names.

nobody mentioned slaves
and yet the curious tools
shine with your fingerprints.
nobody mentioned slaves
but somebody did this work
who had no guide, no stone
who moulders under rock.

tell me your names,
tell me your bashful names
and i will testify.

the inventory lists ten slaves
but only men were recognized.

among the rocks
at walnut grove
some of these honored dead
were dark
some of these dark
were slaves
some of these slaves
were women
some of them did this
honored work.
tell me your names
foremothers, brothers,
tell me your dishonored names.
here lies
here lies
here lies
here lies
hear

— Lucille Clifton

(Teaching Ideas, p. 240)

JEAN-CLAUDE LEJEUNE

RETHINKING SCHOOL CULTURE

To flourish, critical classrooms need to be part of a larger whole. Tackling tough issues like discipline or discrimination, commercialism or cultural bias requires schoolwide approaches and common ground. Too often, schools avoid the hard issues that lie just beneath the surface of schooling. At other times, they "internalize" values and agendas from the larger society and reinforce existing patterns of inequity and failure. In this section, writers examine ways to create a school culture that collectively encourages the sharing, fairness, and mutual respect that classrooms need to pursue a curriculum of social justice.

When Things Turn Ugly

Threats in the student-teacher relationship

By Donn K. Harris

I remember the first time I saw Javier. He had eyes that pierced right through you. Angry eyes, but sad, plaintive eyes too, eyes that asked you for something. He had been thrown out of class for using profanity. He arrived in my office quietly, almost deferentially, and handed me the teacher's referral without saying anything.

"Student refuses to work," the referral read. "Attends irregularly, disrupts class, is on track for failure. Today shouted a profanity as I wrote on the board."

"What happened, Javier?" I asked.

"The teacher called me an idiot," he told me.

His eyes told me that he didn't think I would believe him. I did believe him, but that wasn't enough.

"Do they have a right to say that?" he asked.

I was unable to answer him.

• • •

Our high school was once audited by the California Safe Schools Assessment Team. The state had just recently hired consultants to track data relating to criminal activity in the schools, and the auditors were interested in our reporting procedures and record-keeping systems. As the dean of students, I was responsible for student discipline and campus safety. Our office handled everything from runaway students to missing computer chips.

Near the end of the session the lead auditor asked us if we had any questions or comments. I responded: "You know, I'm surprised you don't have a category that tracks threats against school personnel. We file

JEAN-CLAUDE LEJEUNE

police reports on those, and I thought you'd be interested in that."

"Oh, we are," the auditor assured me. "It's just that we'd be swamped with reports. We'd have to triple our staff."

The audit took place on a day that found an intriguing drama being played out at our school. A teacher had filed a report through me alleging that a week earlier, a student — Javier — had "said something to the effect that he was going to get me." The teacher was filing this report because the student did not appear "contrite."

We had met twice about Javier's disruptive behavior in the hallway outside the teacher's classroom, and the teacher was dissatisfied with the

student's attitude. At one point the teacher had said to me, in the presence of other adults, "I want to get this kid." I had invited the police officer assigned to our school to the second meeting, and the teacher brought in the site union representative.

In a strange twist, during the meeting the police officer felt that it was necessary to admonish the *teacher* for leveling a hard, confrontational stare toward the student, in *the presence of the student's mother*. It also came out that the teacher had said to the student and a group of his friends, "You've got friends, but I've got friends too."

The parent spoke only Spanish, and when this was translated to her, she looked at me beseechingly. What was I going to do about this? Would I allow her son to be railroaded into a possible expulsion? The translator and the police officer looked toward me as well: It was my call.

"I am suspending the student for two days for the disruptive activity in the hallway," I stated in Spanish and English. "I have no documentation of a direct threat against anyone, and I'm recommending that no police report be filed at this time."

The meeting broke up and the student left to collect his work for the two days he would be at home. The teacher wanted 24 hours to think over whether he wanted to file a formal police report.

Matters Escalate

The next morning, in my box, was a referral form filled out by the teacher. It gave a date and time from the previous week, and stated that Javier had "said something to the effect that he was going to get me." I called the police officer back, filed a report, and took the matter to the assistant principal.

"I can't in good faith sit before a disciplinary committee with these charges," I told him. I explained that the report of the alleged threat had come to me after the matter had appeared to be closed. Furthermore, there had been a week's interval between the alleged incident and the documentation, and the teacher had clearly demonstrated hostile and confrontational behavior toward the student. If I were to sit before a disciplinary committee and these issues were raised by the student's family, I could not adequately answer them.

The assistant principal called the teacher in, and the union representative joined us. They wanted action. They wanted the student removed from school. They presented the student's recent history: weapons possession (at another school), incarceration, truancy, academic failure. The teacher's threatening comments and challenging stares, and the lengthy delay in filing charges, were explained as "errors in judgment."

The assistant principal advised me to write up the disciplinary report, but I insisted that the teacher go before the committee to back up his charges. This was agreed upon, but of course the situation continued to escalate once the union was involved. Around the school, the issue took on the somewhat warped proportions of a deep and angry division between two camps: those who wanted the teacher protected and the student removed, and those who felt that the teacher had behaved unprofessionally and had victimized the student. The entire discipline policy of the school became a point of contention. Arguments ensued, teachers argued with teachers, rumors flew wildly about, and the student's family hired a lawyer. The administrative machinery pushed on, and eventually the matter was dropped.

In a similar incident, just before the controversy over Javier and his teacher, a different teacher had asked me to suspend a student for using profanity against her. During our conversation she said to me, "If he were on the street, he'd be dead meat."

Should I have interpreted that as a threat and filed a police report? Was the teacher merely being metaphorical, dramatic, creatively expressive, therapeutically angry? Or was I wrong to try to explain her behavior away, ignoring a genuine threat to the student's safety? Would the district hold *her* responsible in a disciplinary hearing?

I did not act on the teacher's comment. My job as dean of students was a series of judgment calls from 6 a.m. through 5 p.m., and I didn't feel the student was in danger. But I also felt

JEAN-CLAUDE LEJEUNE

that Javier posed no threat to the first teacher. He was, however, perceived as dangerous by a large number of adults in the building, and he had the kind of history that gave their demands for removal some teeth. No school administration wants to be seen as weak in this area; the issue is continually in the public eye, and the call is always for stern disciplinary measures.

Yet what was the actual difference between the incident with Javier and the second teacher's comment? If anything, the statement that the profane student would be "dead meat" was a stronger threat than Javier's "something to the effect...."

This is not the way the world works, though, and we all know that. It is acceptable for teachers to use certain linguistic dramatics; when students use them, we file police reports. Incidents like these are played out daily in schools throughout the country, and teachers' unions flex their muscles and demand consequences and protection, and stands such as mine are wholly unpopular.

I could name a dozen incidents in which students were suspended, and in some cases transferred, for actions that were perceived as potentially violent, but which clearly could have been avoided by better judgment on the part of the adult involved.

Before becoming a dean of students, I had worked in our city's juvenile hall as a teacher, spent a year managing a 50-student dropout prevention program, and taught students with severe emotional disturbances. Over the years, I have been verbally threatened perhaps a dozen times, but have never filed a police report. We have counseling for angry students and a very effective Peer Resource Center where students, trained as peer counselors, advise troubled students on matters like these. Some would call this a lenient approach, and wonder about "appropriate consequences" (a phrase I hear often). But, despite public perception to the contrary, I do not know of a single teacher who has been directly assaulted by a student, and I discuss discipline and violence daily with teachers.

Yet the number of threats is, apparently, off the chart. Could it be that the threats are not connected to acts of violence, but are merely poorly chosen expressions of anger? Wouldn't the two teachers in question — the one with "friends" and the other who told me the student "would be dead meat" — ask to be forgiven for their unfortunate choices of words? And if we forgave them, would we be too lenient?

It could be said that the statement "You're going to amount to nothing" is a threat, particularly when it is made by someone with the power to help that come true, such as a teacher who hands out grades and makes recommendations to counselors and administrators. I hear variations of that kind of comment daily. On a regular basis I hear kids called "jerks," "idiots," "orphans," "psychopaths," or told to "wear diapers" or "buy a broom" (since custodial work is their only future). I have seen a teacher of students with emotional disturbances throw a boy's notebook to the floor because "the dummy has to learn you don't place a notebook on the teacher's desk."

Our state education code gives a vague nod to professional behavior by teachers, and uses catchwords like "dignity" and "respect" to guide educators in their behavior toward students. But the kids have no real recourse when teachers behave otherwise. When the students put these teacher behaviors into writing, I've been accused of soliciting negative information about teachers.

Interestingly, this same education code gives me great latitude in dealing with threats against staff. I can do anything from "counsel" the student to put him or her up for expulsion. I can leave the police out of it or request that the student be cited, even booked and held. I can send the student back to class or place him or her on indefinite suspension. In most cases I ask the teacher how he or she feels. Do they feel endangered? Would they like to file a police report?

I remember the first time I was asked that as a young teacher. A student said he was going to "kick my ass" because I threw him out of class, and the dean had asked me about the police. I was shocked. I didn't think such an incident was a legal problem — but many teachers do. Filing a police report gives a sense of control:

Something is being done to take the schools back from the psychopaths and the future custodians.

There are other troubling aspects to this debate as well. One year, the Union Building Committee asked me to attend a meeting and explain why I hadn't suspended two kids for fighting. Was it because they were African Americans and I had been instructed to keep our minority suspension numbers low?

"Philosophically," I told the group, "I don't believe in suspension." This was to come back to haunt me later, when the incident between the teacher and Javier occurred. I would be criticized for "lax discipline."

Are the Threats Real?

I know I will go out on a limb in saying this, but I honestly believe that 99% of the time, the kids' threats don't mean anything. As I said earlier, but it bears repeating: I do not know of a single teacher who has been directly assaulted by a student, and I am acquainted with many teachers whose careers span three decades.

When I am threatened, I say this to kids: "You don't mean that. Hey, it's me, you don't want to hurt me." And they'll agree. They are angry — they are very angry — and sometimes are filled with a palpable rage. But they don't want to hurt anyone.

The student population in our school is largely immigrant, and many students come from countries recently at war. We have a sizable group who live in public housing, and some of our kids are homeless, or have been homeless. Group-home counselors are in my office continually, checking on the students under their care, students who have been separated from their families for a variety of painful and torturous reasons. Many of these children have heard threats and unchecked expressions of anger their entire lives. We will not teach them differently by transferring them to another school. We will merely lose sight of them.

Who can forget the raging pas-

sions and tormented confusion of their teenage years, even under the best of conditions? Who is unable to predict outcomes when you put the social pressures of the times — the joblessness, the poverty, the troubled streets — into the equation for today's youth?

"I'll get you," was what the homeless kid said to the teacher who had called him an orphan. But all the kid really did was cry. I was in the hallway, standing with the student after

> "I'll get you," was what the homeless kid said to the teacher who had called him an orphan. But all the kid really did was cry.

the teacher had left. When the kid reached into his pocket, there was no weapon there, only a tissue. And a used one at that.

When I was in teacher training, a professor told our class something I never forgot. "You are going to be high school teachers," he said, "and most of you love your subject matter and will try to pattern yourselves after your favorite college instructors. But you would do better to emulate your favorite elementary school teachers." His point was, I believe, that we would be teaching children, no matter how large they might seem, and that the training of the elementary school teacher, with its emphasis on child development and careful nurturing of mind and spirit, was equally meaningful to us.

When I deal with threats and the

sequence of events that precede them, I think of this. How easily we could have avoided the threats, in so many cases, if we had simply met the challenges of the day with an attitude of nurturing instead of punishment, of firm guidance instead of cutting castigation.

I am still groping for answers to these issues, and they are slow in coming. I know this, however: The answer does not lie in police reports, nor in some unfounded idea of "appropriate consequences." Calling a kid a jerk won't do anything except send the kid away, angry and hurt. Suspension only removes a student from your influence and guidance.

But I can begin to see the shape of the answers, and they have to do with respect and truth and the intangible dynamics of the relationship between adult and child. Some might call these intangibles love and understanding and compassion. I just might agree with them.

• • •

Just before the end of the school year, I took my graffiti cleanup crew out for burritos. Javier was among the group, his disciplinary hearing still pending. The mood was joyous and sad at once. It had been a long school year and the approaching summer filled us with varying degrees of excitement and apprehension.

This group of Latino students was not doing well academically. In the small restaurant, as we read the burrito menu on the wall, I noticed Javier pushing his friends aside. "Mr. Harris," Javier said "you order first."

"I'm hungry," Otto complained. But Javier told him, "You gotta show respect. Ain't that right, Mr. Harris?"

We didn't get to see that side of Javier in school. The opportunity just wasn't there in the world of hard desks and loud tardy bells.

"Yes it is, Javier," I answered. "I couldn't agree with you more." ∎

Donn Harris is principal of Raoul Wallenberg High School in San Francisco, California.

Rethinking Discipline

by Jehanne Helena Beaton

"Here we go again, talking about who will guard the prisoners." With that, my colleague Karl Holmquist shook his shaggy head, slammed his grade book on the table, and stormed out of our team meeting.

For two months, we had devoted our middle school team meetings to issues of discipline. We'd even been summoned to a half-dozen "emergency" meetings, called midweek, after school, or during our team's prep hour, to continue the discussions. It seemed we weren't going to talk about anything else, and our frustrations were growing.

"It's out of control up there," the principal at our K-8 school complained, pointing a plum-colored, manicured fingernail to the ceiling and implicating the third floor, which housed our middle school program. "I don't care what you do, but you'd better do something about it."

I've taught seventh- and eighth-grade social studies for eight years in three different middle schools: one rural, one suburban, and one inner-city. Regardless of the setting, it seems that we adults spend an inordinate amount of time, money, and energy dealing with discipline.

Yes, teenagers sometimes spin out of control. They defy, disrespect, and denigrate their peers and teachers. They push buttons, test limits.

Yet you would think that with practice, the adults in schools would improve and get creative in dealing with discipline. Instead, we seem to rely on coercion and compliance, resorting to clamping down, increasing our control, and pulling in the reins.

Every school in which I've taught has espoused this unspoken belief: A good teacher is one who keeps her students quiet.

Discipline policies communicate powerful messages to our students about their worth, value, and power, and our expectations and beliefs about who they are and what they can do. Do we ever step back and examine the hidden curriculum behind our disciplinary policies?

Do we recognize what our disciplinary actions teach our young people about authority, power, and voice? Do we consider how undemocratic most of our disciplinary policies are? Do we realize how we

> **The same kids returned again and again to the portable, and lost more and more of an opportunity to get what they needed and deserved academically.**

reinforce silent compliance and conformity, and squelch individuality, creativity, and critical thinking?

In my first year of teaching, I taught in a border-town school in Arizona. The town's school-age population had exploded and the school district struggled to keep up with its expanding numbers. At every school, somebody had to teach in the portable classroom, usually parked behind the cafeteria or far beyond the gymnasium.

Our principal stationed the portable at the farthest end of campus, the desert-dust no-man's-land beyond the basketball courts and soccer fields. In the first few weeks of my first year, I pitied the poor teacher who had to teach "way out there." Then I found out the portable housed the In-School Suspension (ISS) classroom.

Didn't they do that in 18th-century England, I thought, exiling social outcasts and prisoners out to what "civilized" Brits considered the vast, uninhabitable desert isle of Australia?

My students hated the walk to the portable. The ISS supervisor (I'll call him Mr. Bly) paraded them out during lunch time in front of all their peers, as though they were shackled together like some chain gang.

Bly transformed the ISS portable into his own little kingdom, intensifying its punitive conditions. The thermostat was cemented at 60 degrees, and dark gusts and dank bodies gave the interior a cavernous feel. Desert dirt, broken pencil tips, and dust puffed up from the carpet with each step. Curtains sealed out any rays of the Arizona sun.

Bly built himself a throne, propping up his desk on bricks and installing a black leather swivel chair. From there he peered down on the students, who served their time in

hand-made study carrels with six-foot walls of plywood painted black. Students were cordoned off from one another, isolated in their plastic chairs. Before they were to do any homework or complete any assignments, they had to copy the school rules an unspecified number of times, as determined by their jailer.

No one ever asked the kids why they did what they did. Writing the school rules repeatedly never unearthed the reasons behind their behavior. The same kids returned again and again to the portable, and lost more and more of an opportunity to get what they needed and deserved academically. Our school never prepared them to solve problems on their own. To use words rather than fists. To open themselves up to trusting adults or to understanding themselves. To envision any kind of academic future. We didn't prepare them for anything but jail.

It wasn't hard to determine what my students learned from our school's discipline policy. Discipline equaled punishment. And punishment equaled harm to one's education, one's dignity, and one's soul.

My second school fared no better. Rather than the portable, this suburban Minneapolis junior high school housed its student offenders in "The Crisis Room." Slightly larger than a walk-in closet, the windowless room was just past the main hallway intersection. Teenage passers-by peeped in to memorize and later publicize who sat in attendance.

That year, as part of my building duties, I served as Crisis Room supervisor for one period of the day. Though no one ever told me to require that students regurgitate school policy on paper, veteran teachers passed down Crisis Room procedure like family stories. They recommended that students answer a

condescending series of questions, that they attempt to call their parents upon arrival in the room, and that they keep their mouths shut. Mediation or "counseling" with students as to why they were in the Crisis Room was viewed as counterproductive and "soft," potentially legitimizing the students' conduct. Once again, the disciplinary structure of the school communicated punishment without problem solving.

In my third school, I worked with a gifted team of teachers, all committed and competent in their work with middle school students. Yet despite our collective talents, we were often sucked into that same disciplinary paradigm of coercion, control, and punishment.

Our middle school was located on the third floor of a K-8 magnet program three minutes from downtown Minneapolis. Our student population, which was diverse racially, linguisti-

vide them with opportunities for legitimate power, choice, and self-discipline? What would such a school look like? What would it require of us as educators and adults?

Maybe it's time we begin to imagine. Otherwise, we will continue to communicate powerful messages to our students, especially those who are poor and students of color. We will reinforce their lack of voice, their lack of efficacy in the world. We will reinforce their belief that there exists no democratic, legitimate avenue for them to question authority, to intellectually and personally

> **One of our recurring conversations centered around student defiance. Yet we rarely provided our students with legitimate channels for venting frustrations about school.**

challenge the status quo. We will reinforce their feelings of powerlessness and resignation. We will tell them we expect a life of compliance, control, and silence. And, as a nation, we will be the worse for it. ∎

Jehanne Helena Beaton teaches middle school social studies and writing at the Interdistrict Downtown School in Minneapolis.

cally, and socio-economically, remained small, with fewer than 200 seventh and eighth graders. We followed our students for two years, intending to develop strong relationships with our kids and their families. We adjusted our curriculum regularly to meet the needs of our students and to better relate to our students' lives. We regularly facilitated public performances and presentations, integrating multiple disciplines. We provided a short recess to give the kids the chance to expel some of their age-appropriate energy and to provide us with a more casual environment in which to connect with our students.

Despite these innovations, we often found ourselves caught in the discipline paradigm that permeates most middle schools. If there was criticism as to how loudly our students socialized in the hallway, or if there was a rash of fighting, we would spend the next handful of team meetings "buckling down." We re-hashed the tardy policy, debated about student use of time, locked student bathrooms, and eliminated recess.

One of our recurring conversations centered around student defiance. Yet we rarely provided our students with legitimate channels for venting frustrations about school. Our school's site-based decision process excluded students. Our student council's major responsibility was to decorate the gym for dances.

My students were very attuned to their lack of power. They articulated feelings of confinement, lock-down, and distrust. In their own adolescent ways, they pleaded with us to provide them with a structure that encouraged them to learn to discipline themselves. Unfortunately, we had a difficult time giving up control.

Is it possible to shift ourselves and our schools from a paradigm of control, coercion, and punishment to one where we hold high expectations for our students and simultaneously pro-

Creating Classroom Community

By Beverly Braxton

It was sometime in March when Philip whispered in my ear, "Can I read the class this book?" I still remember trying to hide how surprised I felt as I nodded, OK.

As Philip stood there, tall and confident in front of his peers, I couldn't help feeling proud of the risk he was taking. He had entered my grade 3-4 combination classroom the previous September full of school anxiety. It was clear that he hated school and had difficulty making friends. He regularly neglected or lost assignments, snarled at his classmates, and cried silently when I refused to let him off the hook when work was missing. Philip had strong feelings of inadequacy and was relentless in his efforts to get me to lower my expectations for him.

On that day, Philip, the only African-American student in my class of 27, stood in front of a room of his white classmates to read aloud a story that had touched him. It was a powerful testimony of not only Philip's improved sense of self-esteem but also the trust, intimacy, and connection that we as a class had managed to build.

I was the first African-American teacher that Philip had had in his five years of schooling. And it was probably the first time since attending this semi-rural, nearly all-white school district in the Hudson Valley region of New York that Philip's racial identity was mirrored on the walls of his classroom.

Knowing how easy it is for a child of color to be made invisible by white schools, I go to great lengths to create a multicultural physical setting. I display pictures of people with diverse racial and cultural backgrounds, gender roles, and special needs and abilities. This mirrors the families of the children in the class (which despite the racial homogeneity includes many variations of class and culture) and also reflects the broader diversity within the United States.

Yet having the "right" pictures on the wall and my being a teacher of color were not, by themselves, enough to account for the changes in Philip from September to March. Equally important, Philip had grown by being a member of a learning community that respected differences and focused on empowering children.

This activist teaching integrates

> **Crow Boy is a compelling story that underscores what can happen when differences are respected rather than seen as a problem.**

my interest in multicultural education with my goals of teaching for equality, personal empowerment, and social change. Hence, throughout the school year, I help students to identify their interests, pursue their questions, and collectively address concerns related to curriculum and assignments. I also take time to examine social justice issues as they occur in the context of the school day and the curriculum.

Creating an atmosphere so children feel special, safe, and respected is fundamental to examining more troubling topics and unfair behaviors between children. Helping students learn how to work in groups, develop empathy, and appreciate diversity has taken a lot of hard work. This emphasis on community-building affects how my students hear and see each other. In hindsight, I realize the power that positive group pressure had on helping Philip become a more productive and contributing member of the class.

I recall how one classmate, new to the area and living with relatives, shared his grief about his mom's recent death from cancer and his fear of being abandoned by his distant father. The class sat riveted during the student's revelation of his loneliness and alienation. For several months afterwards, Philip became this child's best friend. Perhaps this bonding happened because of Philip's personal circumstances. He, too, lived with relatives, and until recently, had had minimal contact with his mom and no relationship with his father. Until his classmate shared his grief that day, I don't believe Philip had ever imagined another child's suffering to be equal to his own.

One way I teach critically and, at the same time, work to build a democratic classroom is to choose multicultural children's books dealing with issues pertaining to race, class, gender, or disability. Using such books can be a non-threatening way for children to examine issues of social inequity.

One book, in particular, that mirrored Philip's progress in my class was *Crow Boy*, by Taro Yashima

(1955). This book is about Chibi, a boy who for 5 years is made to feel alienated and isolated at school. In sixth grade, he finally has a teacher who takes an interest in him and ultimately learns of his ability to imitate the sound of crows. The teacher marvels at Chibi's understanding of nature and provides opportunities for his classmates to learn from him. It is a compelling story that underscores what can happen when differences are respected rather than seen as a problem.

A More Critical Approach

When I first began using *Crow Boy* some years back, my objectives were merely to develop cross-cultural appreciation and empathy for what it means to be different. Today, my goals are broader and I use the book to try develop empathy with not only Chibi, but among students in the same class whose life experiences might be different from others. I now provide my students with questions and activities that help them to make a deeper connection between the book's characters and their lives.

When Philip was in my class, I used *Crow Boy* soon after school started, in September. To begin, I had a whole group discussion in which students responded to questions that:

• Identify different ways in. which people reinforce discrimination.

• Consider the power of nonverbal messages.

• Encourage a better understanding of what it feels like to be excluded based on difference.

These questions include: What happened in the first part of the story that led to Chibi feeling left out and unimportant? What kinds of unspoken messages did the boy get from his classmates and previous teachers that indicated what they thought of him? It's important that students identify, when possible, the specific behaviors. For example, if students say, "They didn't like him," I ask them how they showed it. This leads them to point out how children teased the boy or how his classmates did not

An illustration from *Crow Boy* by Taro Yashima.

play with him at recess.

To get my students to empathize with Chibi, I have them describe how they might feel if they were him. I ask: How was Chibi made to feel? How might you feel if you were Chibi? Why might you feel that way?

To help students examine how prejudice and other bias affect them, I ask questions that help them reflect on their own experience. For example, I ask: Has anyone experienced being left out, either here at school or in other areas of your life?

Such questions lead to a powerful sharing, because they usually reveal the extent to which students are regularly made to feel left out of groups both in and outside of school. For instance, one boy said, with tears in his eyes: "Kids tease me because I'm short, and in gym no one wants me on their team." Another boy said he

wasn't short, but was regularly teased because he wasn't good at sports. Embarrassed, he revealed that kids in his neighborhood often called him "sissy" and tried to start fights with him. One girl told how boys teased her when she asked to play basketball with them at recess. She, too, was teary-eyed as she turned to the first boy and said, "I'm not picked because I'm a girl."

By the end of the discussion, many students had spoken about the various verbal and nonverbal ways in which they had been made to feel unpopular or unwanted because they were different in some way. (This discussion has also been a good reference point for a later lesson on put-downs.)

I remember watching Philip's face the day of that discussion in early September. He seemed surprised by the honesty of emotion of some of his

new classmates. Several months later, Philip himself broke down crying when he unexpectedly began talking about an incident in third grade when he was called "blackie" by another student. To see Philip so upset was troubling for the entire class.

Afterwards, I asked, "What is it about Philip's hurt that makes it different than the other name-calling and put-downs we've heard?" It took some time before the other students understood what I was getting at. Finally, one blue-eyed, blond-haired girl said:

> I think I know how Philip might feel. When I went to Jamaica I felt weird because my family looked different than everyone else and people stared at us everywhere we went. I didn't like it sometimes because I was afraid that someone would call us a name or hurt us because we were white. It wasn't fair that Philip was

called a name like that because he can't make his color go away no matter what he does. I wished I wasn't white when I was in Jamaica. And Philip probably feels that way here.

Although this white student's experience in Black Jamaica could not be equivalent to that of Blacks in a white society, the commonality of feeling she expressed was a valid insight and helped to build understanding.

I asked Philip if he felt that way and, with head lowered and face hidden by his hands, he nodded yes. This interaction helped transform Philip's relationship with his classmates. I recognize that issues of a white tourist in Jamaica are vastly different from those of an African American in this country, but for the children such differences were secondary. What was most important at that time was that many students expressed dismay

at the thought that Philip might always be teased about the color of his skin. Philip, meanwhile, seemed relieved that this issue of race was finally out in the open.

Taking Risks

The most important and perhaps most difficult component of an anti-bias teaching approach is empowering students to take risks which will help promote social justice. This crucial step is fostered by getting students to envision the kind of classroom they wish to be a part of. To help do so, I build on the discussions of *Crow Boy* and ask students: "What could the other students in the story have done to better Chibi's experience at school?" As students offer solutions, I record them on a chart for later use.

Most children have an innate sense of what is fair and unfair. They are eager to learn the words to express the inequities they see and to work with others to solve the inequities. So I ask the students: "How should we go about dealing with these issues raised by the story?" Again, I list student responses on chart paper for later reference.

Afterwards, the children break into small groups to discuss and write down ideas of how they'd like our class to be. Concepts of peace and respect are discussed in conjunction with class rules. My ultimate goal is to get my students to see themselves as social change agents. I usually culminate this activity with having them identify areas for personal change.

For instance, last year, we generated a list of "Mean Things That Kids Do To Other Kids." We then brainstormed ideas of what children could do to help stop kids from being mean. Many students said they would like to make a personal goal of speaking up when they see people treated unfairly. A few others spoke about trying not to tease kids about their size or what they bring for lunch. One student said he wouldn't use the word "retarded" anymore. Philip never did say what he was willing to do differently. Yet, over time he ceased teasing kids about the way they dressed and learned to apologize when he treated others unfairly.

Changes in student behavior don't happen overnight. Philip, like the other students new to my room, benefited from working with students who were with me for a second year. These "experienced" fourth graders demonstrated extreme patience with the newer students' adjustment to the classroom, while modeling for them how to solve group conflicts. Regular class meetings provided ample opportunity for students to discuss issues and conflicts as they arose.

In addition, the children were exposed to many readings and history lessons that dealt with race, class, and gender inequities. This led to extensive discussions raising issues of fairness and justice in the world at large. These discussions provided another framework through which the class could view its own issues and conflicts. For example, there were class meetings where classmates expressed concerns about Philip's negative attitude towards girls and his aggressive behavior on the playground. Having a broader understanding of social issues and conflict helped the class to make connections between history and their own lives.

MARILYN NOLT

Philip's Progress

My awakening to Philip's unfolding was like the barely perceptible return of light in spring. Only in retrospect was I able to identify the changes that he had made. As the year progressed, Philip seemed to become more comfortable with his racial difference. His interest in reading changed when he realized he could read what he liked. Nearly every book he chose for his independent reading had to do with an African American or his favorite sport, basketball. I believe that because race issues were dealt with directly in the class, and because Philip had some say in what he could

learn at school, he began to become a more responsible learner and leader.

Gradually I began to notice the changes in Philip's attitude about his schoolwork and his relationships with other students. He readily completed class assignments and was prepared with homework. His contentiousness with classmates eased, and he was able to work cooperatively for longer periods of time. I observed that Philip was friendlier and more responsive to the feelings of the other students, and over time he became increasingly popular.

Eventually, Philip had a new surprise for our class. During a talent day in June, Philip confidently performed four very complicated rap songs, as a class of disbelieving students and parents sat mesmerized by his gift to rhyme. It was a scene

straight out of *Crow Boy,* where Chibi astonishes a similar group with his hidden talents.

Philip, like Chibi, had come full circle this last year of his life in grade school. The standing ovation he received confirmed it. ∎

Beverly Braxton (e-mail address: braxton@warwick.net) is a teacher at Sanfordville School, a parent involvement project of the Partners in Education program in Warwick, New York.

Reference

Yashima, Taro. *Crow Boy.* New York: Viking, 1955.

A Mother Speaks Out

What happens when schools fail to take action

By Leslie Sadasivan

The following is excerpted from remarks at a news conference in September 1998 by the National Education Association and the Gay, Lesbian, and Straight Educators Network (GLSEN). At the news conference, GLSEN released its second annual report card on school district policies toward gay and lesbian students and staff. More than half the nation's 42 largest districts received a failing grade, which meant they did not have a single policy or program to help protect the rights of gay, lesbian, bisexual, and transgendered students.

I am a nurse, a Catholic, and the mother of a gay son, Robbie Kirkland. When my family and I realized that Robbie was gay we let him know immediately that we loved, supported, and accepted him. After all, we had raised him to believe that God loves and accepts everyone despite their differences in race, color, creed, and sexual identity. But our efforts could not protect him from the rejection and harassment he experienced.

As early as first grade, Robbie was teased and harassed because he was noticeably different from the other boys. Robbie was soft-spoken, gentle, creative, and hated sports. Despite his many efforts to fit in with the other boys, such as participating in sports and pretending to have crushes on girls, Robbie was still perceived as different and eventually as gay.

When he did tell us about the early years of harassment, coming home with scratches and torn pants, of being hit by another boy in the locker room, having rocks thrown at him, and of being pushed down in the snow and called "faggot" by a schoolmate, we took him to a counselor and eventually changed his school.

Harassment Escalates

Unfortunately, the teasing and harassment that so humiliated Robbie proceeded to escalate as he got older. Most of the teasing and physical attacks Robbie experienced in school occurred out of the teachers' view in hallways, playgrounds, bathrooms, locker rooms, buses, and unsupervised classrooms.

In a classroom filled with students, but no teacher, a classmate came after him with a sharpened pencil, pointed it in his face and yelled "faggot" repeatedly. Many other acts of aggression were subtle, but persistent. Over time name-calling, pushing, shoving, and general exclusion left him feeling ashamed, insecure, and alone.

It was in 8th grade that Robbie made his first suicide attempt. His suicide note began with, "Whatever you find, I'm not gay," and ended with, "Robbie Kirkland, the boy who told himself to put on a smile, shut up, and pretend you're happy. It didn't work." After that attempt, his therapist confirmed our suspicions that he was gay. Our family rallied around him. My unconditional love and acceptance blinded me from seeing how unhappy he was.

We hoped that high school would be different. Because his new high school was large, he had high hopes that he would not be picked on or singled out. But Robbie's hopes were just that, hope. Although we were not aware, the harassment continued.

Robbie shot himself in the head on Jan. 2, 1997, four months into his ninth grade year. It was the end of Christmas break. He was 14, and was found by my 19-year-old daughter Danielle. I believe his timing to be intentional so that he could avoid the pain of returning to school. Robbie wrote, "I hope I can find the peace in death that I could not find in life." He asked for us to pray for him and to remember him.

Our family has been devastated by this tragedy. Our lives are forever changed for having lost such a loving, gentle, sensitive young man. Since his death, I have told Robbie's story to whomever will listen, in the hope of bringing some good from this tragedy.

Robbie's death has already had an influence on the Catholic school which he attended. After Robbie died, the school's president addressed the student body and explicitly spelled out that gays — and indeed all people — have dignity, and that this is never to be violated. The speech will be given to all incoming freshmen.

My purpose now is to help other gay youth. I sincerely hope that GLSEN's Back To School Campaign can bring about the needed change to make every school environment a safe place for gay youth. ∎

Teaching the Whole Story

One school's struggle toward gay and lesbian inclusion

By Kate Lyman

One fall a teacher in my elementary school returned from a conference with information about the photo exhibit *Love Makes a Family: Living in Gay and Lesbian Families*. The colleague had been part of a team of four teachers at the school, including myself, involved the previous spring in the filming of the video *It's Elementary: Talking About Gay Issues in School (see Resources)*.

We were coming together again to make plans to display the photo exhibit at our school. We discussed organizing activities highlighting gay and lesbian inclusion during the two weeks of the display. I fully supported the plan. But at the same time, something inside me balked at the thought of presenting it to the school district administration. I didn't want to relive all the controversy we had encountered the previous spring, when we did the filming for *It's Elementary*.

But a conversation with the lesbian parents of Paul, one of the students in my second/third grade classroom, renewed my energy. We were discussing a protest to be held at a nearby church, which had invited an inflammatory anti-gay minister to speak. They said that they supported the actions of the protesters but that they were too tired to go themselves.

"I've gone to so many marches, so many rallies," said Jane. "There isn't a day in my life when I'm not confronted with homophobia. I'm just tired of it. I'll let the younger people do it for me. More power to them!"

I knew I wasn't any younger and was also tired of controversy. But I realized that the photo exhibit was an opportunity for me to assist in some of the struggles they faced every day.

Dealing with Student Attitudes

Although I first became aware of gay and lesbian issues through my involvement with the feminist movement in the 1970s, it wasn't until the 1980s that I began to make the con-

> It shouldn't be up to 7-year-old kids, I thought, to defend themselves and their families against irrational fears and hatred.

nection between multicultural education, gender equity, and teaching gay and lesbian inclusion. Under our district's Human Relations Program, I had been working for several years on curriculum for Women's History Month, which included not only learning about women in history, but also challenging traditional gender roles. I began to realize that gay and lesbian inclusion should be a major part of this work, and that it also

should be contained in the discourse on sexism, racism, and other types of discrimination and stereotyping that fell under the district's multicultural umbrella. "Respecting diversity" were words that frequently occurred in the district's mission statements, a commitment that I was to find out later did not fully extend to differences of sexual orientation.

Addressing homophobic name-calling, gay and lesbian stereotypes, and heterosexism became even more of a priority when I found myself teaching children with gay or lesbian parents. During the 1995-96 school year my classroom of 22 children was representative of the school's low-income and working-class urban population, with six African-American, four biracial (African-American/European-American), two Asian-American (Hmong), one Mexican-American and nine European-American children. And, as in the last several years, one of my students, Paul, had two lesbian moms.

Although I was continuing with 15 of the students from my first/second grade classroom the year before, this school year had started out tense, with students challenging each other with teasing and name-calling. After several days of more minor incidents, this culminated in a fight on the playground. I read a poem with the class "Coke-Bottle Brown," by Nikki Grimes (1994) and facilitated a discussion about name calling. We talked about the words that had sparked the conflict and discussed how they fell into certain categories, like racism and sexism. Kendra said, "I know a word. It's homophobia." I

A Kid in My Class

There is a kid in my class and his moms are lesbian. He is a normal kid. There is nothing wrong about being gay or lesbian. Some people are scared of gay and lesbian people. The people that are scared of gay and lesbian people are homophobic. I am not homophobic. The kid in my class is my friend. Here is a little I can add "Hey, hey, ho, ho, homophobias got to go!!"

wrote it on the board and talked about what it meant and how it's related to words that they had mentioned, such as "faggot" and "gay bitch."

There were some negative reactions (among kids new to my class) to the word "gay." Tony said, "I hate gay people." After school he met one of Paul's moms, Anne. Paul went up to Tony and said, "Well, do you like my mom?" He said, "Yeah." Paul said, "Well, my mom's gay, so I guess you don't hate gay people."

Later, I shared with Anne what had happened. She said that she was proud of Paul's efforts to prove Tony wrong. I shared in her wonder at her child's strength and perseverance. Yet I felt uneasy. It shouldn't be up to 7-year-old kids, I thought, to defend themselves and their families against irrational fears and hatred. I felt that I needed to do a more adequate job of

shouldering Paul's burden, of helping the students in my classroom to unlearn negative feelings and stereotypes about gay and lesbian people.

From this initial discussion of name-calling until the last weeks of the school year, anti-bias education was to become a continuous thread woven throughout our curriculum. The photo exhibit opportunity seemed to be a natural conclusion to our year-long efforts. What was clear to me and to most other teachers, however, as well as to many of our students and parents, was problematic for the district administration. As it turned out, the administration's conflicting messages and muddled tactics, along with full coverage by the local press (our school was in the front page headlines for a week and featured on television news and radio talk shows), succeeded in creating

even more of a controversy out of the photo exhibit than I had originally feared.

Conflict in the Community

At an initial meeting about the exhibit with the principal, the assistant superintendent, and a parent, we encountered little opposition. The assistant superintendent assured us, "I have no problems with this." However, after consulting with the deputy superintendent and the superintendent, she sent us a letter that implied otherwise. Along with flowery language extolling our "wonderful work" teaching acceptance of diversity and prejudice reduction was this statement: "Having a picture exhibition that highlights all the many different kinds of families would support your SIP (School Improvement Plan) goal, the larger

Gigi Kaeser

issue of creating an inclusive school, as well as the philosophy of (our) School District. Selecting one family structure only would exclude and not be appropriate given our inclusive goals...." The letter concluded with a suggestion that we meet with interested parents and staff if we intended to proceed with an exhibit within those parameters.

At a hastily called meeting of 17 staff members and 7 parents, it was decided that we needed to preserve the integrity of the photo exhibit by keeping it intact. People agreed that mixing in photos of heterosexual families would dilute the message: that gay and lesbian families need to be recognized and celebrated. It was felt that the exhibit would be an opportunity for gays and lesbians to be highlighted, as has traditionally been done with other groups excluded from the mainstream of school curriculum. But despite the decision of this group and letters sent to the administration from the PTO and local clergy, gay and lesbian groups, university professors, and many parents, the district maintained its stance.

A week later, however, the administrators changed tactics and delegated the decision to the school community. They set up a meeting which, according to a local newspaper, *The Capital Times*, they decided was "not one appropriate for (district) higher-ups to attend." The meeting, which

was announced on television and in the newspapers as a "public hearing," was called for May 1.

Some of the photos from the exhibit, black-and-white images of racially diverse gay or lesbian families in every imaginable family configuration (extended families, two moms or two dads, single parent families, families with stepparents, etc.), were set up in the school library for parents and other community members to preview. Discussion, however, was limited to two dozen parents who had either volunteered or been recruited by the principal to present different points of view.

The meeting, minimally facilitated

by the principal and a district resource person, was described by *The Capital Times* as a "chaotic process." The story began: "A punch was thrown, a moderator lost his cool, and parents were left in an uproar...." Eventually a second meeting had to be scheduled to resolve the issues left unresolved.

Feelings at those meetings were indeed intense. People yelled, cried, interrupted, accused, and sometimes tried to compromise. Having an exhibit of gay and lesbian families was likened by some of the speakers to exhibiting photos of drug dealers or sadomasochists. While many cited religious reasons ("My religion says it's a sin"), a few others gave cultural concerns ("Gays and lesbians are despised in our culture"). One of Paul's moms, Jane, who said later that she was the only gay parent who took part in both meetings, related how difficult it was for her to sit through all the insults and attacks on her family.

At the beginning of the first meeting, our home/school coordinator read a letter signed by 37 staff members supporting the exhibit. The letter said:

> Dear (school) community,
> If we need to be diverse in our thinking and teaching, then we need to teach and talk about gay

Gigi Kaeser

and lesbian families.... This is not about sexuality. This is about family structure.... Additionally, this exhibit addresses a pertinent safety issue. Children are often harassed or intimidated by other children using homophobic terms.

We, as teachers or parents, always challenge a student who is making racist comments or insults. Yet homophobic name-calling — "You're gay!" etc. — is sometimes left unaddressed.... If we are to eliminate discrimination, we need to confront it in all forms.

We, the undersigned [school] staff, are strongly supportive of having the *Love Makes a Family* exhibit at our school. We believe it is educationally sound and supports our SIP goals of prejudice reduction and inclusion.

With the exception of the letter, teachers followed the advice of the union to assert our contractual right of academic freedom by refraining from debate. We joined the observers from the school and the community, who had been instructed by the principal and facilitator to remain silent. About half the parents in the discussion group expressed views similar to those presented by the teachers. They affirmed the need to be inclusive of gay and lesbian families in support of the school's and district's multicultural, anti-bias goals. Several stated that they wanted their children to grow up in a world in which they would be safe from discrimination, regardless of their sexual orientation.

Some parents refuted the parallels to the African-American Civil Rights Movement that had been brought up in the teachers' letter, but other African-American parents supported the comparison. Kendra's mother, for one, said that she had encountered discrimination many times in her life and knew it well. "I can feel it now, again, in this room," she said in an impassioned statement which received resounding applause.

Several alternative proposals were raised: They included leaving out the

GIGI KAESER

words "gay" and "lesbian" in the title of the exhibit, mixing in photos of heterosexual families, and moving the exhibit to the Reach room (a small classroom out of the main stream of traffic). Gigi Kaeser, the photographer who created the exhibit, and several parents deemed these suggestions unacceptable. "This is another case of forcing gays and lesbians back into the closet," Kaeser said.

Toward the end of the second meeting, it appeared that little progress had been made. The 20 parent representatives had not succeeded in narrowing the gap between their widely divergent viewpoints. Suddenly, however, during the last 15 minutes, they reached a consensus. The compromise was very similar to the teachers' original proposal: to display the photo exhibit in the school library; to provide alternatives to children whose parents requested them; and to communicate with parents. This compromise appeared to be more the result of time pressure, exhaustion, and resignation than of genuine conflict resolution. The meeting was adjourned, but the tension continued — in the stuffy and crowded library, in the halls, in the parking lot, and on the sidewalks surrounding the school.

Reactions from the Students

Meanwhile, the students in my classroom were trying to make sense of the conflict. Some children were aware of their parents' support for the exhibit; many of their parents had spoken out publicly. Cassie's dad expressed his opinions in the local newspaper: "Why don't they (the school administration) just say they don't want this in here because it is about gay people?" Jodi's dad was featured in the press as well, because he'd been involved in a scuffle with members of the "Christian Right" who were demonstrating outside the school during the first meeting. Paul's moms lent us their rainbow flag, which we displayed until the end of the school year.

Emily wrote a letter to the local newspaper, which was published.

Dear Mr. and Ms. Editor,
Hi. My name is (Emily). I am 9 years old and go to ... the school that's fighting about gay and lesbian family posters being up in the library.

Lots of teachers and parents think it's a good idea because it shows another kind of family than we usually see. Some school bosses that don't go to (this school) think it's not OK.

There's some kids that live with two moms. I bet they feel pretty bad about this adult fight and I bet they want the posters up too, cuz it's like their families.

Kids don't really know if they are gay or lesbian until they are maybe in high school. I don't think you can tell yet.

What the people are doing when they say "no" about the photo essay is called total homophobia. I hope kids don't learn to be homophobic by listening to the adults fight about this.

Here's a little something I can add, "Hey, hey, ho, ho, homophobia's got to go!"

After Emily read her letter to the class, the dialogue that followed was far more rational and calm than that

GIGI KAESER

of the parents.

Anitra: I didn't know your parents were married.

Lena: What posters are up?

(The student teacher explained the contents of the photo exhibit.)

Cassie: I wanted to stay at the meeting, but my parents wouldn't let me. I think they should go up so people would know that being gay or lesbian isn't bad and then they wouldn't hate them.

Ian: You should fax your letter to all the schools in (our city)!

Samantha: I think two things. I do think they should go up. People can learn that they're not bad, but just the same as us. But I think that there shouldn't only be one kind of family. Just showing them gay and lesbian families looks like they're different and they're different because they're bad.

Emily: If it were Hispanic families or any other kind, they'd say it was okay. They're saying no just because they're gay or lesbian.

Cassie: I know why some people are homophobic. It says in the Bible that gay and lesbian people are bad.

Samantha: It should have been in our school first. A lot of kids tease about being gay or lesbian. Ellen came and reached over me to get something from her cubby and a kindergarten kid who was walking by our room said, "Oh, they're gay!"

Lena: Those kids probably didn't know what lesbians are. Lesbians are girls who love each other and gay means boys. Gay also means happy.

Ian: Oh, I get it. They're together so they're happy. That's why you call them gay.

Cassie: Rob and Tom (a gay couple who are friends with her family) could come and talk to our class about gay rights.

Only two families had expressed opposition to the exhibit. Joel's mom and dad wrote a letter requesting that

their child not participate in the viewing of the exhibit. Ellen's mom and stepdad came into the classroom after school one day, arguing that homosexuality was against their religion and family values. I reiterated the importance of respecting everyone in the school community, regardless of whether we agreed with them or not. They left the room with assurances that their child would not be ostracized for her family's beliefs, and that alternative activities would be available for her.

The Big Day

On the Monday morning following the second parent meeting, we went as a class to view the photo exhibit. After all the discord and tension of the proceeding weeks, the actual event felt almost anticlimactic to me.

I had assigned partners and asked the students to go around the library in pairs to look at the photographs and read the dialogues that went with them. I told them to pick a favorite photo to present to the group and, if they chose, to read parts of the accompanying scripts. Gigi Kaeser, the photographer, joined us for the discussion that followed.

During the discussion, I was somewhat distracted, first by the presence of a parent from another classroom who had been very vehement about his opposing views, and second by the uneasy scrutiny of the principal. But I remember how accepting and matter-of-fact the children's reactions were. Far from seeing something exotic or sinister about the exhibit, the students were interpreting the photos and dialogues as what they were: portraits of families. When we had reconvened in a circle, I let each pair of students show the class the photo of their choice and explain why they had picked it. A typical response was, "Because it looks like a very loving, happy family."

Many members of the class chose families with a racial and/or structural resemblance to their own families. Kendra, who has had a struggle accepting her dad's second marriage to a white woman, picked a family composed of an African-American mom, her two children and her white partner. "I like how the kids didn't like their new mom at first," she said, "but then they changed their minds because she made such good cheeseburgers!"

Emily, on the other hand, laughed when she read from the dialogue accompanying her favorite photo, in which a girl said: "Teachers don't teach the whole story about families in their classrooms. Teachers need to say that most families don't have a mom, a dad, a puppy dog, and a boy and a girl." "That's exactly what I have!" Emily exclaimed. "A mom, a dad, a brother and a dog."

Emily also said she liked the girl's story of how she had dealt with her friends' reactions to her lesbian family. In the exhibit text the girl said: "All of my friends have known about it. Anybody important to me has known about it and is cool about it.... If you can't accept my mom, you can't accept me."

Lena, who has never seen her birth father, was attracted to a photo of a woman alone with a baby. She wanted to know how she got the baby and why she didn't have any partner, male or female. "That's just like me and my mom," said Samantha, whose mom also has been her only parent since birth.

After about a half-hour of discussion, the next scheduled class, a group of kindergartners, came into the library. I invited them to join our class until we finished and they squeezed into our circle, some sitting on the laps of siblings or neighborhood friends. Interrupted only by the squeaks of the library book racks and the voices of children from other classes checking out books, the two classes listened attentively to the remaining presentations by my students.

After the Exhibit

After viewing the photo exhibit, interest was high, so I decided to ask the class to brainstorm related activi-

GIGI KAESER

In our classroom, gays and lesbians had moved a long way from the "other" status that they frequently occupy in school and society.

ties. Someone suggested reading a class book we had compiled during the filming of the *It's Elementary* video the previous year, which was full of stories and pictures about gay and lesbian rights. "That's not fair," Tonisha protested. "We should write stories for a new book!" Other ideas included making pink triangle pins and designing posters for the hallway.

Such activities continued for several weeks. During their free-choice

time, kids made buttons, which they proudly offered to teachers. They started out by copying a pin I had brought in which had a rainbow background and the words "Celebrate Diversity," but soon came up with their own variations in designs and slogans. They used colorful markers to make rainbows overlaid with pink and black triangles and peace symbols. Phrases like "Love one another," "It's OK to be gay," and "Homophobia gots to go!" embellished the pins.

I also read several books about gay or lesbian families to the class. A favorite was a daily "read-aloud" called *Living in Secret* by Christine Salat (1993). Since the book had been suggested by a fourth/fifth grade teacher, I had wondered at first if it might be too advanced. The story, about an 11-year-old girl who runs away to live with her lesbian moms, turned out to be very popular. Students were relating on many levels to the story — to the element of suspense, certainly, but also to the family recombinations, loyalties, and friction that were familiar to many of them. "Read another chapter!" came to be the refrain, as our read-aloud time began to cut into recess and free time.

Adam composed a letter to the editor of a local newspaper:

I think gay and lesbian people aren't respected enough. It's not like they aren't allowed to go to the movies, or restaurants, but it's almost like legal disrespect. I don't know why people have disrespect for gay and lesbian people, because they aren't gay or lesbian so why do they care? I have some advice for you homophobic people out there, don't go out of your homes! There could be a gay or lesbian person anywhere.

On the last day of the two-week exhibit, we went as a class to have another look at the photos. Ian was fascinated by a photo of a gay family with a dog. "They have a Corgi, just like I do!" was his comment. Afterward, we had a quiet writing time to reflect on issues related to the exhibit. As usual, the students chose a variety of ways to approach the topic.

Ian wrote: "I think people should all get along together. I think they should not be homophobic, because it makes gays and lesbian people feel sad. I think our school should have gay and lesbian photos in our school because lots of kids call other kids names and to educate the kids."

Jeremy related the issues of gay and lesbian rights to racist name calling. "One time I got called a nigger and I didn't like it so I went and told the teacher because I don't like being called that name because it is bad," he wrote. "That's why name calling is bad to say (even) when you are just playing around."

Emily wrote a science-fiction story about alien lesbians who encountered homophobia for the first time when they visited Earth. "When they got to Earth they went to an A&W restaurant and a teenager called them 'faggot.' That was the first time that had ever happened, so they said back: '*@#$%^&*!@#$ %^&*!' which means, 'We are proud

to be who we are.'"

When they had finished their stories, the students worked on drawings to go with them. A crowd started to gather around Paul's table. He was drawing a picture of the Capitol

> **People agreed that mixing in photos of heterosexual families would dilute the message: that gay and lesbian families need to be recognized and celebrated.**

building in our city surrounded by little circles that represented the 1,000 people he and his moms had joined for a gay pride march. As he drew he was counting: "... 99, 100, 101...."

As I watched the children cheering Paul for trying to represent all the people who supported his moms, I thought about the progress we had made. In our classroom, gays and lesbians had moved a long way from the "other" status that they frequently occupy in school and society. Gay and lesbian families and individuals had become integral parts of our classroom dialogues and stories. Homophobia, a word now known to all, had become as serious a charge as any other form of discrimination.

On one of the last days of school, Adam and Ian came rushing in from recess, flushed and agitated. "One of the fifth-graders is homophobic!" they said indignantly. "He was teasing us and calling us 'gay.'" I assured them that his teacher would want to hear about it, and, without the trepidation usually shown by members of our class when they approach the 4/5 grade teachers, they confidently marched into the classroom down the hall to report the incident.

I thought back to the name calling incidents and discussions at the beginning of the year, and all the stress and conflict surrounding the photo exhibit. Although as a class and as a school we had felt the divisions and pain, we had come through. The rainbow flag that was flying at our classroom door was a daily reminder of our struggle and testimony to our commitment. ∎

Kate Lyman teaches in Madison, Wisconsin. She can be reached via e-mail at clyman@madison.k12.wi.us. The names of the children in this article have been changed.

References

Chasnoff, Debra and Cohen, Helen (producers). *It's Elementary: Talking About Gay Issues in School.* San Francisco: JPD Communications, 1996.

Grimes, Nikki. *Meet Danitra Brown.* New York: Lothrop, Lee and Shepard Books, 1994.

Kaeser, Gigi. *Love Makes a Family: Living in Gay and Lesbian Families.* Photographs by Gigi Kaeser; interviews by Pam Brown and Peggy Gillespie. Amherst, MA: Authors, 1995.

Salat, Christine. *Living in Secret.* New York: Bantam Books, 1993.

Resources on Gay and Lesbian Issues

Different and the Same, produced by Family Communications. Distributed by Destination Education: 877-347-4047; www.shopdei.com. This series of nine videos for young elementary children uses puppets to explore issues of discrimination and prejudice. Although it does not deal directly with issues of gay and lesbian inclusion, many of the segments could be used to spark discussions about acceptance of family differences or name calling. It includes teachers' guides.

Asha's Mums, by Rosamund Elwin and Michele Paulse. Toronto: Women's Press, 1990. A girl runs into a problem when her teacher doesn't accept the fact that two moms signed her field trip permission slip. This is an engaging story for young elementary students.

How Would You Feel If Your Dad Was Gay?, by Ann Heron and Meredith Maran. Boston: Alyson Publications, Inc., 1991. This story, geared for middle elementary children, presents the story of a third-grade girl who encounters problems at school when she shares the fact that she has three dads (her mother's partner and her dad and his male partner). The book explores the reaction of her classmates and teachers, as well as the reluctance of her older brother to share his family structure.

It's Elementary: Talking About Gay Issues in School, by Debra Chasnoff and Helen Cohen. GroundSpark, 2180 Bryant Street, Suite 203, San Francisco, CA 94110. 800-405-3322. www.groundspark.org. This documentary film is intended for teachers and others interested in educating elementary school children about gay and lesbian issues. It was filmed in elementary classrooms in schools in Wisconsin, New York, California, and Massachusetts.

Love Makes a Family: Living in Gay and Lesbian Families; A Photograph-Text Exhibit, photographs by Gigi Kaeser and interviews by Pam Brown and Peggy Gillespie. Family Diversity Projects, P.O. Box 1246, Amherst, MA 01004-1246. 413-256-0502; fax 413-253-3977. www.familydiv.org. The black and white photographs depict racially diverse gay and lesbian families in a variety of family structures. Included in the exhibit are written dialogues with family members and a teacher resource packet.

Belinda's Bouquet, by Leslea Newman. Boston: Alyson Publications, Inc., 1991. Issues of body image and name calling are explored in a story in which the fact that the child has two moms is secondary to the main plot.

Gloria Goes to Gay Pride, by Leslea Newman. Boston: Alyson Publications, Inc., 1991. Gloria is excited about going to a gay pride march with her moms. She is confused, however, when they encounter protesters with anti-gay signs. This story is helpful in discussing homophobia with young elementary school children.

Heather Has Two Mommies, by Leslea Newman. Northampton, MA: In Other Words Publishing, 1989. This story about a girl with lesbian moms has raised controversy because it explains artificial insemination. However, the question, "How can two women have a baby together?" is natural for students as young as kindergarten to ask. This book gives one possible answer to that question, as well as exploring the variety of families in Heather's classroom.

Overcoming Homophobia in the Elementary Classroom, Lesbian and Gay Parents Association, 260 Tingley Street, San Francisco, CA 94112. 415-337-1629; LGPASF@aol.com. This video package contains materials for elementary teachers, including the video *Both My Moms' Names Are Judy: Children of Lesbians and Gays Speak Out*.

Living in Secret, by Christine Salat. New York: Bantam Books, 1993. This fictional chapter book for older elementary students relates how a girl runs away to "live in secret" with her lesbian mom and her partner.

The Duke Who Outlawed Jelly Beans and Other Stories, by Johnny Valentine. Boston: Alyson Publications, Inc., 1991. These modern fairy tales involve dragons, magic frogs, and girls who defy limitations based on gender. The characters happen to have gay or lesbian families; but only in the last (title) story is this the main issue. In the latter, an autocratic duke decrees that children who have "too many" fathers or mothers will be thrown into the dungeon.

— compiled by Kate Lyman

Playing Favorites
Gifted education and the disruption of community

By Mara Sapon-Shevin

Why are there programs for "gifted" children? Why are some children labeled "gifted" but not others? And what does all this mean for the education of the "non-gifted"?

In discussions about gifted education, the underlying assumption is that gifted students represent an objectively identifiable population, that they are "out there," and that the first step in serving this population is to "find them."

The focus is typically on finding that population that is truly "gifted" and rarely on the integrity or reality of the category itself. "Who is gifted?" and "How do we best find and identify gifted children?" are considered legitimate questions. "Does it make sense to call *any* children gifted?" is not a similarly sanctioned inquiry.

The use of the term "gifted" provides a scientific explanation or label for difference, and, as such, it comes to replace commonsense meaning and understandings of children's behavior and differences. By describing a group of children in ways that emphasize their differences from typical or "nongifted" children, we are encouraged to believe that giftedness is something foreign, outside our daily commonsense frameworks. The parent who exclaims, "Well, I knew my daughter was very smart, but I had no idea she was gifted!" provides evidence of the ways in which official, scientific-sounding, technical terminology replaces our commonsense ways of thinking about and talking about children's differences. Books on "how to raise your gifted child" or "how to live with gifted children" encourage us to see children who are labeled as "gifted" as "others," outside our experience and thus outside our capacity to think about or plan for. This "othering" contributes to the idea that educational programming for children labeled "gifted" is logically considered separate from or apart from educational programming for typical children —

> We can see the category of "giftedness" as a social construct, a way of thinking and describing that exists in the eyes of the definers.

"they're different — they need something special."

Identifying certain children as gifted represents a decision. It represents a decision to attempt to sort children according to specific variables, a decision about how to assess those variables, and then, a decision about what to do with the results of that assessment. Each of these represents a discrete set of decisions. Deciding to identify children as gifted on the basis of tested intelligence is a decision; so is deciding to measure intelligence using a standardized IQ test; and so is the decision to arbitrarily establish a cut-off point along a continuum of scores or behavior and to then act as though those above that point are qualitatively (rather than quantitatively) different from those below.

Defining Giftedness

Giftedness is typically defined as the top 3-5% of the population. Some choose to further subdivide the population into the "gifted," the "highly gifted," and the "exceptionally gifted," and each of these is also generally defined in terms of a percentage of the general population. Efforts by some gifted educators to "liberalize" definitions of giftedness in order to include greater percentages of children have been harshly criticized by others. Nicholas Colangelo, a proponent of gifted education,[1] for example, is concerned that the liberalization of the definition (that is, including too many children within it) will lead to a time when we view every child as either gifted or "potentially gifted" and thereby deny meaning to the term "gifted." Educator Barbara Clark expresses concern that "throwing a wider net may result in children being less well served. ... The attempt to serve 25% of the students must not be allowed to reduce the all-too-inadequate support that is given the top 5%."[2]

Rather than viewing giftedness as a "natural fact," we can see the cate-

KATHY SLOANE

gory of "giftedness" as a social construct, a way of thinking and describing that exists in the eyes of the definers. Children vary along many dimensions; it is a decision (rather than a fact) to decide to focus on one of these varying differences and then to label children according to that dimension. People vary tremendously in height and can be measured with relatively good reliability; nonetheless, deciding to create categories of the "profoundly tall" and the "profoundly short" would mean both deciding that height was a salient characteristic appropriate for describing people and determining where to make the cut-offs along a continuum of heights.

Recognizing giftedness as a social construct means acknowledging that without school rules and policies, legal and educational practices designed to provide services to gifted students, this category, per se, would not exist. This is not to say that we would not have tremendous variation in the ways in which children present

themselves in schools or even in the rates or ways in which they learn. But the characteristic of giftedness, possessed exclusively by an identifiable group of students, only exists within a system that, for a variety of reasons, wishes to measure, select, and sort students in this manner.

The most pervasive method of identifying children as "gifted" is based on the use of standardized intelligence tests. But intelligence testing has come under serious attack as both unreliable and culturally biased. Intelligence tests typically measure a limited range of verbal skills, and these skills are associated with exposure to education and membership in the dominant cultural group of our society. Thus, various cultural groups are disproportionately represented in those categories of exceptionality that are determined primarily by performance on intelligence tests. Children of color and lower socioeconomic levels are overrepresented in classes for the "mentally retarded" and underrepresented

in classes for the "gifted."

But because standardized IQ tests are generally viewed as "objective" and free from the bias we assume would be present if children were identified as "mentally retarded" or "gifted" by their teachers, we neglect both the origins and the continuing uses of intelligence testing to facilitate educational and social stratification.

One of the original uses of intelligence testing (and a major impetus for the development of the testing industry) was to sort out the flood of recent immigrants to this country. Eighty percent of the immigrants tested in the 1920s by test developer Lewis Terman were adjudged "feeble-minded" and channeled into low status, limited educational and employment options.[3] The legacy of defining intelligence as those characteristics possessed by white, upper-middle class students, and the subsequent sorting and selecting of students according to this scale, continues to define gifted education in this country.

Acting as though intelligence is a single continuum along which people can be located masks the embedded decisions to value and measure only certain kinds of intelligence. In fact, the narrow ways in which giftedness is defined and the subsequent limitations on which children are served by gifted programs are directly related to the ways in which classrooms are organized and instruction delivered.

Classrooms and schools that define achievement and ability narrowly produce students who rank one another according to limited variables. When classrooms are organized in multidimensional ways, when many kinds of skills and performance are acknowledged and valued, the kinds of global stratification ("He's smart; she's not") present in unidimensional classrooms is sharply limited. Educational researchers S. Rosenholtz and E. Cohen argue that the conventional "back to basics" classroom structures a narrow view of curriculum and relies on comparative marking and grading as the sole method of evaluation, reinforcing racist beliefs about the intellectual incompetence of minority children.[4]

Identifying giftedness as an inborn, hereditary quality of the individual that can be objectively verified further connects the process of identification to "science" and further removes the decision from common-sense discourse. According to this position, we are not defining intelligence nor making decisions about what kinds of skills we value but are simply identifying and labeling inherent, immutable human characteristics, some of which happen to be highly valued.

Born Gifted?

The belief that certain children are "born gifted" is also used to support gifted education as part of a social justice argument. If certain people are just "born gifted" then you shouldn't discriminate against them because of a characteristic over which they have no control. So if

Jacob was "born gifted," it would be unfair to treat him like "normal" children by providing him with a typical education, just as it would be unfair to penalize children who have diabetes by forcing them to eat a typical sugar-laden diet. The parallel actually raises a compelling set of issues, because it assumes that the typical sugar-laden diet is appropriate for "regular" children who don't have diabetes, just as we assume that the "typical" education provided for students is appropriate for those who aren't identified as gifted.

Marc Gold, a pioneer in education for persons with mental retardation,

> If gifted students and low-achieving, at-risk students all need hands-on, participatory enrichment activities, then who are all the worksheets for?

characterized "retarded students" as those who require more intensive teaching.[5] He evaluated levels of retardation in terms of the willingness of educators to extend the time, energy, and commitment necessary to bring retarded students to higher levels of achievement. This same logic could be extended to gifted children, defining *not* the children but rather the resources that schools and educators would be willing to commit in order to make all children "gifted." Such a definition would see all children as underachieving gifted students, and all students would be

described as varying in terms of the resources needed to help them achieve at high levels. This would substantially alter the conversation, since it would require an explicit discussion of resource allocation and the values that underlie deciding whom to spend money on and who is worth what.

A careful examination of the rhetoric of "what gifted children need" reveals problems not with that wish list of optimum educational options but with its characterization of distinctiveness. Educators of the gifted are counseled that appropriate goals for gifted children include mental flexibility, openness to information, capacity to systemize knowledge, capacity for abstract thought, fluency, sense of humor, positive thinking, intellectual courage, resistance to enculturation, and also emotional resilience.[6] Talented children and adolescents are said to need:

• A maximum level of achievement in basic skills and concepts.

• Learning activities at an appropriate level and pace.

• Experience in creative thinking and problem solving.

• Convergent thinking skills.

• Self-awareness.

• Exposure to a variety of fields.

• The development of greater independence, self-direction, and also discipline in learning.[7]

It is difficult to find much in the above list that is objectionable. The only problem with this list is that these are recommendations for "gifted students," rather than for *all* students. If gifted children need all these things, then what do nongifted children need? Ironically, recent research literature on the educational needs of students identified as "at-risk" and "low-achieving" has produced lists of desirable educational outcomes almost identical to the above list. If gifted students and low-achieving, at-risk students all need hands-on, participatory, enrichment activities, then who are all the worksheets for? Who are the typical kids for whom the standard curriculum is supposedly geared? What evidence do we have that an enriched curriculum and a dynamic environment are not stimulating and educationally appropriate for all students?

Not only are the educational needs of gifted students seen as significantly different from those of typical children but many gifted educators argue that the unique needs of gifted students cannot be met within the regular classroom; gifted children must be grouped together in order to receive appropriate education.

Gifted education proponents argue that the regular classroom as currently organized and implemented is largely not amenable to change, and many teachers and students are hostile to gifted students, thus necessitating the removal of gifted students to a "safe haven" where they can be with other students like them.

While I would never argue that the narrow, often rigid ways in which many regular education classrooms are currently organized make them ideal for meeting the needs of students identified as gifted (or any other students), deciding to remove some children from that setting in order to meet their putative educational needs elsewhere has significant implications. First, it communicates a hopelessness and despair about the ability of teachers to create inclusive, stimulating, multilevel, diverse learning communities that meet the needs of a wide range of students within a unified setting. The message is: third grade was terrible for this child, so we removed him to a better setting. The question should be, however, if third grade was terrible for this child, how was it for other children, and how can we change third grade to make it good for all children?

Second, differentially removing some children whose perceived needs are not being met in the typical classroom makes clear the fact that some parents have the possibility of removing their children from nonideal settings, while others do not. Wealthy parents who are dissatisfied with the education their children are receiving

in public schools have often removed their children to private school settings; poor parents dissatisfied with their children's education do not have the same set of choices. Similarly, children whose test scores qualify them for gifted programs have the option of removal and differential educational opportunities; children whose measured scores are not high enough do not have the same options.

Most significant, however, is that the removal of gifted children in order

> **What evidence do we have that an enriched curriculum and a dynamic environment are not stimulating and appropriate for all kids?**

to meet their educational needs leaves untouched the nature and quality of the regular education classroom.

Evading the Real Problem

As long as gifted programs are described as programs for "gifted children," then their boundaries are arbitrarily and narrowly defined. Books on "Language Arts Activities for Gifted Students," teacher workshops on "Creativity for the Gifted," and similarly labeled efforts all circumscribe the set of students to whom such programming and educational efforts will be directed. Even exemplary gifted programs may impede whole-school reform that is solidly grounded in broader economic and social concerns because they give the illusion that "something is

being done." By siphoning off the efforts and commitment of concerned parents, teachers, and administrators, such stop-gap or partial measures may keep schools from hitting "rock bottom" and thus facing the magnitude and embeddedness of their problems.

Eliminating gifted programs will not solve school or societal problems, because the problems do not result from the gifted programs. Rather, gifted programs are a response to the inappropriateness and inflexibility of schools — a response that creates as many problems as it solves — and to an economic system that depends on the schools to maintain social, educational, and economic stratification. Parents whose children are not well served in regular classrooms often support removing their children to separate classrooms because they have little or no faith that the typical classroom can be altered sufficiently to meet their children's needs. As one parent explained to me, "In the long haul, of course we need better schools for everyone, but for now, I have to think about my child."

This reaction, although understandable, nonetheless contributes to maintaining the status quo. Removing the irritating or irritated child (or parent) does nothing to alter the nature of the overall educational system and sometimes masks the breadth and depth of the problem. The focus becomes on finding a "better fit" for Kyle, rather than on examining the system as a whole. Furthermore, removing the children whose parents typically have the knowledge, resources, and influence to result in their placement in gifted classrooms further segregates the schools and results in even greater disparity between the educational opportunities open to children of varying socioeconomic and racial groups. Removing gifted children and providing a differential education for them will not improve the overall quality of schooling for all children nor will it encourage us to analyze the relationship between schools and broader societal and economic inequities.

Some educational leaders have strongly supported the need to "invest" in gifted children as a way of ensuring America's recovery of economic and political prominence. A changing political climate that attributes many of the nation's educational problems to overinvestment in poor, disadvantaged, and minority students (at the expense of those who are more academically talented) also provides impetus for increased gifted programming. In tracing the history of gifted education in America, gifted education advocates G. Davis and S. Rimm describe the effects of the Russian launching of the satellite Sputnik in 1957 as a landmark event. Suddenly, it appeared that the Russians were gaining on the United States in the fields of science and technology and that we had better pay more attention (and give more money) to promote high achievement in these areas. Davis and Rimm report, however, that "the scare of Sputnik and the keen interest in educating gifted and talented students wore off in about five years."[8] As the United States took the lead in the space race in the 1960s, the panicked need to cultivate gifted students diminished, only to come alive again in the 1970s with the publication of the Maryland Report in 1972, which declared gifted students to be a vastly underserved population.

The spate of national educational reports that appeared in the 1980s proclaiming us to be a "nation at risk of educational failure," again gave rise to new fears about the crisis in the U.S. educational system manifested by its failure to keep pace with other nations. Now the scare came from the progress and successes of the Japanese. While the majority of these reports gave lip service to the twin goals of excellence and equality, some warned that our inadequate educational production was a direct result of "over-investing" in poor, disadvantaged, and minority students. The Heritage Foundation stated in 1984: "For the past 20 years, federal mandates have favored 'disadvantaged' pupils at the expense of those who have the highest potential to contribute to society,"[9] implying that it had been our nation's misguided focus on equality that had led to our crisis of excellence.

While some educators are critical of the ways in which America has retreated from equity, they still cite the need to develop "the best minds," disparaging one kind of meritocracy and substituting another for it. There is little recognition that there are many ways for a child to be "advantaged" and that the overlap between material advantage and perceived educational and intellectual abilities is extensive.

Gifted programs allow society to support differential treatment for a limited group of students and to do so in a way that appears to have a quantitative, unbiased, reasoned, scientific basis. While we would be singularly uncomfortable saying, "We believe rich children deserve a better education than poor children," we are not uncomfortable enough about setting up structures that maintain exactly that outcome.

Restoring schools as communities in which all students learn will take more than small adjustments. Reinventing schools will involve attending to all aspects of school structure, culture, curriculum, instruction, and administration. Expanding gifted programs to include more students or implementing new tests to find gifted students will not bring the large-scale reform that is necessary for all students to succeed. ■

Mara Sapon-Shevin is a professor in the Teaching and Leadership Program at Syracuse University.

This article was adapted from Playing Favorites: Gifted Education and the Disruption of Community *by Mara Sapon-Shevin (Albany, NY: State University of New York Press, 1994). The book may be ordered by calling 800-666-2211.*

Notes

1. N. Colangelo, "A Perspective on the Future of Gifted Education," *Roeper Review* 7 (1) (1984): pp. 30-32.

2. Cited in R.D. Feldman, "The Pyramid: Do We Have the Answer for the Gifted?" *Instructor Magazine*, October 1985: p. 62-66, 71.

3. J. Oakes, *Keeping Track: How Schools Structure Inequality* (New Haven, CT: Yale University Press, 1985), p. 36.

4. S. J. Rosenholtz and E. G. Cohen, "Back to Basics and the Desegregated School," *The Elementary School Journal* 83 (5), (1983): 515-527.

5. M. C. Gold, "An Alternative Definition of Mental Retardation," in *Did I Say That? Articles and Commentary on the Try Another Way System*, ed. M. C. Gold (Champaign, IL: Research Press, 1980).

6. K. Albrecht, "Brain Power: The Human Mind as the Next Great Frontier." Speech presented at the Third Annual Midwest Conference on Gifted and Talented Children, Milwaukee, Wisconsin, April 1983. Cited in *Education of the Gifted and Talented*, eds. G. A. Davis and S. B. Rimm (Englewood Cliffs, NJ: Prentice-Hall, 1985).

7. J. F. Feldhusen and A. R. Wyman, "Super Saturday: Design and Implementation of Purdue's Special Program for Gifted Children," *Gifted Child Quarterly* 24 (1980): 15-21.

8. G. A. Davis and S. B. Rimm, *Education of the Gifted and Talented*, 2d ed. (Englewood Cliffs, NJ: Prentice-Hall, 1989), p. 7.

9. The Heritage Foundation, "The Crisis: Washington Shares the Blame," *The Heritage Foundation Backgrounder* (Washington, DC: The Heritage Foundation, 1984).

Black Teachers on Teaching: A Collection of Oral Histories

With an Introduction by Michele Foster

Prior to emancipation, Blacks held in slavery were forbidden to learn to read. Despite this prohibition and severe punishments, Blacks valued literacy and many learned to read. Some were taught by sympathetic whites; others learned alongside their master's children. But a significant number were taught by free Blacks or by slaves who were literate themselves. Well-regarded and respected, these Black teachers understood both the power and danger associated with literacy.

Leroy Lovelace, a retired high school English teacher, underscores the power of education today: "When a people can think critically, they can change things. They are less likely to be taken advantage of and more likely to be able to avoid the traps that others set for us...."

During the three decades following emancipation and through the first six decades of the 20th century, teaching was one of the few occupations open to college-educated Blacks. "The only thing an educated Negro can do is teach or preach," people would say. One difference between teaching and preaching, of course, was that teaching was open to women on an equal basis. In fact, one of the primary leadership roles available to Black women was as teachers in their communities.

Census data illustrate these patterns. Between 1890 and 1910, the number of Blacks employed as teachers rose from 15,100 to 66,236. In the census years of 1890, 1900, and 1910, Black teachers represented about 44%, 45%, and 45%, respectively, of professional Blacks. In 1910, 76% of Black teachers

JEAN-CLAUDE LEJEUNE

employed were women.

Throughout history, Black teachers have been hired primarily to teach Black students. Because of the large numbers of Blacks who resided in the South, a policy of "separate but equal" schooling, and Southern laws mandating that Black teachers could teach only in segregated schools, greater numbers of Black teachers were employed in the 17 Southern and border states. Of the 63,697 Black teachers in the United States in 1940, 46,381 were employed in the South.

Northern communities did not have laws segregating Black teachers in Black schools. But as more Blacks migrated to the North, the school systems adopted policies that resulted in the de facto segregation not only of Black pupils but also of Black teachers. In cities such as Philadelphia, Boston, New York, and Chicago, it was customary to assign Black teachers to predominantly Black schools or to restrict them to particular grades (usually elementary). In Philadelphia, it wasn't until 1935 that the first Black teacher was appointed to a junior high school, and not until 1947 was the first Black teacher assigned to a high school.

When I began teaching in the Boston public schools in the late 1960s, I encountered similar problems. As a first-year teacher I was assigned only to substitute-teach in predominantly Black schools, and when I finally did secure my own classroom I was assigned as a "provisional" or temporary teacher in predominantly Black schools. It wasn't until 1974, the year Boston public schools were desegregated by court order, that I was offered a permanent teaching position.

The primary reason that Black teachers were prohibited from teaching white children was the widespread belief firmly entrenched since the 19th century that, like others of their race, Black teachers were inferior to whites and not suitable to teach white pupils.

In both the North and the South, however, whites retained the prerogative to teach in Black schools. In 26 all-Black schools in Chicago in 1930, for example, only 34% of the faculty was Black.

The Black community agreed about the importance of schooling for its children. But it has been deeply divided over whether integrated or segregated schools would achieve the best outcome. This was especially true because integrated schools often meant the loss of jobs for Black teachers.

Black communities across the United States have grappled with this dilemma since the early 19th century. Black leaders often weighed in on both sides of the issue. Some believed that by insisting on Black teachers, the community was acquiescing to segregation. But there was still considerable sentiment within the Black community for retaining Black teachers to teach in Black schools....

Perhaps it was W. E. B. Du Bois who best summarized the situation:

And I know that race prejudice in the United States today is such that most Negroes cannot receive proper education in white institutions.... If the public schools of Atlanta, Nashville, New Orleans, and Jacksonville were thrown open to all races today, the education that colored children would get in them would be worse than pitiable. And in the same way, there are many public school systems in the North where Negroes are admitted and tolerated, but they are not educated; they are crucified. To sum up this: theoretically, the Negro needs neither separate nor mixed schools. What he needs is Education. What he must remember is that there is no magic either in mixed schools or segregated schools. A mixed school with poor unsympathetic teachers, with hostile public opinion, and no teaching of the truth concerning Black folk is bad. A segregated school with ignorant placeholders, inadequate equipment, and poor salaries is equally bad. Other things being equal, the mixed schools is the broader, more natural basis for the education of all youth. It gives wider contacts; it inspires greater self-confidence; and suppresses the inferiority complex. But other things seldom are equal, and in that case, Sympathy, Knowledge, and the Truth outweigh all that the mixed school can offer.

— *Michele Foster*

Ruby Middleton Forsythe

Ruby Middleton Forsythe was born in Charleston, South Carolina in 1905. She taught for almost 60 years in a one-room school on Pawley's Island, about 30 miles from Myrtle Beach.

Getting an education has always been hard for Black people. Now that the schools are integrated, getting an education is supposed to be easier, but it is still hard for Black children to get a decent education. The obstacles are different than the ones we faced, but they still exist. Let me give you an example. Not too long ago, they had a science fair at Wacamaw. Out of all the Black children — and some of them had good projects — not one of them got anything. Fourteen ribbons were given and all fourteen went to the whites. Some of the Black children said, "You mean to tell me that with all those good projects we had, no Black got a prize?" Those children just spoke out, said what they felt, and they were suspended because they're not supposed to express themselves even when they believe that what is going on in school is unfair. That just kills their spirit.

When the children were integrated into white schools, they lost something. Integration has helped in some ways, but it has hurt our Black children in some ways. Now, instead of seeing Black children winning prizes for their achievements, you see them all in special education classes. This has caused them to lose their pride, their self-esteem. They have been pushed back, as far as leadership is concerned. Instead of being taught to lead, they are being taught to follow. So we shouldn't be surprised now that when one gets up and does something, then the whole bunch jumps up and follows. Before, I think the older children were a bit more individual. They had a mind of their own. They couldn't be easily led. And when they reached a certain grade, they had a sense of pride or dignity that caused them to act different.

Just like integration has hurt Black children, it has also caused many of our Black teachers not to be sure of who they are and what they are supposed to stand for. In earlier times most of our Black teachers had a sense of purpose and dignity that they tried to instill into students. Some of our Black teachers today are very concerned about our children. But we have too many who will tell the child, "I've got mine.

You'd better get yours — because I know I'll get my paycheck." The Black community doesn't need that teacher.

Lorraine Lawrence

Lorraine Lawrence was born in Haskell, a small town in Oklahoma. She first taught in Cleveland, Ohio, from 1966 to 1972, and later in Orlando, Florida. In 1988, she was named Teacher of the Year.

One of the main criticisms of today's integrated schools is that the Black youngsters do not get pushed enough. In my high school, the few Black youngsters in the honors classes, who are highly motivated and capable, who are active in school, tend to be more affluent. They go out for cheerleading, drama, and debate; they run for student council and get elected. The majority of Black students — those in the regular group — are generally left out. They aren't cheerleaders, they aren't in the choir, which goes on tour every spring. They just don't get pushed to the front.

What I notice about these students is that they are capable of doing many things, and many actually do quite a few things in the community and in church. Many of them play instruments and they are in singing groups, but this tends to be outside of school. Too often their teachers don't know anything about Black kids' lives outside school, so the teachers conclude that these kids don't have anything going for themselves. If the students had a little encouragement, they could not only participate but excel in extracurricular activities.

In order to teach well, you have to think about students as if they belonged to you. If teachers showed the same concern, interacted with their students and treated them as if they were their own children, schools would have more success with greater numbers of students. Instead, teachers sit in the workroom and complain about the kids, how they aren't very smart or how aggravating they are. In class they discourage students, they are punitive, and they teach in such a way that the student hates the subject. In my years as a teacher and as

JEAN-CLAUDE LEJEUNE

department chair, for example, I have seen teachers ridicule students who receive a bad mark, and seat the class according to the grades they receive on a test. It's far too common for teachers not to expend any energy working with students who are labeled "slow learners." These teachers will complain about whatever the students can't do. But teachers ought to be able to work with a student no matter what the level.

The very best teachers can get all students to achieve. These teachers don't waste time complaining about what students can't do. Instead, they create the classroom conditions that enable students to achieve. More often than not, the students singled out for the most punitive treatment, the students considered the most aggravating, the students labeled slow learners are Black. This is a serious problem that has yet to be dealt with satisfactorily in desegregated schools.

Leroy Lovelace

Leroy Lovelace went to school in the farming community of Brewton, Ala., at a time when the public school for Blacks only went up to the tenth grade. He started teaching at Phillips School in Chicago in 1958 and retired from there in 1994.

The one thing that Black students don't need is teachers who let them get away with saying, "I can't do this. I can't do that"— teachers who feel sympathetic because the students are Black, or they are from the inner city, teachers who let them get away with doing nothing. Teachers have to realize that Black students — or all students, but I'm talking about Black students now — are very clever, especially with white teachers. Too many Black students have learned to play the game, to play on a teacher's sympathy in order to get away with doing nothing. Teachers have to demand from Black urban students the same as they would demand from privileged white students, and they have to be consistent. Urban Black students can do the work and in the

hands of skilled teachers they will do it. They may have to work harder to achieve success. All students will con teachers if they let themselves be conned. But it's often easier for Black students to con white teachers because the students know that the teachers will pity them, feel sorry for them, and make excuses that these students can't do this, can't do that, or that there's a problem at home. If teachers aren't careful, every other student will excuse his failure to do his homework by saying he had a

> **Too many Black students have learned to play the game, to play on a teacher's sympathy in order to get away with doing nothing.**

problem at home. I am not saying I never accepted a student's excuse, but I refused to accept every lame excuse they have because that's what they expected.

It particularly disturbs me when I see Black teachers letting Black students get away with doing nothing. Black teachers who do this tell themselves they are doing this sympathetically, but I don't accept that. I believe that Black teachers are doing it because we've become middle class. Once Black folks were poorer than Job's turkey and now that we have joined the white folks, we're talking about "they can't do it." You'd be surprised how many Black teachers do that.

In the past, Black teachers

demanded more of their students and they didn't care whether there was anything in it for them personally. A lot of my Black colleagues thought I was too hard on students. But the students I taught didn't think that, because for several years when the students had teacher recognition I got almost every award. The award I treasure most was the Teacher Who Demanded Most of Students.

Pamela Otis Ogonu

Pamela Otis Ogonu was the first Black person chosen California Teacher of the Year, in 1981. She has taught for 26 years at Samuel F.B. Morse High School in San Diego.

When I was a child, our parents, teachers, and other community members made it clear to us who our heroes ought to be and why. When I was a little girl I used to go to visit my great-grandmother, who was one of the greatest influences on my life. On the walls in her house were pictures she had cut out of *Ebony*. All these pictures used to fascinate me. There were pictures of Jackie Robinson and Roy Campanella. Even though some of the people were athletes, they represented more than that: They were symbols of individuals who had broken the barriers imposed on the Black community by the larger society.

When adults talked about Robinson, their emphasis was not only on his athletic ability. My great-grandmother would say, "There's Jackie Robinson: He's the first Black man to play baseball." All I heard was that he was the first Black man. At the time I didn't see Jackie Robinson only as a Brooklyn Dodger; I saw him as someone who had broken the color barrier. That was how our communities interpreted the meaning of these individuals' achievements. They were able to play with our minds in a positive way. But today when a white person tells Black students about Michael Jordan, they say, "You see Michael Jordan. He can run. Can you see how he can run?" Unfortunately, today's kids think that the reason these sports figures are important is because they play sports. This is why it is important that our community maintain control over the information being conveyed to our children.

Ethel Tanner

Ethel Tanner was born in Austin, Texas and moved as a child to the city of Roxbury, Massachusetts. She later became president of the board of Samaritan House, a nonprofit social service agency in California.

The majority of our students are poor. Many are from immigrant families. Half of them are on reduced-priced or free lunch; some live in motels because they don't have permanent housing. There are 17 languages spoken in the school. But we have created a belief system that our children can learn. We have set high academic standards for kids that we expect them to meet. We have a homework policy. We expect kids to come to school on time.

But we have created an extensive network of support systems to help kids meet our expectations. We have an after-school tutorial staffed by volunteer tutors that is open between 3 and 5 p.m. We have a meal program staffed by volunteers. Each weekday evening, families can come to the school and get a hot meal, no questions asked. In conjunction with the Samaritan House, we sponsor a clothes closet. We created a recreation program which we support with contributions.

As a Black principal, I realized I wasn't reaching many of the Latino families. When I first arrived, few of them came to school, not because

JEAN-CLAUDE LEJEUNE

they didn't care but because they didn't feel comfortable. When I sent home information it was rarely returned. I found out many of the parents were illiterate in their own language. So I organized a Spanish-speaking parent group. Whenever we have meetings I'll have one section in Spanish and one in English. During the meetings we talk about what is going on in school. If there is something that requires filling out forms — summer school, for example — we take the applications to the meetings and help parents fill them out. To reach Latino parents, I developed a close association with Father Isaacs, a priest over at St. Timothy's, the church many of my Latino families attend....

My philosophy of education is that you have to treat the whole child. I didn't get that from any of my teacher education or administrative credential courses, and that's where schools of education need to undergo some fundamental changes. I don't believe kids are really bad. If they become bad it's because of something that society has done wrong....

Teachers have a lot of say-so in this school. I demand quality, but

they have a lot to say about how we get there. Teachers can't just do their own thing: There has to be a cohesion among the faculty. When I interview teachers what's important is their energy level and their acceptance of children. No matter what their other qualifications, I don't want them if they can't accept children and form relationships with them. I want teachers who believe in kids that the society has given up on. A lot of my teachers weren't that way when I came. But if you model acceptance, educate them, they can change. Now I have a group of teachers who are very child-oriented. Not too long ago a teacher told me, "You've taught us that we should give without sitting in judgment of the person." ∎

Michele Foster is an educational consultant and a professor of education at the Claremont Graduate School in California.

This article is abridged and condensed from Black Teachers on Teaching *by Michele Foster, published by The New Press (New York, 1996). It can be ordered by calling book distributor W.W. Norton at 800-233-4830.*

School System Shock

By Melony Swasey

This is my senior year, a time in my life when I am supposed to exhale, to feel like I have accomplished something. When I graduate, I will have completed four years of what I have always been told is college-level education. Since the beginning of high school, I have had all honors classes, have maintained a respectable average, and have attained a top ten academic rank. And because of the type of student I am, I should be able to get into an excellent post-secondary institution and develop into something outstanding. That's what I've been told all along.

In fact, that is what all we high-ranking "scholars" of JFK High School have been told. We have been nourished with the belief that if we remain focused and keep those As, we will have the opportunity to leave the "dumps" and "become somebody." Unfortunately, we haven't been warned of just how far in the dumps we really are.

Unlike many of my classmates, I have seen the other side, a realm that is quite different from what most urban teens experience. I have had the chance to encounter suburbia, and even a little upper-class suburbia. I have made friends with people that some Paterson students mock for being so sheltered, but secretly envy for their money and opportunity. It is this that has made me understand the real flow of things. I once believed we are all equal, no matter what our race or socioeconomic status. But now I have learned the truth, something that has shocked me into a state of sad realization, even paranoia. I now know that students from less affluent areas are greatly deprived of what quality education involves. We are put in a completely different league from our suburban counterparts.

I met my true competition when I went to a more challenging semi-suburban high school for a year. The school has a population of about 1500 students, which is considered large in that area, and the students are challenged by a more rigorous curriculum. There was one girl, for

> **The beginning of success under an unfair system is to see where we fit, and to never be afraid to aim above the low expectations society often seems to have for us.**

instance, who as a sophomore comfortably maintained a high average in the classes I had as a junior. The classes I have as honors at Kennedy are considered only regular college prep classes in other schools. I realized that those of us who are top-notch at Kennedy might be cut down to an average level in more competitive high schools — schools that have higher standards of education and an equally demanding support system from families who often have extra resources and time to invest in their children's education.

I returned to Kennedy with a new view of what my education should be like. I have come to expect more, and I realize now that we have an inadequate library and obsolete books in the classrooms. I have realized that many of the clubs and classes that Kennedy offers bear respectable names or titles, but don't carry the weight or the full challenge that they should. In the supposedly challenging classes that I have, we aren't working at the capacity of students in those same classes on a national level.

Low Expectations

It seems that we are not only given the short end of the stick in terms of facilities and resources; but inner-city students aren't even expected to excel. We are sometimes granted honors for completing only part of a task, while students in more affluent areas are expected to do more to get the same recognition. We are pitied by outsiders who sometimes try to "help" by giving us undeserved praise. Thus, we often don't expect much more of our own selves. We aren't pushed hard enough. We are babied by our teachers for too long, which is why I am concerned about how even the "honors kids" will fare in college next year.

I think about the people who are

ignorant enough to sit around and mock kids from suburbia for being diligent in school, because they are often less aggressive and rebellious than we of the urban sect. We don't even realize that some of these same people we laugh about will be the ones determining our future budgets, controlling our work force, and deciding how long we stay in jail. Then some of us will sit on our behinds complaining that the "white man" is holding us down. Our ignorance feeds on itself and keeps us in the inner-city, where some think we belong anyway, because we are so "crude."

This whole cycle includes our parents, many of whom lack the formal or successful education to guide us educationally, and substantial enough income to support us financially. And as a part of this frustrating cycle, we find ourselves trying to explain to our parents the importance of spending money on the SATs and completing the college admissions process, arguing, at times selfishly, for opportunities many of them never had.

In Paterson, many of us just don't know better. We don't know how to push to get ahead, because we don't realize how far behind we are. Last summer, I took a pre-calculus course, hoping to catch up to some of the better students in my new school. (Until I left Paterson, I wasn't even aware that one could take a summer course to advance to the next level.) Thinking I was getting an edge for my senior year, I went into the class and found that most of the students were sophomores taking the summer course to skip to calculus in their junior year. I sat and compared those students to myself. Their parents had paid for them to go to a summer school outside of their district, and to take SAT courses in the evenings. One girl, in addition to that, played the violin and went to Chinese school. I looked at myself and my Paterson "honors" knowledge and felt like a joke.

I feel for my friends at Kennedy because most of them are focused on a goal — a goal that is easily attainable for better-prepared students — but never stop to look at their competition. I believe, because of our inadequate preparation, many of us will naively go out as confident soldiers and be knocked down before we even reach the front lines.

It is important that we students, even those of us "on top," realize that we are part of an unbalanced society where unequal education is permitted and accepted. We need to understand that the beginning of success under an unfair system is to see where we fit, and to never be afraid to aim above the low expectations society often seems to have for us. ■

Melony Swasey graduated from John F. Kennedy High School in Paterson, New Jersey, in June 1996 and went on to attend Cornell University. This essay originally appeared in Knightlife, *a student magazine.*

Teaching Ideas for "School System Shock"

Discussion Questions:

1. What differences did Swasey find in the schooling she experienced in different communities? What are some possible reasons for these differences?

2. How were the academic expectations for students different in each community that Swasey describes? How were these expectations transmitted or communicated to students?

3. According to Swasey's article, what are some of the effects of low expectations for students? Have you seen similar examples in your own schooling experience?

4. What evidence of tracking, or academic ability grouping, can you find in either of the schools that Swasey mentions? What do you think are some of the effects of tracking or academic ability grouping among groups of students? (For more on this issue, see *Rethinking Our Classrooms, Vol. I.*)

5. Who is responsible for equalizing educational opportunites? What roles do students, teachers, parents, district administrators, community members, business leaders, and government officials have in assuring quality educational opportunities for all? (Divide students into groups to list possible roles for each group.)

Follow-up Activities:

Interview an adult family member about his/her experience in school. Include questions about how the school helped or hindered the person from reaching his/her educational goals.

Swasey writes that "the beginning of success under an unfair system is to see where we fit in" and to "never be afraid to aim above" low expectations. Write an essay explaining where you feel that you "fit in" to the educational system. What expectations do you have for your own educational future? ■

— *Stan Karp*

Arranged Marriages, Rearranged Ideas

By Stan Karp

Jihana was one of my favorite students. By the time she was a senior, we had been together for three years, first in a sophomore English class and then through two years of journalism electives where students produced school publications and learned desktop publishing.

Jihana's bright-eyed intelligence and can-do enthusiasm made her a teacher's dream. Her daily greeting in our busy journalism office was, "Hi, Mr. Karp, what needs to be done?" I used to joke that she'd get straight As until the end of her senior year when I'd have to fail her so she couldn't graduate and leave. It was corny, but she always laughed.

Jihana was one of a growing number of Bengali students in my Paterson, New Jersey high school. Along with increasing numbers of Latin American, Caribbean, Middle Eastern, Central European, and other immigrants, these new communities had transformed the school in the 20 years I'd been there as a teacher. What had once been a predominantly white, then later a primarily Black and Latino student population, was now thoroughly international. The teaching staff, however, remained mostly white, with a limited number of African Americans and Latinos.

Increasingly, some of my best students each year were young Bengali women. Some, like Jihana, covered their heads with scarves in keeping with Muslim tradition. A few wore the full veil. Others wore no special dress. Many seemed reserved and studious. Others gradually adopted

> No matter how I tried to come to terms with it, the custom of arranged marriages was completely alien to my own sensibilities and to my expectations for my students.

the more assertive, outgoing styles of the citywise teens around them.

An Arranged Marriage

By the time Jihana was a senior it was natural to ask, during one of the many extra periods she spent in the journalism office, what her post-graduation plans were. She said she wanted to go to college, perhaps to study medicine, and was considering several schools. But, she added, a lot depended on whether she had to get married.

I knew enough about Jihana, and about the Bengali community, to know that she wasn't referring to a premature wedding prompted by an unplanned pregnancy, but to the possibility of an arranged marriage. Jihana made it pretty clear that she wasn't ready to get married. She was anxious to go to college and to move out of a household where she felt she had too many cleaning chores and child-care duties and not enough personal freedom. She said the outcome partly depended on what happened with her sister, who was several years older and also a candidate for marriage, and on whether her family decided to send them both back to Bangladesh in the summer for possible matches.

I listened sympathetically and made schoolteacher noises about how smart I thought she was and how I hoped she'd get the opportunity to attend college. Unsure of just what my role, as a white, male high school teacher, could possibly be in this situation, I halfheartedly offered to speak to her family about her college potential if she thought it would help. Jihana smiled politely and said she'd keep me posted.

I went home thinking about Jihana's situation. I was seriously upset, even angered by the thought that this young woman's promising prospects and educational future could be sidetracked by a cultural practice that seemed to me hopelessly unreasonable and unfair. No matter how I tried to come to terms with it, the custom of arranged marriages was completely alien to my own sen-

sibilities and to my expectations for my students. I kept thinking of how my own high school-aged daughter — raised at home and, at least nominally, at school, to think in terms of gender equality and independence — would laugh in my face if I ever sat her down and tried to tell her my plans for her marital future.

I also thought, and not for the first time, about what my responsibilities were as a public school teacher, and how I should manage this mix of my own strongly held personal opinions, concern for my students' well-being, and respect for the cultural differences that were increasingly prominent in my school community.

As both a political activist and a classroom teacher, I'd wrestled with these issues often. On the one hand, I'd come to believe that effective classroom teaching, especially in schools with a history of failure and pervasive student alienation, was inherently "political" in the sense that it had to take the social context of schooling and of students' lives as a primary point of departure. I tried to encourage students to "talk back" to the world we studied, and, wherever

possible, take action in response to ideas and issues. These premises informed any number of choices I made daily about curriculum, classroom organization, and about how to channel in particular directions the "oppositional energy" I found in most teenagers. It also meant I frequently tried to take real situations in my students' lives, both in and out of school, as starting points for research, writing, and class discussion.

At the same time, I know it is neither appropriate nor fair for teachers to restrict the curriculum to only those views and ideas that they personally agree with. Since teachers have power over students, it's especially necessary to be sensitive to issues of intimidation, the rights of dissent, personal privacy, and freedom of choice. In some ways, the closer issues hit to home, as in Jihana's situation, the more careful teachers must be, particularly where racial, cultural, and class differences are involved.

At first glance, Jihana's problem seemed personal and private, not readily the stuff of classroom discussion. It had social roots and cultural

dimensions like other student concerns that had become the subject of class assignments or research. But it seemed to call for an individual, personal response on my part, rather than a pedagogical one, and I had real trouble imagining what that response should be.

Reluctant to Intervene

As a rule, I have generally been reluctant to intervene at home when it comes to handling personal and family issues with my teenage students. Though I've always supported parents' participation in their children's education, for me this usually meant support for parent participation in governance and policy-making processes, or finding ways to include parent and family experience in my curriculum. But when personal (as opposed to strictly academic) problems arise with secondary-age students, I've always hesitated to "call home" too quickly. Most of the 15-18-year-olds I deal with are emerging adults who've been semi-independent, to varying degrees, for years: holding down jobs, assuming family responsibilities, traveling the world, dealing with the courts and immigration authorities, and even coping with parenthood themselves. Others come from difficult family situations that are not always supportive or, not infrequently, may even be the source of the problems they choose to share with me. In the normal course of a year, it's not unusual for me to deal with teenagers who are wrestling with everything from homelessness, pregnancy, and sexual identity to depression, domestic violence, and drug abuse.

When my students bring such issues to me, I've always felt that my first allegiance was to them, to listen sympathetically and to offer whatever advice or access to services I could manage, and not, primarily, to act as a surrogate for — or even mediator with — parental authority. Yes, there have been occasions when my judgment, or the legal responsibilities that are periodically spelled out in nervous memos from central office, compel me to pick up the phone or make a home visit. But in general I take my signal about whether home intervention on my part makes sense from my students, and most of the time it doesn't. There have also been times when I've passed on information about where to get birth control or other kinds of counseling services, (e.g., for gay teens) that I knew might not be fully endorsed at home.

In Jihana's case I tried to imagine what I could possibly say to her family about the situation: "Hi, I'm Jihana's teacher, and as a politically progressive, pro-feminist, privileged white male, I think your plans for Jihana are a medieval abomination." I don't think so. But the more I thought about it, the more I realized that the problem wasn't finding more diplomatic ways to voice my opinions; the problem was figuring out the dividing line between responding to the needs of my students and interfering inappropriately with "other people's children."

I also thought about another student I'd had some 10 years earlier, Rafia, who faced this same situation.

Rafia was the youngest of four daughters in a Bengali family. Smart, sophisticated beyond her years, and ambitious, Rafia was anxious to go to college despite her family's objections. As I encouraged her and helped her fill out applications during her junior and senior years, it was Rafia who first made me aware that many Bengali families did not think girls should go to college, and that she and her sisters were facing, with varying

> **The problem wasn't finding more diplomatic ways to voice my opinions; the problem was figuring out the dividing line between responding to the needs of my students and interfering inappropriately with "other people's children."**

degrees of dread, the prospect of arranged marriages.

I was horrified at the idea, and said so. In fact, as I recall, my main reaction consisted of expressing my outrage that women were oppressed this way in her culture. I told her I didn't think anyone had the right to tell her whom to marry, and that it was much more important for her future to go to

college than to please her parents. I even suggested that it was more important to choose college than to avoid a break with her family, and that, even if they got upset, they would probably get over it. I somewhat flippantly told her she could stay at my house for a while if she decided to run away.

Learning A Lesson

When Jihana's story jogged my memory, it was with more than a little embarrassment that I recalled how my reaction to Rafia had been foolish and not a little arrogant. At the time, I had acted as if the most important response to Rafia's dilemma was to show her that not everyone was so "backward" as her parents, and that there were swell, "enlightened" folks like myself who believed in her right to shape her own future and education. In effect, I was showing off the "superior" values and "advanced" thinking of "progressive western culture," especially of radicals like myself, and contrasting it to the "underdeveloped practices" of her own community, which I encouraged her to reject. I had also reacted as if what I thought and how I felt about the issues raised by her predicament were of paramount importance, and should be the point of departure for my response.

Looking back, it seemed that the problem wasn't that I was wrong to oppose the custom of arranged marriages or make my opinions known, but that I did it in a way that was essentially self-serving, and as a practical matter, not very helpful. I had basically denounced what I, as an outsider, saw as "deficient" in her culture and encouraged her to turn her back on it. While my sympathies may have been well-meant, my advice was culturally insensitive and wildly impractical. And it probably just reinforced Rafia's sense of alienation and being trapped.

Fortunately, Rafia was sharp enough to appreciate my personal support and ignore my advice. Instead of running away or openly breaking with her family, she steadfastly argued for her chance to attend college while continuing to excel in school. Eventually, she got her father's permission to go to college (though she was forced to study engineering instead of the humanities she preferred). The experience had stayed with me over the years, and now that a similar situation had arisen, I was anxious to do better by Jihana.

A couple of weeks passed after our first conversation, and it became clear that nothing decisive would happen with Jihana's situation until the summer came. Still looking for a way to lend support, one day I suggested to Jihana that she consider writing a story about arranged marriages for our student magazine. I mentioned briefly my experience with Rafia and asked how the growing community of female Bengali students in the high school felt about this and related issues. Instead of dwelling on my own opinions, I tried to emphasize that she wasn't the only one facing these issues, and that she could perform a service for both Bengali students and the rest of the school by focusing on a set of concerns that had gotten little attention.

Jihana seemed interested but hesitant. She was a good writer but generally took less ambitious assignments like covering school news or activities. She expressed some concern that her family would be offended if they found out, and that, in the tightly-knit Bengali community, it might be hard to keep it a secret even if she published a piece anonymously. I asked her to think it over and told her she could get credit for writing the article even if she decided in the end not to publish it. I also told her, as I did all my students, that we could consider the implications or consequences of going public later, but she should write what she really thought and not censor herself in advance. I was hoping to use the tremendous potential that writing has, not only to help students express their ideas and feelings, but also to help them develop the skills, and sometimes the dis-

tance, needed to analyze complicated topics and clarify issues. While I hoped Jihana would eventually publish, it seemed valuable to have her organize and express her thoughts for her own purposes as well. After a few days, and after double checking that she wouldn't have to publish the piece if she wasn't comfortable, she agreed. She asked for help making an outline, so we arranged a story conference.

A Broader Context

When we started discussing how to organize the article, Jihana said she wanted to deal first with stereotypes and misconceptions that Westerners had about Muslims. She said she wanted to put the issue of arranged marriages in a broader context of Muslim culture, which had a variety of customs and practices that she felt were misunderstood. Muslim women were not "slaves," she said, and not everyone did things the same way. When it came to marriage, there were a range of practices, and in many cases, Muslim women did have choices and varying degrees of input in the decision.

This led to a discussion of women and marriage customs in general, and how women have faced oppression and male supremacy in all cultures. We also talked about the generational conflict between young Bengalis (and other younger immigrants) raised in the United States, and their parents, rooted in more traditional, "old country" customs, and how this exacerbated the struggle over marriage practices. Jihana told me stories about families that had been torn apart by these differences, and others where parents and children had found common ground and happy endings.

As we talked, several things started to become clear. By locating the issue of arranged marriages inside the broader issue of woman's rights, which cuts across all cultures and countries, it became easier for Jihana to address the topic without "stigmatizing" her own community. If Bengali women had to wrestle with

arranged marriages and male dominance, the supposedly more "liberated" sexual culture of the United States presented women with its own set of problems: higher levels of sexual assault, single teenage parenthood, divorce, and domestic violence. Generational conflict between old ways and new also cut across cultures and made the issue seem more universal, again allowing it to be addressed in a context that didn't demonize one particular group.

Finally, it was clear that speaking on behalf of Bengali women, instead of just against the practice of arranged marriages, tended to make Jihana feel more empowered than isolated. She was still determined to question the imposition of marital arrangements against the woman's will, but would do so in the context of defending Muslim culture against stereotypes and as part of a critique of women's oppression as a whole. Added to the protection she felt from not having to publish her work if she chose not to, assuming this positive stance on behalf of herself and her peers seemed to give her the safe space she needed from which to address these difficult issues. By the end of our conversation, she seemed ready to go. Within a week or two, Jihana was back with her article.

"Do Muslim women have any rights?" she began. "Do they make their own decisions? Are they allowed to think? Are they prisoners in their own homes? There are many stereotypes held by Westerners about the position and role of Muslim women.... These notions are based upon the lack of knowledge Westerners have of Islam."

She continued:

Women, regardless of their culture or society, have suffered tremendously over inequality and have had to fight for a firm place in their society. During the Roman civilization, a woman was considered to be a slave. The Greeks bought and sold their women as merchandise rather than accept them as human beings. Early

JEAN-CLAUDE LEJEUNE

Christianity regarded their women as "temptresses," responsible for the fall of Adam.

In pre-Islamic times, as well as in certain places today, a female child is thought of as a cause for unhappiness and grief. Baby girls were sometimes buried alive after birth. But gaps in wealth, education, and justice between men and women can be found everywhere and just can't be explained by religion.

Jihana went on to discuss "some issues about the rights of a Muslim woman [that] stem from the issue of marriage." She wrote about the varying degrees of choice women may have in different families, the generational conflict, the problems associated with patterns of marriage in the United States. ("Some Muslim families say that while the Westerners seem to be 'more free,' their society is not working too well.") She cited examples to show that "as in all marriages, whether arranged or not, some work and some do not."

Though many of the Bengali students Jihana spoke to declined to be quoted by name, she did find one senior who "extremely disagrees with arranged marriages" and who thought "all Muslim women should be given an opportunity and the privilege to choose the person that they want to spend the rest of their lives with."

After exploring the issues from several sides, Jihana came to a balancing act that suggested her own personal struggle:

Arranged marriages and other Muslim customs of life, like the covering of the body and not dating, may seem to be burdensome to women of most Western cultures, but for Muslim women it's their way of life. We were brought up to follow and believe that these practices were the right ways of life. It is up to us as individuals to see that we follow what is expected of us.... The Muslim religion, in my opinion, can include double standards.... In many cases males are allowed to do certain things that females can't.... For example, when a male does get married without his parents' permission, it is okay, but if a female does the same thing it is not okay. This is so because in the Holy Koran it states that a woman has to follow certain things. For example, it is a woman's duty and obligation to bring up her children according to the ways of Islam. She has to look after the family and has absolute control over domestic affairs. She must wear a covering cloak when meeting adult men outside her family. She is her husband's helpmate. Islam recognizes the leadership of a man over a woman, but that does not mean domination.

In conclusion, women should have the freedom and right to do something they're interested in doing or accomplishing. They should go forward with their education if they want to continue it, with the help and support to do so. Women can cook and clean, but they could also do more.

At bottom, Jihana's "balancing act" was an affirmative statement about her place and her rights in her community. And though writing the article didn't resolve her dilemma, it did, I think, support her in her efforts to speak up for herself, and offered a way for her to develop some useful perspectives on her situation. It also helped focus attention on issues that she and her Bengali peers were wrestling with inside the school community.

New Pride

Though Jihana had originally balked at the idea of publication, by the time she was done she used the computer skills she'd learned in class to create a two-page layout for our magazine with her article, her byline, and her picture under the title, "Muslim Women: Where Do We Belong?" She seemed proud of it, and so was I, especially as I reflected on what I'd learned myself.

Switching the focus from my own reactions to my student's point of view, and developing a deeper appreciation of the need to deal with issues of cultural difference with more humility and care, had led me to a more effective and more appropriate response. I was still just as opposed as ever to arranged marriages, and still saw pitfalls and contradictions in Jihana's balancing act about the codes of Islam. But, because I hadn't begun with an attack on the cultural norms of her community, I had managed to find a way that, to some degree at least, both supported and empowered her.

As it turned out, Jihana's willingness to raise such issues was not limited to our magazine. One morning in the spring, I found her working feverishly in the journalism office on a list of "Bengali Concerns" for the next student government meeting. The list had a tone familiar from earlier days of student activism, but it had specifics I'd never seen before. It read:

1. How come there aren't more Bengali SGA members?

2. There is a lack of Bengali students involved in school activities. We need more participation and more representation of the Bengali people.

3. We need Bengali-speaking guidance counselors and teachers.

4. We need Bengali mentors.

5. How come the history teachers never teach about Bangladesh and its culture when they teach world history?

6. Why isn't there Bengali student representation when the school presents a panel of students to represent the school?

7. How come all the newsletters that go home from the school are either in Spanish or in English? How come you can't send letters home that are in Bengali; that way the parents will know what is going on in their children's school. The lack of communication with the Bengali parents is a reason why many don't attend the Home-School Council meetings.

New Steps for Jihana

Around the same time that these concerns were being presented to the student government, preparations were underway for an assembly pres-

entation of Bengali dance and traditional dress. Like many other schools, my high school was still in the relatively superficial stages of addressing multicultural issues, and tended toward food festivals and holiday celebrations. But the assembly program tapped the energy of many Bengali students, and Jihana had gotten

> Because I hadn't begun with an attack on the cultural norms of her community, I had managed to find a way that, to some degree at least, both supported and empowered Jihana.

involved. One afternoon, soon after our magazine had appeared, she came to the journalism office and asked if I could fax a copy of her article to a reporter from a local newspaper. She said she'd been interviewed in connection with the upcoming assembly program, but had left some things out. "I was trying to explain myself to the reporter and couldn't get the words out right," she said. "I told him I had written an article explaining what I thought, and it was all in there. I promised to send it to him." The article she had been hesitant to write and reluctant to publish had become a personal position statement.

As we headed into the last weeks of the school year, I occasionally asked Jihana if there were any new developments. There weren't any on the marriage front, but she did get accepted to several colleges and began to make plans to attend a state university. When we parted at year's end, I made her promise to let me know how things turned out.

About a month later, I returned from a trip to find a slightly ambiguous message. Jihana had called to say hello and to invite me to a wedding. Taken aback, and fearing that this might be her way of letting me know that marriage had won out over college, I called her at home. She was in good spirits and busy getting ready to move into the dorms on her new campus. The invitation was to her sister's wedding, Jihana explained, and if I could come I'd get a chance to see some more of how Bengali marriage customs worked. Unfortunately, I wasn't able to attend, but Jihana promised to show me the proceedings on videotape.

In September Jihana started college classes. A few weeks later, I got a note describing her new life. "College is OK," she wrote, "not that great as everyone said it would be. Maybe it is just me. I never realized how difficult my classes would be and so large in lectures!! I am taking an Arabic class so that I can be trilingual!

"I have to go home every weekend, but I don't mind. I have a new status in my family; everyone respects me more, and I also don't have to do any more housework. Isn't that great??!!"

I had to agree that it was. ∎

Stan Karp (stan.karp@gmail.com) taught English and Journalism to high school students in Paterson, New Jersey for 30 years. He is a Rethinking Schools editor, and currently Director of the Secondary Reform Project for New Jersey's Education Law Center. The names of the students in this article have been changed.

Out Front

What schools can do to fight homophobia

By Annie Johnston

My prep period was half over. I still had to prepare for a sub the next day and copy the materials for my next class when a student appeared at my door. Nervously clutching a bathroom pass as her eyes darted from the room number to me, she asked, "Are you the one who does that support group for...." Her voice trailed off.

"The lesbian, gay, bisexual, and questioning youth support group?" I answered. "Yes. They meet Thursdays at lunch. They are working on a conference of gay/straight alliances around the Bay Area. It's not a large group ...." As my explanation continued I could see I had lost her.

"That's not what I want," she said. "I need to talk to someone, right away."

Oh dear, I thought, crisis management. This is not what I can do today. I had to leave early to get my daughter to an appointment.

Instead I said, "What do you need to talk about?"

Slowly and hesitantly it came out. A good friend was attracted to her. She might actually be interested. That scared her to her very core. She sought me out because my room number was announced weekly as the location of the support group meetings. I took her name, found out what period she could stand to miss, and spent the rest of my prep period finding someone in the health center who would be positive about the possibility that this child might have feelings for someone of the same sex. I was lucky. More often, I end up playing amateur psychologist.

I teach history at Berkeley High School, considered one of the better schools for queer-identified youth (an all-inclusive term, preferred by the students, for queer and questioning youth).[1] Yet even at Berkeley, there are limits to the school's openness to queer youth, who tend to graduate early or to leave for a semester or two of "Independent Studies." The

> The club of homophobic ridicule is held over the heads of all young people — it is one of the main means by which gender roles are enforced.

Independent Studies program is an alternative track in which students only meet with each teacher for one half-hour per week and do all their work on their own.

I have been teaching at Berkeley eight years and have been coming out to my classes since my first year. There are a few other staff in this school of 3,000 students who do not hide our sexuality. We know that we have to be seen — that it's important not just for the gay youth but for all the students to have gay role models. We also know that at Berkeley, because of district and city policies forbidding discrimination on the basis of sexual orientation, we won't be fired.

The situation is better at Berkeley than at most schools across the country. But even at Berkeley, homophobia is a constant reality. Girls who are close friends and lean over each other's desk are called "lezzies." Boys who seem in any way weak or "womanly" are called "faggots." Despite advances in the struggle against homophobia in our schools, there is still a long, long way to go.

One teacher recently described a situation in which a young man, who had been consistently called "faggot" by his peers, took an all-too-typical approach to stop the taunting. He came into her class one day and went up to a shy, relatively unpopular girl and, in front of his buddies, proceeded to make sexually humiliating remarks. He was conforming to teenage male culture, in which "Hey, baby, why don't you suck my...." means, "See, I'm a real man." The club of homophobic ridicule is held over the heads of all young people — it is one of the main means by which gender roles are enforced.

Backlash Era

In this backlash era, out teacher role models are an endangered species. Even in the progressive Bay

Area, there have been major flaps over a teacher allowing a brief discussion of the *Ellen* coming-out episode, and a teacher simply letting it be known to her classes that she is lesbian.

At the same time, Gay/Straight Alliances are growing at a phenomenal rate. When students in Salt Lake City formed a Gay/Straight Alliance in 1995, the district banned all clubs rather than allow the alliance to meet. But protesting students walked out en masse and marched to the state capital, forcing the state legislature to intervene and countermand the district. In addition, there have been significant legal victories in recent years — in particular the case brought by Jamie Nabozny, which held school administrators liable when a gay student was harmed by harassment that the administrators had ignored despite the existence of a district anti-harassment policy. Many districts have also been more open to training staff on how to create a safe environment for lesbian and gay youth.

At my school, the lesbian, gay,

bisexual, and questioning youth support group is an important place for students to find each other and establish a supportive community. It is difficult, however, for those students to be activists around gay issues at school. They face constant harassment and ridicule. It is equally difficult for students who are unsure of their sexual identity to take the radical step of coming to such a gay-identified group.

Take the situation facing Jake, who was ridiculed by other students the entire semester two years ago in my World History class. He came midyear, he said, because he had been so ostracized in his last school. He had a manner about him that just spoke of weirdness and difference. By the end of four months, students would write things on the board about him, no one would work with him, and he would take it all in as if he deserved it. After he brought in a crucifix he'd made in shop class and announced to me that the bloody body hanging from it was himself, I redoubled my efforts to get him seen by a

counselor, but to no avail. It was May by that time, the university interns who helped out at the health center were gone for the year, and there was really no one who could help.

Jake spent time hospitalized over the summer for severe depression and on suicide watch, I think. He spent more time hospitalized in the fall. After he left the hospital, he came by to tell me he had known he was gay since he was seven years old. He'd been in denial, hoping and praying that something would change him.

I'm not sure where Jake got the strength, but he finally decided to stand up for himself, to shove the hatred and ridicule back at his tormentors. He also began reading books about gay male sexuality, and came to a staff development inservice I had organized to speak to teachers about the damage a homophobic environment does to youth.

Jake started to like himself, and it changed his life. He is now a junior at Berkeley High and has a number of friends. And while he still gets gay-bashed, the last time he got kicked

Gay &
Lesbian
Equality

SKJOLD PHOTOGRAPHS

and punched he lodged an official complaint rather than just turning the other cheek.

Jake could have been a statistic. According to a study done by Paul Gibson for the U.S. Department of Health and Human Services, gay youth are two to three times more likely to commit suicide and comprise up to 30% of all completed suicides.

Help!

As an openly gay teacher, I do what I can to help the Jakes of our school. I talk to the social living classes, work with others to organize staff inservices, get students to speak on panels about their experiences, and advocate for the youth who end up on my doorstep. I struggle with how to make support services available to all students, not just those who come to the lesbian, gay, bisexual, and questioning youth group. This is particularly crucial for students of color, for whom the issue of identity is much more complex.

I know I should do more, but I can't. "Out lesbian teacher" is not my only identity. I can take the lead on these issues for only so long without getting burned out. I need allies, and

so do the youth. I need young gay teachers who are supported and encouraged to act as out role models in the schools, instead of being scared that they will be persecuted and driven from their jobs. I need straight teachers to sponsor forums on the issue and push for an "anti-slur" policy .

You don't always get what you need, but you don't get much of anything unless you ask. So here are a few things I would ask of other teachers:

• Set a clear anti-homophobic standard for what is acceptable language and behavior in your classrooms and your schools.

• Incorporate gay issues into the curriculum — not just in social living classes when talking about sex, but in history, English, science, and Spanish.

• Support gay teachers' ability to be out role models for our youth.

Anti-Slur Policy

Establishing policies on language and behavior is sometimes the best place to start. Even at Berkeley, it has been difficult to develop a culture in which anti-gay language in unacceptable. When I recently asked a group of

queer-identified youth what teachers had done to make a positive difference in combating homophobia, they could not think of a single thing. One teacher tried last year to make an issue of anti-gay language, but she was quickly overwhelmed by students' negative responses. For the remainder of the semester, not a single student in her class suffered any consequences for using anti-gay language.

Once, after a 45-minute argument with students in my class over why anti-gay language is harmful, Ryanna, still unconvinced, said, "I'll do it, Ms. Johnston, because I respect you. But I just want you to know that none of my other teachers ever has demanded this of me. It is extremely difficult to remember to watch my language here when this is the language I use at home all the time, and when every other teacher in the school considers it acceptable."

Despite her reluctance, however, Ryanna has managed to watch her language since. Moreover, during the initial class discussion, many other students expressed their disapproval of anti-gay language, and reevaluated words they had been using.

Such conversations and policies have a ripple effect. One closeted bisexual student told me that he later felt able to raise gay issues in a current events discussion, knowing a large number of the students in the room would take them seriously. In this case, events that affected gay people became a normal, acceptable thing to talk about.

These conversations require a large chunk of class time. Further, policies must be backed up by immediate consequences when students forget or violate the rules. For instance, many students don't understand why calling a test they hated "gay" is insulting to gay people. They don't connect the emergence of "gay" as a slang word, meaning "really yucky," to homophobia. It takes teaching to make that connection. Usually a talking-to in the hallway is adequate, although not always. Once in awhile, a student will be unwilling to suppress his or her homophobia and will use homophobic remarks to seriously taunt another student. In such cases, teachers need to be aware that gay-baiting is a form of sexual harassment and that state education codes require schools to create a safe place for all students.

Curriculum Issues

An anti-slur policy reduces the amount of negative vibes but is not sufficient to create a classroom that welcomes the existence of queer people. To take this further step, teachers must include queers and queer issues in their curriculum. It's likely that a tenth of the population is gay in this country, and gay people play a major role in our society. Students must see that fact reflected in what we teach. "Gay" has to be integrated into our picture of current events, historical reality, literary themes, and scientific exploration. We need curriculum in which "gay" is not relegated to the "Sexuality and Sexually Transmitted Diseases" discussion in health and social living classes.

Every subject area has openings for such curriculum, but it takes a conscious effort to develop or access and incorporate the materials. In U.S. history, for instance, when we teach the Civil Rights Movement, we can examine the role of Bayard Rustin, who helped organize the 1963 March on Washington, as an out civil rights activist. We can include the gay liberation movement as a civil rights movement. We can have students study the Black Panther Party's position on homosexuality. Here is what Huey Newton approved as the official Black Panther position on the subject:

> Homosexuals are not given freedom and liberty by anyone in this society. Maybe they might be the most oppressed people in the society..... A person should have the freedom to use his body whatever way he wants to. The Women's Liberation Front and Gay Liberation Front are our friends, they are our potential allies and we need as many allies

as possible....We should be careful about using terms which might turn our friends off. The terms "faggot" and "punk" should be deleted from our vocabulary, and especially we should not attach names normally designed for homosexual men to men who are enemies of the people, such as Nixon or Mitchell. Homosexuals are not enemies of the people.

There are countless pieces of literature with lesbian and/or gay themes, ranging from *Coffee Will Make You Black* by April Sinclair, to *Giovanni's Room* by James Baldwin, to *Rubyfruit Jungle* by Rita Mae Brown. A multitude of famous literary icons are or were lesbian or gay, such as

> If we acknowledge gay people's contributions in every area of our society, young people's perceptions of what it means to be gay can go beyond the often-threatening issue of sexuality.

Sappho, James Baldwin, Adrienne Rich, and E. M. Forster. Biology classes that discuss human reproduction can include the role of artificial insemination in allowing a growing number of lesbians and gay men to

become parents. The ongoing "biology versus environment" debate — i.e., whether sexual preference is determined largely through genetics or environmental factors — can be one of the topics students can choose to research and debate. Physical education teachers can talk openly and respectfully about gay athletes such as diver Greg Louganis and tennis star Martina Navratilova.

If we acknowledge gay people's contributions in every area of our society, young people's perceptions of what it means to be gay can go beyond the often-threatening issue of sexuality.

From elementary school on, teachers need to talk about gay people so children learn they are a normal part of our society. Many students have lesbian and gay family members whom they love. They must not feel they have to hide or be embarrassed by these relationships.

My eight-year-old daughter, for instance, has decided she will not compromise on telling the world she has two moms, no matter what the consequences. Last year, she had a confrontation with a bunch of kindergarten boys who accused her and her friend of being gay because she was leaning on her friend's shoulder for support due to a twisted ankle. She told them there was nothing wrong with being gay. Then she announced that, besides, both her moms were gay.

The boys really went to town on that. The ridicule they subjected her to reduced her to tears. After 10 minutes of crying in the bathroom she returned to class and was given detention — her first — for tardiness. She called it the worst day of her life and said, "And Mom, how am I going to make it through high school?"

In every class, every semester, after I come out I find out about the aunts, cousins, brothers, and friends that young people are normally forced to be silent about. Children desperately need teachers to counter these taboos, to talk about gay people naturally, unabashedly, and positively.

Role Models

A queer-friendly school is one in which there are positive lesbian and gay role models, not just for queer students but for all students. Whether students are gay or bi or straight, they need to experience gay teachers as people who enrich their lives and care about them. An environment in which lesbian, gay, and bisexual teachers can be out to their students is critical to breaking down the culture of homophobia.

But it is extremely difficult to be out in a school setting. You feel isolated and pegged. In many districts, you can be fired for being out in the classroom. At the least, one risks censure by the administration and homophobic reactions from parents. Every gay teacher fears being targeted and persecuted if word gets out.

Consider my experience with Calley, who was a bright, energetic 14-year-old when first she came to my classroom. She had spent junior high fighting with the little league coach to be able to play on the all-boys baseball team. She spent her freshman year trying out boyfriends and sporting large hickeys. By her sophomore year, she'd had enough of all that. She began attending the lesbian/gay support group meetings in my classroom and signed up to be a proctor for me. Her mother searched her backpack and read her journal, in which she had a number of poems that made her feelings about sexuality quite explicit. Calley's mother immediately wanted to drag Calley to a therapist. And her mother was looking for someone to blame. I was a handy target.

In a conservative community hellbent on targeting gays, I'd have been mincemeat. But at Berkeley, where there is no such organized opposition to the rights of gays, and where many straight colleagues and administrators are supportive of gays, Calley's mother could do little about me.

Calley ran away from home that summer, returning to an uneasy truce in the fall. She is out and has a strong circle of friends, but clearly it will be

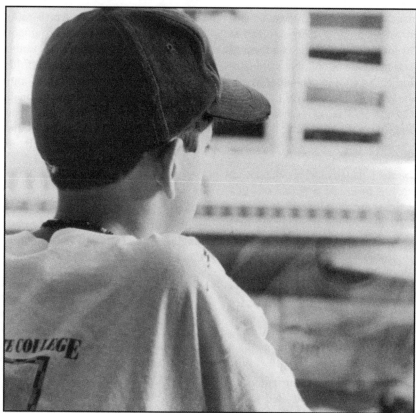

many years before she feels again the support of a loving family.

Gay teachers need to take more risks to provide strong out models of what it means to be gay. We cannot do that, however, without a supportive environment. Straight teachers can help to create such support.

If straight faculty members at my high school would raise a concern about the homophobia they so constantly see in their classes, it would be easier to develop an anti-slur policy. If there were any other teachers developing curriculum that included gay issues (besides when discussing HIV), I would feel supported. These actions do not require a particular sexual orientation. They only require concern and a commitment to act against homophobia. ■

Annie Johnston is a teacher at Berkeley High School in Berkeley, California.

Note

1. For many years, "queer" was a pejorative only acceptable when used among gay people. But as the definition of this movement has expanded to include lesbian, bisexual, transgendered, and questioning people, many youth openly began using "queer" as an all-inclusive term. This was probably popularized by the short but exciting existence of the group, "Queer Nation," which did a lot of in-your-face type guerrilla theater against heterosexism. "Gay," on the other hand, was an acceptable term in general usage denoting all homosexual people and had a respectful connotation. Among youth now, however, "gay" is a slang adjective with extremely negative overtones. I use "queer" when talking about youth, partly because it covers so many bases, and so many youth aren't sure what base they'll end up playing. I use "gay" when talking about older people because we came of age when "gay" (or lesbian-gay-bisexual-transgender) was the proper term.

Staying Past Wednesday
Helping students cope with death and loss

By Kate Lyman

The first time that death took a seat in my classroom was about 15 years ago. Jessica, a kindergartner in my class, and her brother had died over the weekend in a fire at a baby-sitter's house. I prepared to return to school on Monday, to face the empty seat at her table, answer the inevitable questions, and deal with my students' fears and grief.

When I got to school, the staff was told to go to the library for a brief meeting. The principal announced the tragedy and warned teachers not to broach the subject. "Trained personnel" (the school psychologist and social worker) would talk with the children. Teachers could answer questions but were to get on with school business as soon as possible.

"I'm giving this until Wednesday," whispered the teacher of my student's sibling. "After Wednesday, we won't talk about it anymore."

Death — like sex, AIDS, genocide, racism and poverty — is silenced in the elementary classroom. That silence sends a strong message to children: This may be your reality but it is not the truth that we honor in this institution. You must set aside your classmate's death or your ancestor's history or your 13-year-old sister's pregnancy. You are here to discuss and write and learn about matters of more importance.

The Monday after Jessica's death, my students gathered on the rug. Many had heard about the fire. They burst out with facts (many erroneous), questions, and feelings. There was an undertone of fear for

From *The Tenth Good Thing About Barney* by Judith Viorst.

ERIK BLEGVAD

their own safety.

I took the students' lead and, ignoring the principal, I moderated a sharing session. After about 30 minutes, the tone switched from curiosity and fear to sadness. What about Jessica? Where was she now? How could we remember her and tell her that we miss her? I asked the students for ideas. They wanted to decorate her table space, to write about her, to draw pictures of her, and to send something to her family. I told them I

would clear off a bulletin board for remembering Jessica and sent them to their tables to draw and write.

The bulletin board stayed up until the end of the school year. Questions, stories, and projects about Jessica did not end on Wednesday.

Death and Loss

Since then, I have often included a unit of several weeks on death and loss in my curriculum. Some years,

The AIDS Memorial Quilt stretches out before the U.S. Capitol in 1996. Handmade sections commemorate thousands of victims of the disease.

ASSOCIATED PRESS

especially when I taught kindergarten, the unit was precipitated by the death of a classroom guinea pig or by a robin found dead on the playground. Books, such as *The Tenth Good Thing About Barney*, sparked student discussions on a range of topics: the loss of a favorite pet (Barney was a cat), the death of a grandparent, and the many different views on afterlife.

More recently, when teaching first through third grade, I have incorporated the unit as a regular part of my curriculum, sometimes as part of a discussion on AIDS awareness. The unit's immediacy invariably becomes clear. One year, for example, while I was preparing for the unit, a student who had been in my classroom the year before died in a car accident. A few years later, the mother of a girl in my class came in to tell me that her cousin was dying of AIDS and probably would not survive the night. Several days later, as part of our unit, this student solemnly shared her eulogy of her mother's cousin.

This year, in my second/third grade classroom, I planned for the class to create a "death and loss quilt" as a follow-up to a field trip to view panels from the NAMES Project (AIDS Memorial) Quilt. For students who had several stories to tell, we talked about whom they would choose for their quilt panel; we discussed hard questions like who had meant the most to them and whom they missed the most. For several students, the loss of a parent through separation was akin to death because the parent had dropped out of their lives.

On that particular day, Lisa came in late, which was not atypical. She is often quiet and withdrawn, but she appeared unusually upset and on the verge of tears. She sat down at her seat and laid her head on her arms. With some coaxing, she agreed to meet with me in the hall.

"What's the matter?" I asked.

"Nothing."

"You seem to be feeling very sad." No response. "Did something happen at home?"

"Yeah, but it's nobody's business," Lisa said, her body wracked with sobs. I sat with her a while and asked how I could help. She blurted out, "Well, my aunt killed herself last night, but my mom says it's nobody's business."

I suggested that Lisa speak with a counselor but she didn't want to. She wanted to go back to the classroom. Feeling as if I were in a movie, I told her what the class was writing about. She sat down and wrote about her dog who had run away. Being unsure myself if it were too soon, I tentatively suggested she write about her aunt.

"No. Too hard," was her tearful answer.

Then I noticed that Mariah was also in tears. Usually a prolific writer, she had written only her name and the date. I went over to talk to her.

"I want to write about my mom, but it makes me too sad," she confided.

I told her that Lisa was having a similar problem and suggested they share their feelings. They went to the bench in the hall. When they came back, they were both ready to write. Lisa quickly wrote her story:

My aunt, Linda, lived in Stevensville for a long time, since she was a kid. When my grandma moved out, she had to move out. She got an apartment. And it was very small. It was one room. Everybody said she was a slob because she left cigarette wrappers around. Everybody said she was crazy. She died and I miss her.

When Mariah finished her story, she shared it with the class:

Brenda was my mom. I will never see her again. I loved her and I still do. I always will. Whenever I came over she gave me sea shells because I hadn't seen her for too long.

When they got divorced I was four. We went out for ice cream from Dairy Queen. We don't know where she lives. That's why I'll never see her again. I have to stay with my dad. I want to stay with her, but I can't.

She loves Cheetos. I know she loves me. My mom couldn't take care of me. But my dad could. My mom and dad probably had a fight over me. But I don't know. I was only four. I wished it never happened.

I wished on a star. It was the first one; I know it. I wished on Lauren's sea shell that was painted.

I know she loves me. I know it. I just know it. She is a friend and a special mom. She is special because she's my mom, and I love her. And she's part of my family.

I love you mom!!

Struggling Through

I was having a hard time handling the intensity of the girls' feelings. I struggled through the day and the rest of the year. Students worked on their quilt squares in art class. They wrote and decorated acrostics (poems or short stories formed around the letters of a person's name) about their loved ones. I read the chapter book *Words of Stone* by Kevin Jenkes, which paralleled Lisa's and Mariah's issues. In this book, two children who have experienced the loss of a parent (one through death and the other through abandonment) discover what they have in common and become friends.

Lisa and Mariah also became friends and continued to write about their losses. While Lisa's writing seemed to serve as a private emotional outlet, Mariah asked again and again to read her stories to the class. She welcomed questions and input from classmates. She seemed relieved to discover that her loss was not unique.

"Oh, that's just like me," contributed Jamie. "But my mom's in jail. I hardly ever can see her."

The support that Mariah gained from the class enabled her to begin to heal from her loss. Lisa, however, went on an emotional spiral downward, was treated for depression, and was briefly institutionalized. As the school, her family, and her therapists struggled to deal with her mental illness, writing was one of the few activities that sustained her. She wrote stories about her aunt at every opportunity, even on paper towels used to serve snacks.

For both girls, writing had become necessary and cathartic. As I watched them write about their pain and grief, I wondered what would have happened if I hadn't made room for their stories. Would they and the other children have learned that grieving, compassion, and working through loss have no place in school, perhaps no place in life?

I have always believed that the most powerful lessons are those relevant to the students' lives. Death, tucked away in the "life cycle" part of our science standards, has never been a major part of our official curriculum. But ever since Jessica's death 15 years ago, it has forced its way into my classroom. It has taken a seat and proclaimed its presence. It refuses to move out on Wednesday. ■

Kate Lyman teaches in Madison, Wisconsin. She can be reached via e-mail at clyman@madison.k12.wi.us. The names of the students in this article have been changed.

JEAN-CLAUDE LEJEUNE

Earth's Last Cry

By Rachel M. Knudsen

The earth
can't save the people.
Branches of willow
have no fingers
to pick up broken glass
from city streets.

Grains of sand
have no hearts
to pump oil out
of darkening water.

Blades of grass
have no knives
to cut away
thickening pollution.

Roots of trees
have no feet
to trample
drug needles.

Petals of lilac
have no arms
to carry away
nuclear waste.

(Rachel M. Knudsen was a junior at Jefferson High
School in Portland, Oregon when she wrote this poem.)

(Teaching Ideas, p. 240)

RETHINKING ASSESSMENT

The testing craze that has swept over the country in recent years represents an attack on the critical, multicultural teaching advocated in the pages of this book and its predecessor. How can we "rethink our classrooms" when state authorities dictate a standardized curriculum and threaten students, teachers, and administrators with "high-stakes" consequences should they fail to perform as required? Writers in this section critique the new testing regime. They point out some of the flawed premises of top-down, multiple-choice assessments, and propose innovative classroom-based alternatives. Rethinking our classrooms requires teachers to be activists, requires us to defend our right to engage students in a rich curriculum that promotes academic achievement and social justice.

Failing Our Kids: What's Wrong With the Testing Craze

By the Editors of Rethinking Schools

"How is my child doing?" is the most frequent question a parent asks a teacher. "How are our schools doing?" is an equally common question asked by community members.

Both are important questions. But standardized tests can't adequately answer either of them. Decades of experience and research show that relying on standardized tests distorts student learning, exacerbates inequities for low-income students and students of color, and undermines true accountability between schools, parents, and the community.

The tests, often tied to state standards, can narrow curriculum and impose a restricted, official view of what constitutes knowledge. In addition, standardized tests are often "high-stakes" measurements. This high-stakes approach mandates that students who fail a particular test be retained, placed in low-track remedial classes, denied access to a preferred high school, or in some cases, even refused a high school diploma. Some districts and states also use standardized test scores to evaluate principals, teachers, and entire schools — which lends an additional meaning to the expression "high-stakes" testing. In some locations, schools have been "reconstituted" on the basis of low test scores.

And standardized tests will never answer the question of what our children need to learn to be leaders and informed citizens in a multicultural, ever-changing world.

Accountability or Discrimination?

Many of the political and corporate backers of standardized tests skillfully use the language of high standards to promote an agenda

> Standardized assessments come packaged with demands for more standardized curriculum.

that, contrary to the rhetoric, will increase divisions between the haves and have-nots. They cynically promote reform on the cheap, suggesting that we not "throw money at the schools," but instead simply "raise the bar" with high-stakes tests.

But some advocates of standardized testing genuinely hope to use tests to improve the level of education in low-achieving schools. They argue that uniform standards and measurements of student achievement will increase the likelihood that all students will be served more equally — that without some *measurable* targets, many children will continue to be ill-served by schools.

Clearly, many schools do not adequately serve low-income students, students of color, students with special needs, and students who do not speak English as their first language. These are problems that require urgent attention and our best thinking and organizing. The irony is that a reliance on standardized tests is likely to make matters worse for such students.

African-American and Latino students, for example, are disproportionately failing "high-stakes" standardized tests. Such failure may lead to lifelong consequences. Dropout rates are increasing. In places like Texas, many schools that serve communities of color spend most of the year teaching students to pass tests. As one researcher noted, the high-stakes test regime "reduces both the quality of what is taught and the quantity of what is taught, because commercial test-prep materials are substituted for the regular curriculum." Students may learn techniques that allow them to score higher on reading or writing tests, but students are not becoming readers or writers.

From the earliest uses of standardized tests in American schools, inequality was the expectation. Educational leaders used "mental ability" tests at the turn of the century to sort and rank children, especially along racial and class lines, and to rationalize giving more privileges to the already privileged. The supposed

Dear President Bush,
Thank you for your plan to test all students.
The tests are very useful...

objectivity of test scores gave this stratification a scientific veneer. Indeed the first standardized tests were developed by eugenicists to support theories of the intellectual superiority of northern European whites.

Given the historical use of standardized tests, it is not surprising that the latest testing craze coincides with a resurgence of the view in some quarters of the intellectual inferiority of African Americans, as manifested most starkly in the 1995 publication of the book *The Bell Curve*. This trend paralells a conservative upsurge that opposes programs designed to counter institutionalized discrimination, and justifies a growing division between the rich and poor despite unprecedented economic prosperity.

Tests Shape Curriculum

Standardized tests do more than legitimate and preserve existing power relations. Standardized tests often shape teaching and learning in ways that harm children. As mentioned, teachers are increasingly pressured to drill students on the tests, even when they know that the tests don't assess the most essential aspects of thinking and learning. Entire subject areas — such as music, art, social studies and foreign languages — are de-emphasized in some schools because they aren't tested. Students often internalize the judgments of the tests, as if test scores were the final word on one's knowledge or potential. What is tested becomes "what counts" as knowledge.

In addition, when standardized tests become the engine of school improvement, they divert attention from what is truly needed to make schools better: reforms involving funding equity, lower class sizes, improved teacher education, and addressing unconscionable levels of child poverty.

Standardized tests also come packaged with demands for more standardized curriculum. These calls are part of a broader movement to promote a narrow version of patriotism and "family values," and to silence the critical voices of feminists, environmentalists, labor activists, and advocates of racial justice. As scholar and activist Harold Berlak notes in a recent essay, state-mandated standards and tests "are an effort to put an end to the most valuable asset of a multicultural society: its vibrant cacophony of views about what constitutes truth, knowledge, and learning, and about what young children ought and ought not to learn at school. Standardized curriculum and tests insist upon one set of answers, and only one."

Implicitly, the tests teach students — and everyone else, for that matter — that the purpose of education is to become technically proficient at the manipulation of data. Can you look at a paragraph and locate the "topic sentence"? Can you look at a map and determine "which kind of climate would Area 4 have?" The tests discourage us from seeing that a vital aim of schooling is to engage students in thinking critically about vexing social and ecological crises — that the point of education ought to be to make the world better and more just.

To critique the origins and consequences of standardized tests is not, however, to dismiss parent and community concerns about how well our children are learning.

Alternative Assessment

Developing more equitable forms of assessment is essential to defeating calls for standardized curriculum and testing. Critical educators do not oppose all forms of schoolwide, districtwide, or statewide assessment. Historically, social justice activists have used such aggregate data to show how schools fail to provide a quality education to all children — to highlight schools' "savage inequalities."

There are many potential benefits of "authentic assessments" or "performance assessments" — assessments built into instruction that evaluate how children perform on important tasks, not just on a multiple-choice test, and which can "drive" the curriculum in ways that promote genuine student achievement. These

types of assessment can offer more helpful models of "accountability" than those provided by the testing establishment.

As we develop new ways of assessing our students, we mustn't lose sight of the critical perspective that is vital to the larger project of "rethinking our classrooms." Alternative assessments should reinforce, and be integral to, a broader curriculum of equity and social justice. For example, students in a science class could make presentations, write articles, perform skits, or create audio or video tapes on ecological conditions in their community. Students in a history class studying the Oregon Trail could design a museum display or other commemoration, with the requirement that they must include the perspectives of African Americans, Native Americans, and women, and note the consequences for the environment. Students in one New York City school were required to design a social change project. One group of students surveyed the attitudes of police officers toward Dominican youth, and then led workshops for the cops, after which they re-administered the survey.

There are numerous challenges. How can assessments help teachers to better know the strengths and weaknesses of their students' work, so that the students' work may become more thoughtful and complex? How can assessments be used to nurture critical inquiry, problem-solving, and multiculturalism — so that students are better prepared to understand the world and change it?

And how can alternative assessments become a way to build partnerships between educators and parents/community members as we work together to refine our ideas about what constitutes a "good" education?

The question, as is the case with so many areas of school reform, is:

What will best foster more equitable schooling and promote skills and values that are necessary for a more just society?

Resistance to High-Stakes Testing

As important as it is to develop alternatives to high-stakes standardized tests, this alone will not make these tests go away. High-stakes tests also need to be directly resisted.

Such resistance has taken many forms. In Ohio, for instance, a "Say No" campaign was organized to let parents know they could exempt their child from the 4th, 6th, or 12th grade Ohio Proficiency Tests — tests used to determine graduation and grade advancement. In Portland, Oregon, teachers publicly challenged the state's standards and tests; they have sought to develop alternatives to the social studies component, which makes no mention of race, gender, or labor. In Texas, the Mexican-American Legal Defense and Educational Fund (MALDEF) asked the courts to declare unconstitutional the requirement that students must pass the Texas Assessment of Academic Skills in order to graduate from high school. MALDEF was particularly concerned about the requirement's discriminatory effect on Latino and African-American students. The legal challenge failed, but it helped to draw attention to the tests' biases. Across the country students have boycotted standardized tests and have spoken out on their harmful effects.

The movement to challenge high-stakes standardized tests is still in its infancy. We urge students, teachers, parents, counselors, administrators, community members, and social justice activists to join this movement. And we urge you to use the pages of the quarterly journal *Rethinking Schools* to share analyses, tactics and strategies. ■

Basketball and Portfolios

By Linda Christensen

It was 5:30 on finals day. Most students had left the building at noon, giving teachers a chance to work on their grades before the weekend or prepare for the new classes starting on Monday. They had three hours; the possible uses for their time were endless. I was in the library's prehistoric computer lab with a roomful of students who were still writing, revising, and polishing work for their portfolios.

Lloyd had walked out of the lab and into the adjoining library. At 5:30 college basketball comes on cable. Lloyd slid onto the library table, obviously through with portfolios for the day. "Hey, Linda, why do we have to write these evaluations anyway? You've got all my work in there. You're the teacher. Just read my work and give it a grade. Why do I have to evaluate it?"

His eyes moved back to the TV, where Arizona was playing UCLA.

I looked over at him. Somehow this year he'd moved from his one or two line papers without punctuation to essays, scrappy and sometimes not quite full enough to be called "done," but a big improvement over last year's meager output. He wasn't ready for college writing yet, and our class was ending.

"Do you watch videos after your basketball games?" I asked, knowing that the coach always scheduled mandatory post-game reviews.

"Yeah, every day after our game we got to go watch those videos," he answered without taking his eyes off Damon Stoudamire.

"Why do you think Coach Harris makes you watch your game after you already played it? Couldn't he just tell you what you did?"

"Because then we can see our mistakes — and what plays we're running that work. We look at videos of teams we're going to play, too, so we can see what kind of offense and defense they've got. We can see who to match our players up with. We learn their plays so we can outwit them at the basket." He shifted on the table, still not seeing how his writing portfolio had anything to do with post-game videos. I turned off the TV and we sat and made comparisons between basketball videos and writing portfolios.

With Lloyd it was basketball, with Harold it was wrestling, with Tawni and Aaron it was dance. The connection between teaching, practicing, performing, reviewing, and critiquing is a common thread between disciplines. It also gives me a way to connect the student's passion with learning to evaluate their own writing.

Portfolios: Grading, Evaluation, Assessment?

I've had students make portfolios for years. When I first started keeping writing folders, I called them portfolios, but they were really glorified work folders, where students stored everything from false starts and ugly "I didn't want to write that poem anyway" fragments along with polished pieces. Now I've come to see portfolios as places where students keep the journey of their writing, but also as a place where they analyze both their work and their process, so they can take what they know and apply it to the next piece that comes along — just as my basketball players view their videos to improve their next game.

JEAN-CLAUDE LEJEUNE

While most students enjoy rummaging through their folders and don't mind tossing their work from one folder to another, they are resistant to reflection. Lloyd's comment that I'm the teacher, therefore I should just do the evaluation, is common. Most students aren't accustomed to standing back from their work and assessing it. The routine has been write it, turn it in, the teacher grades it, get it back. End of cycle. When the teacher evaluates a piece, it takes an essential part of the learning experience away from the student and gives the act of judgment and power to the teacher. Ultimately, students learn a great deal more about their writing if they learn to "watch the post-game video" and critique their "play." But it's hard to get them to that point.

Portfolios are hot items in the educational marketplace today. They abound in education catalogues, teaching and assessment journals, and conference book fairs. Vermont has a statewide portfolio assessment which other states are eyeing, as "authentic assessment" becomes a way to tie "workplace skills" to classroom outcomes.

As a classroom teacher and director of the Portland Writing Project, I'm skeptical of legislators and school bureaucrats mandating portfolios. The ones I've seen designed for English classrooms too often dictate types of writing students must include, and then provide ways to score them so that once again student achievement can be reduced to a single-digit number — easily compared across cities, states, and the nation.

I'm not interested in reducing my students to a single digit. I am concerned about their growth in writing and thinking. Frankly, I've never found district or state reading and writing scores to be reliable or useful in my classroom practice. I use portfolios to shape my instruction for individual students, but I also see portfolios as a tool to move students from object to subject in their education. For a critical teacher, portfolios are an evaluation method that pushes students to participate with their teacher in their assessment, rather than being judged by teacher-as-outside-authority.

But let me be clear, I'm not a hands-off kind of teacher. Some of my colleagues believe the portfolio belongs to the student; therefore, the student should be allowed complete freedom to select and control the content. I disagree. There are places and times when students have control; for example, at the end of my class, students make a book of their writing where they can choose the pieces. Jessica, a terrific poet, put poetry and pictures in her book; Aaron made his a collection of fiction writing. With portfolios, I try to

establish and negotiate higher expectations. I'm setting the standards. Each grading period in each class, I determine the kinds of writing that students must include in their portfolios.

One term in Literature and U.S. History class, they needed a literary analyis, a historical fiction piece, and a research paper on either a resistance

> **Most students are not accustomed to standing back from their work and assessing it.**

movement or a person who worked for change. Students also included poetry, interior monologues, film critiques that we worked on, but unless they completed satisfactory drafts of the requirements, they didn't pass. I provided lots of work time, models, and demonstrations; these tasks were not assigned; they were taught. I spent two to three afternoons a week in the computer lab after school working with students who either needed extra help or who wanted more work time.

Partly, my insistence on variety and standards comes from real world concerns: I'm at the high-stakes end of education; I work mostly with juniors and seniors. Tyrone, a thoughtful rapper, would like to write every assignment — from museum critique to historical fiction — as a rap, but if I allowed that, I wouldn't be providing him a rigorous education. He already knows how to write raps. He doesn't know how to write essays. As more colleges move toward portfolios as entrance criteria in addition to SATs, I want my students, who tend to score poorly on these tests, to be

able to demonstrate their range.

Beyond the college connection I want to push students to think more deeply about the world, to make connections in their essays between literature and life in their neighborhood. I don't just want pretty words and adept dialogue; I want searing analysis. My students walk out the school door into a social emergency. They are in the center of it. I believe that writing is a basic skill that will help them both understand that emergency and work to change it.

The portfolio in my classroom fulfills several duties: It showcases students' work in a variety of genres; it demonstrates their journey as a writer — from early to polished drafts as well as stumbling first attempts at poetry, fiction, and essays to later, more accomplished pieces. But it also provides a space for student and teacher to reflect on the change and growth in writing and thinking as well as pointing out a trajectory for future work.

Over the years, I've made some discoveries and fine-tuned my approach to portfolios. Some terms I'd end up with amazing evaluations — where students had obviously internalized discussions on craft and content. Other terms, the analysis was thin — even when I could see remarkable changes in students' writing. Sometimes I knew I'd crammed too much work in at the end of the term; other times, it was obvious that the portfolio prompts were too meticulous or too broad, and still other times it was clear that my teaching was off target. Although I'm still struggling with the evaluation process — as well as the teaching process that precedes it — I've learned some lessons along the way.

Time is Important

Students need enough time between their entry into the class and the analysis of their writing to see change or growth. Often the portfolio evaluation written after the first nine weeks of class is weak. Students are just "finding the basket," learning to dribble. I'm still working at moving them from perfunctory "for-the-teacher writing" to committed writing, from all-rhyming poetry to free verse, from aimless diatribes to essays with support, but after nine weeks, the pathway has not been traveled often enough to see it clearly. Still, it's important to begin the process, so they are critiquing their own work. They also need to begin noting how they work, what they do to move out of a block, how to get a first draft finished. In short, they need to become critics of their own learning.

I used to jump into the writing evaluation at the end of the quarter without giving students time to reread their pieces. Now I devote a 90-minute class period for students to transfer papers from their work folder to their writing portfolio.

Before they begin, I bring in one of my portfolios and talk about pieces I chose to put in and why. Some are samples of my best writing, others are pieces I want to work on, while some show how much my writing has improved. I show them all the drafts of my pieces — including the false starts and comments from my writing friends. I want them to see that most people do not create a perfect draft the first time. This is a noisy 90 minutes, as students read and talk about their writing (mostly, but not always on task). It's when I hear students say, "I didn't realize how much work I completed." Or, "Look, I didn't even know how to line my poetry out." And sometimes, "I wrote better pieces last year."

I learned that if I expect a thorough analysis of their writing, then I need to give that signal by weighting the evaluation as heavily as I do a major writing assignment. I need to give models, criteria, set standards, and give them adequate time to complete the task.

I also need to practice patience. It takes as much time to teach students how to think about and write a reflection on their writing as it takes to teach them how to write a literary or historical analysis. Older students with more experience tend to write better analyses than younger, less experienced writers.

I have to praise the effort and push them to the next level.

Models and Prompts for Portfolio Reflection

When I first started asking students to critique or examine their own writing, I underestimated their need for models of self-reflection. I expected them to "do it" without knowing what they were doing. Bobby Harris, Jefferson High School's basketball coach, wouldn't spend two hours watching a game video without telling his players what to look for — or developing the criteria together with them.

"What is self reflection?" Johnny asked, "What do you mean, 'What did I learn from my writing?'" Amber didn't understand how to use examples from her work for support. Students need to see what I want. They need models of past portfolio evaluations so they can gain a sense of how to look at their writing. Just as they needed examples of former students' essays or historical critiques so they could see what embedded and block quotes look like in text.

I discovered that students took their own writing more seriously after they listened to conversations by writers about writing. For this reason, I read selections from William Stafford, Tess Gallagher, Donald Murray, and Toni Morrison writing about their writing. Students are fascinated, for example, to discover that the idea for Toni Morrison's novel *Beloved* came from an old news article explaining how a woman killed her children because she didn't want them to grow up in slavery.

I also save samples from previous years. I provide guidelines to get students started, but leave them loose enough so that students have room to follow their passion. Sometimes inexperienced writers take the model and copy it exactly, substituting examples from their writing, but using the knowledge of the model. They are not really thinking deeply — they are mimicking. I've come to see this as a stage in their evolution.

Some students like more specific prompts, while others find them stifling — so I vary them and allow them choice. When a student says he/she can't get excited about this (or any) assignment, I say, "Find your passion." They know they have to write an evaluation of their work. Renesa, for example, couldn't put pen to paper until I showed her an article by a local columnist on writing. She wrote her evaluation as an advice column for writers, and typed it in newspaper format — including her picture and examples from her writing to prove her point. Frank wrote his as a letter to my future students telling them what they could expect to learn about writing, then giving examples from his own writing.

Some terms I ask my class to focus their evaluation on one genre — essays or fiction, perhaps. Using colored pencils or highlighters, they have to identify types of evidence, introduction styles, block and embedded quotes, and they must analyze their content and conclusion in essays. In fiction, they have to point out dialogue, blocking, imagery, flashback, interior monologues. Aaron discovered that he rarely used dialogue. Shameica realized that she didn't use blocking and wondered if that was why people got confused about who was speaking in her story. Tony saw that he didn't use evidence from Andrew Jackson's speech on the Cherokee removal; in his critique, he had no quotes to support his position that Jackson was a "racist pig." The act of coloring their drafts made the holes concrete.

Sometimes I ask students to draw pictures or write poems that describe themselves as writers, and then write a paragraph explaining the image for me. Gabriella drew a sculptor with a block of clay. She wrote, "I am the potter with clay, molding, shaping, by taking off pieces and discarding pieces until I have a piece of art." Jim wrote that he was a chef and his writing is dough that he pinches and pulls into just the right shape. Licy drew a jar full of candy to describe herself as a contributor to the class:

My writings and contributions are like the taste of candy itself — some sweet, some sour. Like melting bits of chocolate, I melt cultural information to teach the class something about Mexicans. Like the wrinkled wrapper, I make a sound so everyone knows I am aware. I am here.

One obvious lesson I learned was that students should share their insights with the class. At the beginning of the new term, students showed their metaphors and drawings. These became conversation starters about the craft of writing. As students talked about their drawings or poems, they also shared their roadblocks and their detours. Johanna was a planner who ran into difficulty because her drafts never went as she predicted. The information didn't lay itself out as neatly as she initially hoped it would. Lisa needed to doodle to get started. Anthony said that seeing all of my drafts freed him to get started because he knew he didn't have to get it right the first time. Peter taught some classmates his method of outlining, which was flexible enough to allow for surprises, but gave his piece "river banks" to contain the flow.

The point of our class discussion wasn't to make students all work the same way through a piece of writing, but rather to encourage them to find alternative strategies, so if they weren't successful they could try someone else's for a spell to see if it helped.

Portfolios are one small part of the total classroom, but an important part, because it's where I "measure" not only the students' success and growth, but my own as well. I can lay the foundation of expectations at the beginning of the grading period and help students meet those criteria. The compiled work and the evaluation of it allows both student and teacher to reflect on what worked, on our mistakes, what we can do better next time.

Perhaps because evaluations give us time to pause and look back, they also rehearse us for our next performance — whether it's writing an essay or making a three-point outside shot in the state tournament. ■

Linda Christensen is Language Arts Coordinator for the Portland, Oregon public schools and is a Rethinking Schools editor. This article was adapted from her book Reading, Writing, and Rising Up: Teaching About Social Justice and the Power of the Written Word, *available from Rethinking Schools.*

SKJOLD PHOTOGRAPHS

One Size Fits Few

Why we shouldn't force 15-year-olds to read Moby Dick

By Susan Ohanian

Standardistos in most of the 50 states are high on skills amphetamines, engaged in what amounts to a standards arms race. These days, every Standardisto is looking for 10 minutes of fame, proving "my standards are tougher than your standards."

If John Silber, former chairman of the Massachusetts State Board of Education, had his way, students would read from a core list, including Milton's sonnets and *Moby Dick*. Now you know and I know that anyone who says high-schoolers should read *Moby Dick*:

1) doesn't know any 15-year-olds,

2) has never read *Moby Dick*,

3) has read *Moby Dick*, has a 15-year-old in the house, and wants to get even.

I worry that a whole lot of the Standardistos' curriculum exists on this "get even" premise. I suffered, so why should today's kids get a break? The sad thing is that *Moby Dick* is a great book. It wasn't until I was 42 years old that I'd sufficiently recovered from my college experience to try it again. Okay, I confess: At 42, I still skipped the rope-tying stuff. It just seems a pity that in the name of Standards, we ruin so many wonderful books by forcing them prematurely on kids.

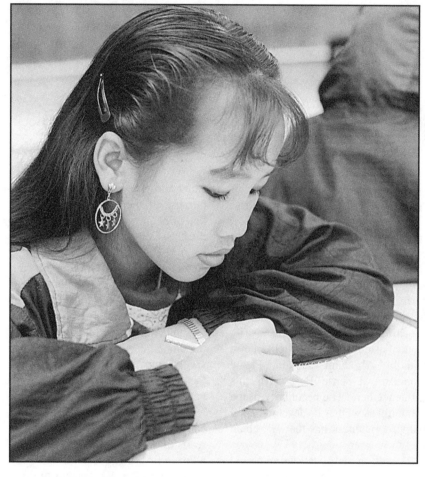

California's Standards

Sometime back, a number of blue-ribbon commissions expressed concern that American kids were getting too little history. Now California pro-duces a document showing us how to give them too much.

Here, for example, is section 1.6 of the California History/Social Science Standards:

Students understand basic economic concepts and the role of individual choice in a free-market economy, in terms of:

1. The concept of exchange and the use of money to purchase goods and services.

2. The specialized work that people do to manufacture, transport, and market goods and services and the contribution of those who work in the home.

Remember, this is Grade One.

JEAN-CLAUDE LEJEUNE

Second graders label a map of North America from memory: Countries, oceans, Great Lakes, major rivers, mountain ranges. Second graders also read the biographies and "explain how heroes from long ago and the recent past make a difference in others' lives." The Standardistos suggest: George Washington Carver, Marie Curie, Louis Pasteur, Albert Einstein, Indira Gandhi, Abraham Lincoln, Jackie Robinson. I sense E. D. Hirsch's influence here. The peculiarity of the grouping as well as its developmental inappropriateness has that Hirschian feel to it.

Fourth graders get latitude and longitude and the Spanish missions. Many California teachers won't see much new here. I remember studying the Spanish missions in fourth grade eons ago. Of course, the text then, like the text today, does not talk about Father Serra's missions as a system of forced labor.

In the new California standards, fifth graders "describe the entrepreneurial characteristics" of early explorers such as Columbus and

Coronado. They also "understand the purpose of the state constitution, its key principles, and its relationship to the U.S. Constitution (with an emphasis on California's Constitution.)" Actually, I, a native Californian, have vague memories of learning — no, memorizing — all that California Constitution stuff. I wonder today how much poorer a life I lead for not remembering a bit of it for longer than six minutes after regurgitating the facts on a test. All I remember is the bear on the flag.

There is more matter here than I can possibly describe. This document reads like the outline for at least half a dozen fat college texts.

Standard 7.9, for seventh graders, is the penultimate standard. As fifth graders, students had to learn the history of civilization in medieval times. Now, under 7.9, they will analyze the historical developments of the Reformation, in terms of:

1. The causes for the internal decay of the Catholic church (e.g., tax policies, selling of indulgences),

2. The theological, political, and economic ideas of the major figures during the Reformation (e.g., Erasmus, Martin Luther, John Calvin, William Tindale),

3. The influence of new practices of church self-government among Protestants on the development of democratic practices and ideas of federalism,

4. The location and identification of European regions that remained Catholic and those that became Protestant, and how the division affected the distribution of religions in the New World,

5. How the Counter-Reformation revitalized the Catholic Church and the forces that propelled the movement (e.g., St. Ignatius of Loyola and the Jesuits, the Council of Trent),

6. The institution and impact of missionaries on Christianity and the diffusion of Christianity from Europe to other parts of the world in the early modern period, including their location on a world map,

7. The "Golden Age" of cooperation between Jews and Muslims

in Medieval Spain which promoted creativity in art, literature, and science, including how it was terminated by the religious persecution of individuals and groups (e.g., the Spanish Inquisition and the expulsion of Jews and Muslims from Spain in 1492).

Seventh graders meet John Calvin! William Tindale! The Council of Trent! The prospect leaves me breathless. Surely a person must be unusually dense to think seventh graders can be forced to drink of this brew. I confess I thought it wonderfully apt that William Tindale is of such secondary significance that he isn't even in my Merriam Webster's Collegiate Dictionary: Tenth Edition. But I kept checking and discovered that he's there. Standardistos, ever esoteric, employ the third-alternate spelling.

Seeking Asylum for Seventh Graders

Time out. Does anybody out there know any seventh graders? As a refresher course, let's hear from premier New Hampshire middle school teacher Linda Rief. This description of emerging adolescence as both the best of times and the worst of times is from her book, *Seeking Diversity: Language Arts with Adolescents* (Heinemann, 1992):

Working with teenagers is not easy. It takes patience, humor, and love. Yes, love of kids who burp and fart their way through eighth grade. Who tell you "Life sucks!" and everything they do is "Boring!" Who literally roll to the floor in hysterical laughter when you separate the prefix and the suffix from the word "prediction" and ask them for the root and what it means. Who wear short, skintight skirts and leg-laced sandals, but carry teddy bears in their arms. Who use a paper clip to tattoo Jim Morrison's picture on their arm during quiet study, while defending the merits of Tigger's personality in Winnie the Pooh. Who send obscene notes that would make a football player blush, written in pink marker, blasting each other for stealing or not stealing a boyfriend, and sign the note "Love, ____ . P. S. Please write back."

No one who knows seventh graders would insist that the subject matter will take precedence for longer than about 12 minutes a period; that's on good days. "Bad-mannered little shits" is a phrase that seventh-grade teachers understand. It was coined by Noel Coward, referring, not to seventh graders, but to the Beatles.

The above is just one of 11 standards that California Standardistos say seventh graders will master in their history classes. If I were a parent in California, I would be looking for a transfer out-of-state rather than face the savage reality of the homework these standards will generate. A class-action lawsuit against the Board of Education might be another option.

An interesting footnote: No history/social studies standards have been written for ninth graders in California "in deference to current California practice in which grade nine is the year students traditionally choose a history/social studies elective." I have read all the standards documents, including the minutes of commission meetings, produced by the Standardistos. In twelve grades on imperatives and explications, this is the only mention of students getting a choice.

California Standardistos were very conscious that these are the first-ever statewide academic standards for history. In announcing the California Academic Commission's approval of its standards, History/Social Science Committee Chair Lawrence Siskind said, "Our History/Social Science Standards are balanced and academically rigorous. I am especially proud of the civic values and virtues which they impart. When they graduate high school, California students will be ready to vote, to serve on juries, and to take their place in society as responsible citizens. Should they ever be called upon to fight for their country, these standards will teach them why their country is worth fighting for."

No comment. ■

Susan Ohanian is a teacher and author of more than a dozen books.

This article is excerpted and condensed from Chapter 5 of her book One Size Fits Few: The Folly of Educational Standards *(Portsmouth, NH: Heinemann, 1999). To order call: 800-225-5800.*

Tracking and the Project Method

Reflections on alternatives to tracking

By Bob Peterson

SKJOLD PHOTOGRAPHS

Children enter my fifth-grade classroom at so many levels that at times I feel I'm teaching in a one-room schoolhouse in the 1800s. A few of my students who are learning-disabled struggle with basic sounds and letters, while other students read at close to a high school level. The same is true with math, writing, artistic, athletic, and verbal skills — although not all students remain at one end of the spectrum. Sometimes, for instance, I will have a student who has difficulty reading but is quite adept at math.

This range of skills is one of the most difficult dilemmas that I grapple with as a teacher. To deal with it, I draw not only on my years of classroom practice, but also my own experience as a student and my grounding in progressive educational philosophy. The result is an approach that combines curricular projects with an eclectic grouping of students, with the twin goals of promoting equity within my classroom and of pushing each child to perform their best.

The issue, however, is much broader than how I, as an individual teacher, decide to organize my classroom. Fundamentally, the issue involves important questions of how schools, especially schools in urban areas, can provide equal educational opportunities to all, and avoid the tracking and ability grouping that are all-too-popular despite their stereotypical assumptions and their disastrous consequences.

My Student Experience

I grew up in Madison, Wisconsin, and I recall how some of my teachers dealt with the varied skill levels in their classrooms. In elementary school, we were placed by "ability" in reading and math groups named after birds and animals, a thinly veiled attempt to mask who the teacher thought was smart and who was not. There was virtually no chance of moving from one group to another, a rigidity I remember well because my best friend and I were always in different groups.

As we moved into junior high, this tracking became more pronounced. Every kid in the school knew where they fit in the intellectual pecking order, and teachers held different expectations for different groups.

There were five gradations for the seventh grade student body — 7-1 being "the best and the brightest," with the "losers" grouped in 7-5. Each gradation started the day together in homeroom and traveled as a group to all classes, except gym and industrial arts. Interestingly, during this time my family moved overseas for 18 months, and upon my return I was placed into the lowest track. School officials quickly changed my academic classes, but left me in the lower-track homeroom. It was there that I made my first African-American friends — not surprisingly, since then as now, racist assumptions about intelligence led to a tracking system in which African-Americans were often segregated and grouped into the lower tracks.

By high school, the tracks were even more rigid: vocational, general education, and college bound. It's not hard to guess which kids were in the top track at my school, Madison West High School — the middle-class and upper-middle-class whites.

During my sophomore year, in a fit of progressivism, Madison West detracked the social studies courses. I have no clue whether school officials deemed the effort "successful," but one incident in particular made me realize the negative impact of tracking on some of my friends. While I was leaving my tenth-grade U.S. history class one day, a "lower-track" student — a cheerleader — approached me and apologized for being in the class. She told me she was sorry for "slowing down the class with her questions" and wondered why they put all the "smart and dumb" kids together in the same history class. I was taken aback by her comments, but recovered enough to tell her the problem wasn't her lack of smarts, but the less-than-capable teacher that bored all the students to tears every day.

The teacher took the dreary but pervasive approach that students are empty vessels who need to be "filled up" with "facts" about names, dates,

Today, with the stress on "high standards" and "back to basics" — and decreased emphasis on issues of equity and multiculturalism — the pendulum appears to be swinging back to tracking as an acceptable way to group students.

and places, so they can regurgitate those "facts" on tests filled with true and false, multiple choice, and short-answer fill-in-the-blank questions. In fact, according to researcher John Goodlad in his seminal work, *A Place Called School,* less than 1% of instructional time in high school is spent on discussion that requires students to form an opinion or use any reasoning skills.

Criticisms of Tracking

In the late 1970s and early 1980s, there was a growing awareness of the negative consequences of ability grouping in the elementary grades and tracking in secondary schools. Research by Robert Slavin of Johns Hopkins University, and books such

as Jeannie Oakes' *Keeping Track: How Schools Structure Inequality* and Anne Wheelock's *Crossing the Tracks: How "Untracking" Can Save America's Schools,* helped alert educators and policy-makers to the problems with tracking; they also pointed toward potential alternatives. People such as Slavin, Oakes, and Wheelock argued that in many schools, tracking institutionalizes inequality and leads to lower expectations and less rigorous course work for students in the bottom tracks. They also found that such tracking does not benefit the students in the upper tracks, as is commonly assumed. As Oakes, an assistant dean in the Graduate School of Education and Information Studies at UCLA, wrote: "No group of students benefits consistently from being in a homogeneous group."

At the same time, community groups in some areas took up the issue, even to the extent of going to court. In essence, they viewed the struggle against tracking as a continuation of the movement to abolish separate but unequal schools — although in this case the focus was on nominally integrated schools that were highly segregated by classroom. In both cases, the unequal and segregated schooling denied African Americans full access to equal opportunities.

Today, with the stress on "high standards" and "back to basics" — and decreased emphasis on issues of equity and multiculturalism — the pendulum appears to be swinging back to tracking as an acceptable way to group students.

Recently, the influential Thomas B. Fordham Foundation (headed by conservative education guru Chester Finn) published a 27-page report arguing that tracking isn't really all that bad, and in fact may be good. The report, "The Tracking and Ability Grouping Debate," was written by Tom Loveless, an associate professor of public policy at Harvard. In the report, Loveless argues that criticisms of tracking are "mostly unsubstantiated by research" and that "evidence does not support the

SUSAN LINA RUGGLES

charge that tracking is inherently harmful."

This swing back toward tracking is complemented by rightward trends such as increased reliance on standardized testing, an obsession with phonics-based reading instruction, attacks on multicultural and bilingual education, and attempts to "decertify" the teaching profession and undermine schools of education, which are seen as bastions of child-centered pedagogy.

What unifies these rightward shifts is a conservative conception of education itself — a view that education is little more than a transfer of subject matter and facts from the adult society to the next generation, best done through drill and rote memorization. The conservative approach stands in stark contrast to a progressive view of education, perhaps most notably articulated by John Dewey at the turn of the century. Dewey held that schools should start with the child, build on his or her interests, and link them to broader intellectual and social concerns through a curriculum that poses problems and actively involves the student.

If one's conception of education is the "subject matter set out to be learned" approach (as the conservative approach has been character-ized), then it's understandable why ability grouping and tracking might be viewed as the most efficient and easiest way to "deliver" an education. If, on the other hand, one's educational goal is to develop independent thinkers who can look critically at the world and solve real-world problems, heterogeneous groupings might make more sense. To cite just one reason: The more social diversity there is in a class, the more the classroom mirrors the real world, and the more students learn to draw upon each others' strengths to analyze and solve problems.

Let me explain by looking at my own classroom.

Grouping in My Classroom

I admit that I group students. I can't imagine a teacher who has two or three dozen children in a classroom who never does so. But my groups vary a lot. Some are homogenous — kids who need work on certain skills or kids who are dominant in Spanish or English (I teach in a two-way bilingual school). But most often the groups are heterogeneous, with kids of varying skill levels working in cooperative groups on a common project such as a role play, dramatization, critique, or discussion.

Sometimes students work in pairs, such as in peer conferences in which they give feedback on each other's writing. Occasionally, I allow the students to choose their own groups.

But the most important thing is that the groups are always changing. No student is forever "stuck" in a "lower" group, as my best friend was in elementary school.

Take my reading groups. Every two weeks or so, we start a new children's novel as part of my guided reading instruction. I show the children four or five different books of varying levels, and they write their top three choices on a file card. I make up two or three groups based on student interest, my assessment of their reading skills, and their background knowledge about the book's subject.

The composition of the groups changes every two weeks, and the activities vary as well. Sometimes the groups are self-directed "literature circles." Other times I take a more active role and use the time to reinforce basic reading and vocabulary skills. I usually make sure that all the books for any two-week period have a common theme that relates to something else we are studying (for example, homelessness, the American Revolution, the Underground Railroad, immigration experiences of Asian Americans, and so forth). This way, the groups can adopt additional projects that extend into other parts of the curriculum, and can discuss common themes regardless of which book they are reading.

I take a similar approach in math, sometimes working with the entire class, sometimes in small groups, sometimes with pairs of students, and sometimes one-on-one. I especially use a varied approach when introducing a new topic, such as fractions, to ensure that students get as many opportunities as possible to understand the new concept. Depending on the concept and skill being taught, I might group by "ability" for a week or two (for instance when reviewing long division and it becomes clear that some students need extra help) and then rearrange both the groups and my approach. Sometimes the students do group math projects, such as using data they collect from their classmates to make graphs or solve problems. (See "Teaching Math Across the Curriculum," p. 84.)

In other curriculum areas, I group kids depending on the purpose, whether it's brainstorming ideas, critiquing, or discussing. In social studies, for example, as we start studying a topic such as the American Revolution or the abolition movement, groups of three to five might generate a list of things they know about the subject, or what they'd like to learn. Often when I have an assignment for the children — such as writing a dialogue poem or doing a book report — we look at examples of similar assignments by my previous students. Afterwards, the students break into different groups to evaluate what they think of the previous students' work and generate ideas on how they will evaluate their own work. Students working in groups have also critiqued things like the bias in children's books about Columbus, or the number of put-downs and stereotypes on popular TV shows.

These varied approaches to grouping and classroom organization are a beginning step toward dealing with the "range of skills" dilemma. I believe, for example, that cooperative groups done well, especially when there is a component of individual accountability, can boost academic achievement and improve the classroom's sense of community. If done in a slipshod fashion, however, cooperative groups can lead to a situation in which the harder-working, more committed students do most of the work and little learning takes place for the students who might need it the most.

Even if done well, however, cooperative grouping is insufficient as a teaching strategy. My goal is not just to push each student to learn to the best of their ability, or to have students understand the value of working together. I also want to promote an anti-racist, social justice curriculum that encourages children to criti-

> **The more social diversity there is in a class, the more the classroom mirrors the real world, and the more students learn to draw upon each other's strengths to analyze and solve problems.**

cally think about — and help change — the world. Cooperative learning is a worthwhile method, but we need to ensure that it isn't used to more effectively teach a traditional curriculum replete with Eurocentric biases and stereotypes.

Structured-Project Approach

Perhaps the most useful curricular approach that I have found is what I call the structured-project approach.

The projects are interdisciplinary assignments in which each student must make a booklet using reading, writing, geography, research, and other skills. Throughout the year, my fifth-grade students make a total of five magazine-size booklets; they follow a prescribed outline developed over the past several years by my partner teacher, Jesús Santos, and me.

The projects include a student autobiography, a report on an endangered animal, a bilingual poetry anthology, a report on a famous person who fought for social justice, and a report on the student's journey through elementary

school. The topics allow for significant student input so that the specific theme of each book is generated by the student. While each student is expected to complete their individual project, many components of the project are approached collaboratively in groups. For example, one part of the student autobiography is to write about their neighborhood. In groups, students will list all the things they might look for in their neighborhood — such as the type of buildings, the different kinds of people, and what they like and don't like about their neighborhood — then write a draft in the evening and come back the next day and share their drafts in their group.

For the project on a famous person who worked for social justice, the students start by interviewing family and friends for suggestions of who might fit the category. As a class, we compile lists and I use mini-lectures to teach children about dozens of possible choices. Continuing as a class, we read parts of biographies on a few people. Then we break into groups and the students take notes on what we've read. Each student has to write down at least three things they've learned, but the whole group must compile a master list. Each group then shares its notes with the entire class and we draw lessons about how to take good research notes. Eventually we do the same kind of activity for turning notes into rough drafts.

The modeling and group practice help teach all students basic research and writing skills. The process also challenges the most skilled and assists the least skilled — so that no child is left behind, and no child is left bored.

Ultimately, the completed projects are shown at student-led parent-teacher conferences in fall and spring, and also at an end-of-year fifth grade exhibition. These demonstrations of their work provide additional motivation for the students to do quality work. (See "Motivating Students to Do Quality Work," p. 219.)

Interestingly, it was not until I was well into the third year of using this project approach that I recalled — and ultimately recovered from my parents' attic — some similar projects I had done while in fifth and sixth grade. My favorite was on jet airplanes, and I had written to a range of corporations and officials, from North Central Airlines to the U.S. Air Force, to get photos. I show the 84-page report to my students when we start our work on projects. (They seem to comment most on the impeccably neat cursive handwriting, which is in sharp contrast to my current scrawl. More than one of my students has asked whether I had a serious accident with my hand at some point after 6th grade, which might account for my current handwriting.)

Other Projects

Students do their book projects in the context of other project-like activities in my classroom. I try to make sure that some of those projects are more group-based than the books. I also try to ensure that some of the projects don't take very long, so that students can see immediate results and build their self-confidence.

In the first few days of school, for example, each of my students does a name poem in which they reflect on how they were named, their name's significance, and how they feel about their name. I do the poem in the context of a social studies lesson about the power of naming, and how enslaved Africans and many immigrants were forced to take on new names as they arrived in the Americas. Working in pairs, the students edit, type, and print their poems, which are then framed on colored paper, laminated, and displayed. Later, a version of that poem will be incorporated into their autobiography and their bilingual poetry booklets.

Students also do lots of drama and role plays in my classroom. Drama projects range from reenactment of scenes from the literature books we are reading, to problem-posing situations where groups of students show how they might peacefully resolve peer conflicts, such as a playground quarrel or who gets to use a computer first.

In our study of U.S. history, I use more involved role plays to highlight key conflicts. Such role plays have specific parts and involve several days of student preparation. Some of my most successful role plays have been a trial of Columbus, a mock Constitutional Convention that includes groups not invited to the original convention, (see p. 63) and a trial of a runaway slave.

Projects have also emerged out of discussions of current events. One year, for example, a few students were particularly concerned after reading a *Weekly Reader* article about child labor. They did more research, writing, and discussing, which led to a couple of them speaking at a community rally against child labor and NAFTA. As a spin-off, I helped them form a Stop Child Labor Club that met weekly during lunch hour.

These various projects help me deal with students who are at different skill levels. First, because of the combination of group and individual activities, the more-skilled students can help the lesser-skilled students, and in so doing both benefit. The student who is a good writer, for example, can help to revise and edit a weaker writer's essay, and in the process learn more about writing. Second, because the book projects are individualized, each student can be challenged according to my assessment of their capabilities. For example, the learning-disabled or English-as-a-second-language student might write considerably less in English than another student. Nonetheless, both projects can challenge those students to the maximum. Third, because I do a variety of projects in my classroom and not all the projects are writing-based, students have a chance to shine in different contexts. For example, students who have difficulty writing sometimes are among the best verbal acrobats in the class. They are sought after by other students to be in their groups when we do dramas or role plays. I remember how one year, a learning-disabled student who could barely write excelled in social studies because in the group work, role plays, and dramatizations he was among the most articulate. Had I just expected him to show what he learned through "end of chapter tests," he would have been perceived as a poor student and quite likely would have been turned off to learning.

Final Reflections

I am convinced that tracking and rigid ability grouping lower expectations unfairly for many students and channel them away from rigorous class work. But proponents of equality must not only work to end tracking. We must also ensure that teachers in untracked classrooms use techniques that are effective with all students. Tracking and ability grouping can't be ended overnight with dictates from above. We must create school cultures and staff development programs that help teachers deal effectively with their students' wide-ranging level of skills. It should be unacceptable for teachers to rely on traditional whole-class approaches which use the textbook as a crutch and a substitute for good teaching. Such approaches either bore the more-skilled students or leave the less-skilled students behind.

If we don't boldly confront this issue, dissatisfied parents and students will fall prey to the idea that the best way to resolve such problems is to promote admission standards for schools, increase tracking within schools, and use strict ability grouping within classes.

Our students demand more of us, and we must rise up and meet that demand. ■

Bob Peterson (repmilw@aol.com) teaches fifth grade at La Escuela Fratney in Milwaukee, Wisconsin and is a Rethinking Schools editor.

Motivating Students To Do Quality Work

By Bob Peterson

There is a sense of excitement in the air. Fifty-two fifth graders sit at desks throughout the gymnasium. A few boys wear suits and ties; girls are in their Sunday best. At each desk, student-made books and projects are neatly arranged on colorful cloths brought from home. Large math projects and artworks adorn the walls. Freshly cut flowers brighten the sunlit room.

La Escuela Fratney's fifth-grade student exhibition is about to begin.

"It was the best day of my life,"
commented one student the next day. Another reflected: "I liked staying after school and showing my projects to students, parents, and teachers. It made me feel important."

The exhibition is the culmination of the students' academic career at Fratney, a kindergarten through fifth grade Milwaukee public school. The success of the exhibition depends on several other activities, including student-work portfolios, student reflection, a project approach to learning, and student-led parent/teacher conferences. The exhibition's goal is to increase students' intrinsic motivation to do quality work and to ensure that authentic forms of assessment help drive the curriculum.

My teaching philosophy holds that classroom environments and lessons should be structured so that students become intrinsically motivated to do schoolwork, instead of being motivated mainly by extrinsic rewards or punishments. If students are genuinely interested in the work and find it meaningful, its quality will be much

Fifth Grade Exhibition Checklist

Name _____

_____

Mandatory

❏ Autobiography

❏ Endangered Animal Project (Spanish)

❏ Bilingual Poetry Book

❏ Famous Person Report

❏ Journey through Elementary School Booklet

❏ English Math Problem Solving Notebook

❏ English Reading Response Journal

❏ Bilingual Exhibition Script — What You Will Say and Show

Optional

❏ Art Project _____

❏ Large Math Project/Display _____

❏ Other Writings (books, poetry display, rough drafts, from previous grades as well) _____

❏ Other: _____

---

richer than if they work solely for a grade. That's one reason I use a structured project-approach in which students have considerable latitude to choose what they study and research. Nonetheless, I have found that while student involvement in choosing topics spurs an interest in doing the project, it does not automatically translate into completion of the project or the production of high-quality work.

Lack of student motivation and low-quality work are nemeses for most teachers, but I became particularly aware of them a few years ago when I returned to the classroom after four years as program implementor for Fratney's two-way bilingual program. Despite my creative activities and participatory lessons, too many of my students seemed to be indifferent to the quality of their work. After a year back in the classroom, my frustrations were such that I knew I had to try something different.

I recalled two visits, some years before, to high schools in New York City associated with the Coalition of Essential Schools. In those schools,

students were expected to maintain a work portfolio and participate in an exhibition at the end of their school career. Their portfolios and the exhibition gave greater purpose to their school projects and allowed the students to show off publicly what they had accomplished. It also allowed others to assess how well the students (and the school) were doing.

I decided to try the same approach with my fifth-graders, who end their elementary school career with me and move on to middle school. I figured such a public exhibition of work would help motivation. It would also help me maintain high expectations for my students. If teachers know that their students are going to present their work so publicly, they're less likely to fritter away the days assigning worksheets. Their curriculum will be more oriented to projects and the real world, and their standards will be higher. This is a good example of the idea that if the "test" is a good one, it's fine to have it drive the curriculum. Finally, I knew that an exhibition would fit well with the

already established policy at Fratney of maintaining language-arts portfolios. And so Fratney's fifth-grade exhibition was born — at least in my mind.

La Escuela Fratney has about 360 students, more than 80% of whom are eligible for free or reduced-cost lunch. The student body is multiracial, with the majority being Latino. Fratney, a two-way bilingual school with approximately 50% Spanish-dominant speakers and 50% English-dominant speakers, teaches students either English or Spanish as their second language. In fourth and fifth grade, students spend two weeks in an English-language classroom learning their basic subjects in English and then two weeks in a Spanish-language classroom working in Spanish. There are two fourth-grade classrooms and two fifth-grade classrooms, so there are "partner teachers" for each grade level. I am the English-language fifth-grade teacher, sharing responsibility with my Spanish-language partner teacher, Jesús Santos, for about 50 students. We prepare joint plans and report cards and conduct joint parent-teacher conferences.

The First Year

The first year, the student exhibition was almost an afterthought and suffered from lack of planning. The expectations were vague, and the results were disappointing. It happened this way: After spring break I told the children that on the last day of school before the completion (graduation) ceremony, kids would display the projects and work they had completed throughout the year. A few students worked very hard on their displays. One girl, Jade Williams, brought a beautiful table-cloth and flowers to accompany her work, which included a couple of books of poetry that she had published in my classroom. The day before the ceremony we transformed our classroom into a display area and each fifth-grader put out a name card and work to display. Unfortunately, the day's completion ceremonies and emotional good-byes overshadowed the exhibition; by the last day of school, fifth grade, for my students, was history.

But a number of staff members showed interest in the students' work. Their encouragement, and the proud smiles of Jade and her mother, convinced me to try again.

Changes in the Exhibition

Some important changes the following year paid off. I explained the exhibition at the start of the school year, showing photos of Jade and her mother standing beside her display. I moved the exhibition into the third floor gymnasium and scheduled it a week before the end-of-the-year completion ceremony. The third- and fourth-grade students visited the exhibition, not only so that they would know what to expect in fifth grade, but also to provide a non-threatening audience and a practice opportunity for the fifth-graders. Also, I invited other staff, members of Fratney's site-based council, and other community members, ranging from university people to school board members to local business people.

The afternoon before the exhibition, the fifth-graders moved their desks into the gymnasium and set up their displays. The following morning they completed preparation; that afternoon the third- and fourth-graders visited. They were quite impressed, especially proud of any sibling who was exhibiting work. For an hour after school, parents and staff came.

The results, though better, were still uneven. Some students excelled; others had little to show. Moreover, a former partner teacher and I differed regarding what constituted worthwhile display work. At the last minute she had students bind their math worksheets from throughout the year. This was symptomatic of a larger problem: Some students focused on the quantity of work instead of the quality. Moreover, despite attempts to encourage students to reflect on their growth as learners, there were few written reflections, and what there was was shallow. This was due to a combination of factors, including my not allocating adequate time for this complex task, failing to model quality reflections, and not developing the vocabulary necessary for more nuanced thinking and critiquing.

But, just as Jade had in the previous year, some students shone. They proudly exhibited several projects which showed thoughtful planning, writing, and revision. Students displayed detailed research projects on famous people who fought for social justice, such as Langston Hughes, Sitting Bull, Malcolm X, Elizabeth Cady Stanton, John Brown, and César Chávez. Many had poster-size math projects with the results of surveys of classmates on topics such as TV viewing habits, ethnic background, and favorite Green Bay Packers players — using bar and circle graphs, percentages, and fractions. Others proudly displayed simple alphabet books and stories they had made in kindergarten and first grade.

Further Refinements

In more recent years the exhibition has improved considerably. My partner teacher, Jesús Santos, and I collaborate closely on the entire project and share similar expectations. At the beginning of the year we inform our students of end-of-year exhibition requirements (see checklist in box). To ensure better quality reflections, we and the students develop rubrics and evaluation guides for all major projects — so that students reflect on their work regularly throughout the year. Such reflections are important because they help students step back and think about what they have done, what they've learned, and how they might improve on similar projects in the future: Students can start to see themselves as learners, and in charge of and responsible for their own learning, a sharp contrast to their traditional role of completers of tasks and recipients of grades.

The reflections, however, vary greatly from the almost meaningless "I did nice work on this project" to more thoughtful statements. One boy reflected on his poetry anthology by writing: "This book of poetry taught me plenty. Not only punctuation, but making pictures with words. I learned how to make people feel the poem, taste the poem, and see it in its many different forms." Another wrote: "I learned that poems have no limits."

One year, in order to develop more substantive dialogue at the actual exhibition, each student created a bilingual script and practiced it with a partner. By doing this, students

> Students can start to see themselves as learners, and in charge of and responsible for their own learning, a sharp contrast to their traditional role of completers of tasks and recipients of grades.

thought out in advance what they would say about their work and themselves as learners. It also focused them on the exhibition and their own learning.

A professor from a local college who visited told me: "The students are very motivated to show their work and proud of it. It's clear that the projects are engaging for the students, and most of them are quite articulate in explaining what they learned from them."

Fratney's student exhibition takes place in a very supportive school environment. Classroom teachers maintain portfolios with student work and reflections, and non-classroom teachers and the principal provide crucial logistical support. One of our parents, who owns a Mexican restaurant, supplies food at the exhibition and volunteer teachers serve it. The exhibition in turn has affected the entire school. Both teachers and students in the lower grades, for example, have a better sense of why it's important to keep quality portfolios.

Project Approach

The exhibition's success also rests on the teaching method in our fifth grade, which I call a "structured-project approach." (See "Tracking and the Project Method," on p. 214.) Throughout the year, fifth-grade students are expected to complete major projects. These projects include a student autobiography, a report on an endangered animal (in Spanish), a bilingual poetry anthology, a report on a famous person who fought for social justice, and a report on the student's journey through elementary school. In each case, the student chooses specific topics and how each will be presented, following clear guidelines established by the teacher.

The guidelines vary from project to project but always include a core set of requirements and options for additional work. For example, the autobiography has 17 core items which include everything from a cover, title page, and table of contents to short essays on the student's heritage, neighborhood, and preschool experience. Also required is a self-portrait (done with the help of the art teacher), a name poem, a timeline, and a description of numbers in the student's life. In groups, students brainstorm other things to write about, coming up with another 30 or 40 items. I type up both lists as

checklists and staple them into manila folders which become the student's working folder for the project. We talk about what constitutes quality work, review examples from previous years, and create both student and teacher evaluation forms that are included in the book when it is finally spiral-bound.

The last project of the year is the most original. Students go through their entire elementary school portfolio, choose at least one piece of work from each year, and reflect on it. They also create a "postcard" for each year, on one side drawing a picture of a memorable event and on the other writing about it as they would have at the time. The students reflect on their growth; we teachers chuckle at the bizarre incidents that stick in their minds: Four dead tadpoles floating in the aquarium, the shape of the pumpkin chosen at the pumpkin farm, the lone compliment or joke from a substitute teacher. In fact, this project is an additional incentive for other staff members to visit the exhibition, to find out how their former students remember their classrooms.

The written booklets are tied to other, non-writing projects in my student-centered classroom. For example, as part of the fifth-grade U.S. history social studies curriculum, my students do role play re-enactments of key conflicts. We hold a trial of Columbus, recreate the U.S. Constitutional Convention including social groups that were excluded at the time (see p. 63), and conduct a trial of a runaway slave. Students also participate in literature circles, reading a variety of children's novels, and critiquing children's books and TV shows for bias and stereotypes. These group activities provide a broader context for the students when they tackle their individual projects. So, for example, when doing their poetry anthology their "dialogue" poems might not only include a traditional cat and mouse duo, but also Columbus and a Taíno, or a slave master and an abolitionist. Similarly, when the students choose their person for the project on a historical figure

who fought for social justice, they have a broader range of people to choose from. The individual written projects in turn spawn other classroom projects. For example, after the famous person project, students present a videotaped monologue pretending to be their person — an activity that helps prepare them for the districtwide oral language proficiency assessment. In addition, students often share selected parts of their written project in our biweekly oral sharing time with the fourth grade.

The students also reflect on each project in its entirety. Roberto Villafuentes wrote about his final project of the year: "I learned that to be in each grade is not easy and also that my life is long. I learned that it is better to study than to be on the street like some people." Eduardo Díaz reflected: "Most of my handwriting is neat and my drawings are decent. I'm pretty original and creative. I learned that I'm a fast learner."

This project approach helps motivate students because it allows them significant input into what they study and write. It also assumes that learning should be active, with much of the students' time spent in learning through creating something meaningful, whether it's a booklet or class debate.

The project approach also meets the needs of varying skill levels. In my class, children read and write at levels from first through eighth grade. The project approach allows me to challenge the most skilled students, and yet see to it that the lesser-skilled meet with some success. This of course is what all schooling should do and is essential for educators who create alternatives to tracking of students by alleged ability.

Student-Led Parent/Teacher Conferences

One problem with the end-of-year exhibition is the timing — we only do it once and it's at the end of the year. While we try all year to entice students to do their best, the exhibition occurs too late for it to be an incentive for some kids. By the time they realize that they have not completed some of their projects, no amount of rushing around will enable them to complete their work. Yet we teachers know that we can't pull off multiple exhibitions throughout the year. So we have decided to use the parent-teacher conferences, which in Milwaukee are traditionally held in October and March, to help students focus on their end-of-year exhibition and become more reflective about themselves as learners.

Several Fratney teachers attended a Wisconsin State Assessment Institute and read the book *Changing the View: Student-Led Parent Conferences* by Terri Austin (1994). As a result, third-, fourth-, and fifth-grade teachers decided to restructure our traditional conferences to involve students, a change that fit in well with our philosophy of student reflection and of students taking responsibility for their learning.

We made a distinction between a three-way conference and a student-led conference. At the former, the student participates by taking some responsibility for leading the discussion, but the teacher is always present. In the student-led conference, the student leads the entire conference, with several occurring simultaneously in the same room. The teachers move from conference to conference, participating occasionally. We also decided which aspects of the curricula would be focused on at each grade level.

In fifth grade, we provide each student with the skeleton guide for what they will say at their conference, requiring that students talk to their parents about their current projects (which are due just prior to the conference) and how they are doing with reading, math, homework, and self-discipline. Finally, they have to decide on three goals for the next marking period and share them with their parents.

The response of the parents has been very favorable. In a survey conducted one year by our school's parent organizer, all 26 sets of parents surveyed were satisfied with the new format and thought it should be con-

SKJOLD PHOTOGRAPHS

tinued. Common themes in their comments were that the conferences "develop responsibility and make them [the students] want to do better each day," that it's informative for parents to see "students present their own achievements," and that it was good that the students "could make observations about themselves."

The one drawback that was mentioned is that the format seemed to cut into the time available for parents and teachers to talk.

Conclusion

After several years of student exhibitions, we've seen their potential. Students are more motivated in doing their work and more reflective in analyzing it. Parents are definitely pleased to see what their kids have accomplished. One comment we often hear is: "I wish I would have gone to a fifth grade where I did proj-

ects like this." Because of what the students exhibit, I, as a teacher, am more aware of what I am teaching and how well I am reaching all students.

But despite our successes, we continue to struggle with problems. Students are still apt to be too task oriented, especially near the due date of an assignment, and tend to rush, short-changing the quality and reflective aspect of their work. We are trying to more consciously teach our fifth graders how to keep major projects organized and how to make a timeline to ensure that they complete their projects on time.

Second, we realize that, for whatever reason, some parents don't come to conferences or to exhibitions. Because of that, some children feel less motivated to plan to show their work. We have tried to solve this by having other adults in the school hold a conference with the student as surrogate parents.

IMAGE PRODUCTIONS

Third, we need to figure out how to "exhibit" oral-language based projects. Our students perform a lot — biweekly sharing sessions, social studies role plays, and in-class dramatizations, some of which we videotape. Nonetheless, we haven't figured out an effective way to include this work in our exhibition.

Fourth, as teachers who believe in conveying the importance of social justice and activism to our students, we still need to figure out how to incorporate these values into the exhibition and the conferences. Letter writing, group projects, and dramatizations that might reflect social justice issues are not well represented in the exhibition.

Finally, we struggle daily with the problem of time. With the increasing demands placed on classrooms by district, state, and national entities to test and assess, and to cover ever-greater amounts of curriculum, time is at a premium. And time is just what is required to prepare these student-centered exhibitions, conferences, and projects. We have decided that despite the time crunch, the time we invest in these student-centered, reflective activities is justified.

Moreover, when parents have so much real information about their children's progress, and when community leaders see the concrete work of students at exhibitions, people don't feel as compelled to support test-based "accountability" schemes. The challenge, of course, is for educators to not only find the time to create these broader forms of assessment, but to popularize such models to help undercut the testing juggernaut. Only through this popularization will teachers build a strong enough constituency to fight the standardized testing craze, which consumes the very time needed for this kind of teaching and genuine assessment.

While this takes extra effort, it's worth it. As one of my students said in evaluating the year in my classroom, "I had fun in this class and I learned a lot. I never thought I would be able to do so much." ∎

Bob Peterson (repmilw@aol.com) teaches fifth grade at La Escuela Fratney in Milwaukee, Wisconsin and is a Rethinking Schools editor.

Resource

Austin, T. *Changing the View: Student-Led Parent Conferences*. New York: Heinemann, 1994.

RESOURCES

This list includes books and curricula, children's books, audio/visual resources, catlogs, organizations, websites, and periodicals to promote justice.

In our earlier volume, *Rethinking Our Classrooms, Volume 1*, readers will find an extensive listing of valuable classroom resources. They include: videos; books for children; curricula; literature anthologies; maps and posters; organizations; periodicals; and books on history, policy and theory. With the exception of organizations and periodicals, by and large, the resources included in these categories have not been repeated here in *Rethinking Our Classrooms, Volume 2*. Please see *Volume 1* for the full listing.

The resource list and links to supplemental materials are available on the Rethinking Schools website: www.rethinkingschools.org/ publication/roc2/roc2links.shtml

Teacher Resources

Books and Curricula to Promote Justice

All starred resources (*) are available from the Teaching for Change Busboy and Poets webstore: www.bbpbooks.teachingfor change.org; or by calling toll-free at 800-763-9131.

*Affirming Diversity: The Sociopolitical Context of Multicultural Education, Sonia Nieto. White Plains, NY: Longman, 1996, second edition. Of the scores of books on multicultural education, Nieto's is one worth reading. The central message of this 422-page book is that multicultural education is essential to promote the academic achievement of students of color; it is a message that comes through powerfully in her clear explanations of related issues of bilingual education and critical pedagogy, and her numerous case studies that give voice to students of different backgrounds.

*Anti-Bias Education for Young Children and Ourselves, Louise Derman-Sparks and Julie Olsen Edwards. Washington, DC: National Association for the Education of Young Children, 2010. Perhaps the best book for the early child/primary level on how to teach about all forms of bias and what to do about it.

*Beyond Heroes and Holidays: A Practical Guide to K-12 Anti-Racist, Multicultural Education and Staff Development, edited by Enid Lee, Deborah Menkart, and Margo Okazawa-Rey. Washington, DC: Teaching for Change, 2004. A 434-page collection developed by educators, parents, and activists determined to create a valuable resource for change. Lesson plans and staff development activities are included, as well as critical examinations of controversial school issues such as bilingual education and tracking. Contains an extensive resource guide of teaching and learning resources and many helpful websites.

*Caribbean Connections, edited by Catherine Sunshine. Washington, DC: Teaching for Change, 1991. Stories, interviews, songs, drama, and oral histories, accompanied by lesson plans for secondary language arts and social studies. Separate volumes on: Puerto Rico, Jamaica, Regional Overview, and Moving North.

Chicano! The History of the Mexican American Civil Rights Movement, F. Arturo Rosales. Houston: Arte Público Press, 1997. A comprehensive account of the struggle of Mexican Americans to secure and protect their civil rights, starting with the U.S. invasion of Mexico and subsequent annexation of most of what is now the U.S. Southwest. The book is designed to accompany a PBS series that is available on video.

*Child Labor is Not Cheap, Amy Sanders and Meredith Sommers. Minneapolis, MN: Resource Center of the Americas, 1997, (information available online at **www.maslibraries.org/Publications/samplers/childlabor.html**) A three-lesson unit for grades 8-12 on the 250 million children throughout the world who spend most of their day on the job. First lesson is designed to accompany the video, *Zoned for Slavery* (see more informnation under Audio/Visual Resources).

*Colonialism in the Americas: A Critical Look (1991), and also **Colonialism in Asia: A Critical Look,** Susan Gage. Victoria, BC: VIDEA. Sophisticated descriptions of colonialism in an easy to read, comic book format. Through dialogue and cartoons, each booklet traces the development of colonialism and its legacy. Teaching ideas are included in each volume.

*A Different Mirror: A History of Multicultural America, Ronald Takaki. Boston: Little, Brown & Co., 1993. Beginning with the colonization of the "New World" and ending with the Los Angeles riots of 1992, this book recounts U.S. history in the voices of Native Americans, African Americans, Jews, Irish Americans, Asian Americans, Latinos and others. Takaki turns the Anglocentric historical viewpoint inside out and examines the ultimate question of what it means to be an American.

*Days of Respect: Organizing a Schoolwide Violence Prevention Program, Ralph Cantor, et al. Alameda, CA: Hunter House, 1997. Step-by-step instructions for putting together an event that unites students, parents, teachers and community leaders for a common goal: preventing violence and creating an atmosphere of respect in school.

De Colores **Means All of Us: Latina Views for a Multi-Colored Century**, Elizabeth Martinez. Cambridge, MA: South End Press, 1998. Martinez's more than 30 years of experience in the movements for civil rights, women's liberation, and Latina/Latino empowerment are reflected in these readable essays. Particularly good on the struggles of Mexican Americans.

*Education Is Politics: Critical Teaching Across Differences, K-12, edited by Ira Shor and Caroline Pari. New York: Heinemann, 1999. In memory of Paulo Freire, the essays in this collection describe critical practices by teachers committed to transformation in and beyond the classroom. They show culturally diverse educators constructively taking sides and refusing to fit students or themselves quietly into the status quo.

*Failing Our Kids: Why the Testing Craze Won't Fix Our Schools, edited by Kathy Swope and Barbara Miner. Milwaukee, WI: Rethinking Schools, 2000. More than 50 articles provide a compelling critique of standardized tests and also outline alternative ways to assess how well children are learning. The long arm of standardized testing is reaching into every nook and cranny of education. Yet relying on standardized tests distorts student learning, exacerbates inequities for low-income students and students of color, and undermines true accountability.

*The Field Guide to the Global Economy, Sarah Anderson and John Cavanagh, with Thea Lee. New York: The New Press, 1999. Illustrated with charts, graphs, and political cartoons, this accessible and engaging guide reveals the harmful effects of corporate-driven globalization. It explains current trends in the global economy, the driving forces behind globalization, and the organizations and individuals working to reverse these destructive forces.

*Finding Solutions to Hunger: Kids Can Make a Difference, Stephanie Kempf. New York: World Hunger Year, 1997. Engaging, interactive, and challenging lessons for middle school, high school, and adult education on the roots and solutions to domestic and global hunger. Examines colonialism, the media, famine vs. chronic hunger, the working poor, and more.

*Flirting or Hurting? A Teacher's Guide on Sexual Harassment in Schools for 6th through 12th Grade Students, Nan Stein and Lisa Sjostrom. Washington, DC: National Education Association, 1994. An excellent teacher-friendly curriculum, with stories and role plays. Widely used.

*Freedom's Unfinished Revolution: An Inquiry Into the Civil War and Reconstruction, The American Social History Project. New York: The New Press, 1996. Lively prose, primary documents, illustrations, and photographs bring this key period of U.S. history to life and invite students to study Reconstruction in depth. This 302-page book includes exercises and discussion questions. By the authors of *Who Built America?*

*Funding for Justice: Money, Equity and the Future of Public Education, edited by Stan Karp, et al., Milwaukee, WI: Rethinking Schools. 1997. Presents the complicated issues of school finance in a readable form for teachers, parents, and the community. In more than 25 articles packed with information, background, and analysis, *Funding for Justice* makes a strong case for providing adequate and equitable funding to all schools.

*Honoring Our Ancestors, edited by Harriet Rohmer. San Francisco: Children's Book Press, 1999. A must for teachers of all grade levels. Through portraits and stories, 14 outstanding artists from diverse communities honor the ancestors who touched their lives. This 32-page book includes Joe Sam's beautiful portrait of his three aunts who raised him in Harlem during the 1940s while working as maids in the white neighborhoods of Manhattan; and Hung Liu's portrait of her grandmother who made shoes for the family in China. Can be used at any grade level.

*Hope and History: Why We Must Share the Story of the Movement, Vincent Harding. Maryknoll, NY: Orbis, 1990. A series of essays from Harding's consultation on the Public Broadcasting Service's *Eyes on the Prize* series. The 246-page book provides good ideas and poses challenging questions for a course or a teacher study group.

*Keepers of the Earth: Native American Stories and Environmental Activities for Children, Michael J. Caduto and Joseph Bruchac. Golden, CO: Fulcrum Inc., 1988. Features a collection of North American Indian stories and related hands-on activities designed to inspire children. An interdisciplinary approach to teaching about the earth and Native-American cultures.

*Lies My Teacher Told Me: Everything Your American History Textbook Got Wrong, James W. Loewen. New York: New Press, 1994. Loewen's book is an entertaining and eye-opening de-mything of key aspects of American history. It's both an effective critique of some of the most widely used history texts and an alternative history.

*The Light in Their Eyes: Creating Multicultural Learning Communities, Sonia Nieto. New York: Teachers College Press, 1999. Nieto takes us beyond individual learners to discuss the social context of learning, the history and manifestations of educational equity, the influence of culture on learning, and critical pedagogy. Centering on multicultural education as a transformative process, the text includes reflections of teachers who have undergone this process.

*The Line Between Us: Teaching About the Border and Mexican Immigration, Bill Bigelow. Milwaukee, WI: Rethinking Schools, 2006. Using stories, historical narrative, role plays, and videos, veteran teacher Bill Bigelow shows how he approaches immigration and border issues in his classroom.

Making the Grade: A Racial Justice Report Card, Applied Research Center, 1999. 510-653-3415. Free. An extremely user-friendly tool to measure racial equity in schools. The heart of this CD is an interactive reporting mechanism through which the user inputs raw data that are available from most school districts. The program then issues a "racial justice report card." Designed for anyone who wants to document patterns of institutional racism in schools, the CD has everything from sample letters to send school administrators to background information on racial inequality in schools. [Although this resource is no longer available in CD format, it is available on the ARC website, at www.arc.org.]

*Making the Peace: A Violence Prevention Curriculum, Paul Kivel and Allen Creighton. Hunter House, 1997. A comprehensive teaching handbook with all the information needed to implement a 15-session core curriculum. It offers step-by-step instructions for sessions, anticipates difficult issues that may arise, and suggests ideas for follow-up both within the classroom and within the school or youth program.

*Multicultural Education as Social Activism, Christine Sleeter. Albany, NY: SUNY Press, 1996. Sleeter connects multicultural education with issues of power. Chapters include: "This curriculum is multicultural ... isn't it?" "Teaching science for social justice," "Reflections on my use of multicultural and critical pedagogy when students are white," and more.

Multicultural Voices in Contemporary Literature: A Resource for Teachers, Frances Ann Day. Portsmouth, NH: Heinemann, 1999. Day's updated book provides classroom teachers and librarians with a quick reference for hundreds of multi-

cultural titles, as well as some thoughtful writing prompts.

The Norton Anthology of African American Literature, edited by Henry Louis Gates, Jr. and Nellie V. McKay. W.W. Norton, 1996. Too many teachers have never read African-American literature. Most who have read individual works have not systematically explored the tradition and come to understand how it draws upon the vernacular language of African Americans. This anthology is where teachers who work with African-American children can find direction in their study of the African-American literary tradition.

*One Size Fits Few: The Folly of Educational Standards, Susan Ohanian. Portsmouth, NH: Heinemann. 1999. This hilarious, unsparing, and touching narrative recounts the author's quest to make sense of the Standards movement. Ohanian explores the ironic results of the movement in schools (e.g., failure to pass students who lack "necessary knowledge" on topics such as covalent bonds and the Edict of Nantes), discusses the absence of critical dialogue in the media regarding standards, and ultimately issues a call to action.

*Open Minds to Equality: A Sourcebook of Learning Activities to Affirm Diversity and Promote Equity, (third edition) Nancy Schniedewind and Ellen Davidson. Milwaukee, WI: Rethinking Schools, 2006. This resource both inspires teachers to teach for justice and provides classroom-ready ideas that work. The lessons integrate various curricular areas and are presented in a sequential fashion. Includes an excellent resource bibliography. Also by Schniedewind and Davidson is *Cooperative Learning, Cooperative Lives: A Sourcebook for Learning Activities for Building a Peaceful World*, W.C. Brown Company, 1987.

*Other People's Children: Cultural Conflict in the Classroom,

Lisa Delpit. New York: The New Press, 1995. Gives an excellent background on issues related to language and literacy. Delpit shows how educators' unconscious assumptions about race and culture play out in classrooms with harmful, if unintended, consequences. A vital resource for teacher education.

*Peters Projection World Map, New York: Friendship Press. This is a map, not a book, but it comes with a teaching guide. It presents all countries according to their true size. Traditional Mercator projection maps distort sizes, making Europe appear much larger than it actually is. *A New View of the World* by Ward Kaiser is a handbook on the Peters map.

* A People's History for the Classroom, Bill Bigelow. Milwaukee, WI: Rethinking Schools, 2008. Examplary teaching articles and lesson plans emphasize the role of working peple, women, people of color, and social movements in shaping U.S. history.

*A People's History of the United States: 1492 – Present, Howard Zinn; New York: HarperCollins; revised 1995. The best single volume history of the United States. No teacher should be without a copy. Some sections are readable by high school students.

*The Power in Our Hands: A Curriculum on the History of Work and Workers in the United States, Bill Bigelow and Norm Diamond. New York: Monthly Review Press, 1988. role plays and writing activities help students explore issues about work and social change. An essential curriculum for history and economics teachers, or for school-to-work programs.

Preventing Prejudice, Marta Hawthorne, et al. Buena Vista Lesbian and Gay Parents Group. 1999. Age-appropriate gay-positive curriculum for grades K-5. A valuable resource for teachers to talk openly and respectfully with their students about gays and lesbians and to take concrete steps to diminish homophobia.

*Putting the Movement Back into Civil rights Teaching: A Resource Guide for Classrooms and Communities, edited by Deboarh Menkart, Alana Murray, and Jenice View. Washington, DC: Teaching for Change, 2004. Provides lessons and articles on how to go beyond a heroes approach to the Civil Rights Movement.

*Reading, Writing, and Rising Up: Teaching About Social Justice and the Power of the Written Word, by Linda Christensen. Milwaukee, WI: Rethinking Schools, 2000. In this practical, inspirational book, Christensen draws on her 20-plus years as a high school teacher to describe her vision of teaching reading, writing, and language courses that are rooted in an unwavering focus on social justice. Includes essays, lesson plans, and a remarkable collection of student writing.

*Readings for Diversity and Social Justice: An Anthology on Racism, Antisemitism, Sexism, Heterosexism, Ableism & Classism, edited by Maurianne Adams, et al. London: Falmer, 2000. An invaluable anthology of over ninety readings by some of the foremost scholars in the fields of education and social justice, including Gloria Anzaldua, Patricia Hill Collins, bell hooks, Michael Omi, Ronald Takaki, Beverly Daniel Tatum, Cornel West and Iris Marion Young. Covers the scope of social oppressions, emphasizing interactions among racism, sexism, classism, anti-Semitism, heterosexism, and ableism.

*The Real Ebonics Debate: Power, Language and the Education of African-American Children, edited by Theresa Perry and Lisa Delpit. Milwaukee, WI: Rethinking Schools, 1998. Educa-

tors, linguists, writers and students examine the lessons of the Ebonics controversy and unravel complexities of the issue that have never been widely acknowledged.

Reinventing the Enemy's Language: Contemporary Native Women's Writings of North America, edited by Joy Harjo and Gloria Bird. New York: W.W. Norton, 1997. This anthology includes works from such notable authors as Leslie Silko and Louise Erdrich and lesser-known writers from a variety of Native cultures. It is groundbreaking in its depth, breadth, militancy, and beauty.

*Resistance in Paradise: Rethinking 100 Years of U.S. Involvement in the Caribbean and the Pacific, edited by Deborah Wei and Rachael Kamel. Philadelphia: American Friends Service Committee, 1998. In 1898, the United States annexed the Pacific Islands of Guam, Hawai'i, and Samoa, as well as Cuba, Puerto Rico, and the Philippines. This major event in U.S. history is barely mentioned in school textbooks. *Resistance in Paradise* fills the gap with over 50 lesson plans, role plays and readings for grades 9-12. Includes illustrations, cartoons, maps, and photographs.

*Rethinking Columbus: The Next 500 Years (second edition), edited by Bill Bigelow and Bob Peterson. Milwaukee, WI: Rethinking Schools, 1998. This widely acclaimed book asks educators to think about the racial and cultural biases in traditional tales of "discovery," and provides numerous teaching ideas that encourage students to think critically about these myths. An essential volume for teacher education. Greatly expanded from the first edition, which sold a quarter of a million copies.

*Rethinking Early Childhood Education, edited by Ann Pelo. Milwaukee, WI: Rethinking Schools, 2008. This inspiring anthology shows

how educators can nurture empathy, an ecological consciousness, curiosity, collaboration, and activism in young children.

*Rethinking Globalization: Teaching for Justice in an Unjust World, edited by Bill Bigelow and Bob Peterson. Milwaukee, WI: Rethinking Schools, 2002. "A treasury of ideas and information," according to historian Howard Zinn. Includes role plays, interviews, poetry, stories, background readings, and hands-on teaching tools.

*Rethinking Mathematics: Teaching Social Justice by the Numbers, edited by Eric Gutstein and Bob Peterson. Milwaukee, WI: Rethinking Schools, 2005. Shows how to weave social justice issues throughout the mathematics curriculum, and how to integrate mathematics into other curricular areas.

*Rethinking Multicultural Educaton: Teaching for Racial and Cultural Justice, edited by Wayne Au. Milwaukee, WI: Rethinking Schools, 2009. Collects the best articles dealing with race and culture in the classroom that have appeared in *Rethinking Schools* magazine. A powerful vision of anti-racist, social justice education.

*Rethinking Our Classrooms: Teaching for Equity and Justice (Volume 1), edited by Wayne Au, Bill Bigelow, and Stan Karp. Milwaukee, WI: Rethinking Schools; 2007. This new edition includes creative teaching ideas, classroom narratives, and hands-on examples of ways teachers can promote values of community, justice, and equality — and build academic skills.

*Rethinking Our Classrooms, Volume 2: Teaching for Equity and Justice, edited by Stan Karp, Brenda Harvey, Larry Miller and Bill Bigelow. Milwaukee, WI: Rethinking Schools; 2001. Supplements the first volume of *Rethinking Our Classrooms,* which has sold over 180,000 copies. Practical from-the-classroom stories from teachers about how they attempt to teach for social justice. Extends and deepens many of the themes introduced in the first volume of *Rethinking Our Classrooms*.

*Rethinking School Reform: Views from the Classroom, edited by Linda Christensen and Stan Karp. Milwaukee, WI: Rethinking Schools, 2003. Puts classrooms and teaching at the center of the debate over how to improve public schools.

*Roots of Justice: Stories of Organizing in Communities of Color, Larry R. Salomon. Chardon Press. 1998. *Roots of Justice* recaptures some of the nearly forgotten histories of communities of color. These are the stories of people who fought back against exploitation and injustice — and won. From the Zoot Suiters who refused to put up with abuse at the hands of the Navy to the women who organized the welfare rights movement of the 1970s, *Roots of Justice* shows how, through organizing, ordinary people have made extraordinary contributions to change society. In a time of cynicism, this is an especially needed book.

*Talkin and Testifyin: The Language of Black America, Geneva Smitherman. Detroit: Wayne State University Press, 1986. This wonderful book is still the best introduction to the study of Black language. It is required reading for teachers who work with African-American children.

*Teaching for Diversity and Social Justice: A Sourcebook, edited by Maurianne Adams, Lee Anne Bell, and Pat Griffin. New York: Routledge, 1997. A compilation of course syllabi, lessons, and resources for college courses and staff development on issues of racism, sexism, classism, anti-Semitism, heterosexism, and ableism.

*Teaching for Joy and Justice: Re-imagining the Language Arts Classroom by Linda Christensen. Milwaukee, WI: Rethinking Schools, 2009. Demonstrates how to draw on students' lives and the world to teach poetry, essays, narratives, and critical literacy skills.

*Teaching Economics As If People Mattered: A High School Curriculum Guide to the New Economy, Tamara Sober Giecek. Boston: United for a Fair Economy, 2000. Field-tested by high school teachers, this innovative economics curriculum looks at the human implications of economic policies. These 21 lesson plans are designed to stimulate dialogue and encourage active student participation in the high school or college classroom.

*Teaching for Social Justice: A Democracy and Education Reader, edited by William Ayers, Jean Ann Hunt and Therese Quinn. New York: Teachers College Press/New Press. 1998. A unique mix of hands-on, historical and inspirational writings. The topics include education through social action, writing and community building, and adult literacy.

*That's Not Fair: A Teacher's Guide to Activism with Young Children, Ann Pelo and Fran Davidson. St. Paul, MN: Redleaf Press. 2000. Children have a natural sense of what's fair and what's not. This book helps teachers learn to use this characteristic to develop children's belief that they can change the world for the better. Includes real-life stories of activist children, combined with teachers' experiences and reflections. Original songs for children and a resource list for both adults and children.

*Transforming Teacher Unions: Fighting for Better Schools and Social Justice, edited by Bob Peterson and Michael Charney. Milwaukee, WI: Rethinking Schools,

1999. A vital tool for anyone working in or with teacher unions today. The 25 articles look at exemplary practices of teacher unions from the local to national level, and present new visions for the 21st century. Addresses the history of teacher unionism and connects issues of teacher unions, classroom reform, local communities, and social justice.

*We Can't Teach What We Don't Know: White Teachers, Multiracial Schools, Gary Howard. New York: Teacher's College Press. 1999. With 25 years of teaching experience as a multicultural educator, Howard looks into his own racial identity to search for what it means to be a culturally competent white teacher in racially diverse schools. His lively stories and compelling analysis offer a healing vision for the future of education.

*Who Are the Arabs: The Arab World in the Classroom, Steve Tamari. Washington, DC: Center for Contemporary Arab Studies, Georgetown University, 1999. History, poetry, photographs, maps, short stories, and articles by and about the Arab-speaking world. This 12-page booklet is available free if requested along with an order for other titles from the Teaching for Change catalog, www.teachingforchange.org.

*"Why Are All the Black Kids Sitting Together in the Cafeteria?" and Other Conversations About Race, Beverly Daniel Tatum. New York: HarperCollins, 1997. In 270 pages, Tatum, a psychologist and a professor at Mount Holyoke College, provides a detailed explanation of racial identity development for people of color and whites. This remarkable book, a road map filled with wisdom and humanity, tells those looking to explore issues of race where to begin.

Women of Hope. New York: Bread and Roses Cultural Project. A poster and curriculum series on African-American, Native American, Latina, and Asian American women. The posters and study guides provide a powerful tool for challenging stereotypes by teaching about the real history and contemporary reality of extraordinary women of color.

Children's Books

América Is Her Name, by Luis Rodríguez, illus. by Carlos Vásquez. Simultaneosly published in a Spanish edition, *La Llaman América,* trans. by Tino Villanueva. Willimantic, CT: Curbstone, 1998. These books are the first children's picture books to be published by Curbstone, which has long published quality books by Latin-American and Latino authors. The story, by prize-winning poet and journalist Rodríguez (author of the memoir *Always Running*), deals with life in urban neighborhoods, but with a positive theme: You can succeed despite odds against you.

*The Birchbark House, Louise Erdrich. New York: Hyperion Books for Children. 1999. Omakayas, a seven-year-old Native American girl of the Ojibwa tribe, lives through the joys of summer and the perils of winter on an island in Lake Superior in 1847. This is the first in a series of young adult novels based on noted author Louise Erdrich's own family history. This book begins to tell the story untold in the Laura Ingalls Wilder *Little House on the Prairie* series.

*Dreams of Looking Up, Cindy Goff; art by Paul and Mary Fricke.Onamia, MN: Mille Lacs Band of Ojibwe. 1999. This educational comic book teaches the meaning and importance of tribal sovereignty. Through the Ojibwe oral tradition, a young girl learns about her people's culture in conversations with her deceased grandmother. She passes on these vital lessons to her skeptical older brother.

From Slave Ship to Freedom Road, Julius Lester, paintings by Rod Brown. New York: Puffin Books, 1998. A beautifully illustrated book that presents the slave experience — from auction block to freedom.

*Gathering the Sun: An Alphabet Book in Spanish and English, Alma Flor Ada and Simón Silva. Lothrop, Lee and Shepard Books. 1997. In children's poems and sun-drenched paintings, *Gathering the Sun* take us into the fields and orchards, and the lives of the people who work them. Using the letters of the Spanish alphabet as a template, Alma Flor Ada has written 28 poems that celebrate honor and pride, family and friends, history and heritage, and, of course, the bounty of the harvest.

*Get Real Comics, Philadelphia: COLLAGE/Tides Center. 1997. Popular culture that helps kids 8-14 rethink issues like gender, sexuality, self-esteem, race, violence, friendship, and family. Award-winning series used in classrooms and community groups nationwide.

Grab Hands and Run, Frances Temple. New York: HarperTrophy, 1992. Set during the civil war in El Salvador, a family flees north to escape the government soldiers. 4th/up.

Home to Medicine Mountain, Chiori Santiago. San Francisco: Children's Book Press, 1998. Based on a true story, this picture book tells the story of how two young members of the Mountain Maidu and Hamawi Pit-River tribes in California escaped from the government-run boarding school and came back home.

I, Too, Sing America: Three Centuries of African American Poetry, Catherine Clinton, illustrated by Stephen Alcorn. Boston: Houghton Mifflin, 1998. A beautiful collection of poetry from 25 of the greatest African-American poets, accompanied by striking colored drawings. Appropriate for all age groups.

*In My Heart, I Am A Dancer, Chamroeun Yin. Philadelphia Folklore Project. 1996. Through photos and large print, traditional Cambodian dancer Chamrouen tells the story of his life. Children learn that not only does he dance, but he also sews, gardens, cooks, spends time with his friends, and is a teacher. *In My Heart* is as a model for teaching about cultural traditions. Bilingual in English and Cambodian.

*The Long March: A Famine Gift for Ireland, Marie-Louise Fitzpatrick and Gary WhiteDeer. Hillsboro, OR: Beyond Words Publishing, 1998. Based on a true story of solidarity, this picture book for all ages tells of the Choctaws in 1847 who collected $170 from their meager savings for the people of Ireland during the Potato Famine. Readers learn the story of the Choctaw who were forced by the U.S. government to leave their ancestral home in Mississippi. In the Long March west, thousands died of cold and starvation. The story's protagonist, Choona, a young Choctaw, grapples with whether he is willing to extend help to a group of Europeans after the pain his own family has experienced.

Moon Over Crete, Jyotsna Sreenivasan. Duluth, MN: Holy Cow! Press, 1994. This novel for young adults is about the mixed messages society sends to young girls, and the double standards and sexual discrimination it subjects them to. The story centers on 11-year-old Lily, and her "travels" back to ancient Crete, an egalitarian culture that did not have gender-specific roles or jobs.

*My Name is Maria Isabel, Alma Flor Ada. New York: Atheneum,

1993. For Maria Isabel Salazar Lopez, the hardest thing about being the new girl in school is that the teacher doesn't call her by her real name. Named for her Papa's mother and for Chabela, her beloved Puerto Rican grandmother, Maria must find a way to make her teacher understand that if she loses her name, she's lost an important part of herself.

Passage to Freedom, The Sugihara Story, Ken Mochizuki. New York: Lee and Low Books, 1997. A children's picture book which describes the true story of Hiroki Sugihara, the eldest son of the Japanese diplomat in Lithuania who, at great risk to his family, helped save hundreds of Jews from the Nazis.

The Pasteboard Bandit, Arna Bontemps and Langston Hughes, illustrated by Peggy Turley. New York: Oxford University Press, 1997. Written 60 years ago by two great African-American poets, this beautifully illustrated children's book depicts a white American boy and a Mexican boy in an intercultural adventure in which both cultures and languages are equal, although the Americans are viewed as the "strange" ones. Never published before, this is a must for all elementary school libraries.

The Red Comb, Fernando Pic, illustrated by María Antonia Ordez. Ri Piedras, Puerto Rico: Ediciones Huracán, 1991. In a story set in Puerto Rico, two women conspire to save a young woman from a slave catcher. Based on historical documents, this beautifully illustrated book brings to children another aspect of the struggle against slavery in the Americas. Spanish version also available.

Richard Wright and the Library Card, William Miller, illustrated by Gregory Christie. New York: Lee & Low Books, 1997. A wonderfully illustrated picture book that describes the struggle of the great African-

American author Richard Wright's attempt to get access to all-white libraries. Appropriate for all ages and a good way to introduce Wright's works to older students.

Stolen Spirit, Peter Hays and Beti Rozen, illustrated by Graça Lima. Fort Lee, NJ: Sem Fronteiras Press, 2001. One interpretation of how a Native boy might have reacted to the first encounter in 1500 with Portuguese explorers who chop down trees that the boy's people think are sacred. Beautifully illustrated.

*The Story of Colors/La Historia de los Colores, Sub-comandante Marcos. El Paso, TX: Cinco Puntos Press. 1999. A beautifully illustrated, bilingual folktale from the indigenous people of Chiapas. This story celebrates diversity as it tells how all the colors of the earth were born.

*The Streets are Free, Kurusa. Toronto: Annick Press, 1995. An illustrated story based on the experience of children in a low-income neighborhood in Caracas, Venezuela who fought for the right to turn an empty lot into a playground. Useful at all age levels to raise discussion about how people can organize to defend their rights.

Sweet Words So Brave: The Story of African American Literature, Barbara K. Curry and James Michael Brodie, illustrated by Jerry Butler. Madison, WI: Zino Press, 1966. Inspired by African-American literature and history, this colorful work reflects the magic of the Harlem Renaissance and the influence of African-American writers.

*Talking Walls: The Stories Continue, Margy B. Knight and Anne S. O'Brien. Gardiner, ME: Tilbury House. 1996. Illustrations and text tell the stories of walls, and the people they divide, throughout the world. Includes the stories of:

Chinese detainees who wrote poetry on the walls of Angel Island, children who write poetry on the fence around the home of Pablo Neruda in Chile, children who created a garden in Philadelphia from an abandoned lot and painted a mural on the surrounding wall, children in Belfast who are divided by a wall constructed by the army in the 1970s, and more.

The Turtle Watchers, Pamela Powell. New York: Puffin Books, 1992. A chapter book set in the Caribbean where three sisters work to protest the killings of the giant leatherback turtle. Grades 4 and up.

*We Can Work It Out: Conflict Resolution for Children, Barbara K. Polland. Berkeley, CA: Tricycle Press. 2000. An invaluable tool for parents and teachers. Through beautiful color photographs and questions, this book encourages conversations between adults and children about typical conflicts children encounter, such as teasing and sharing. It helps children develop problem-solving skills they need to resolve conflicts independently.

The Well, Mildred Taylor. Dial, 1995. The newest book in Taylor's saga of the Logan family introduced in *Roll of Thunder, Hear My Cry*. This story is of the grandfather's childhood, when his family is the only one in the county that has a functioning well. Racial tensions erupt between two teenage kids exposing the early 1900s Southern power structure. Highly recommended. Grades 4 and up.

We Shall Not Be Moved: The Women's Factory Strike of 1909, Joan Dash. New York: Scholastic, 1996. A readable nonfiction account of one of the most important women's strikes in US history. Grades 5 and up.

What Do You Know About Racism, Pete Sanders and Steve Meyers. Copper Beach Books, 1995.

A children's book from England that directly addresses racism with clear definitions and realistic comic strips. Grades 4 and up.

Audio/Visual Resources

(The prices below are current as of Spring 2001, and in most instances apply only to individual purchases from the Teaching for Change Busboy and Poets webstore: www.bbpbooks.teachingfor change.org; or by calling toll-free at 800-763-9131. Institutional purchasers should contact the distributors, if listed.)

*Act of War: The Overthrow of the Hawaiian Nation, by Puhipau and Joan Lander. 1993, 60 min., $65. Comprehensive documentary on the events surrounding the overthrow of the Hawai'ian monarchy in 1893 from the perspective of Native Hawai'ians. *Act of War* explores colonialism and the conquest of a Pacific Island nation by western missionaries and capitalists.

*The Ad and the Ego, by Harold Boihem and Chris Emmanouilides; California Newsreel (www.newsreel.org), 1996, $70. This is the best video-critique of the social and ecological effects of advertising. Blending MTV-style editing with brilliant narration, *The Ad and the Ego* can be a real awareness-raiser for many high school students.

*Ancient Futures: Learning from the Ladakh, based on the book by Helena Norberg-Hodge. Produced by John Page with International Society for Ecology and Culture. 1993, 60 min., $25. Through the story of Ladakh, a Himalayan region in India, this video enables students to confront the devastating impact of "development." They see the root causes of environmental, social, and psychological problems that arise when a traditional society is invaded by Western investment, culture, and consumer goods. This is an extraordi-narily useful film that uses one case study to consider some of the intimate meanings of "globalization."

*Arms for the Poor, Maryknoll. 1998, 25 min. $20. This video presents an international spectrum of dignitaries and activists who share the belief of one Nobel Laureate that "the poor are crying out for schools and doctors, not guns and generals." Through interviews and footage of the impact of massive amounts of weapons throughout the world, students learn who benefits and who loses from the military-industrial complex.

*At the River I Stand, California Newsreel. 1993, 56 min. $50. Martin Luther King, Jr. saw in Memphis an opportunity to use nonviolence to challenge the economic power structure of the North and South. *At the River I Stand* documents Memphis' Black community support for a path-breaking strike by 1,300 city sanitation workers for a living wage. This film joins together many critical issues: violent vs. nonviolent struggle, white privilege vs. Black poverty, and grassroots mobilization vs. national politics.

*Banking on Life and Debt, narrated by Martin Sheen, Maryknoll World Productions, 1995. $20. More than 90% of the world's population lives in countries directly affected by World Bank and International Monetary Fund policies. This video takes students to Brazil, Ghana, and the Philippines to see the results of these policies. A valuable resource for classes in economics, global studies, and U.S. government. 30 minutes. (A longer version, *The Money-lenders*, is also available.)

*Barefoot Gen, (DVD format; video out of print), 1983, 83 min $24.99. Chronicles the devastating impact of the bombing of Hiroshima as experienced by a family in Japan. A stylistically close adaptation of Keiji Nakazawa's graphic autobio-graphical novel, this animation brings home the horrors of the war and the strength of people who survived.

*Bus Riders Union, by Haskell Wexler. Strategy Center (213-387-2800, www. busridersunion.org). 2000, 86 min., $30. Video documentary tracing three years of the Los Angeles Bus Riders Union, one of the nation's most dynamic social movements formed to fight transit racism, clean up L.A.'s lethal auto pollution, and win billion-dollar victories for real mass transit. *Bus Riders Union* is a rare mix of fine filmmaking, astute political awareness, and a complex portrayal of a multiracial grassroots movement that is taking on some of the most powerful forces in Los Angeles — and winning.

*Business of Hunger, Maryknoll. 1984, 28 min., $20. In many countries, crops are exported while the poor go hungry. This phenomenon, one of the major causes of world hunger, is examined in Latin America, Africa, Asia, and North America. The film proposes a more just distribution of the earth's resources offering a vision of a world where all have enough to eat.

Civil Rights: The Long Road to Equality, The Duncan Group, AGC/United Learning, 1999. 800-323-9084. $95. "The Civil Rights Movement: The Role of Youth in the Struggle" is the first video in this helpful two-video set. The second video, "Overcoming Racism," has middle- and high-school youth reflecting on their own racial identity and discrimination. The producers are aware of the limitations of any short video on such a complex subject. Upper elementary through high school.

*Earth and the American Dream, by Bill Couturie. Direct Cinema Limited, 1993; $95 (individual or institution). This extraordinary

77-minute film examines U.S. history from the standpoint of the earth. Beginning with Columbus, it effectively blends contrasting quotes from Native Americans and European "settlers" with images of the environmental consequences of these ideas. We've never seen a film that does this so powerfully. A vital classroom resource.

Freedom On My Mind, by Connie Field and Marilyn Mulford. Clarity Educational Productions, 800-343-5540, $69.95 for high schools and public libraries; others inquire. A mesmerizing 115-minute video that puts the Civil Rights Movement into the context of the daily lives of Mississippians and of Black and white activists. What distinguishes this documentary is its willingness to delve into complicated issues. Activists discuss the joys of struggle and the community it creates, as well as the implications of difficult decisions like the one to bring white northerners down to Mississippi to increase media and government attention.

*Freedom Song, starring Danny Glover. Directed by Phil Alden Robinson. 2000, 150 min., $20. Inspired by accounts of the women and men on the front lines of the Civil Rights Movement, *Freedom Song* chronicles a family nearly torn apart by the struggles of a nation and the impact of the movement on a small Mississippi town. In documenting the complexity and effect of the movement on the volunteers, their families, and their community, *Freedom Song* places heroism squarely on the shoulders of the local people — the unsung volunteers who risked their lives to make change at the grassroots level. Effective for young people as the story is seen through the eyes of a grade-school student.

Gay Lives & Culture Wars, produced by Elaine Velazquez and Barbara Bernstein. Democracy Media, P.O. Box 82777, Portland, OR 97282; 503-452-6500. $20, plus $2.50 s+h for individuals. $50, plus $2.50 s+h for institutions. A powerful 27-minute video that looks at the relationships between gay and lesbian youth and their families against the backdrop of the intolerance of the religious right.

*Global Village or Global Pillage? How People Around the World are Challenging Corporate Globalization, by Jeremy Brecher with Tim Costello and Brendan Smith. 1999, 28 min., $25. This documentary explores the impacts of globalization on communities, workplaces, and environments. Narrated by Ed Asner, *Global Village* weaves together video of interviews, music, and comics to show that, through grassroots organizing and international solidarity, ordinary people can empower themselves to deal with the global economy.

*It's Elementary: Talking About Gay Issues in School, by Debra Chasnoff and Helen Cohen. New Day Films, 888-367-9154. 1997. This video provides a window into what really happens when teachers address lesbian and gay issues with their students in age-appropriate ways. It shows how addressing anti-gay prejudice is connected to preventing violence, supporting families and promoting social equality.

*Off the Track: Classroom Privilege for All, by Michelle Fine, et al. New York: Teachers College Press, 1998, $50. This 30-minute video takes the viewer into a World Literature classroom where all the students — lower income, middle class, and affluent; white, African American, Asian-American, and Latino; girls and boys; those automatically "advanced" and those who have been labeled in need of "special education" — receive and produce high quality education. Useful for staff development.

*Regret to Inform, by Barbara Sonneborn. Sun Fountain Productions. 1999, 72 min., & teacher's guide by Bill Bigelow, $25. This beautifully filmed Oscar-nominated documentary follows director Barbara Sonneborn as she travels to Vietnam to the site of her husband's wartime death. Woven into her personal odyssey are interviews with American and Vietnamese widows who speak openly and profoundly about the men they loved and how war changed their lives forever. *Regret to Inform* is ideal for classes taking a critical look at the Vietnam War.

*Rethinking Columbus Slide Show, by Bill Bigelow. Teaching for Change. $70. Slides and script provide a critique of the story of the "discovery of America" as it is told in most children's literature and textbooks. Ideal for workshops for teachers or students on critiquing bias.

*Scarves of Many Colors: Muslim Women and the Veil. Audiotape by Joan Bohorfoush and Diana Dickerson. Curriculum by Bill Bigelow, Sandra Childs, Norm Diamond, Diana Dickerson, and Jan Haaken. 2000, audiotape 24 min., curriculum 54 pages, $10. This award-winning audiotape and curriculum engage students in thinking critically about stereotypes of "covered" Islamic women. The audiotape introduces a range of U.S. and Middle Eastern women who tell stories and offer insight. The curriculum offers four classroom-tested lessons, including an excellent role play/tribunal on "Women and the Veil," with accompanying student handouts. A lively addition to any Global Studies, psychology, sociology, women's studies, world history, or teacher education curriculum.

The Shadow of Hate: A History of Intolerance in America, by Charles Guggenheim. Order Dept., Teaching Tolerance, 400 Washington Ave., Montgomery, AL 36104. $25, free to middle and high school principals and college history department chairs upon written request. A teaching kit that details the legacy of prejudice toward ethnic and religious minorities, immigrants and other groups. The kit includes a 40-minute video, teacher's guide, and a student handbook. While the video has technical shortcomings, the teacher's guides and student handbook are excellent.

*Some Mother's Son, starring Helen Mirren, 1995, 112 min., $20. From start to finish, students are riveted by this poignant dramatization of the hunger strikes initiated by imprisoned Irish Republican Army members in 1981. Based on true events, it explores the struggle in Northern Ireland from the standpoint of two mothers of IRA prisoners — each of whom responds very differently to her son's political involvement and incarceration. Although this film was unfairly slapped with an R rating for some harsh language and violence, this should not deter teachers who want to expose students to the complexities of the Irish "Troubles".

*Sweating for a T-Shirt, Medea Benjamin. 1999, Global Exchange, 24 min., $25. An excellent classroom resource. Arlen Benjamin decides to travel to Honduras with her mother, activist/writer Medea Benjamin, to find out the conditions of workers who make T-shirts and sweatshirts for college students. Her narration deftly responds to a number of the myths about life in poor countries, and we meet several women workers who share powerful descriptions of their living and working conditions.

*Trinkets and Beads, by Christopher Walker. First Run/Icarus, 1996. This powerful 52-minute video examines the impact of oil "development" in the rainforests of eastern Ecuador. Unforgettable images weave in and out of interviews with Huaorani Indians, oil company officials, and missionaries. The video has been used successfully with middle and high school students throughout the country. Accompanying teaching guide to *Trinkets and Beads*, by Bill Bigelow, available from the Teaching for Change, www.teachingforchange.org.

*Viva La Causa! 500 Years of Chicano History, by the SouthWest Organizing Project and Collision Course Video Productions, SouthWest Organizing Project, 211 10th Street S.W., Albuquerque, NM 87102; www.swop.net; 505-247-8832; fax 505-247-9972; swop@swop.net. $112.50, includes s&h. A multicultural kit that includes the 238-page bilingual book *500 Years of Chicano History in Pictures*, the two-part video *Viva La Causa! 500 Years of Chicano History,* and a teacher's guide for elementary and secondary schools. The kit spans pre-Colombian times to the present, focusing on ancient Mexican societies, Spanish colonization, the U.S. War against Mexico and the resistance to U.S. colonization, and other significant events in Chicano history.

*Zoned for Slavery/The Child Behind the Label, National Labor Committee, 1995, $20. This 23-minute video looks at the exploitation of children and teenagers working in factories in Central America that make clothes for U.S. companies such as the GAP, Eddie Bauer, J.C. Penney and WalMart. Some of the young workers earn only 12 cents to make a shirt that retails for over $20. The video works with students as young as 5th grade but is also excellent for high school students.

Catalogs

Asian American Curriculum Projects: www.asianamericanbooks.com; 529 East Third Avenue, San Mateo, CA 94401; 800-874-2242; fax: 650-357-6908; aacp@asianamericanbooks.com. An extensive catalog of resources and services that underscore the importance and diversity of the Asian-American experience. Books for students of all ages.

Center For Media Literacy: www.medialit.org; 23852 Pacific Coast Hwy. #472, CA 90265; 310-456-1225; fax: 310-456-0020; cml@medialit.org. A catalog that offers educators and parents a means of evaluating, understanding, and challenging our media culture. It contains literacy workshop kits, videos, books, guides and other resources designed to help parents and teachers through the media maze.

The National Women's History Project catalog: www.nwhp.org; 3440 Airway Drive, Suite F, Santa Rosa, CA 95403; 707-636-2888; fax: 707-636-2909; nwhp@nwhp.org. A nonprofit distributor of multicultural, women's history books, CDs, videos, posters, and curricula.

Northern Sun Merchandising: www.northernsun.com; 2916 East Lake Street, Minneapolis, MN 55406; 800-258-8579; fax: 612-729-0149; info@northernsun.com. A distributor of valuable resources on environmental, gay/lesbian, multicultural and feminist themes. Beautiful, classroom-friendly posters.

Peoples Publishing Group: www.peopleseducation.com; P. O. Box 513, Saddlebrook, NJ, 07663; 800-822-1080; fax: 201-712-0045; customersupport@peoplesed.com. A distributor of valuable K-12 resources, especially from an African-American perspective.

Syracuse Cultural Workers: www.SyracuseCulturalWorkers.com; P.O. Box 6367, Syracuse, NY 13217; 800-949-5139; fax: 800-396-1449; scw@syracuseculturalworkers.org. A long-time distributor of multicultural, social justice resources, including the Peace Calendar that should adorn all classrooms.

Organizations

Adbusters Media Foundation: www.adbusters.org; 1243 West 7th Avenue., Vancouver, BC, V6H 1B7, Canada; 604-736-9401; fax: 604-737-6021; info@adbusters.org. Adbusters describes itself as "a global network of artists, activists, writers, pranksters, students, educators and entrepreneurs who want to advance the new social activist movement of the information age." Adbusters publishes a magazine of the same name, sponsors Buy Nothing Day and TV Turnoff Week, produces clever "uncommercials" and seeks to agitate so that folks "get mad about corporate disinformation, injustices in the global economy, and any industry that pollutes our physical or mental commons."

American Federation of Teachers: www.aft.org; 555 New Jersey Avenue, NW, Washington, DC 20001; 202-879-4400; fax: 202-879-4545; online@aft.org. Resources and information from the national teachers union.

The Applied Research Center: www.arc.org; 900 Alice Street #400, Oakland, CA 94607; 510-653-3415; fax: 510-986-1062; arc@arc.org. ARC is an important public policy, educational and research institute whose work emphasizes issues of race and social change. Publishes the acclaimed *ColorLines Magazine* — see the listing under Periodicals.

Center for Law and Education: www.cleweb.org; 99 Chauncey Street, Suite 700, Boston, MA 02111; 617-451-0855; fax: 617-451-1167; kboundy@cleweb.org. See especially *NewsNotes*, the Center's newsletter, for up-to-date information on vocational education legislation.

Children's Defense Fund: www.childrensdefense.org; 25 E Street NW, Washington, DC 20001; 800-233-1200; fax: 202-662-3510; cdfinfo@childrensdefense.org. This website offers a great deal of information about the CDF and its positions on critical issues affecting children, especially minorities and the disabled. Also includes position papers and background materials on many topics, and a host of links to other resources.

Corporate Watch: www.corpwatch.org; 2958 24th Street, San Francisco, CA 94110; 415-641-1633; corpwatch@corpwatch.org. A must-visit site for activists who want to keep tabs on the behavior of corporations. Lots of timely news and impressive archives of past corporate misdeeds.

Defence for Children International–Canada: www.dci-canada.org; 25 Spadina Road, Toronto, Ontario M5R 2S7, Canada; 416-907-7432; fax: 416-907-7432; contact@dci-canada.org. Defence for Children international (DCI) is an independent non-governmental or-ganization that was set up during the International Year of the Child (1979) to ensure ongoing, practical, systematic and concerted international action specially directed towards promoting and protecting the rights of the child.

Designs for Change: www.designsforchange.org; 814 South Western Avenue, Chicago, IL 60612; 312-236-7252; fax: 312-236-7927; info@designsforchange.org. Detailed reports on Chicago's site-based reform, the country's most ambitious governance reform. Materials for parents, teachers.

Economic Policy Institute: www.epinet.org; 1333 H Street NW, Suite 300, East Tower, Washington, DC 20005; 202-775-8810, fax: 202-775-0819; epi@epi.org. The mission of the Economic Policy Institute is to provide high-quality research and education in order to promote a prosperous, fair, and sustainable economy. The Institute stresses real world analysis and a concern for the living standards of working people, and it makes its findings accessible to the general public, the media, and policy makers.

Facing History and Ourselves: www.facing.org; 16 Hurd Road, Brookline, MA 02146; 617-232-1595; fax: 617-232-0281. An education project that targets hatred, prejudice, racism, and indifference by focusing on teaching students about the Holocaust. Resources, workshops, and newsletter.

Fairness & Accuracy In Reporting: www.fair.org; 104 West 27th Street, Suite 10B, New York, NY 10001; 212-633-6700; fax: 212-727-7668; fair@fair.org. FAIR is a national media watch group that has been offering well-documented criticism of media bias and censorship since 1986. FAIR publishes the indispensable *Extra!*, an award-winning magazine of media criticism, and regular updates, available via their listserve. FAIR also produces a weekly radio program, CounterSpin. An excellent source to get students thinking critically about media coverage of world events.

Food First/Institute for Food and Development Policy: www.foodfirst.org; 398 60th Street, Oakland, CA 94618; 510-654-4400; fax:510-654-4551; foodfirst@foodfirst.org. Since its founding in 1975, Food First has published some of the most useful books on food and hunger issues. Through their publications and activism they continue to offer leadership to the struggle for reforming the global food system from the bottom up. Their catalog is on-line at their website.

Gay, Lesbian, Straight Educators Network (GLSEN): www.glsen.org; 90 Broad Street, 2ndFloor, New York, NY 10004; 212-727-0135; fax: 212-727-0254;

glsen@glsen.org. GLSEN is the leading national organization fighting to end anti-gay bias in K-12 schools. The organization offers many useful resources. The GLSEN-initiated student organizing project provides support to young people as they "form and lead gay-straight alliances — helping them to change their own school environments from the inside out."

Global Exchange: www.globalexchange.org; 2017 Mission Street 2nd Floor, San Francisco, CA 94110; 415-255-7296; fax 415-255-7498; info@globalexchange.org. Global Exchange is a human rights organization dedicated to promoting environmental, political, and social justice around the world. In the late '90s it was perhaps the most important organization drawing attention to Nike's sweatshop abuses. Their expansive website will be valuable for students researching just about any important global issue.

International Education and Resource Network (iEARN): www.iearn.org; 475 Riverside Drive, Suite 450, New York, NY 10115; 212-870-2693; fax: 212-870-2672; iearn@us.iearn.org. iEARN is a non-profit organization made up of almost 4,000 schools in over 90 countries. It aims to empower teachers and young people (K-12) to work together online at low cost through a global telecommunications network.

Media Education Foundation: www.mediaed.org; 60 Masonic Street, Northampton, MA 01060; 800-897-0089; fax: 800-659-6882; info@mediaed.org. The Media Education Foundation is a nonprofit educational organization devoted to media research and production of resources to aid educators and others in fostering analytical media literacy. Their mission: "We believe that a media-literate citizenry is essential to a vibrant democracy in a diverse and complex society."

National Association for the Education of Young Children: www.naeyc.org; 1313 L Street NW, Suite 500 Washington, DC 20005; 800-424-2460; fax: 202-328-1846; naeyc@naeyc.org. Publishes *Young Children* and other useful materials.

National Center for Fair & Open Testing (*FairTest*): www.fairtest.org; 15 Court Square, Suite 820, Boston, MA 02108-9939; 857-350-8207; fax: 857-350-8209; info@fairtest.org. The major clearinghouse for information and activism on countering testing injustice. See especially *FairTest Examiner,* a quarterly news-letter on assessment issues.

National Association for Multicultural Education: www.nameorg.org; 2100 M Street, Suite 170-245, Washington, DC 20037; 202-679-6263; fax: 214-602-4722; name@nameorg.org. Founded in 1990, NAME provides resources and support that help educators promote "a philosophy of inclusion that embraces the basic tenets of cultural pluralism," and "promoting cultural and ethnic diversity as a national strength."

National Clearinghouse for English Language Acquisition: www.ncela@gwu.edu; 2011 I Street NW, Suite 300, Washington, DC 20006; 800-321-6223; fax: 800-531-9347; askncela@gwu.edu. News, discussion groups, and resources for educators working with linguistically and culturally diverse students.

National Education Association: www.nea.org; 1201 16th Street NW, Washington, DC 20036; 202-833-4000; fax: 202-822-7974. The nation's largest teachers union.

National Labor Committee: www.nlcnet.org; 5 Gateway Center, 6th Floor, Pittsburgh, PA 15222; 412-562-2406; e-mail: nlc@nlcnet.org. The National Labor Committee is the

producer of some of the most valuable videos and reports on sweatshop and labor rights issues around the world. (See, for example, the videos *Zoned for Slavery* and *Mickey Mouse Goes to Haiti*.)

National Women's History Project: www.nwhp.org; 3440 Airway Drive, Suite F, Santa Rosa, CA 95403; 707-636-2888; fax: 707-636-2909; nwhp@aol.com. The project has a variety of K-12 curriculum materials, and also holds workshops and training seminars.

New Mexico Media Literacy Project: www.nmmlp.org; 6400 Wyoming Blvd. NE, Albuquerque, NM 87109; 505-828-3129; fax: 505-828-3142; nmmlp@nmmlp.org. Excellent materials on critical media literacy teaching.

People For the American Way: www.pfaw.org; 2000 M Street, NW, Suite 400, Washington, DC 20036; 800-326-7329; fax: 202-293-2672. A national progressive organization that fights school vouchers and other right-wing policy initiatives.

Rainforest Action Network: www.ran.org; 221 Pine Street, 5th Floor, San Francisco, CA 94104; 415-398-4404; fax: 415-398-2732; answers@ran.org. RAN works to protect the earth's rainforests and support the rights of their inhabitants through education, grassroots organizing, and nonviolent direct action. Theirs is a must-visit comprehensive website that includes a wealth of information, including ideas for activities and activism with students, classroom-friendly factsheets, and links to indigenous rainforest groups.

Teaching for Change: www.teachingforchange.org; P.O. Box 73038, Washington, DC 20056; 800-763-9131; 202-588-7204; fax: 202-238-0109; e-mail: info@teachingforchange.org. Publisher of excellent multicultural, social justice teaching materials, such as the widely-used collection *Beyond Heroes and Holidays*. Excellent cource of social justice, multicultural teaching resources through their Busboys and Poets webstore: www.bbpbooks.teachingforchange.org; or order by calling toll-free at 800-763-9131.

TURN – Teacher Union Reform Network: www.turnexchange.net; 30 N. Union Street, Suite 301, Rochester NY 14607. 585-546-2681; fax: 585-546-4123. Network of progressive AFT and NEA locals engaged in educational reform. Includes contract language of innovative contracts.

United for a Fair Economy: www.ufenet.org; 29 Winter Street, Boston, MA 02108; 617-423-2148; fax: 617-423-0191. UFE provides numerous resources to organizations and individuals working to address the widening income and asset gap in the United States and around the world. They publish useful training and curriculum materials, and their website features an economics library, research library, and fact sheets.

ZNet / ZMagazine: www.zcommunications.org; 18 Millfield Street, Woods Hole, MA 02543; 508-548-9063; fax: 508-457-0626; zmag@zmag.org. Z Net is one of the most amazing websites we know of. Forums, commentaries from around the world, song lyrics for 530 songs-with-a-conscience, courses, analyses on global issues of all kinds. Many pre-college students might find some of the writing a bit hard-going, but there is an awful lot here. *Z Magazine* is available the old-fashioned way — see Periodicals.

Periodicals

Adbusters: www.adbusters.org; 1243 West 7th Avenue, Vancouver, BC V6H 1B7; 800-663-1243; fax: 604-737-6021; info@adbusters.org. Canadian journal that promotes critical thinking about consumer culture. See Adbusters Media Foundation under Organizations.

ColorLines Magazine: www.arc.org; 900 Alice Street, Suite 400, Oakland, CA 94605; 510-653-3415; fax: 510-653-3427; arc@arc.org. Published quarterly; subscriptions $24/year. An award-winning national magazine that covers race, culture, and community organizing, with a particular focus on issues that affect communities of color.

Dollars and Sense: www. dollarsandsense.org. 29 Winter Street Boston, MA 02108; 617-447-2177; fax: 617-447-2179; dollars@dollarsandsense.org. Dollars and Sense provides easy to understand articles on the economy from a critical perspective. Indispensable for economics teachers.

The Ecologist: www.theecologist.org; 102 D Lane House Studios, 116–118 Commercial Street, Spitalfields, London E1 6NF, UK. An outstanding journal that challenges basic assumptions about "development," "progress," and "growth." Important articles that can help students and teachers consider the environmental consequences of globalization.

FairTest Examiner. See the National Center for Fair & Open Testing (FairTest), in Organizations.

Green Teacher: www. greenteacher.org; 95 Robert St., Toronto, Ontario, M5S 2K5; 416-960-1244; fax: 416-925-3474; info@greenteacher.com. Emphasizes hands-on education on issues concerning the environment.

In These Times: www. inthesetimes.com; 2040 N. Milwaukee Ave., Chicago, IL 60647; 773-772-0100; fax: 773- 772-4180. A weekly news magazine that promotes an anti-corporate perspective on national and international issues.

Labor Notes: www.labornotes.org; 7435 Michigan Ave, Detroit, MI 48210; 313-842-6262 fax: 313-842-0227. labornotes@labornotes.org. An excellent monthly newsletter of news and analysis dealing with ongoing labor union and rank-and-file activities.

The Nation; www.thenation.com; 33 Irving Place, New York, NY 10003; 212-209-5400; fax: 212-982-9000 Weekly. Important articles on world and national events from a progressive perspective.

New Internationalist: www.newint.org; P.O. Box 1062, Niagra Falls, NY 14304; 905-946-0407; fax: 905-946-0410. A colorful monthly magazine on issues of global inequality. Articles reproducible for students. Each issue has a different theme: child labor, global warming, the AIDS crisis, etc.

New Youth Connections: www.youthcomm.org; 224 W. 29th Street, New York, NY 10001; 212-279-0708; fax: 212-279-8856. Monthly newspaper written by high school students. Also publishes Foster Care Youth United.

NACLA Report; www.nacla.org; North American Congress on Latin America, 38 Greene Street, 4th Floor, New York, NY 10013; 646-613-1440; fax: 646-613-1443. 5 issues a year. Detailed analyses on Latin American and Caribbean issues.

Radical Teacher: www. radicalteacher.org. University of Illinois Press, Journals Division, 1325 S. Oak Street, Champaign, IL 61820; 217-244-0626; fax: 217-244-9910; info@radicalteacher.org. Offers many valuable articles and teaching ideas from a critical standpoint.

Rethinking Schools: www. rethinkingschools.org; 1001 E. Keefe Avenue, Milwaukee, WI 53212; 800-669-4192; fax: 414-964-7220; office@rethinkingschools.org. A quarterly journal put out by classroom teachers with a focus on social justice and equity. Rethinking Schools Online contains this entire resource list with all website addresses hot-linked so all you have to do is click on them and you are taken to the site. Rethinking Schools also publishes a number of the books listed in these Resources, including *Rethinking Our Classrooms,* volumes 1 and 2, (see descriptions above.)

Sex, Etc: www.sexetc.org; Rutgers University, 100 Joyce Kilmer Avenue, Piscataway, NJ 08854; 732-445-7929; fax: 732-445-4154. An award-winning website by and for teens about health and sexuality issues. Sponsored by the Network for Family Life Education.

Teaching Tolerance: www. teachingtolerance.org; 400 Washington Avenue, Montgomery, AL 36104; 334-956-8200; fax: 334-956-8488. Mailed twice a year to teachers at no charge, this magazine has a range of popularly written articles and a useful resource section. Published by Southern Poverty Law Center, which

also has a film and curriculum package on the Civil Rights Movement.

Z Magazine: www. zcommunications.org. 11 issues a year. Detailed articles on current events from a critical perspective. Valuable column on the politics of the media. See description of ZNet under Organizations. ■

JEAN-CLAUDE LEJEUNE

Poetry Teaching Guide

By Linda Christensen

Discrimination Poems

"Waiting at the Railroad Café"
by Janet Wong
(p. 72)

Janet Wong's poem is powerful because it portrays a moment in history experienced by a father and daughter on an ordinary outing. This poem can be used to emphasize the struggle of Chinese railroad workers as depicted in Lawrence Yep's moving novel *Dragon's Gate,* complement a lesson about the lunch-counter sit-ins of the Civil Rights Movement, or demonstrate how to write about a personal experience with discrimination.

1. After reading the poem out loud, ask students to locate the two different forms of discrimination in the poem: One is passive — the waitress ignoring them; the other is active — the drunk yelling at them.
2. Encourage students to talk about the difference between how father and daughter react to the discrimination.
3. After discussing the content of the poem, point out how Janet Wong creates a movie close-up of the moment. We see the father with his arms folded; we hear them talk; we watch the waitress ignore them. To make the action in the poem come alive, ask for volunteer students to act the poem out as someone else reads it.
4. Ask students to create a poem full of details about a historical event or an incident from their own lives when they encountered discrimination. Encourage students to use details to help their readers see and hear the story in their poem.
Janet Wong has a student-friendly website at www.janetwong.org.

History Poems

"at the cemetery,
walnut grove plantation,
south carolina, 1989"
by Lucille Clifton
(p. 154)

Museums or historical markers can be great places for poetry to erupt. I can imagine Lucille Clifton lifting the "curious tools" at the "walnut grove plantation" or standing beside a marker in a cemetery, her body full of pain as she created this poem out of an urgent need to honor in death those who were not honored in life.

Too often, museums mask real history, making the museum an accomplice of past injustice. Exhibits use passive language to hide what really happened or they place a tersely worded marker like Clifton notes in her poem: "the inventory lists ten slaves but only men were recognized."

Clifton's poem makes a powerful prompt prior to a field trip. If you take students to popular historical sites, her poem will help students investigate whose history is valued, whose lives are celebrated at the site. Encourage students to look at how language can simplify or erase some voices and celebrate others.

1. Read Clifton's poem out loud. Ask students to write a response to the poem. What's going on? Who is the poem written to? Why do they think Clifton wrote it? What is their response to the poem?
2. After sharing student reactions, discuss the idea of historical perspective. In Clifton's poem she writes, "nobody mentioned slaves," ask students why they think nobody mentioned slaves. Ask why nobody mentioned women slaves.
3. Point out the physical details Clifton uses from her visit to the plantation: rocks, tools, finger prints. Encourage students to use physical details from their visit as well.
4. Note how Clifton writes her poem to the slaves who are not mentioned. Who could they write their poems to? Also note her lines: "tell me your names/ tell me your bashful names/ and i will testify." Who can they "testify" for? Whose history can they restore?

Letter Poems

"In Response
to Executive Order 9066"
by Dwight Okita
(p. 75)

Dwight Okita's poem is a wonderful example of a letter poem. Okita writes "In Response to Executive Order 9066" from the point of view of a young girl responding to the U.S. government's orders to Japanese Americans to report for relocation. The poem puts a face on the supposed "enemy," but it also provides a model for students to imagine themselves a literary or historical character from any historical period. They could also write these poems to people connected to their own lives — teachers, parents, friends, principal, superintendent or from one literary character to another.

1. If students aren't familiar with the Japanese-American internment, they will need to understand the historical context of the period prior to reading the poem.

2. After reading the piece, ask students to write a list of what they learn about the letter writer — her age, her interests, etc. What are her concerns? Point out how the poet uses specific details to build the girl's character. You might ask students if they think she might be considered dangerous enough to be imprisoned for the safety of the United States.

3. If you are studying another historical period, brainstorm potential recipients for a letter poem. For example, students could take on the persona of one of the Little Rock Nine and write a letter poem to Governor Faubus or the principal of Central High School. Students reading *Poisonwood Bible* could write a letter from Ruthie Mae to her father or from an African to Ruthie's missionary father.

Environmental/Social Problem Poems

"Earth's Last Cry"
by Rachel Knudsen
(p. 202)

Rachel Knudsen's poem demonstrates that art and science make powerful allies. "Earth's Last Cry" provides the perfect prompt for students to write a poem from the point of view of the earth or to highlight social problems.

1. Engage students in a critical examination of local or national environmental problems (see the article on toxic waste p. 144) or social problems (see "The Trial" p. 140).

2. Ask students to read "Earth's Last Cry." Talk with students about the poem. What is Knudsen's message? What does she want people to do? To whom is the poem directed?

3. Point out the list of environmental problems Knudsen outlines — from broken glass to pollution and nuclear waste. Ask students to choose an environmental or social issue and create a list of the problems associated with it.

4. Encourage students to find a hook to pull their poem forward. Knudsen uses two hooks. First, she demonstrates how the earth can't save itself because it lacks fingers, a heart, feet, and arms. She also uses the repetition of the word no — no fingers, no hearts, etc. These two devices pull her through the poem, give her a structure from stanza to stanza. ■

Linda Christensen is Language Arts Coordinator for the Portland, Oregon public schools and a Rethinking Schools editor.

Index

Notes

Notes

Notes

Notes

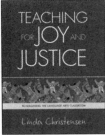

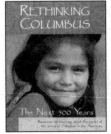

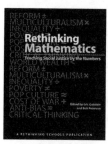
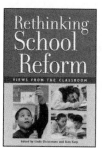

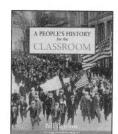
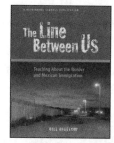
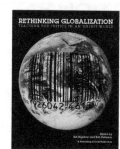

RETHINKING SCHOOLS
FOUR EASY WAYS TO ORDER

❶ **CALL TOLL-FREE:** 1-800-669-4192 8am-9pm (ET) M-F
❷ **SECURE ONLINE ORDERING:** www.rethinkingschools.org
❸ **FAX ORDER FORM TO:** 802-864-7626
❹ **MAIL ORDER FORM TO:** Rethinking Schools, P.O. Box 2222, Williston, VT 05495

MASTERCARD, VISA AND PURCHASE ORDERS ACCEPTED

Name _____

Organization _____

Address _____

City/State/Zip _____

Phone _____

E-mail _____

METHOD OF PAYMENT

☐ Check or money order made payable to Rethinking Schools
☐ Purchase order   ☐ MasterCard   ☐ Visa

Credit Card No._____

Exp. Date _____

Authorized Signature _____

QUANTITY	TITLE/ITEM	UNIT PRICE	TOTAL

MAIL TO: Rethinking Schools, P.O. Box 2222, Williston, VT 05495
FAX TO: 802-864-7626
CALL 1-800-669-4192 FOR A FREE CATALOG OF ALL OUR MATERIALS

* U.S. shipping and handling costs are 15% of the total (minimum charge of $4.00). Canadian shipping and handling costs are 25% of the total (minimum charge of $5.00). Subscriptions already include shipping costs. Payment in U.S. dollars.

Subtotal $ _____
Shipping $ _____
Donation $ _____
TOTAL $ _____

2BROCV2

If you liked *Rethinking Our Classrooms, Volume 2,* then *Rethinking Schools* magazine is for you!

Take advantage of this special discount coupon to receive the country's leading magazine for school reform.

"Rethinking Schools is a teacher's close friend — insightful, intelligent, and compassionate. I have read, used, and loved this publication for over a decade. I'm a better teacher because of it."

—MICHELE FORMAN, 2001 National Teacher of the Year

INTRODUCTORY OFFER!
Subscribe today and save!

☐ **$22.95** Two-year subscription *(Save $24.65 off cover price!)*
☐ **$14.95** One-year subscription *(Save $8.85 off cover price!)*

☐ **Print version**   ☐ **Digital version**

☐ Please send me a free catalog of all your materials
☐ Bill me
☐ Enclosed is my check payable to Rethinking Schools

Name _____

Organization _____

Address _____

City/State/Zip _____

Phone _____

E-mail _____

RETHINKING SCHOOLS

P.O. Box 2222, Williston, VT 05495 • toll-free: 800-669-4192 • fax: 802-864-7626

2BROCV2

BUSINESS REPLY MAIL
FIRST-CLASS MAIL   PERMIT NO.2222   WILLISTON VT

POSTAGE WILL BE PAID BY ADDRESSEE

RETHINKING SCHOOLS
PO BOX 2222
WILLISTON VT 05495-9940